MODERN HUMANITIES RESEARCH ASSOCIATION
NEW TRANSLATIONS
VOLUME 1
General Editor
ALISON FINCH

Mademoiselle de Montpensier
(La Grande Mademoiselle)

MEMOIRS

Selected, translated, and introduced by
P. J. Yarrow

Edited by
William Brooks

Mademoiselle de Montpensier
(La Grande Mademoiselle)

MEMOIRS

Selected, translated, and introduced by
P. J. Yarrow

Edited by
William Brooks

MODERN HUMANITIES RESEARCH ASSOCIATION
2010

Published by

The Modern Humanities Research Association,
1 Carlton House Terrace
London SW1Y 5AF

© The Modern Humanities Research Association, 2010

P. J. Yarrow and William Brooks have asserted their right under the Copyright, Designs and Patents Act 1988 to be identified as the authors of this work.

Parts of this work may be reproduced as permitted under legal provisions for fair dealing (or fair use) for the purposes of research, private study, criticism, or review, or when a relevant collective licensing agreement is in place. All other reproduction requires the written permission of the copyright holder who may be contacted at rights@mhra.org.uk.

First published 2010

ISBN 978-1-907322-01-3

Copies may be ordered from www.translations.mhra.org.uk

CONTENTS

Foreword, by *Jean Garapon*	vii
Introduction	xi
Four Notes: Titles; Royal Residences; Coinage; Places and Distances	xxiv
Chronological Table	xxix
Genealogical Table	xxxii

MEMOIRS

Part I (1627–1659)

1. Childhood and Youth (1627–1647)	1
2. The Fronde: (1) Matrimonial Projects (1648–1652)	24
3. The Fronde: (2) Military Exploits (Orleans and Paris, 1652)	43
4. Exile and Country Life (1652–1657)	74
5. Return to Court (1657–1659)	99

Part II (1659–1671)

1. The Treaty of the Pyrenees and the King's Marriage (1659–1660)	130
2. Mademoiselle's Second Exile (1662–1664)	144
3. Lauzun and the Journey to Flanders (1670)	148
4. The Death of Madame and its Aftermath (1670)	166
5. The Match Made (1670)	175
6. The Match Unmade (1670–1671)	190

Part III (1680–1684)

1. Lauzun's Release (1680–1681)	200

2. Reunion and Final Break-Up (1681–1684)   203

Further Reading   210

Index   213

Foreword

I am delighted to welcome this new edition of extracts from the memoirs of Mademoiselle de Montpensier, translated by Philip Yarrow and edited by William Brooks. The princess whose memoirs readers can now approach in English might well have become Queen of England. She was the granddaughter of Henry IV, King of France, and the niece of Queen Henrietta Maria, Charles I's wife. Frequently sought in marriage, she very nearly married her cousin Charles II, who, however, was not much attracted to her. She got to know Sophia, Duchess of Hanover — mother of the future George I — who, in 1679, visited Paris and Versailles, and she was well acquainted with Sophia's niece, Louis XIV's sister-in-law Madame Palatine, whose juicy and shameless correspondence is justly celebrated. All these great ladies on the fringes of the world of literary culture enjoyed a special rank in society, and they all shared a taste for writing. They belong to a European tradition that goes back to Renaissance Italy and the princesses whom Castiglione evokes in *The Courtier*. It includes Marguerite de Navarre and Marguerite de Valois, queens of France, and it was continued by many others in different ways — in Mademoiselle de Montpensier's own time by Christina, Queen of Sweden, and Sophia of Hanover, and in the second half of the eighteenth century by Catherine the Great, Empress of Russia, who is known to have been a reader of Mademoiselle de Montpensier's memoirs. Princesses or rulers in their own right, they all chose to write in French, in those days the universal language of the aristocracy of Europe, and they all did so without any literary pretensions, still less any idea that their writings might be published — but, paradoxically, it is their uncomplicated avoidance of sophistication, their carefree informality when dealing in confidences, that makes their work so appealing to modern eyes. When after the passage of hundreds of years we read these texts with their rich flavour of improvisation, they come across as astonishingly fresh and quite unlike official literature of the kind that so clearly betrays its age, so much so that, irrespective of fashions and of the passage of time, their authors are on intimate terms with us. And it is indeed the intimate private life of a princess that is brought to us here, someone to whom birth and good fortune gave everything she could possibly want — she was considered the richest marital prize in the whole of Europe — and yet whose whole life was one of disappointment and failure. Perhaps that was what interacted with her own reading of other women's memoirs to inspire her to write, and to vouchsafe a lifetime's worth of sisterly confidences as though bending the ear of a friendly listener.

It is hard to imagine more enchanting surroundings than those in which the young Mademoiselle de Montpensier grew up, in the original Tuileries, Catherine de' Medici's marvellous Renaissance palace barely a stone's throw from the Louvre — it was later rebuilt by Louis XIV — the very centre of the elegant Paris of Louis XIII's day, a setting wholly devoted to festivities and the pursuit of refinement. Thanks to Philip Yarrow's account of the young princess's experiences, I have no need to rehearse them again here. Lacking in formal education — her father, Gaston d'Orléans, the king's brother, took no pains to provide one for her — she is a good example of the benefits of being immersed in a culture of politeness, the desire to be like her peers, as La Bruyère put it, that characterized the upper echelons of society. From architecture to painting, from music to theatre, in the subtleties of salon conversation or at the ball, from the very beginning the young princess experienced an effortless grounding in matters of taste that stayed with her all her life. We can still see it today in the magnificent building work she undertook at Saint-Fargeau in Burgundy or at Eu in Normandy (soon to become a home for her collection of paintings once more). It is further attested by the presence at her side of the young tiro Jean-Baptiste Lully, who in 1648 came from Florence to teach her Italian, her long-lasting patronage of a theatre company, the existence — long-lasting also — of her own little coterie of men and women of letters who kept her abreast of the latest literary developments. This exceptional environment made her aware of her capabilities, broadened her imagination, and gave her the confidence to express herself.

That is why Mademoiselle de Montpensier has such a developed self-awareness, one that exhibits both pride and sensitivity, allied to a richness of language that, when the time came, was to make an author of her. Her unhappy experiences stem from her haughty insistence upon her own freedom of action, bolstered by an awareness of history and a love of romantic fiction that led her to the conviction that her fabulous Bourbon heritage gave her the absolute freedom to choose a husband for herself. The trouble with such an outlook was that such freedoms simply did not exist in the princely houses of Europe in those days, and she ended up condemned to spinsterhood. A sense of self-worth typical of the plays of Corneille, her favourite dramatist, underscored the feudal aspect of her personality and made her despise the king's chief minister Mazarin (that foreigner!), thanks to his apparent usurpation of powers that could legitimately be exercised only by the young Louis XIV. With the failure of the Fronde, inevitable as it was to our modern way of thinking, she discovered instead the unexpected rewards of solitude during a period in which she at last asserted her individuality by means of architectural enterprises — such as the reconstruction and embellishment of the château of Saint-Fargeau — and her writing; but her writing propelled her towards a state of mind into which she perhaps would have preferred not to venture, towards an uneasy sense of self-questioning, every bit as much as it drew her into composing the wonderful account she gives us of her life. Incapable of expressing regret, Mademoiselle de Montpensier prefers to reflect on her failures and to meditate on her fate. Writing, for her, turns into an opportunity to exhibit ever greater honesty about herself and to acquire the kind of self-awareness that conflicts, sometimes cruelly, with her sense of self-esteem, not to mention its role as the private realization of her personal freedoms. Back once more in a court in which Louis XIV had evolved into the brilliant and authoritarian monarch of legend, she encountered other moments of happiness and other disappointments, not least in her private emotions, before returning to her memoirs and to the outpouring of ever more confidences. This time the cause was the obligation she felt to extricate herself from what had been an intolerable emotional experience by examining the whole question of her moral, spiritual and religious freedom — something she succeeded in undertaking even while the sincerity of her Christian faith, strengthened as it was both by her readings of Saint François de Sales and her advancing years, brought about the renewal of the more thoughtlessly automatic piety of her younger days. Thus it was that she was able to come to terms with a duty which she now saw as living out her days in the ambit of her royal cousin at the magnificent and oppressive court of Versailles; at the same time, and right up until her death, maintaining the right to absent herself whenever she pleased, to travel about and stay in her many other places of residence, activities that amounted to an affirmation of her independence that did nothing to please His Majesty. A rebel in the days of the Fronde, and recklessly so, Mademoiselle de Montpensier never, in the last analysis, ceased to be one.

When all is said and done, these memoirs with their ever-changing reflections of the life of a princess are the privileged memories of someone with a ringside seat as a witness of more than half a century of French history. They are full of striking and intimate glimpses and whimsical accounts of the doings of the men and women who played central roles in the politics of their times. They focus on the destiny of one special individual in their portrayal of an unsettled and anxious dreamer of nostalgic dreams and they are vividly modern in their feminist outlook. They are also a powerful if unconscious pre-echo of what we now call autobiography, and, what is more, in the context of the seventeenth-century clash between the old princely aristocracy of France and the new monarchical authoritarianism, they read like an allegory of liberty of conscience. Well aware of her rank as a granddaughter of France and determined that the demands of etiquette should always be respected, Mademoiselle de Montpensier has left us with a set of memoirs that breathe a healthy spirit of nonconformism, and we should be grateful to Philip Yarrow for his translation and to William Brooks for his work in preparing it for publication.

Jean Garapon
University of Nantes

Introduction

Anne-Marie-Louise, duchesse de Montpensier (la Grande Mademoiselle), began working on her memoirs at the age of twenty-five when she was exiled from Paris following her involvement on the 'wrong' side in the Fronde, the civil war that threatened for a time to dislodge the young king from his throne. She was an accomplished writer of novels and literary portraits and she also wrote at least one manual of pious Christian behaviour. For a time, she hosted one of the most prominent of the literary salons in the capital; but we remember her best for her colourful life both at court and in exile. She resumed her memoirs when Louis XIV, who had initially agreed to her marriage to Lauzun, withdrew his permission. She took them up for a third time towards the end of her life. On each occasion, she picks up the thread of the narrative where she left it so that, in the end, it covers a period of sixty years. Saint-Simon is known to have possessed and used a manuscript copy; many subsequent historians and modern linguists have used them. They are well written and they provide an informative, outspoken, and, at times, exciting account of the life and times of one of the most active (and richest) women of the seventeenth century.

The Mademoiselle specialist Jean Garapon writes of 'the modern reputation of la Grande Mademoiselle [...] a woman who excites fascination and controversy in equal measure and seems to represent in some mysterious way the contradictory charm of her whole era' and observes that she was both lionized and denigrated, sometimes at one and the same time. She was 'a character who belongs as much to the literature of her period as to its history' — his reason for so saying being that

> [although] sometimes she lacks the critical distance necessary to formulate a disinterested judgement, the very naivety and the palpable sincerity of her account marks her out as a major writing talent [...]. Above and beyond her sense of self-worth, pride in her social position, and royal prejudices, her evident human warmth captures the sympathy of modern readers.

Quite so; and moreover, says Garapon, if some literary critics decline to date the origins of autobiography earlier than Rousseau's *Confessions*, Mademoiselle's memoirs certainly prefigure the genre.

Garapon himself, of course, would argue that they constitute the first genuine example of it.[1]

As one reads the memoirs of this niece of Louis XIII and cousin of Louis XIV, the phrase 'poor little rich girl' springs to mind. Indeed, though she herself, of course, does not use these words, she expresses the idea: 'Born with all possible greatness and the advantages God has given me, I have been so unhappy all my life.'

Her life being the subject of her memoirs, little need be said of it here. She was born on 29 May 1627. Her mother, Marie de Bourbon, died a few days afterwards, leaving her daughter a very wealthy woman — sovereign princess of Dombes; duchess of Montpensier, Saint-Fargeau, and Châtellerault; dauphine of Auvergne; princess of La Roche-sur-Yon and Joinville; marchioness of Mézières; baroness of Beaujolais; countess of Bar-sur-Seine and Mortain; viscountess of Auge, Bresse, and Domfront; and Lady of Champigny-sur-Veude, Combrailles, and Montaigu. Her father, Gaston d'Orléans,[2] the brother of Louis XIII (childless until 1638) was heir presumptive to the throne, and the rallying point for opposition to the king's chief minister, Cardinal Richelieu. For his part in the conspiracy known as the Day of Dupes, he fled from France in 1630. He made his peace, and was allowed to return four years later; but he had remarried in the meantime, and does not seem to have cared much for his eldest daughter. Although she expresses her dutiful affection for him, she soon became aware of his weak, indecisive, unreliable, and treacherous nature. Her grandmother, Queen Maria de' Medici, who had befriended her, another of the dupes, also left France, leaving Mademoiselle (as Anne-Marie-Louise was known) to the care of governesses. This neglected childhood may well have left her with an unfulfilled need for affection, and in later life made her easy prey to Lauzun.

The civil war known as the Fronde — in part a reaction against the centralizing policy of Richelieu, in part a protest against the high taxation necessitated by participation in the Thirty Years' War — broke out in 1648. In its later stages, Gaston d'Orléans and his eldest daughter threw in their lot with the rebels, and she, on behalf of her vacillating father, performed the exploits at Orleans and Paris

---

[1] The quotations in this paragraph are translated by William Brooks from Jean Garapon, *La Grande Mademoiselle mémorialiste* (Geneva: Droz, 1989), pp. 11–14.

[2] Gaston, duc d'Anjou from birth, was created duc d'Orléans et de Chartres in 1626 in consideration of his forthcoming marriage. The city and château of Blois were awarded to him at the same time as part of his apanage.

that she narrates with not unjustified pride, but which destroyed any chances she might have had of marrying her cousin, Louis XIV, and becoming Queen of France.

When the court returned to Paris in triumph in 1652, Mademoiselle and her father were ordered to leave. They lived in exile for several years, he mainly in Blois, she at Saint-Fargeau, occasionally visiting her father, or taking the waters at Forges in Normandy. She hunted; she enjoyed building; and she was fond of the theatre and liked to have actors with her. She corresponded with Condé, now fighting for Spain against France. She also acquired a taste for reading, and began to write — a collection of satirical pieces, *Histoire de Jeanne Lambert d'Herbigny, marquise de Fouquerolle* (1653),[3] and the first part of her memoirs. Relations with her father were strained, partly because of his mismanagement of her estates during her minority and his unwillingness to render an account of his stewardship (their dispute was finally settled, to Mademoiselle's detriment, in 1657), and partly because of his constant meddling with her household. Mademoiselle was allowed to return to court in 1657, but, as we shall see, she underwent a further period of exile five years later.

The chief interest in the later part of her memoirs is provided by the moving story of her passionate love for the comte de Lauzun, a spiteful, insolent, little man, but a good soldier and attractive to women.[4] Elisabeth Charlotte, duchesse d'Orléans, Louis XIV's second sister-in-law, who knew her well and seldom left her during her last illness, says that she fell in love with him because he enjoyed the king's favour more than she, but this sounds like an over-simplification; besides, Elisabeth Charlotte had very quickly come to despise him just as she admired Mademoiselle for having spent a lifetime behaving in a manner that was not consistent with what was expected of women in those times. Louis XIV at first consented to Mademoiselle's marriage to Lauzun; but the outcry at this unequal match was so great, and so much pressure was brought to bear on him — his mistress, Mme de Montespan, finally tipped the scales — that, a few days later, he withdrew his consent. Mademoiselle's reaction has something of the schoolgirl frustrated in her first crush, and we

---

[3] Spelt thus in the title of the story, but as 'Fouquerolles' when Mademoiselle refers to the person in the course of her memoirs.
[4] Antonin Nompar de Caumont, comte de Lauzun, a captain in the king's bodyguard (1633–1723). References to Lauzun in general works of history often style him 'duc de Lauzun', which is correct, but he did not acquire the higher rank until 1692.

do well to remember, as we read her account, that she was forty-three years old. Some months afterwards, Lauzun, who had learnt of Mme de Montespan's share in the overthrow of his plans, and insulted her, was arrested and imprisoned in the Piedmontese fortress of Pinerolo, which was in French hands at the time. Ten years later, Mademoiselle was induced to buy his release by transferring her title to Dombes and Eu, which she had previously donated to Lauzun, to the duc du Maine, Mme de Montespan's son — 'tricked into giving her property to the king's bastard just to save that little toad Lauzun', as Elisabeth Charlotte put it, never one to mince words.[5] It is generally supposed that, at some point after his release, Mademoiselle secretly married Lauzun, chiefly on the grounds that, if he had not been her husband, he would not have treated her so badly, partly because of a report that at the château d'Eu, of which she retained the use during her lifetime, and where they lived together for a while, their rooms were connected by a concealed staircase, and partly because, after her death, he went into deep mourning like a widower. Whatever the truth may be — and Lauzun seems to have been so unbalanced that it is difficult to draw any conclusions from his behaviour — they led a cat and dog's life until she finally sent him packing in 1684. It is, withal, hard to avoid concluding that the queen and others who had opposed her marriage were all along in the right.

Lauzun regained the favour of the king for his services to James II — he helped the Queen of England to escape to France with her baby son in 1688, and he commanded (without conspicuous success) the French expeditionary force in Ireland in 1690. Not wishing to see him, Mademoiselle gave up going to court. She died in 1693. It was the custom for the body, the heart, and the entrails of royal personages to be buried separately; the explosion of Mademoiselle's entrails in the urn into which they had been put caused first consternation at Versailles and then mirth. Poor little rich girl![6]

The *Histoire de Mme de Fouquerolle* had given her a taste for writing; reading the memoirs of Marguerite de Valois made her think of writing her own; and she was encouraged in this project by Mme de Fiesque, Mme de Frontenac and her husband, and Préfontaine. The first part of her memoirs, by far the longest, covers her life up to

---

[5] *Correspondance de Madame duchesse d'Orléans*, ed. by Ernest Jaeglé, 3 vols (Paris: Bouillon, 1890), I, 64.
[6] The episode is related by Saint-Simon in his account of her funeral. See *Mémoires*, ed. by Yves Coirault, 8 vols (Paris: Gallimard, 1983–1988), I (1983), 52–55 (p. 54).

1659 and, moreover, towards the end of that period she was writing quite soon after the events she narrates;[7] the second part, begun, she tells us, at Eu on 18 August 1677, after a break of seventeen years, deals with the years up to 1676; and the third part, written — in all probability — in 1689 and 1690, carries the story up to 1688.

Mademoiselle wrote her memoirs for herself alone, as she several times makes clear: 'As I am writing these memoirs only for my own amusement, and as they will never, perhaps, be seen by anyone, at least during my lifetime, I shall not bother to correct them.' This is what gives them their particular interest. They are, it is true, a valuable contribution to the history of seventeenth-century France, full of information about court life, the Fronde, social life, manners, and glimpses of historical characters in their more human moments — Louis XIII in love; Gaston d'Orléans, his brother, playing with his daughter, dithering and feigning illness at moments of crisis, or putting his gloves on his head in the cool of the evening, in the vain hope that the king would invite him to put his hat on; Mazarin fawning on Mademoiselle when she returned to court; Louis XIV and his brother hiding, lest Christina of Sweden should make them go to the fair with her; Monsieur throwing a plate at his brother's head; Queen Maria Theresa disgruntled at having to rough it in Flanders; Madame on her deathbed (Henrietta Anne, daughter of Charles I, always known as Henriette d'Angleterre), and so forth. Nevertheless, Mademoiselle's memoirs are an autobiography, not a chronicle — indeed, they are an intensely personal record, and, as such, unique at that time: she states explicitly that she will relate only what she herself witnessed, and although she does, in fact, report news she has received from third parties, she always creates the impression of being personally interested in events; and it is above all, perhaps, what they have to tell us about her own life and what they reveal about her far from commonplace personality that chiefly appeals. Mademoiselle appears as a complex, not entirely consistent, person. One of her most obvious characteristics is pride in her birth, rank, and connections. Discussing the demands made by the parlement during the early months of the Fronde,[8] she declares that she naturally believes in

---

[7] Garapon, pp. 48–51. None the less, a reference to her 'late' father in her account of the closing week of 1658 shows that she was still working on that part of her text after his death in February 1660.

[8] The parlements were the main lawcourts; that of Paris (the one that is meant here) had the widest jurisdiction. As they had the task of registering edicts, treaties, and so forth, and claimed the right of remonstrance in consequence, they

absolute monarchy, '[for] it seems to me that the authority of one man partakes so much of divinity that one should submit joyfully and respectfully to it of one's own free will, even if God had not willed us to be born under it' (C, I, 191).[9] Loving monarchy, she says, is loving herself, since French monarchy originated with her house. She attaches great importance to the privileges of her rank, and in her memoirs we read more about matters of status and precedence than we do in the writings of anyone else save Elisabeth Charlotte, the second Madame, and, of course, in a later period, Saint-Simon. She makes a fuss, for instance, when she hears that the princesse palatine, Anne de Gonzague,[10] intends to wear a train at the royal wedding in 1660, and appeals to Louis XIV, who examines precedents, and puts a stop to it (C, III, 476–77). When in 1665 a contract is drawn up to settle a dispute with her stepmother, the latter signs the contract with her maiden name, Marguerite de Lorraine, instead of plain Marguerite. To the surprise of Colbert, who is present, Mademoiselle boldly writes her own name above that of her stepmother, arguing that by repudiating her status as her father's widow Marguerite has also repudiated her superior rank. On hearing of it, Louis XIV considers that it is Mademoiselle who has acted correctly (C, IV, 19). On other occasions, he appeals to her judgement in matters of propriety. She is fond of ceremonies, and is sure that she cuts a fine figure in them, although normally she dislikes formality and dresses negligently. She expects to be treated with respect, likes marks of respect, and resents being treated disrespectfully. She says, indeed, that it is wrong to use threats against the dependants of people like her, 'whose least scullion is to be treated with respect' (C, II, 487).

She is confident that she is worthy of her rank: 'God ordained that I should be born in a lofty station; he gave me feelings proportionate to it, and no one has ever detected any base ones in me, thank God' (C, IV, 412). She is eager to distinguish herself — a side of her character that destroyed her chances of marrying Louis XIV. She is confident of

---

had a certain political importance, particularly when the government was weak and unpopular — during the Fronde, for instance.

[9] In order to enrich our portrait of Mademoiselle, we have drawn on parts of her memoirs that are not included in the present volume. We indicate the whereabouts of the original text in the edition by Adolphe Chéruel, referred to, in our Introduction only, as C. (For details, see 'Further Reading'.)

[10] Anna Gonzaga, daughter of the duc de Nevers, who had married Edward, Prince Palatine of the Rhine, the brother of Prince Rupert and of Karl Ludwig, the Elector Palatine, all of whom were grandsons of James I of England. We call her Anne de Gonzague, a name more familiar to both French and English readers.

her own worth and appearance; and she is sure that Charles II, after hoping to marry her, could not stoop to Mlle de Longueville (C, III, 95–96). Indeed, she never comes across as modest. She thinks she is handsome enough to have no need of jewellery: 'I have so much confidence in my good looks that I think they adorn me more than all the diamonds of a thousand creatures who are not made like me' (C, III, 355); elsewhere, too, she praises her own shapely figure and good looks. And she does not like people to find fault with her. At times she prides herself on her self-control, as when she overcomes her aversion to Condé, or is delighted to find, on passing near Paris during her exile, that she can look at it without regretting that she cannot go there. On another occasion, she claims to be impassive: 'I pretended, however, to be very cheerful; and as my face seldom changes, and neither sadness nor joy affects it, people are used to that. So no one noticed my conflicting emotions at this moment' (C, III, 46). Yet it is doubtful whether self-control and impassivity are her dominant characteristics. A few pages after that last remark, she observes: 'I think that they saw in my face that I am sensitive and that kindness and unkindness affect me' (C, III, 59); and the general impression left by her memoirs is that of a woman who is emotional, impetuous, natural, sincere, and, it must be conceded, rather naive.

She is affectionate, and seems to have been genuinely fond of her unworthy, indecisive, self-interested, and frequently unkind father. She sheds tears easily, and is capable of pity. After the Battle of the Faubourg Saint-Antoine, for instance, she cannot sleep for thinking of the dead (C, II, 113), and she sends to ask after the wounded on behalf of her father and Condé. 'It would never have occurred to them, but attentions of this kind win hearts, maintain the affection felt for the great, and make friends and servants for them' (C, I, 154). She is loyal to her dependants, and gives them her support. She is horrified by the plight of the galley-slaves in Marseille, and, unwilling that a paralytic old man should be moved from his chair by the fireside in a billet allotted to her, sleeps in the closet. She is of a sanguine and melancholic temperament (and might have ended mad, she tells us), inclined to pessimism and to fear the worst (C, III, 55).

Mademoiselle is active, and seldom bored: 'I am the person least liable to be bored, always occupying myself, and even enjoying day-dreaming. I am bored only with people I do not like, or under constraint.' Grief makes her even more active than usual. There is a vein of common sense and practicality in her: she likes to look after her own affairs, and not leave them to her man of business; and, in later life, at least, she puts health before pleasure. She is generous, however. 'Money will never hold me back in any of my actions, since I have the will and the power to use it well' (C, II, 187), she says; and her gifts to Lauzun show that she was not mean. She is hasty, and quick to anger, but slow to carry out threats, and forthright. Being allowed to witness the wedding by proxy of Louis XIV and Maria Theresa, she forgets that she is incognita, and orders her compatriots about (C, III, 458).

She makes no attempt to conceal her feelings. If she is proud of her exploits or her regiment or her splendid mourning for her father, she says so; she clearly enjoyed queening it in Dombes; and she tells us exactly what her successive emotions were in the course of her expedition to Orleans. Her account of the death of Mme de Fiesque is a good example of her realism and freedom from sentimentality. She does not disguise the fact that she felt little grief when her grandmother, Mme de Guise,[11] died. 'The mourning I wore was as deep as if I had felt it in my heart; for in this world we must always keep up appearances as far as possible' (C, II, 383). When there was talk of marrying one of her half-sisters to the king, she admits that 'no woman likes seeing her younger sister above her' (C, III, 62). Her description of the same sister when the court visited Blois in 1659 and Louis was on his way to marry someone else is not without a certain satisfied cattiness. A similar jealousy of her half-sisters comes out when their mother tries to arrange for them to live with the queen (C, III, 450). It is noteworthy that she does not go back and alter her memoirs to give an impression of consistency. If, at first, she is sympathetic to her stepmother, whose marriage to her father seems, unusually for those times, to have been a love match, she later views her with a mixture of hostility and disdain — but she does not revise her earlier references to her. Having insisted in the earlier parts that she disapproved of love, she relates in the succeeding parts both how much she loved and admired Lauzun, in no way concealing or disguising the depth of her love for him. Later, she says how disappointed she is in him, and how demanding, unreasonable, faithless, and ungrateful she finds him.

---

[11] Henriette-Catherine de Joyeuse, Mademoiselle's maternal grandmother by her first husband Henri, duc de Montpensier, had taken as her second husband, in 1611, Charles de Lorraine, duc de Guise.

Nor does she conceal her defects and weaknesses, even the comic aspects of her behaviour — locking her hated governess in her room, for example, and taking away the key, or the fit of piety brought on by her desire to marry the emperor, or the occasion when, despite her apparently boundless self-confidence, she tells the Orleans councillors to stand behind her so that she cannot see them and become flustered into saying the wrong thing. She fears being poisoned by the act of opening and reading a letter — a device worthy of the world of French fiction — simply because it is addressed in the handwriting of Goulas, her father's secretary, and she holds it over the fire to drive off anything with which it might be impregnated (C, III, 50). The only passages in which she seems to want to prove that she was in the right are those that relate to her childhood experiences, though even in later life, the idea of getting her own back for some perceived slight or other is not often far from the thought processes she reveals to us and, however sincerely (and often) she claims that she is writing for herself alone, she does call into question such an apparently disinterested approach when she writes, for example, of her dealings with the présidial in Orleans,[12] that 'I leave you to judge whether I would not have done better to follow my original feelings in the matter'; a few pages earlier she has mentioned that she is 'pretty resolute by nature, as will sufficiently appear in these memoirs' — surely again an acknowledgement that they may come to be read by people other than herself. She admits to being timid. She is afraid, not only of death, but of being given a room or remaining in a house in which someone has died. She is afraid of water, of ghosts, and of going to see a woman possessed of the devil (C, III, 297). She has faith in astrology, fears that Fridays are inauspicious, and thinks — until undeceived by experience — that it is lucky to see the crescent moon on the right (she probably means the new moon). She confesses more than once that her handwriting is atrocious. We learn something of her interests, too. She acquired a taste both for reading and for writing in her exile, but does not care about foreign languages. She is fond of horses and, later, of dogs. She dislikes long prayers, and sometimes falls asleep during them.

Mention should be made, doubtless, of the conversations she records. Writing, in some cases, many years after the event, she can scarcely have remembered them verbatim, but the fact that she did not attempt in any part of her memoirs to eliminate, for the sake of

---

[12] A regional lawcourt with lesser powers than those of the parlements.

history, the pomposity and naivety of which she was capable lends weight to our belief that she tried seriously and responsibly to give the very words that were spoken. At any rate, there is nothing inherently unconvincing or out of character in any of them.

Mademoiselle being a woman, and her friends and associates being chiefly women, her memoirs have a good deal to tell us about women in seventeenth-century France, the possibilities open to them and the restrictions to which they were subject. Was it because she was a woman that her father felt free to interfere in the affairs of her household, even after she had attained her majority? His secretary, Goulas, went so far as to say to him in 1657: 'But, Monseigneur, the Romans had the power of life and death over their children; are you not a great enough prince to treat Mademoiselle as you like?' Instead of throwing him out of the window, comments Mademoiselle, her father merely said nothing (C, III, 54-55). Would this conversation have taken place about a son?

It was not fitting, Mademoiselle tells us, for a woman to talk about theology; nor was it proper, she says when speaking of the Battle of the Dunes, for a lady to discuss military matters. It is therefore remarkable that she herself, previously, during the Fronde, had played some part in military affairs, and that, at the end of her life, she wrote two devotional works. It is not without some satisfaction that she reports that Brûlart, the First President of the parlement of Dijon who harangued her in November 1658 in that city as she was travelling with the court towards Lyon, told her that, had it been possible to foresee that France would have a princess like her, the Salic Law would never have been introduced, or would have been abolished in her favour (C, III, 295).

The great affair in the life of a woman — of a great lady, at least — was marriage. The list of suitors or possible husbands mentioned in Mademoiselle's memoirs is formidable. It begins with the comte de Soissons, who, however, rebelled against Richelieu and was killed. Then marriage with the Cardinal-Infante was arranged, but he died.[13] Other matches proposed or discussed concerned Charles II of England, both when he was in exile and after the Restoration; Philip IV of Spain; Ferdinand III, Emperor of Austria, on two occasions; his brother, Archduke Leopold; both the great Condé, known as

---

[13] Cardinal-Infante Ferdinand, a Spanish prince and the brother of Anne of Austria, was Governor of the Spanish Netherlands. Even though rumours of his impending marriage to Mademoiselle may have been false, they were believed in influential quarters.

Monsieur le Prince (his wife was ill more than once, but she always recovered) and his son, known as Monsieur le Duc; the Duke of Neuburg; Charles Emmanuel, Duke of Savoy; Charles Leopold of Lorraine; the King of Portugal; Frederick, Prince of Denmark; the young duc de Longueville; and the king's brother, Monsieur, both when he was a bachelor and when he became a widower. The Duke of Savoy's mother told Mademoiselle that her son had a closet in which were the portraits of all the marriageable princesses in Europe — an interesting sidelight on these matrimonial arrangements.

None of these marriages came to anything for various reasons; but some of them, which is not so common in the period, foundered solely on Mademoiselle's reluctance. She makes her attitude to marriage clear:

> I have never much cared about being married without greatness equal to my own (an ambition with which I was born) or even superior to my birth (if there can be any house above mine, but the vivid imagination God has given me has always carried things to excess), or without an inclination of a kind I had not then experienced. (C, III, 393–94)

She disdained Charles II and the Duke of Savoy, and suffered a second period of exile from court (1662–1664) rather than marry the repulsive King of Portugal, Alfonso VI.

One name has so far been omitted from the list, that of her cousin, Louis XIV. When he was a baby, his mother told Mademoiselle: 'You shall be my daughter-in-law'; and that match she would certainly not have refused. But, on the day she turned the guns of the Bastille on the royal army, and a cannon ball landed near her cousin, she ruined her chances. 'That gun has killed her husband,' observed Mazarin, if we are to believe Voltaire.[14]

Other women appear in the memoirs, less strong-minded than Mademoiselle. Richelieu married his niece, Mlle de Maillé-Brézé, to the duc d'Enghien (later prince de Condé — the great Condé).

> Shortly after his wedding, he fell so seriously ill that he was expected to die, and everyone attributed it to the chagrin this marriage had given him, as well it might, if only because of the

---

[14] Voltaire, *Le Siècle de Louis XIV*, in *Œuvres historiques*, ed. R. Pomeau (Paris: Gallimard, 1957), p. 663, a work published nearly one hundred years after the event. So many historians have quoted Mazarin's words that they have become a received truth. Voltaire always did his homework, and may have believed what he wrote, but there is no contemporary evidence.

person of his wife; for not only, as regards beauty and intellect, had she nothing that placed her above the average, but she was such a child that, over two years after being married, she was still playing with dolls; in consequence, all her husband's family rather looked down on her, and treated her badly. (C, I, 51)

The year after (Mademoiselle continues), she had to be sent to the Carmelite nuns of Saint-Denis to be taught to read and write.[15] Nevertheless, when her husband was arrested during the Fronde, she showed her mettle by raising Bordeaux against the government. Condé's sister, Mlle de Bourbon, was married by her father to the duc de Longueville — a cruel fate, says Mademoiselle, since he was old, and she 'very young and as beautiful as an angel' (C, I, 53–54). She was later La Rochefoucauld's mistress, and, like Mademoiselle, played an important part in the Fronde. Mlle de Gramont was married to the grandson of the Prince of Monaco. He was 'young, handsome, and a great nobleman; despite that, he did not please Mlle de Gramont; she was very sorry to be married. There was someone at court [Lauzun] who pleased her more' (C, III, 404). Mme de Monaco's affair with Lauzun endured just until she became, for a time, the mistress of Louis XIV himself. Perhaps the saddest story is that of Mlle d'Orléans, Mademoiselle's half-sister, married in 1661 to the Grand Duke of Tuscany, with love for Charles Leopold in her heart. She and her husband got on badly, and in 1675 she left Florence and returned to France. Louis XIV would not allow her to return to court, and relegated her to a convent.

There were ways of avoiding arranged marriages. Abduction or elopement was one. Mademoiselle relates how Mlle des Marais was abducted by her lover, with the connivance of her mother, and lived idyllically with him. Mlle d'Épernon, on the other hand, who had a vocation for the religious life, slipped into a convent and became a Carmelite in order to evade marriage with the heir presumptive of the King of Poland.[16] 'She preferred the crown of thorns to that of Poland', comments Mademoiselle, and she was proof against her stepmother's supplications: 'Neither tears nor entreaties had any effect on Mlle d'Épernon' (C, I, 185).

The lot of a king's mistress was not a bed of roses, either. Here is Louise de la Vallière in childbirth at Vincennes in 1666:

---

[15] The Carmelite convent of Saint-Denis, north of Paris, founded in 1625, had a reputation for piety and discipline. The premises still stand, having become the Musée d'Art et d'Histoire of Saint-Denis.

[16] John II Casimir, heir presumptive to his half-brother Ladislas IV.

> I have many times since heard how, as she was in labour, Madame passed through her room to go to mass in the Sainte-Chapelle; they concealed Boucher, who was delivering her, behind a curtain. She said to Madame: 'I am dying of colic!' And when Madame had gone, she said to Boucher: 'Hurry: I want to be delivered before she comes back.' It was a Saturday; cards were played in her room till midnight. She ate like the others at supper afterwards, and was bare-headed, just as if she had not given birth that morning. (C, IV, 48)

As Mlle d'Épernon demonstrated, the religious life was another possibility. Other women who opted for a similar course of action are Mlle de Saujon, who entered a convent but was persuaded to come out again, Mlle de Remenecourt, and Louise de la Vallière. A visit to Port-Royal des Champs is described. That the life of nuns was not always austere is shown by the example of the nuns of Perpignan. Without becoming nuns, many women interested themselves in good works: Mademoiselle founded a hospital in Saint-Fargeau and schools in Eu.

One thing that women could do — that Mademoiselle did do — was to write. Besides the *Histoire de Mme de Fouquerolle*, she published *Divers Portraits* (1659), a collection of descriptions of the appearance and analyses of the character of friends and acquaintances, by Mademoiselle and her friends.[17] In 1659, too, she published two stories, *La Relation de l'isle imaginaire* and *L'Histoire de la princesse de Paphlagonie*. She conceived the idea of a community of men and women leading a life of cultured seclusion, and corresponded with Mme de Motteville about it; their letters appeared in Cologne in 1667 in a *Recueil de pièces nouvelles et galantes*. In the last years of her life, she wrote two devotional works, *Réflexions sur les Huit Béatitudes du Sermon de Jesus-Christ sur la Montagne* (1685), and *Réflexions morales et chrétiennes sur le Premier Livre de l'Imitation de Jesus-Christ*, published posthumously in 1694.

A volume entitled *Nouvelles françoises, ou les Divertissements de la Princesse Aurélie* appeared in 1656 under the name of Segrais, Mademoiselle's secretary and a man of letters. Aurélie

---

[17] Just under a third were composed by Mademoiselle herself, and they include portraits of people we shall meet in the extracts translated here: Brays and Guilloire, two of her men of business, the chevalier de Béthune, the comtesse de Brienne, the chevalier de Charny (an untitled portrait, but there can be no doubt), the elder Mme de Choisy, Condé, the duchesse d'Epernon, the marquise de Montglat, Philippe d'Orléans, Mme de Thiange, Mlle de Vandy, and Louis XIV.

(Mademoiselle) and her five companions and their life at Saint-Fargeau are described. The ladies talk about novels, and Aurélie suggests that, unlike the romances of the day, fiction should be set in contemporary France. The ladies decide that each shall tell a story. Aurélie begins with a love story of the time of the Fronde. The five other stories also deal with love, and, with one exception, are set in medieval or modern France. They are not free from improbable or romantic situations, but in representing a transitional phase between the romances then fashionable and Mme de Lafayette's masterpiece, *La Princesse de Clèves*, the collection — reflecting, as it does, Mademoiselle's tastes and ideas — contributed to an important development in the French novel.

In the correspondence with Mme de Motteville, Mademoiselle attacks marriage and wishes to exclude married people from the proposed community: 'In short, let us withdraw from slavery; let there be one corner of the world in which women may be said to be their own mistresses.' Apart from that, she did not openly proclaim the rights of women, or insist on the equality of the sexes, but asserted her independence, refused to be a pawn in marriage, and distinguished herself not only in the field of literature, but also in the masculine preserve of war. In so doing, she furthered the cause of women.

Four Notes

1. *Titles*

The king's brother was known simply as 'Monsieur', his wife as 'Madame', and their daughter as 'Mademoiselle', a title she retained while unmarried, after which it passed to the eldest of any younger sisters she might have. In Mademoiselle's memoirs, there are thus two 'Monsieurs', her father, Gaston d'Orléans (also referred to as His Royal Highness), and, later (but with some overlap), Louis XIV's brother, Philippe, duc d'Anjou, who, after Gaston's death, became duc d'Orléans; and four 'Madames', her mother, her stepmother (Marguerite de Lorraine), Philippe d'Orléans's first wife Henrietta Anne (Henriette d'Angleterre), who died in 1670, and his second wife (Elisabeth Charlotte). Mademoiselle, the author of the memoirs, came to be known as the Grande Mademoiselle to distinguish her from Marie-Louise d'Orléans, the daughter of her cousins, Philippe d'Orléans and Henrietta Anne, who was also known as Mademoiselle until her marriage to the King of Spain in 1679. Thereupon the title passed to Marie-Louise's sister, Anne-Marie, until her marriage to Victor Amadeus II, Duke of Savoy, in 1684. After that, while the Grande Mademoiselle remained the Grande Mademoiselle, the title Mademoiselle devolved upon Elisabeth Charlotte d'Orléans, the half-sister of Marie-Louise and Anne-Marie and daughter of their father's second wife.[18]

2. Royal Residences

The king had two palaces in Paris, almost adjoining each other, the Louvre and the Tuileries (in which Mademoiselle was brought up). The court resided from time to time outside Paris at Saint-Germain or (more rarely) Vincennes. In summer or autumn, it might go to Fontainebleau, Chambord, or Versailles. Gradually Louis XIV developed Versailles, staying more and more frequently before establishing the court there permanently in 1682.

When Richelieu died in 1642, he left his palace, the Palais-Cardinal, to the crown; it was renamed the Palais-Royal. Anne of Austria lived there until she left Paris, during the Fronde, in 1651. On her return, in 1652, she moved back into the Louvre, and handed the Palais-Royal over to Henrietta Maria, the exiled Queen of England. When, in 1661, the Queen of England's daughter Henrietta Anne married Philippe, duc d'Orléans, the young couple moved into the Palais-Royal, and Henrietta Maria moved out.

The Luxembourg palace in Paris, built by Maria de' Medici, was the residence of Gaston d'Orléans, who, however, spent his last years in exile, mostly in Blois. After his death, Mademoiselle shared it with her stepmother and, after the latter's death, with her widowed half-sister, the duchesse de Guise, with whom she was on bad terms. In conformity with contemporary practice, Mademoiselle called it just *Luxembourg* ('I went to Luxembourg'), but, mindful of the ambiguity thus created, we have followed the modern tendency to call it 'the Luxembourg'.

3. Coinage

The unit of currency was the livre (or franc), subdivided into twenty sous and 240 deniers, in the same relationship to each other as the

---

[18] *Grand[e]* can mean 'great' (Le Grand Condé), and it is certainly found meaning 'senior' when distinguishing two people with similar titles, but Saint-Simon (III, 436), without ever quite sounding as though he believes it, advances the idea that Mademoiselle was so called because she was tall.

English pounds, shillings and pence that were in circulation until 1971. A silver écu was worth three livres. The louis or louis d'or, a gold coin so called from the image of the king's head on the obverse (originally that of Louis XIII), was worth ten livres in the early part of Mademoiselle's life; she prefers the word 'pistole' to indicate the louis d'or. Originally designating a Spanish coin, pistole became the more common word in unofficial French parlance in the 1640s. The pistole or louis d'or drifted to a value of eleven livres, and then twelve, as the century progressed. When John Locke was in France between 1675 and 1679, the rate of exchange was thirteen livres to an English pound.

4. *Places and Distances*

Mademoiselle mentions numerous places, mostly in France. Where we judge that readers will not locate them easily in an everyday atlas, we have explained where they are. Likewise, we have explained the position of buildings and streets that she names in Paris and Orleans so that they can be located by anyone with an ordinary modern street map. She gives distances in leagues. One French league was a little over two-and-a-half English miles. We have generally converted her leagues into miles, but in our notes we have used kilometres. One mile is 1.6 kilometres.

Notes on the Translation

The source text is that of the Chéruel edition (see 'Further Reading' for details). Occasionally, where it seemed appropriate to do so, original French terms have been retained; unless their meaning is obvious, an explanation is added, usually in a footnote. Although archaic English terms are avoided where there is a modern equivalent, some archaisms remain where they correspond to French objects and concepts that are themselves archaic. Our rule of thumb has been that words that appear in the Concise Oxford English Dictionary do not require an explanation.

Special consideration had to be given to names and titles, where a compromise has to be achieved between translating and retaining the French flavour of the text for readers who, we expect, will appreciate it. While it did not strike us as odd to write of the French kings Francis I and Henry IV, the fashion for calling their two great successors Lewis XIII and Lewis XIV has surely passed; consequently, while anglicizing Francis and Henry, we left Louis alone. As to titles, were we to write 'the Duke of Épernon', 'the Princess of Guéméné'? Perhaps so; but we preferred 'the duc d'Épernon', 'the princesse de Guéméné', and we took a similar decision in relation to comte, comtesse, duchesse, and so on, also respecting the French rule that the title takes the lower case.[19] Since the duchy of Lorraine, though not strictly part of France, was repeatedly occupied and was formally annexed by the Treaty of Montmartre in 1662, regaining a measure of flimsy independence only in 1697, we treated the titles of the house of Lorraine similarly. In other cases, we anglicized titles. We adopted the modern practice of giving some French cities their French names — such as Lyon and Reims — but we retained the spelling Luxemburg for the country in order to distinguish it from Mademoiselle's palace in Paris (the Luxembourg). We sought to resolve differences in the spelling of proper names in order to avoid creating the wrong impression: Mademoiselle, for example, writes Barail and Baraille — at least, she does so in Chéruel's edition; on the other hand, we did not intervene when her idiosyncratic spelling is internally consistent, as, for example, when she writes 'Saujon', a name elsewhere given as 'Saugeon'. When she writes 'château', she sometimes means a medieval fortification and sometimes a more modern grand residence; conscious that 'the castle of Chambord' looks strange to modern readers and that 'château' has become naturalized in English, we used that word where it seemed more appropriate.

Mademoiselle does not always trouble to avoid the kind of repetition that a careful writer might shun ('the next day ... the next day'; 'the prince was attacked ... where he was attacked'); we have not intervened, since our purpose is to capture Mademoiselle's style, not to improve it; neither have we intervened when she switches the time frame from the past to the present within the same paragraph, or even within the same sentence, so long as her meaning is clear. Often, she allows her sentences to run on excessively; we have intervened only in a number of places where misunderstandings could occur. She also places dialogue all in the same paragraph, not an uncommon arrangement in her day anyway, and we have left well alone.

---

[19] Mademoiselle often gives the full formal style of address, viz 'Madame la marquise de', 'Monsieur le duc de', and so on. We have not retained this practice in our version.

It was impossible, within the confines of a single volume, to provide the entire text of the memoirs; besides, even the most determined admirer of Mademoiselle would, we think, be willing to concede that some passages add little or nothing to our understanding either of the woman or of the social and historical context of the matters she relates. Consequently, we have translated just under one quarter of the original text by word count. We have placed in square brackets short descriptions of passages that we chose to omit on the grounds of length. Among them are several lengthy and discursive passages dealing with the court and courtiers, the court's travels, and military adventures in which she took no part personally. Numerous other much shorter passages, never exceeding 300 words and containing digressions and amplifications that we felt could be omitted, are represented by suspension marks, also within square brackets. The choice of what to translate must, in the end, be subjective. We have given, above, some pointers to the reasons for that choice.[20]

The memoirs form one continuous whole: that is to say, Mademoiselle does not divide her text into chapters or sections. Consequently, most of her editors and translators have felt the need to insert divisions of their own making. We have done likewise.

Whilst the source text is Chéruel's, the explanatory footnotes are our own. In addition, we have sometimes inserted a comment or explanation in square brackets in the text itself. Matter in parentheses represents Mademoiselle's own text.

The translation is the work of P. J. Yarrow, who also drafted the Introduction. William Brooks made some adjustments to the translation, revised the Introduction, added the footnotes and the suggestions for Further Reading, and compiled the index.

---

[20] Broadly, we have translated large parts, although not the entirety, of the following sections of Chéruel's edition: I, 1–75, 135–50 (forming 'Childhood and Youth'); I, 175–235, 290–330 ('The Fronde (I)'); I, 346–65 and II, 30–35, 90–125 ('The Fronde (II)'); II, 195–250, 280–308, 355–70, 430–62 and III, 67–74 ('Exile and Country Life'); III, 112–37, 156–223; 253–55; 272–300, 330–45 ('Return to Court'); III, 370–455 ('The Treaty of the Pyrenees'); III, 540–78 ('Mademoiselle's Second Exile'); IV, 92–137 ('Lauzun and the Journey to Flanders'); IV, 146–69 ('The Death of Madame'); IV, 169–232 ('The Match Made'); IV, 234–310 ('The Match Unmade'); IV, 400, 452–57 ('Lauzun's Release'); IV, 457–510 ('Reunion and Final Break-Up').

Chronological Table

1601	(27 Sept.) Birth of Louis de France, eldest son of Henry IV, dauphin and future Louis XIII
1607	(16 April) Birth of a second son, often called 'Nicolas', who died in 1611
1608	(24 April) Birth of Jean-Baptiste Gaston de France, duc d'Anjou, third son of Henry IV, known to history as Gaston d'Orléans
1610	(14 May) Assassination of Henry IV; accession of Louis XIII with his mother, Maria de' Medici, as regent
1615	(28 Nov.) Marriage of Louis XIII and Anne of Austria
1624	(April) Richelieu becomes Louis XIII's chief minister
1626	(6 Aug.) Marriage of Gaston d'Orléans and Marie de Bourbon, duchesse de Montpensier
1627	(29 May) Birth of Anne-Marie-Louise d'Orléans (4 June) Death of her mother
1630	France enters the Thirty Years' War (10 Nov.) The Day of Dupes: Gaston d'Orléans and Maria de' Medici leave France
1632	(3 Jan.) Gaston d'Orléans marries Marguerite de Lorraine
1634	Gaston d'Orléans returns to France
1638	(5 Sept.) Birth of Louis de France, dauphin, and future Louis XIV
1640	(21 Sept.) Birth of Philippe de France, brother of the future Louis XIV
1642	(4 Dec.) Death of Richelieu

1643	(14 May) Death of Louis XIII; accession of Louis XIV, with his mother, Anne of Austria, as regent and Mazarin as her chief minister
1648	(Aug.) Beginning of the Fronde, which lasted until 1652
	(Oct.) Treaty of Westphalia, which ended the Thirty Years' War — but France and Spain remained at war until 1659
1652	(27 March) Mademoiselle enters Orleans (2 July) Battle of the Faubourg Saint-Antoine (21 Oct.) The king returns to Paris
1652–1657	Mademoiselle exiled from court
1659	(Nov.) Treaty of the Pyrenees
1660	(2 Feb.) Death of Gaston d'Orléans (3–9 June) Marriage of Louis XIV and Maria Theresa of Spain
1661	(9 March) Death of Mazarin (31 March) Marriage of Philippe d'Orléans and Princess Henrietta Anne, sister of Charles II of England (1 Nov.) Birth of Louis XIV's son Louis de France, the dauphin (known to history as 'the Grand Dauphin')
1662–1664	Mademoiselle in exile again
1666	(20 Jan.) Death of the queen mother, Anne of Austria
1667–1668	War of Devolution: Louis XIV annexes Southern Flanders
1670	(April) The court tours Flanders (30 June) Death of Madame (Henrietta Anne) (Dec.) The king agrees to the marriage of Mademoiselle and Lauzun, then changes his mind

1671	(16 Nov.) Marriage of Monsieur and Elisabeth Charlotte of the Palatinate
	(25 Nov.) Arrest of Lauzun
1672	(13 April) Death of Marguerite de Lorraine
1672–1679	Dutch War
1680	(7 March) Marriage of the dauphin and Anne-Marie-Christine-Victoire of Bavaria
1681	Release of Lauzun
1683	(30 July) Death of Queen Maria Theresa
1684	(4 May) Mademoiselle dismisses Lauzun
1693	(5 April) Death of Mademoiselle

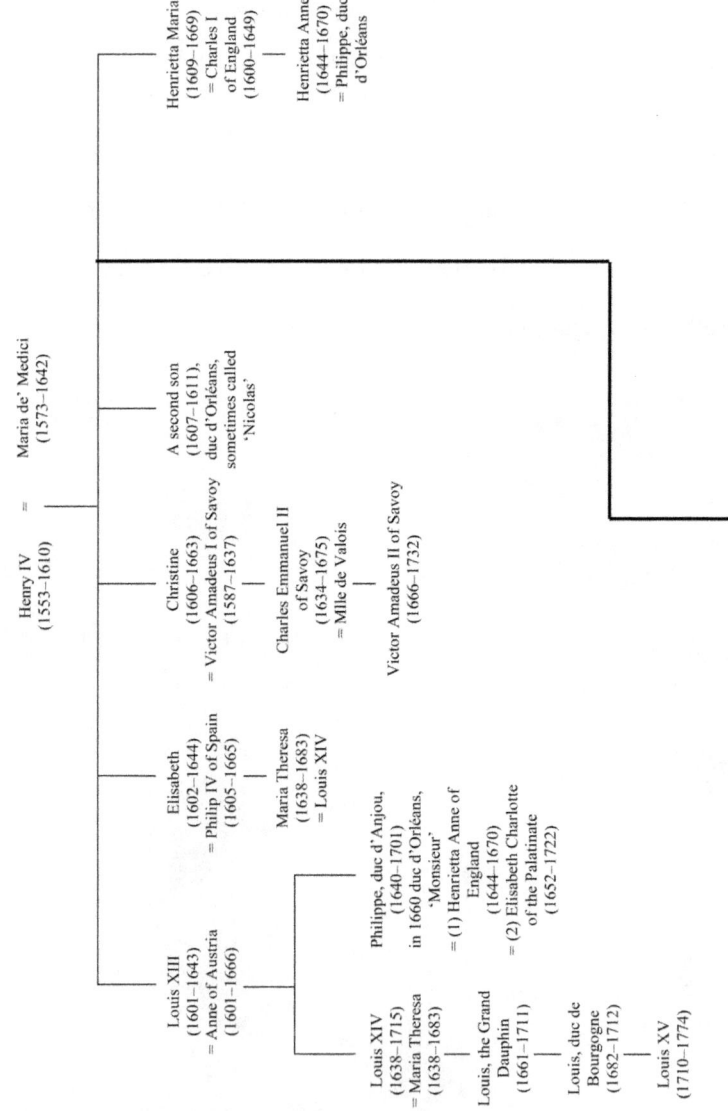

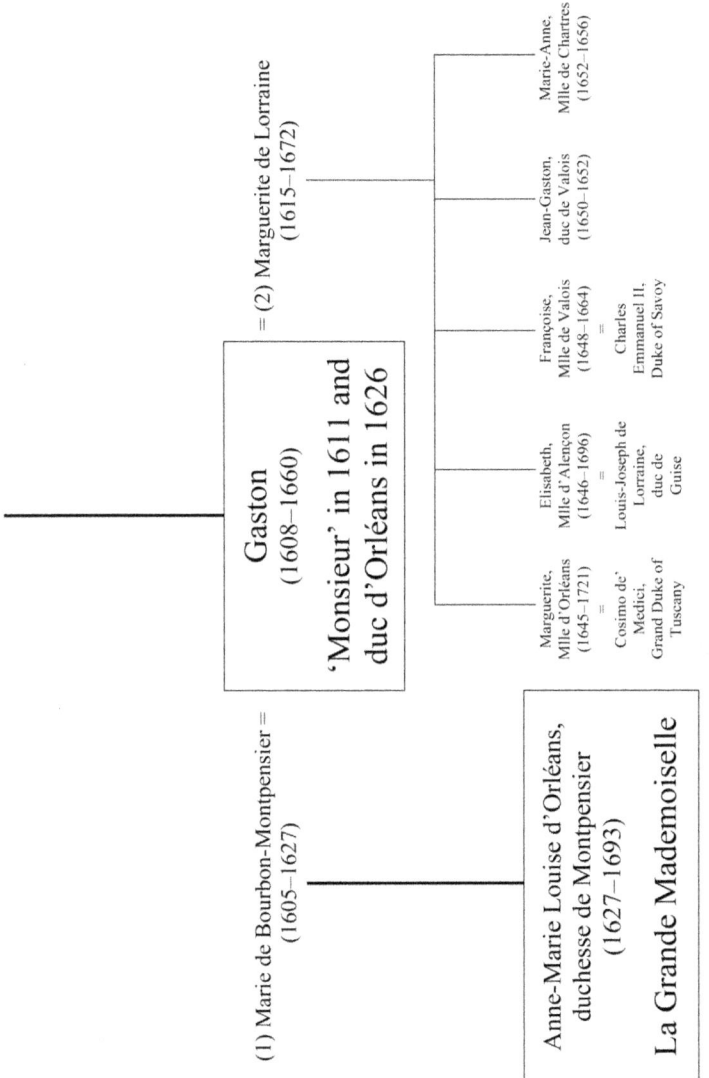

Part I

(1627–1659)

Chapter 1
Childhood and Youth (1627–1647)

I used to have great difficulty in imagining how the mind of someone accustomed to the court, and born to live at it with the rank that my birth confers on me, could occupy itself when that person found himself condemned to live in the country; for it had always seemed to me that nothing could entertain one during an enforced exile, and that, for the great, to be away from the court was to be in utter solitude, despite the number of their dependants and the company of those who visit them. However, since I have been secluded on my estates, I have had the pleasant experience of finding that remembering everything that has happened during one's lifetime is a sufficiently enjoyable occupation for the period of seclusion to be considered by no means the least agreeable in one's life. Not only is this state highly conducive to recalling events in order, but one finds the necessary leisure to write them down. Thus, the ease with which I can call to mind everything I have seen, and even what has happened to me, makes me today, at the request of some of whom I am fond, undertake a labour to which I should never have believed I could bring myself. I therefore set down here, as accurately as I can, everything I have had the opportunity of witnessing from my childhood until now, without, however, observing any other order than that of time. I hope, in view of the excellent memory that God has given me, that few of the things I have learnt will escape me; and my natural curiosity has led me to discover some that are sufficiently curious to make me think that they will not bore the reader.

The misfortunes of my house began soon after my birth (29 May 1627), since it was followed by the death of my mother, which spoiled my chances of the lofty station to which my rank entitled me. The great wealth which my mother left at her death, and of which I am the sole heiress, might well, in the opinion of most people, have consoled me for losing her. I, however, who realize today how invaluable her supervision would have been in my upbringing, and her influence, together with her affection, in establishing me in life, cannot sufficiently mourn her loss.

Soon after she died, my household was set up, and I was given a greater establishment than any daughter of France ever had, not even any of my aunts, the Queens of Spain and England and the Duchess of Savoy, before they were married.[1] The queen, my grandmother, gave me as governess the marquise de Saint-Georges, whose husband was of the house of Clermont of Amboise; she was the daughter of the marquise de Montglat, who had been governess of the late king, of Monsieur, of my late uncle, the duc d'Orléans,[2] and of all my aunts; and she was a woman of great virtue, intelligence, and worth, and thoroughly acquainted with the court. [...] My mother was brought to bed in the Louvre; I was lodged in the Tuileries, connected with it by the great gallery, which was the usual passage through which I was carried to Their Majesties, and through which they quite often, too, took the trouble to come and see me.[3]

The queen, my grandmother, Maria de' Medici, was very fond of me, and showed, as I have been told, much more affection for me than she ever had for her own children; but, as Monsieur had always been her favourite, and as she had always esteemed and loved my mother, her fondness for me need occasion no surprise. None the less, I was unfortunately deprived of its effects by the disgrace that made her leave France, for I was so young at that time that I cannot even remember having seen her. This was no less serious a loss than that which I suffered at my birth, since, in this great queen, I should most likely have found what I had lost by the death of my mother. Not that Mme de Saint-Georges, my governess, did not possess, for the satisfactory performance of her duties, all the qualities that could have been desired; but although ability, good conduct, and birth are often found in women chosen for this position, those of my degree, however young, are so rarely afraid of those beneath them, that it is more or less necessary for a superior authority to second their efforts. This emboldens me to say that, if there are any good

---

[1] Her aunts, in the order in which Mademoiselle mentions them here, were Elisabeth, Henrietta Maria, and Christine, the daughters of Henry IV and Maria de' Medici.

[2] By 'late uncle' she means her father's elder brother, often referred to as 'Nicolas' (1607–1611); in fact, the child was never officially named. The governess, the mother of Mademoiselle's governess, had been the baronne (not the marquise) de Montglat.

[3] The great gallery or 'waterside gallery', stretching for over 400 metres alongside the Seine, was completed in the reign of Henry IV and linked the Louvre to the Tuileries. The upper floor provided access from one to the other, while the lower floor accommodated artists and writers.

qualities in me, they are innate, and none of them must be attributed to my upbringing, excellent as it was; for I never feared the least punishment. Moreover, children who are looked up to and to whom people talk only of their high birth and their great wealth usually come to be filled with false pride. My ears were so frequently assailed by talk of those two things that I was easily persuaded, and I retained a highly disagreeable spirit of vanity until reason taught me that the greatness of a well-born princess consists in not being content with the greatness for which I had so often and for so long been praised. The frankness with which I mean to talk about everything I am going to tell leads me to set down here an anecdote of my childhood. When they spoke to me of Mme de Guise, my grandmother, I would say: 'She is only remotely my grandmother; she is no queen.'[4]

The disgrace of the queen, my grandmother, gave rise to many dissensions at court. Monsieur was one of the malcontents; he fell out with the king, and left France soon after her. His exile affected me much more than that of the queen, and, on that occasion, my behaviour was beyond my years: I refused to be amused by anything, and I could not even be induced to go to the assemblies in the Louvre; my misery increased when I learned that Monsieur was with the army, because the danger he was in filled me with apprehension. Monsieur's relations with the court did not stop them from taking all possible care of me; the king and queen treated me with unequalled kindness, and showed me all kinds of marks of affection. When they came to Paris, they gave orders that I should often be taken to see them; and that never happened but that I talked to the king about Monsieur. His absence obliged the king to appoint commissioners to administer my property: M. Favier and M. d'Irval, members of the conseil d'Etat,[5] and a councillor in the parlement called Grasteau were selected, all men of ability and probity, who took great care that I should lack nothing that I might want; and they behaved so honourably in their commission that they gave Monsieur, on his return from Flanders, a considerable sum that they had put by.

Many things occurred during that period; I was but a child at the time, and I was not in a position to observe anything. The only thing I can remember is seeing the ceremony of the installation of the

---
[4] On her father's side, Mademoiselle's grandmother was, of course, Queen of France, but her sardonic comments about Mme de Guise must also have been influenced by the knowledge that that great lady's second husband, who died in 1640, nursed pretensions to the French throne.
[5] The conseil d'Etat or Council of State existed to advise the king.

knights of the Order at Fontainebleau, at which the duc d'Elbeuf and the marquis de Vieuville were simultaneously expelled.[6] I saw the panels with their coats of arms, which were in line with the others, taken down and smashed. I asked the reason for this; I was told that they were being insulted in this way because they had followed Monsieur. I burst into tears, and was so upset by this treatment that I insisted on going out, saying that I could not with propriety witness this deed. My annoyance, however, did not make me hate the court; I was delighted when it was at Fontainebleau and Their Majesties sent for me. When that happened, I would blissfully stay there for three or four weeks because of the continual entertainments I enjoyed. Certainly, the king, by the affection he showed me, assuaged the grief that his dislike of Monsieur occasioned me. The queen's feelings did not concur with his in this respect. I think that her good will towards me was only the consequence of her liking for Monsieur. I was so used to their caresses that I called the king 'little papa' and the queen 'little mamma'; I thought she was, because I had never seen my mother. When I was in Paris, all the girls of noble birth came and played with me; but the most assiduous were Mlles de Longueville, d'Épernon, de Brissac,[7] M. de Gramont's daughters,[8] Mlles de Lannoi, du Lude, Séguier (the chancellor's daughter),[9] de Rancé,[10] de la Ville-aux-Clercs, Jarnac,[11] and many others, and they were my particular friends.

---

[6] 15 May 1633. The Order was the Ordre du Saint-Esprit (Order of the Holy Ghost), the knights of which wore a blue ribbon or *cordon bleu*.

[7] This must be Élisabeth de Cossé, Mlle de Brissac, because her older sister Marie was already married, having become the second wife of Marshal de la Meilleraye. If Mademoiselle means to indicate more than one daughter of the duc de Brissac, she must also have in mind one or both of Élisabeth's much younger sisters Ursule-Anne and Marguerite-Guyonne.

[8] By his second marriage, the marquis de Gramont had a son (Philibert), whom we shall meet later, and three daughters, Suzanne-Charlotte, Anne-Louise, and Charlotte-Catherine, two or all of whom must have been the daughters whom Mademoiselle mentions here. The last-named is not to be confused with Catherine-Charlotte, daughter of their half-brother Antoine, Marshal Gramont, who was to marry the grandson of the Prince of Monaco.

[9] Chancellor Séguier had two daughters who survived infancy, Marie, the future duchesse de Laval, and Charlotte, the future duchesse de Sully. Charlotte was closer to Mademoiselle's age.

[10] One or both of the daughters of Denis de Boutheillier de Rancé. They were Charlotte, the elder, and Marie. Their brother Armand-Jean was the future abbot of La Trappe.

[11] One or more of the daughters of Guy Chabot, comte de Jarnac, by his second wife. They were, respectively, Claire, who was born in 1620, Charlotte, and Marie, who were about ten years younger. All three became nuns.

I was not so much taken up with play that I did not listen carefully when there was talk of Monsieur's reconciliation. Cardinal Richelieu, who was chief minister and in control of everything, was determined to handle this matter himself — with such shameful terms for Monsieur that I could not even hear of them without being in despair. He spread a rumour that, for Monsieur to make his peace with the king, he would have to divorce the princess Marguerite of Lorraine, and marry Mlle de Combalet, the Cardinal's niece, now Mme d'Aiguillon.[12] I could not help weeping as soon as anyone spoke to me about it, and, in my rage, to get my own back, I would sing all the songs I knew deriding the Cardinal and his niece; it even made me like Princess Marguerite better and talk of her incessantly. Monsieur, however, made his peace and returned to France without this ridiculous condition. […]

As soon as I learned that Monsieur had come back, I went to Limours to meet him.[13] I was only four or five when he left. He wanted to see if I should know him again after such a lengthy absence; and, in order that nothing should distinguish him from his courtiers, he had his blue ribbon taken off, and then I was told: 'Pick Monsieur out from all those.' The force of nature guided me so well in this that, without a moment's hesitation, I ran to him and flung my arms round his neck, which seemed to give him great joy. While I was with him, he delighted in everything that delighted me, and, hearing that I should very much like to dance in a ballet, he made up his mind that I should, since I had been too little to be in the one the king and queen had got up at this time. Accordingly, for this ballet, which might have been called a pygmies' dance, a company was formed of little girls, princesses and noblewomen, and of all the gentlemen who were of the same size as we. Because of the magnificent jewellery and dress of each of the dancers, the ballet — the steps and entrees of which, of course, were not too complicated — was much appreciated. There was one entree in which birds were brought in cages and set free to fly round the room — an invention worthy of such a ballet. One of these birds became entangled in a fold in the ruff of Mlle de

---

[12] Mademoiselle refers to 'Mlle' Combalet, but must mean 'Mme' because the future duchesse d'Aiguillon was the widow of Antoine de Combalet. (She did not remarry; her title was a creation.)

[13] Limours is about 30 kilometres south-west of Paris. Louis XIII had purchased its château from Cardinal Richelieu and, in 1627, added it to his brother's apanage. Gaston had returned there on 8 October 1634, but without Marguerite. Richelieu and the king were furiously opposed to the marriage. Gaston, for once, held firm, but even so, she was not allowed to join him in France until 1643.

Brézé, Cardinal Richelieu's niece, who was one of us. She shrieked and wept so passionately as greatly to increase the laughter that this unexpected incident had excited in the whole assembly. From that you may judge of the age of the ladies in the ballet. The king's was not so entertaining. [...]

Had I not had a child's mind, I should not have seen the comte de Soissons's assiduous attentions to me at that time without drawing conclusions. He was then on excellent terms with Monsieur, and treated him with great deference, the point of which I did not learn until long after it had come to an end, and shortly before his death. His purpose was to marry me. Monsieur, when he was at Sedan, had promised his consent, and this aim made him alert to anything that could help to make me remember him. He asked a gentleman named Campion to remain behind in Paris, and often come and ask after me, and give me the count's good wishes. In order to acquit himself the better of these duties, he sometimes brought me different varieties of sugared almonds sent to me from Sedan by his master.

Monsieur, who remained at Blois after the count had withdrawn to Sedan, ordered me to go and join him there. Before setting off, I sent to ask for the permission of the king, who was at Chantilly; he agreed, merely telling me to go and take leave of him. [...] On arriving at Chantilly, I put the whole court in a good humour. The king was then deeply unhappy, because his suspicions of the queen had been aroused, and it was not long since the discovery of the casket, which occasioned what happened at the Val-de-Grâce, of which only too much has been heard.[14] I found the queen ill in bed — one might well be made ill by less than the insult she had received. The chancellor had come to interrogate her the day before; her distress was still in its first freshness, and the presence of Mme de Saint-Georges had the power to soothe it. She was the intermediary between the queen and Monsieur, and the queen was delighted to see a confidante to whom she could open her heart. In order that no one could suspect anything, they called me in as a third person, believing that no one could imagine that they would risk talking of such weighty matters in the presence of a child. Necessity compelled them to confide in me;

---

[14] The queen was suspected of being in correspondence with Spain. She was interrogated at Chantilly by the chancellor, Séguier, on 24 August 1637. Earlier, the king had had the Val-de-Grâce (founded, and often visited, by the queen) searched by the Chancellor and the Archbishop of Paris, Jean-François de Gondi; a casket was found, but, according to Mme de Motteville, it contained only gloves, a gift from the Queen of England, Henrietta Maria.

and if I had attended as much to what they were saying as I have since regretted not doing, I should be able to set down here details that I suppose no one knows. Besides, they urged me in every possible way to say nothing about their conversations. One of their ploys was to praise secrecy continually, and I took it into my head that the real and safest way to keep a secret was to forget what I had heard; and I was so successful in that, that I have never remembered it. [...]

Monsieur came as far as Chambord, ten miles from Blois, to meet me; this is a château belonging to him, built by Francis I in a most extraordinary manner in the middle of a park some twenty-five or thirty miles round, with no courtyard other than a space surrounding part of the main building, which is round. One of its most curious and remarkable features is the staircase, so constructed that one person can go up and another come down without meeting, though they can see each other. Monsieur straight away amused himself by teasing me with this. He was at the top of the staircase when I arrived; he came down when I went up, and laughed heartily to see me run, thinking that I should catch him. I was very pleased with his enjoyment, and even more so when I had joined him. Immediately afterwards, we got into a coach together, and went to Blois, where the municipal bodies came to welcome and compliment me like those of all the other towns I passed through, as is customary. Monsieur himself was good enough to think of ways of amusing me, and kept coming to my room, even though I was in a block separated from his by the courtyard, and there was a staircase to climb. I did as he intended: I spent my time doing whatever could amuse me, usually playing at shuttlecock or some other active game, that being what I like best in the world. Monsieur condescended to join in, and to play at forfeits with me. I usually won, and was paid in watches and all sorts of jewellery to be found in the town. [...]

Monsieur left Blois and went to Tours, drawn by his fondness for Louison Roger.[15] He ordered me to join him two days later, but an attack of fever prevented me from going for a week. [...] I went as soon as my health allowed. I set out on the river in a little galley of Monsieur's, who had had it built to go sailing on the Loire, and which was, in every respect, like those on the sea. I stopped it some ten miles short of the city, and went the rest of the way by coach. I found Monsieur in a house near the city, known as La Bourdaisière,

---

[15] Gaston's mistress, Louison Roger de la Marbillière, born in 1621. In 1653, she entered a convent.

made ready for me.[16] All the ladies had come, and Monsieur took the trouble to present them to me himself, particularly Louison, who was dark, and of medium height, and had a good figure, a very attractive face, and a good deal of wit for a girl of that class who had never been to court. Monsieur praised her liberally, instructed me to treat her well, and informed me that she would often come and play with me, and that she was not too old for that; she was about sixteen. Mme de Saint-Georges, who knew of Monsieur's passion, asked him if she was a good girl, because, if not, although Louison had the honour of his good graces, she would not like her to come to my house. Monsieur gave her every assurance, and told her that, unless she were, he would not wish it himself. Even at that time, I had such horror of vice that I said to Mme de Saint-Georges: 'Mamma (so I called her), if Louison is not a good girl, although my father loves her, I do not wish to see her; or, if he wants me to, I shall receive her coldly.' She replied that she was a very good girl, and I was delighted. I liked her very much; she was as good-humoured as she was attractive; so I often saw her. The marquise de Fourilles, who was at Tours while I was there, also saw me very often; she was a very well-bred woman, whose company I enjoyed enormously. Although I ought to have been more at home with children of my age, when I met adults who were to my taste, I would leave my games and amusements to converse with them. In short, both there and in Blois, I passed my time most agreeably. It was autumn, and I had the pleasure of driving out. Monsieur sent for actors, and we had plays nearly every day.

[Monsieur went to Paris. After a few days in Richelieu, Fontevrault, and Saumur, Mademoiselle returned via Chenonceaux to Blois, where her father was waiting for her and where they spent All Saints' Day, 1 November 1637.[17] After recalling events in Tours that she had previously forgotten to mention, Mademoiselle briefly relates her journey to Paris later that month.]

I spent the winter in Paris in the same way as the previous ones. I went to the receptions given twice a week by the comtesse de

---

[16] It belonged to the marquis de Crèvecœur, and still stands today, just south of Montlouis-sur-Loire.

[17] Fontevrault is 10 kilometres east of Saumur, and Richelieu about 30 kilometres south-east of Fontevrault. The disputed property of Champigny, which will be mentioned below, was between Fontevrault and Richelieu, 6 kilometres from the latter.

Soissons in the hôtel de Brissac;[18] plays were the usual amusements; I loved dancing, and there was often dancing for my sake, and Mlle de Longueville enjoyed it most. She and I were in the habit of laughing at everyone, though it would have been easy to pay us back in our own coin; we dressed as ridiculously as anyone could, and we made every possible face, despite the merciless scoldings of her governess and mine. The only way of stopping us was to forbid us to see each other; everyone knew that this would be a really harsh punishment, because of the great friendship between us. The princesse de Condé and Mme de Longueville (who was then Mlle de Bourbon), who were in Paris, did not come to our balls; I was delighted, for at that time I had the greatest dislike for them both.

Towards the end of the winter, the queen became pregnant; she wanted me to go and live at Saint-Germain. During her pregnancy, which was veiled in mystery, Cardinal Richelieu, who disliked Monsieur, was unwilling that anyone connected with him should be with Their Majesties; and although he had been one of my godparents together with the queen, although he told me that this spiritual relationship obliged him to look after me and that he would find me a husband (he spoke to me in this way as one speaks to children, saying the same thing over and over again), and although he claimed to be very fond of me, it was with great difficulty that the scruples his mistrust gave him were removed. When he had agreed, I went to Saint-Germain with great delight. I was so innocent that I was overjoyed to see the queen in that condition, and did not at all think of the injury it was doing to Monsieur, who had such a warm affection for the king and queen that he was genuinely glad and said so. Because of my attentiveness to the queen, she gave me many marks of kindness, and kept saying: 'You shall be my daughter-in-law'; but of all that was said to me, what was beyond my age passed over my head.

The court was very pleasant at that time; the king's love for Mme de Hautefort, whom he endeavoured to entertain every day, had a lot to do with it. Hunting was one of the king's greatest pleasures; we often went with him: Mme de Hautefort, Chemerault, and Saint-

---

[18] The seventeenth-century hôtel de Brissac is not to be confused with the well-known eighteenth-century building that became the *mairie* of the seventh arrondissement of Paris. Rather, it lay close to the hôtel de Soissons, occupying a site on the north side of the rue des Deux Écus. The street no longer exists, but its position can be imagined as a westward extension of the modern rue Berger beyond its junction with the rue du Louvre in the first arrondissement.

Louis, maids of honour to the queen, D'Escars, Mme de Hautefort's sister,[19] and Beaumont came with me. We were all brightly dressed, on fine, richly caparisoned palfreys, and, to keep the sun off, each of us had a hat trimmed with many feathers. The hunt always went in the direction of some fine houses, in which we would find substantial collations, and on the way back the king would get into my coach between Mme de Hautefort and me. When he was in a good humour, he conversed very pleasantly with us about all manner of things. At that time, he allowed people to talk quite freely to him about Cardinal Richelieu; and a sign that that did not displease him was that he spoke about him in the same way himself.

As soon as we got back, we would go to the queen's apartments; I took pleasure in serving her at her supper, and her maids carried the dishes in. Regularly, three times a week, there was a musical entertainment, given by the musicians of the king's chamber, and most of the songs sung at it were composed by him; he even wrote the words, and the subject was always Mme de Hautefort. The king was always so gallant that, at the collations he gave us in the country, he never sat down at table, and he served nearly all of us, though his civility had but one object. He ate after us, and seemed to affect to pay no more attention to Mme de Hautefort than to the rest, so afraid was he that his love might be noticed. If they fell out, all entertainments were suspended; and if the king visited the queen at such times, he spoke to no one, and no one dared to speak to him either; he would sit down in a corner, where usually he yawned and fell asleep. His melancholy cast a chill over everyone, and while his ill humour lasted, he would spend most of the day writing down what he had said to Mme de Hautefort, and what she had said to him in reply; indeed, after his death, detailed accounts of all the disagreements he had had with his mistresses were found in his casket, to the credit of whom (and of him) it may be said that he never loved any that were not highly virtuous.

Towards the end of the queen's pregnancy, the princesse de Condé and Mme de Vendôme came to Saint-Germain and brought their

---

[19] Marie de Hautefort was Louis XIII's mistress. As mistress of the wardrobe to the queen, she was entitled to the courtesy title 'Madame'. Her sister Charlotte, called Mlle d'Escars, and a third sister, Françoise, Mlle de Ségur, who will be mentioned later, were in the queen's service as well. We shall also meet their brother, the comte d'Escars.

daughters with them.[20] This was fresh company for me; they drove out with me, and the king was very embarrassed; he was always shy when he saw anyone to whom he was not used, just like an ordinary country gentleman freshly come to court. This is an unfortunate quality in a great king, particularly in France where he often has to show himself to his subjects, whose affection is won more by affability and familiarity than by the austere gravity which the members of the house of Austria never abandon. Monsieur also came to court, and shortly afterwards the queen bore a son. The birth of the dauphin [the future Louis XIV] gave me a new occupation; I went to see him every day and called him 'my little husband'; the king was amused, and approved of everything I did. Cardinal Richelieu, who did not want me to become familiar with the court, nor the court to grow accustomed to me, ordered me to return to Paris. The queen and Mme de Hautefort did everything they could to keep me there; they were unable to get permission, for which I was very sorry. I wept and screamed when I parted from the king and queen. Their Majesties expressed much affection, especially the queen, who showed me particular fondness on this occasion.

After this blow, I had to suffer another. I was made to go to Ruel to see the Cardinal, who usually resided there when the king was at Saint-Germain.[21] He so deeply resented my having called the dauphin 'my little husband', that he reprimanded me severely. He said that I was too old to use such expressions, and that it was unbecoming of me to talk in that way. He spoke to me so seriously, as if I had been grown up, that, without answering him, I burst into tears. To pacify me, he gave me a collation. That did not stop me from going away very angry about everything he had said.

When I had gone back to Paris, I went to court only once in two months; and when I did, I dined with the queen and came back to Paris to sleep.[22] [...] When the queen learned what the Cardinal had said to me, she expressed her displeasure, and said to me good-naturedly: 'It is true that my son is too little; you shall marry my brother.' She meant the Cardinal-Infante [Ferdinand], who was then

---

[20] The daughters were, respectively, Anne-Geneviève de Bourbon-Condé, the future duchesse de Longueville, and Élisabeth de Vendôme, the future duchesse de Nemours. It is, indeed, for Anne-Geneviève and her mother that Mademoiselle has evinced the greatest dislike only four paragraphs earlier.
[21] Ruel, later Rueil (and now Rueil-Malmaison), lies west of Paris, roughly half way to Saint-Germain; its château belonged to Mme d'Aiguillon.
[22] We should remember, throughout these memoirs, that one *dined* at around midday, and that *dinner* is the midday meal.

in Flanders, Captain-General of the country, and in command of the armies of the King of Spain. Not caring about being married, I heeded these projects less than I thought about dancing and the entertainments of that winter. [...]

While we thought of nothing but passing our time, there were more important intrigues at court than those which sowed dissension in our balls. Cardinal Richelieu gave M. de Cinq-Mars a post about the person of the king, who made him his favourite in place of M. de Saint-Simon, master of the horse, who was relegated to Blaye [about 30 kilometres north of Bordeaux], of which he was governor. M. de Cinq-Mars was no sooner established, than the Cardinal made him his confidant, and used him to dismiss Mme de Hautefort and Chemerault from court. This was a great blow to me, especially as I did not dare to go and see them. [...]

That was not the only aspect of court affairs that interested me: I was also very much concerned about those of the comte de Soissons, which grew worse every day. The king went to Champagne to wage war against him; and during this expedition, Mme de Montbazon, who was very fond of the count, who was very fond of her, came to see me regularly every day, spoke to me about him with much affection, told me that she would be overjoyed when I had married him, that boredom would then be banished from the hôtel de Soissons,[23] that he would think of nothing but giving me balls and plays, that we should drive out, and that I should have his respect and unrivalled affection. She overlooked nothing that could make this condition a happy one, and nothing that, at my age, might incline me towards it. I listened to her with pleasure, and I had no aversion from the count's person. However, without knowing why, I had no inclination to be married. The unhappy fate with which his projects met shows clearly that we were not born for each other; none the less, I wept bitterly at his death, and when I went to Bagnolet [just east of Paris] to see his mother, M. and Mlle de Longueville and all the household did nothing but express their grief by continual lamentations. The

---

[23] The large and luxurious hôtel de Soissons, on a site that can best be described as partly overlapping that of the present-day Bourse de Commerce in the first arrondissement of Paris, was constructed by Catherine de' Medici in the sixteenth century, when it was called the hôtel de la Reine and considered the only palace in Paris to rival the Tuileries and the Louvre. In those days, the rue du Jour continued in a south-south-westerly direction beyond the rue Coquillière until it met the rue Saint-Honoré. The hôtel occupied roughly two-thirds of its western side, and extended westwards along the south side of the rue Coquillière. Charles de Bourbon-Condé, comte de Soissons, bought it in 1606.

king's wrath against him was so great that he would not allow his memory to be honoured, and forbade mourning for him to be worn at court.[24]

Apart from the disproportion between my age and his, my marriage with him was perfectly suitable: he was very gentlemanly, and endowed with great qualities, and, although a younger son, had nevertheless been engaged to the Queen of England.[25] No one can gainsay that the loss of such an accomplished prince of the blood was a great loss to the state. Shortly before the Battle of Sedan [the Battle of La Marfée], in which he was killed, he had sent the comte de Fiesque to Monsieur, to remind him of his promise to him about me, and that the arrangement could now be carried into effect; he begged him most humbly to agree to his eloping with me, as the only means of bringing the marriage about. Monsieur refused to agree to this expedient, so that the answer taken back by the comte de Fiesque greatly affected the count.

[Mademoiselle recalls events at court in 1641 and 1642, including the marriage of the duc d'Enghien, the future Grand Condé, and — not in its correct chronological place — the birth in 1640 of Philippe, duc d'Anjou, brother of the future Louis XIV. News came of the death, on 3 July 1642 in Cologne, of her grandmother, Maria de' Medici.]

This news was followed by that of the trial and execution of M. de Cinq-Mars, the king's master of the horse, and of M. de Thou, which I deeply regretted, both on their own account, and because Monsieur was unfortunately involved in the affair that led to their deaths:[26] indeed, it was believed that his evidence to the chancellor was what weighed most heavily against them and was the cause of their deaths. This memory is too painful for me to say any more about it. Mourning for my grandmother compelled me to be shut up in a room hung with black. I observed this retreat with all possible conscientiousness. I had no difficulty in keeping out visitors. What all unfortunates experience happened to me: no one came to see me.

---

[24] Louis, the rebel comte de Soissons, defeated a royal army at the Battle of La Marfée, near Sedan, in July 1641, but was killed, reputedly by accident, after the battle was won.

[25] Henry IV had agreed that Soissons should marry his daughter, Henrietta Maria. When Louis XIII married her to Charles I in 1625, Soissons wanted to marry Mlle de Montpensier (the future mother of Mademoiselle).

[26] Cinq-Mars plotted against the government and signed a treaty with Spain. He and his friend, De Thou, were beheaded at Lyon in September 1642. Gaston d'Orléans was implicated in the conspiracy.

I may say, to my credit, that I showed more feeling for this misfortune of Monsieur's than might have been expected from someone of my years. [...]

As soon as I heard of the death of Richelieu [4 December 1642], I went to see the king to beseech him to relent towards Monsieur. I thought this a very favourable opportunity to mollify him: he refused, and went to the parlement next day to have the declaration against him registered; its subject is well known,[27] and I need not explain it here. I intended to go and throw myself at his feet when he entered the parlement, to beseech him not to go to such lengths; he was warned and sent an order forbidding me; nothing could deter him from this insulting measure.

[Soon afterwards, the Cardinal-Infante died. Monsieur made his peace with the king and was permitted to return to Paris, where he came to stay with his daughter.]

I started by complaining of abbé de la Rivière, who was beginning to enjoy his favour; he did not heed my complaints as I had expected, which did not lessen my joy on seeing him. He supped with me to the accompaniment of the twenty-four violins;[28] he was as merry as if M. de Cinq-Mars and M. de Thou had not fallen by the wayside. I confess that I could not see him without thinking of them, and that, in my joy, I felt grieved by his. Next day he went to Saint-Germain, where he was well received by the king. As for the queen, no one can doubt it, since they had both been involved in the last affair that had made Monsieur leave court.[29] He did not stay long with Their Majesties; he went to see them occasionally, and spent the winter in Paris. Never were there so many balls as that year [the winter of 1643]. The marriage of M. de Montglat with Mlle de Chiverni was the occasion of many; I was at them all. I was all the more pleased with this marriage as, after it, this girl, who was excellent company, was always with me, since she came to live with Mme de Saint-Georges, her mother-in-law. I did not long enjoy her company, because of the death of Mme de Saint-Georges. She had been ill all the winter. Soon after her son's wedding, she was compelled to take to her bed, and

---

[27] The exclusion of Monsieur from the regency.
[28] This was the name given to the king's string orchestra, strictly the twenty-four violins of the king's chamber. They played during the king's dinner and at balls, and they could be hired by other people.
[29] The conspiracy of Cinq-Mars.

her complaint grew worse. On 13 February, she had a stroke, and lost consciousness. In the morning, when I awoke, I learnt of her condition; I got up hurriedly to go and show her by my solicitude how grateful I was to her for having so worthily fulfilled her duties to me ever since I came into the world. I arrived as all possible remedies were being tried to bring her round. After a great deal of effort, her attendants succeeded, and immediately the last sacrament and extreme unction were brought, which she received with all the marks of a truly Christian soul. Her responses to all the prayers were admirably devout, which did not surprise those who knew how piously she had lived.

That done, she called her children to give them her blessing, and asked my leave to give it to me, too; she told me that the honour she had of serving me since my birth, made her dare to take this liberty. My affection for her was equal to that which she had showed in all the trouble she had taken over my education. I knelt down by her bedside, my eyes bathed in tears; I heard her mournful farewell; I embraced her. I was so much affected by her death and all the kind things she had said to me, that I was unwilling to leave her till she had expired. She begged her attendants to make me withdraw, and her children, too; she was too much moved by our tears and lamentations, and said that I alone was all the subject of the regrets she was capable of feeling. I went to my room, which I had no sooner entered than her death throes began, and she died a quarter of an hour later.

Monsieur came about that time, found me greatly affected, and told me that I must not remain in a house in which there was a dead body, particularly that of someone whose loss I felt so deeply. He ordered me to sleep in the hôtel de Guise, where he was then staying; he gave his room up to me, and went to a bathing establishment.[30]

[Ignoring his daughter's preferences, Monsieur chose Mme de Fiesque to succeed Mme de Saint-Georges.]

I have since learnt that the reasons which made him prefer the comtesse de Fiesque to the comtesse de Tillières and everyone else was that she was a widow, and more suitable for the post than

---

[30] 'Chez les baigneurs', in Mademoiselle's words. Bathing establishments, kept by *baigneurs*, also provided accommodation in which well-heeled individuals could reside luxuriously. The hôtel de Guise was in the rue du Chaume, roughly where the north-west corner of the Archives nationales lies in the modern rue des Archives in the third arrondissement of Paris.

a married woman.³¹ She had been mistress of the wardrobe to my mother; he wanted to deprive her of any possible claim to be that of his wife, because, while she had been in his house, she had been an intriguer — indeed, had my mother not died, he would have dismissed her: I speak from first-hand knowledge. Thus, His Royal Highness, who wanted to remove such people, of whom there were already too many, from his household, made her my governess, and rightly foresaw that my dislike of her would stop me from following her example.

When she arrived at Saint-Denis, I received her kindly. I expressed considerable gladness at being in her hands, and said that I had wanted it and helped to bring it about. She told me that she well knew it and felt much obliged to me. Thus, the first days passed pleasantly, largely because of her intellectual gifts; she told me a great many, highly entertaining, stories of her youth, which made me greatly enjoy her conversation, and, indeed, though old, she is as good company as anyone. She entered on her duties by having an inventory made of all my jewels, to stop me giving any away without her permission, particularly several that were in a separate cabinet, which she was afraid I might give to Mme de Montglat. Then she took away the key of my writing desk, which was usually left in it (so that it was always open), and kept it, because it was not seemly, said she, that it should be in my keeping, and she ought to see everything I wrote, and to whom.

This made me really cross, and I thought her authority most oppressive. However, although unaccustomed to such subordination, I put up with it without saying anything. But I could not behave in the same way soon afterwards in a matter concerning the interests of Mme de Saint-Georges's children,³² whom she treated badly. I then recalled all my grievances, and mentioned them to her, respectfully enough. That gave rise to some acrimony, and, after this tiff, instead of enjoying her company, I regarded her as a nuisance. Henceforth, we tended to quarrel frequently. One day I had a cold; my doctor prescribed some remedy, which, as my custom was, I refused to take. She took it into her head, although I was over fifteen, to treat me like a child; she locked me in my room, and visitors were told that I was

---

[31] Anne Le Veneur, comtesse de Fiesque, the mother of the comte de Fiesque whom we met earlier. The comtesse de Tillières's second husband, Henri Le Veneur, was Mme de Fiesque's brother.
[32] François-de-Paule, marquis de Montglat, and his brother Victor de Clermont de Saint-Georges.

ill and could not be seen. I thought this behaviour as high-handed as it was disagreeable, and yet I did not otherwise rebel. I merely expressed childish resentment. I managed to escape from my room; I went to her closet, where I knew she was, locked her in, and took away the key. She was worried for some hours, because locksmiths could not be had, and her sufferings were all the greater because I had locked her grandson in another room, and he screamed as if I had been ill-treating him. I very much enjoyed her discomfort. There was no mischief I did not devise to get my own back on her; and my only consolation for her treatment of me was the tricks I was able to play on her. She relented a little, and let me see people, but not without taking the opportunity to find fault. My usual visits were from the girls I have mentioned, and when we were all together, the comtesse de Fiesque would come and listen to our conversation: she thought we only talked about trifles that did not develop our minds, as if at our time of life we should have conversed about the most serious matters in the world.

[Mme de Guise returned from Italy, and Mademoiselle took to visiting her, her daughter, and her sons.[33] At the hôtel de Guise, she also met other people.]

I was so fond of Mme and Mlle de Guise that I could not bear not to see them every day. One day, having not done so, I insisted on going after supper. The comtesse de Fiesque objected; despite all the difficulties she made, I got my way. That visit cost me five or six days' imprisonment. I took it into my head that that could not have happened without the connivance of Mme de Guise, became less eager to go and see her, and felt less warmly towards her.

As I was such a nuisance to the comtesse de Fiesque, she decided to obtain orders from Monsieur to back up her authority, and, with this object, she took him a long memorandum about the way I was to behave. The first article of it was that I was to cross myself when I awoke, and the rest suitable for a child, although I was already sixteen. What hurt me most was an irritating rule, imposed on me purely for her own convenience. Her age and tastes made her loth to go out in the evening. She dared not directly stop me from going

---

[33] Mademoiselle's maternal grandmother and her youngest surviving children by her second marriage: Marie, Mlle de Guise, Louis, duc de Joyeuse, and Roger, chevalier de Guise.

to the Cours,[34] which was the only opportunity I had to stay up late: she forbade me to go without asking Monsieur's permission. The distance between the Tuileries and the hôtel de Guise, where he was staying, often prevented me from seeing His Royal Highness or from having a reply in time; and so, on many days, I was deprived of the pleasure of this outing. She also used Monsieur's authority to mortify me, when her own was inadequate.

[Louis XIII died on 14 May 1643 at Saint-Germain. The queen, Anne of Austria, became regent.]

After the queen settled in Paris, I went to the Louvre every day, often twice. When I was there, I usually played with the king or the duc d'Anjou,[35] who was the prettiest child in the world and for whom I have always had a great liking. Of all the queen's maids of honour, the one with whom I most liked to spend the time was Neuillant, who was very amiable and very witty.

[The Queen of England, Henrietta Maria, escaped to France in 1644. She reached Paris on 5 November and was lodged in the Louvre. She was joined in 1646 by the Prince of Wales, whom his father, Charles I, had sent to France for his own safety. Around this time, Mademoiselle's particular friend, Mlle d'Épernon, had been summoned to Bordeaux, along with her stepmother, to join her father, the Governor of Guyenne.]

The absence of Mme and Mlle d'Épernon was still on my mind more than anything else. [...] Even the attentions of the Prince of Wales made me think of them more than of the feelings he was supposed to have. I mention that, because they had vouched for them, and during their absence he appeared to be devoted to me; we saw each other frequently, because it was a season when there were often plays at the Palais-Royal. The Prince of Wales never missed one, and always sat next to me; when I went to see the Queen of England, he always took me in his coach, and, whatever the weather, he did not put his hat on until he had left me. His civility towards me was evident even in the merest trifles.

---

[34] The Cours-la-Reine, laid out in 1618 by Maria de' Medici, was a broad avenue along the Seine, closed off to ordinary citizens by ditches and gates, where people of fashion rode or drove. It ran west from the Tuileries to a point close to the present-day place de la Reine-Astrid, and could take eight coaches abreast.
[35] Philippe, the younger brother of the king (Louis XIV), who became duc d'Orléans after the death of Mademoiselle's father.

One day when I was to go to a reception at the house of Mme de Choisy — she was the wife of Monsieur's chancellor and she gave me one every year — the Queen of England, who insisted on having my hair dressed and adorning me herself, came to my house in the evening on purpose, and took every possible trouble over my toilet. The Prince of Wales held a candle near me all the while, to give light, and wore that day crimson, white, and black ribbons,[36] because my jewellery was fastened with ribbons of those colours; I also had a feather like that; everything was as the Queen of England had ordained. The queen, who knew whose hand had adorned me, sent for me before the ball, which she never failed to do whenever I was going to a reception, because she wanted to see if I was dressed to her taste.

The Prince of Wales arrived at Mme de Choisy's before me, and came and gave me his hand when I alighted from my coach. Before joining the assembly, I stopped in a room to rearrange my hair in a looking-glass, and he held a candle the whole time; he almost dogged my footsteps, and, what is remarkable — believe it who will — according to Prince Rupert, his cousin, a near relative of mine,[37] who was acting as his interpreter, he understood everything I said to him, although he did not understand French.

When the reception was over and I left, I was taken aback to find that when I reached home, he had followed me to the door; and when I had gone in, he went his way. His devotion was so obvious that it created a sensation; it went on like that all the winter. It appeared again, very clearly, at a famous entertainment in the Palais-Royal towards the end of the winter, at which there was a magnificent Italian play with machines and music,[38] and a ball afterwards, for which the queen insisted on adorning me. It took three whole days to get my jewellery ready: my dress was all studded with diamonds and with crimson, white, and black tassels; I was wearing all the crown jewels, and those of the Queen of England, who still had some left at that time. No one can be better or more magnificently arrayed than I was that day, and many people told me, appropriately enough, that my shapely figure, my good looks, my white skin, and the sheen of

---

[36] Mademoiselle writes *petite oie*, the term used to denote the ribbons that decorates a man's suit, hat, gloves, stockings, and sword.
[37] Charles, Prince of Wales, was the son of Charles I of England, and Prince Rupert the son of Charles I's sister, Elizabeth (the 'Winter Queen'). Mademoiselle, first cousin to Charles I, was consequently first cousin once removed of both men.
[38] Francesco Cavalli's opera *Egisto*.

my fair hair adorned me no less than all the riches that glittered on my person.

That day, everything helped to throw me into prominence, because we danced on a large stage, specially erected for the purpose, decorated and illuminated, to the utmost degree, by candles; at the back of the stage, in the middle, was a throne with three steps, covered with a canopy, and, all around the stage, benches for the ladies who were to dance, at the foot of which were the male dancers; and the rest of the hall was arranged as an amphitheatre directed at us. Neither the king nor the Prince of Wales would sit upon the throne; I remained alone on it, so that I saw at my feet those two princes and all the princesses of the court. I did not feel embarrassed in this situation, and those who had flattered me when I went to the ball found more to say to the same purpose next morning. Everyone told me that I had never seemed more at my ease than I was on that throne; and that, as my pedigree fitted me to occupy it, when I had one on which I should have to remain longer than that at the ball, I should occupy it with even greater self-confidence than I had that one.

While I was on it, and the prince at my feet, my heart looked down on him no less than my eyes; I was then contemplating marrying the Emperor, which seemed not improbable, if the court had acted in good faith, because Mondevergue, who had been sent by Their Majesties to convey their condolences on the death of his wife,[39] had reported that, all over the country and at the court of Vienna, there was a strong desire that I should be Empress; and that some ministers had even said to him that the queen had the means of providing the Emperor with all the consolation he could find. What made my mind dwell all the more on the matter was that the queen, while dressing me that evening, had spoken of nothing else but that marriage, and had told me that she passionately wanted it, and that she would do everything to promote it, convinced that it was a considerable piece of good fortune for her house. Thus, the thought of the Empire so filled my mind that I no longer regarded the Prince of Wales as anything but an object of pity. [...]

I must not forget to say that at the ball of which I have just been speaking, the Queen of England had noticed me looking disdainfully at her son; as soon as I saw her after she had found out the reason, she reproached me, and afterwards she even kept saying that I had the Emperor on my mind. I protested as vigorously as I could; I was so

---

[39] Maria Anna of Spain, first wife of Ferdinand III, died in 1646.

incapable of keeping the feelings of my heart from my countenance, that it was not difficult for anyone who saw me to know what they were. Cardinal Mazarin often spoke of marrying me to the Emperor, and though he did nothing about it, he emphatically assured me that he was attending to it. Abbé de la Rivière, also, to worm himself into my good graces, officiously assured me that he was not neglecting to speak to Monsieur and the Cardinal about it. What has made me since conclude that all that was merely to mislead me was that Monsieur said to me one day: 'I have been told that the project of marrying the Emperor pleases you; if that is so, I shall further it to the best of my ability. I am convinced that you will not be happy in that country: they live in the Spanish manner there; the Emperor is older than I am; so I think it is not a good thing for you, and that you can be happy only in England, if matters improve, or in Savoy.' I replied that I wanted the Emperor, and that it was for me to choose; that I begged him to approve of what I wanted; that I was thus speaking of it quite properly; that he was not a young gallant, and so it was clear, which was the truth, that I was thinking more of the position than of the man. Nevertheless, my desires were unable to affect any of those who had the authority to settle the matter, and I had nothing from it all save the unpleasantness of hearing it talked of longer. After Easter [1647], a ball was given in the Palais-Royal for the wife of a Danish ambassador. [...] The Prince of Wales having forgotten to dance a second courante with me, as is customary, I told Prince Rupert, in a tone that showed him that I was displeased, that that was, indeed, the mark of a clever man; and straight away he made me every conceivable excuse.

Shortly afterwards, the court left for Compiègne, and then went on to Amiens; and the desire to be Empress, which pursued me everywhere, and which I always expected to take effect imminently, made me think that it was incumbent on me to adopt in readiness the habits that might fall in with the Emperor's humour. I had heard that he was pious, and, following his example, I became so pious, after pretending to be so for a time, that, for a week, I wanted to be a Carmelite nun, a desire which I confided to no one. I was so obsessed with it that I neither ate nor slept, and it worried me so much that, coming on top of my own worrying nature, people were very much afraid of my falling dangerously ill. Whenever the queen visited convents, as she often did, I remained in the church alone; and, thinking of all who loved me and would regret my retirement,

I would burst into tears; what, in that, seemed an effect of my detachment from myself, was an effect of my natural tenderness. But I can say that, during that week, the Empire was nothing to me. I was not without a little vanity in leaving the world at such a moment — so that it would be said that it was only my perfect acquaintance with it that led me to give it up, despite the prospect of such a considerable establishment, with which I was satisfied. I could not be accused of having come to this decision out of pique. Daily confirmed in this purpose, I determined to speak to Monsieur about it. I went to his house; but, as he was at the gaming table, I merely paid my respects, and put off the communication of my purpose to another day. Next day, he came to me, but I was at mass.

After I had several missed opportunities of speaking to him, he came to me one evening, and I asked him to hear me on a matter about which I had to speak to him. He immediately took me aside, and, mentioning my worthy impulse, I asked his permission to examine this idea, and to carry it out, if it, and the feelings that had given rise to it, persisted. He told me that it was due to the fact that, to my mind, sufficient efforts were not being made to marry me to the Emperor. I answered that that could not be, since I no longer cared about it, and that I preferred serving God to all the crowns in the world. I followed that up with a host of similar remarks, which finally made him angry. He blamed the people who saw me most, and said: 'It is Mme de Brienne and suchlike bigots who put that into your head; you shall not speak to them any more, and I shall ask the queen not to take you to convents with her.' When I saw him take my announcement like that, fear of his making a fuss determined me to beg him not to talk about it any more, and I assured him that I should only do what he should order me to; indeed, no one has ever been more obedient than I was on that occasion. Three days later, I had forgotten what I had said to him [...] and Mondevergue, who kept talking about this marriage, and who had noticed my fit of piety, would sometimes say: 'I am the devil that tempts you.' Eventually the court came to have some inkling of my intention of withdrawing from the world, and when I heard that they had laughed about it, I laughed, too, and denied that I had even thought of it.

[Mademoiselle recalls the progress of the war in Flanders and in Catalonia. The court undertook its usual visit to Fontainebleau in the late summer of 1647. The chances of Mademoiselle's marriage to the Emperor receded. In the summer of 1648 she fell out with the queen and took herself to the château of Bois-le-Vicomte, from where she also went to stay with Mme de Bouthillier in Pont.]⁴⁰

---

⁴⁰ The château of Bois-le-Vicomte, since destroyed, lay in what is now the commune of Mitry-Mory (Seine-et-Marne), near the eastern boundary of Charles de Gaulle airport. During this period, it was in the *de facto* care of Mademoiselle, but it was one of two properties — the other was Champigny — that were the subject of a dispute between her father and the duc de Richelieu, heir to the Cardinal. Bois-le-Vicomte was eventually restored to Richelieu. Pont, nowadays Pont-sur-Seine, lies a few kilometres east of Nogent-sur-Seine.

Chapter 2
The Fronde (1): Matrimonial Projects (1648–1652)

One day while I was at Bois-le-Vicomte, news came of Condé's victory [over the Spaniards] at the Battle of Lens [20 August 1648]. As my people knew how much I disliked Condé, no one dared to tell me. They left on my table the account that had been sent from Paris. When I got out of bed, I saw the document on my table; I read it with much surprise and annoyance. As I was obliged not to confuse my aversion to him with an event of such advantage to the state, I was at a loss to disentangle the one from the other; in this regard I felt to be less of a good Frenchwoman than an enemy; I took myself off and concealed my distress by means of the sorrow I expressed for some of the officers I knew who had been killed; and, since good nature is praiseworthy mainly in great persons who are accused of hardly having any, and especially in great persons belonging to the House of Bourbon, I found myself being praised, instead of being blamed as I deserved. I do not know how I could have been moved by Condé's victories; he won them so often that I ought to have been able to accustom myself to them; but one does not become accustomed to things that one finds displeasing.

[Monsieur ordered Mademoiselle to come back to Paris to celebrate Condé's victory. She did so reluctantly, and heard the Te Deum in Notre-Dame on 26 August. The Fronde began that same day.]

I had no sooner returned home [to the Tuileries] than I heard the news that was spreading around the city, according to which people were taking up arms and erecting barricades because President Blancmesnil and M. de Broussel had been arrested. The latter was more popular than the former, and the people called him their father. He was an honest, virtuous man, though without much intelligence. When I saw him, I was astounded that, with so little ability, he had managed to sustain such a reputation for so long. I went to the Luxembourg. I passed along the quayside by the gallery of the Louvre, where I found nothing but companies of the Swiss and French regiments of guards under arms. When I crossed the Pont-Neuf, I had found a great many chains stretched across it. The people of Paris have always been very fond of me, because I was born and bred there; that has given them more respect and affection for me than they usually have for people of my rank, so, as soon as they saw my footmen, they lowered the chains.

After paying my visit to Madame, I went to the Palais-Royal, where there was a great commotion, everyone alarmed by the disturbance, serious, not in itself, but only because of the possible consequences and the example of the past events that fill all our history books. As for me, who had seen none, and who was not old enough to think seriously, I enjoyed these novelties; and as, at that time, I was not very pleased with the queen and Monsieur, I was delighted to see them at a loss. However important a thing might be, providing it could entertain me, that is all I thought about all the evening; and during the days that followed, I did nothing but look at all the men with swords, who were unaccustomed to wearing them, and who wore them awkwardly. That is how, while all France trembled, even though I had a vested interest in her preservation, I spent my time. The Swiss and French regiments of guards I have mentioned remained the whole night where I have said, and in the street in front of the Tuileries, in case the citizens should seize the Conference gate.[41]

On the evening of that day, the citizens were in arms in all districts, with detachments of guards at all the crossroads; and, with dreadful daring, they had stationed one at the Saint-Honoré sergeants' gate,[42] where there was a sentry only ten paces from the one belonging to the king's guard. Next day, I was awakened early by the drum beating to action for an attack on the Tour de Nesle,[43] which some scoundrels had taken. I sprang out of bed, and ran to the window to see them march off. The expedition was soon over; seasoned troops soon get the better of scoundrels. However, they wounded a few soldiers, who straggled after their company on the way back to its post. I looked at these wounded men through the window with great pity and alarm; I had never seen any; the misery of the times that came after inured me to the sight of the dead and the wounded without destroying the first feelings of pity I had for those.

As all history books and the memoirs of a great many writers relate everything that happened — how the chancellor went to

---

[41] The name popularly given to the gate at the western end of the Tuileries, hard by the river bank. It was through this gate that the Queen Mother and the young Louis XIV were later to make their escape when the mob burst into the palace in 1649.
[42] The entrance on the north side of the Louvre that was used by members of the king's guard.
[43] Opposite the Louvre, alongside the present-day quai de Conti, the Tour de Nesle was part of the medieval fortifications of Paris. It was demolished in 1663.

the law-courts and was then forced to take refuge in the hôtel de Luynes,[44] and all the other circumstances of the barricades — I shall say nothing further about it, except that I was in the Palais-Royal when the whole parlement came to see the king there. After it had been decided that the prisoners should be restored to them, they walked out very haughtily, looking as if they would take advantage of it, and knew with whom they had to deal. From that moment, they began to attack the Cardinal, and even while they were speaking to the king, I found myself next to one, whom I did not then know, who spoke to me very freely about him. That was where the trouble began. [...]

Although the word Fronde[45] came from a trifle, I must set its origin down here. One day, at the beginning of the disorders, when the parlement was meeting frequently, Bachaumont spoke of a lawsuit he had; he said of his adversary: 'I shall pepper him properly with my sling', and, when everyone was in his seat, they began to speak against the Cardinal, though without naming him, but making it clear whom they meant. Barrillon the elder[46] began to sing:

> Un vent de *Fronde*
> S'est levé ce matin.
> Je crois qu'il gronde
> Contre le Mazarin.
> Un vent de *Fronde*
> S'est levé ce matin.

[A Fronde wind | Rose this morning. | I think it is rumbling | Around Mazarin. | A Fronde wind | Rose this morning.]

Shortly afterwards, the king and the queen left Paris on the pretext of having the Palais-Royal cleaned, and went to Ruel. The château of Saint-Germain was occupied by the Queen of England, whose son, the Prince of Wales, had gone to Holland. Monsieur did not leave Paris, nor I; I merely went twice or thrice a week to pay my court. [...]

---

[44] The hôtel de Luynes was on the quai des Grands-Augustins, on the left bank of the Seine, just west of the present-day place Saint-Michel.
[45] The word *fronde* means a sling.
[46] Antoine Barrillon, whose nephew Jean-Paul was also a member of the parlement.

While the court was at Ruel, the parlement met every day about the subject with which it had begun: the revocation of the paulette,[47] and it continued to criticize the Cardinal, which had more to do with the court's going to Ruel than the cleaning of the Palais-Royal. The king's absence greatly increased the licence and the freedom of speech in Paris and in the parlement. This body even took some measures that displeased the court, so that it was compelled to go to Saint-Germain, which the Queen of England vacated and came to Paris. Monsieur, who sometimes slept at Ruel, was there at this time, and ordered Madame to leave Paris and take with her her two daughters, who were very little, my sister d'Orléans and my sister d'Alençon. The princesse de Condé sent for the duc d'Enghien, her grandson; and I felt somewhat embarrassed to be the only member of the royal family in Paris to receive no instructions.

As one must never hesitate to do one's duty, however unpalatable, I went to Ruel, and arrived as the queen was about to leave for Saint-Germain. She asked me whence I came; I said that I came from Paris, that, on the rumour of her departure, I had gone to her to have the honour of accompanying her, and that, though she had not done me the honour of giving me an order, I had felt that I could not fail in my obligations, and that I hoped she would be good enough to approve. She replied, with a smile, that what I had done did not displease her, and that it was good for me, after the way I had been treated, to see that I was tolerated, although my behaviour was such as to deserve an obliging response to make up for the past. I told Monsieur and abbé de la Rivière that I was not pleased that they had even sent for little children and not said a word to me; they hardly knew what to reply. When one lets down people who, themselves, never let people down, their conduct can embarrass one, and generally, when that happens, one says things that are best forgotten. During my stay there, I paid my court only because I had to; I lodged in the same house as the queen; I could not help seeing her every day; it was not with the same attentiveness and assiduity as at the beginning of the Regency; nor had I the same pleasure.

---

[47] An annual payment by officers of the Crown of a sixtieth of their salary, in return for which their offices could be passed on to their heirs. It took its name from the tax farmer Paulet, who collected it on behalf of Sully, Henry IV's great minister, who instituted it in 1604.

[The Peace of Saint-Germain was signed on 24 October 1648, and the court returned to Paris. It decided, however, to leave the capital again on the night of 5–6 January 1649.]

I had supped with Madame that day [5 January], and all the evening I had been in Monsieur's room, where one of his household came and told me in great secrecy that we were leaving next day; which I could not believe because of the state of Monsieur's health.[48] I went and told him this news in jest: he made no comment, which gave me grounds for suspecting the reality of the journey; he bade me goodnight a moment later, without making any reply. I went to Madame's room; we talked about it for a long time; she was of the same opinion as I, that Monsieur's silence indicated that the journey was settled. I went home quite late.

Between three and four in the morning [of 6 January], I heard a loud knock on the door of my room; I guessed what it was. I awakened my women, and sent one of them to open the door. I saw M. de Comminges come in; I asked him: 'We must go, must we not?' He answered: 'Yes, Mademoiselle; the king, the queen, and Monsieur are waiting for you in the Cours; and here is a letter from Monsieur.' I took it, put it under my pillow, and said to him: 'To make me obey, there is no need to add an order from Monsieur to those of the king and the queen.' He urged me to read it; it merely said that I was to do as I was told without delay. The queen had wanted Monsieur to give me this order, thinking that I should not obey hers, and that I should have been delighted to remain in Paris, in order to join a party opposed to her — for I never met anyone who admitted to opposing the king; it is always someone other than the king. Had she made no more grievous errors in her prognostications than this, she would have been more fortunate, and would have had fewer worries: nothing was ever so true as what I have thought a hundred times since.

At the time when M. de Comminges spoke to me, I was quite overcome with joy to see that they were about to make a blunder and that I should witness the misfortunes it would bring on them. That repaid me a little for the persecutions I had undergone. I did not then foresee that I should belong to a considerable party in which I could do my duty and take my revenge at the same time. However, revenge of this kind rebounds upon one.

---

[48] He had gout.

I got up as quickly as I could, and departed in Comminges's coach; mine was not ready, nor the comtesse de Fiesque's. The moon was setting, and it was not yet dawn; I urged the comtesse de Fiesque to bring my baggage as soon as possible.[49] When I got into the queen's coach, I said: 'I want to be in the front or at the back of the coach; I do not like the cold, and I want to be comfortable.' My intention was to dislodge the princesse de Condé, who was usually in one of those two seats. The queen replied: 'The king, my son, and I are there, and the dowager princesse de Condé.' I replied: 'She must stay there; the young must give the good seats to the old.' I remained near the door with the prince de Condé; his wife the princesse and Mme de Senecey were at the other. The queen asked me if I had not been very much surprised; I said no, and that Monsieur had told me, though this was not true.

She nearly found me out in this fib, because she asked: 'And yet you went to bed?' I replied: 'I wanted to get some sleep, not knowing if I should have my bed tonight.' I have never seen anyone so merry as she was: if she had won a battle, captured Paris, and had all those who had displeased her hanged, she could not have been merrier, and yet she was very far from all that.

When we arrived at Saint-Germain (it was Twelfth-Day), we straightway alighted at the chapel in order to hear mass, and the rest of the day was spent questioning newcomers about what was being said and done in Paris. I was very worried about my baggage; I knew that the comtesse de Fiesque had an unseasonably timid nature, and I was afraid of being the victim of it — as, indeed, I was. She was unwilling either to leave Paris during the disturbances, or to despatch my baggage, which was what I most needed. As for her, I could well have dispensed with her. She sent me a coach, which passed through the most unruly mobs without a word being said — the rest would have passed through in the same way. Those in it were very civilly treated, although by people who are not normally civil, and that was reported to me. In this coach, she sent me a mattress and some linen.

Seeing myself so badly provided for, I went to seek help at the Château-Neuf,[50] where Monsieur and Madame were lodged. She

---

[49] Having been Mademoiselle's governess, Anne le Veneur, comtesse de Fiesque, became her lady-in-waiting. They still did not get on with one other.
[50] At Saint-Germain-en-Laye, Francis I had built what came to be known as the Château-Vieux. A second château (Château-Neuf) was built by Henry IV. It is the older one that survives today.

lent me two of her chambermaids; as she, like me, had not all her clothes, we had an amusing time. I went to bed in a very fine garret, well painted, well gilded, and large, with a tiny fire and no glass or windows, which is not pleasant in January. My mattresses were on the floor, and my sister, who had no bed, slept with me. I had to sing her to sleep, and her sleep did not last long; she disturbed mine a great deal; she would turn over, feel me near her, wake up, and cry out that she could see the evil spirit; so I would sing her to sleep again, and the night passed in this way. You may judge if this was pleasant to one who had not had much sleep the night before, and who had suffered all that winter from sore throats and a violent cold. However, all this fatigue cured me.

Fortunately for me, Monsieur's and Madame's beds arrived: Monsieur was good enough to give me his room; he had slept in a bed that the prince de Condé had lent him. While I was in Monsieur's room, where no one knew that I was, I was awakened by a noise I heard; I drew back my curtain, and was astounded to see my room full of men in great buff collars, who were astounded to see me, and who were as complete strangers to me as I to them. I had no linen to change into, and my nightgown was washed by day, and my shift overnight; my women were not there to do my hair and dress me, which is highly inconvenient; and I ate with Monsieur, whose fare is poor. Nevertheless, I was in good spirits, and Monsieur was surprised that I did not complain about anything. As for Madame, she was very different; indeed, I am a creature whom nothing puts out, and far above trifles. I stayed like this with Madame for ten days, at the end of which my baggage arrived, and I was extremely glad to have all my comforts. I went and lodged in the Château-Vieux, where the queen was. I had made up my mind, if my baggage had not come, to send to Rouen to have some clothes and a bed made, and for that purpose asked Monsieur's treasurer for some money; and Monsieur might well give me some, since he was enjoying my property. If he had refused, I should nevertheless have found someone to lend me some.

[Mademoiselle briefly recounts some military manœuvres.]

There was little magnificence at Saint-Germain: no one had all their baggage; those who had beds had no tapestries, and those who had tapestries had no clothes, and we lived in a poor way. For a long time, the king and the queen had only furniture belonging to the Cardinal.

Since the Parisians were afraid that the Cardinal's belongings might be passed off as those of the king and the queen, they would not let anything out, so great was their aversion. It is not unprecedented for nations to be able to hate and love the same people in a short space of time, the French particularly. The king and the queen lacked everything, and I had everything I liked, and lacked nothing. Passports were given for everything I sent to Paris for; it was escorted; nothing was equal to their civility to me.

The queen asked me to send a cart to bring away some of her clothes. I sent it joyfully: one is joyful enough to be able to do a good turn to people like that, and to see that one is of some consequence. Amongst the clothes the queen sent for, there was a chest of Spanish gloves; as they were searched, the citizens entrusted with the search, unused to such strong scents, sneezed a great deal, according to the page I had sent, who was my usual ambassador. The queen, Monsieur, and the Cardinal laughed heartily at that part of his narrative that related the honours he had received in Paris: he had gone into the parlement, into the great chamber, where he had said that I had sent him to fetch the clothes I had left in Paris. They told him that I had only to let them know whatever I wanted, and that I should always find the company full of all the respect it owed me — in short, they said a great many kind things about me.

[Further manœuvres are described, and Mademoiselle refers to various love affairs and rumoured affairs among members of the court.]

When there was talk of peace, I paid little attention; for, as I cared for nothing at that time save enjoying myself at Saint-Germain, I should never have wanted to stir from it, and I did not know much about the public weal or that of the State; for, although I was born with a good deal of interest in them, when one is very young and very thoughtless, one is concerned with nothing but the pleasures of one's age.

[The Peace of Ruel was signed in April 1649, and the court returned to Paris. In the interim, Charles I had been executed,[51] and the Prince of Wales was now King Charles II. The queen and the Cardinal urged Mademoiselle to marry him.]

I told the queen that he was doing me a great honour in wanting me; but that, though the affairs of the King of France did not allow him to give the King of England the considerable help he needed to

---

[51] On 30 January by the old-style English (Julian) calendar, or 9 February in France.

be restored to his states, I should, nevertheless, do whatever she and Monsieur ordered. The queen rallied me in front of Lord Jermyn; she teased me, and I blushed. M. de la Rivière came and saw me again about the matter, and told me that Jermyn, going to Holland to fetch the King of England, who was there, was asking for a positive reply, because his affairs obliged him to go to Ireland promptly. If I agreed to the match, this is how the King of England would come to court: he would be there for two days; he would marry me, and, after the wedding, he would stay there as long again to give me the pleasure of preceding the queen, and after that I should go with him to Saint-Germain, where, now that the court had left, the Queen of England had returned. He would not stay there long; and, as for me, I should live in Paris as usual, if I wished. I told him that this last point was out of the question. I should go to Ireland with the king, if he wished. If he did not wish, I should remain with the queen, his mother, or in one of my houses, since it would not be proper for me to go into society and enjoy its pleasures (which involves people of my rank in expense), when I ought to be denying myself everything so as to send him money; I could not be free from anxiety, knowing him to be exposed to such a war; and finally, if I married him, I should eventually have to form resolutions more difficult to carry out, and I should not be able to refrain from selling all my property and risking it to conquer his kingdom; but, having always been fortunate and brought up in the lap of luxury, these considerations alarmed me a good deal. He told me that I was right, but I must reflect that there was no other match for me in Europe; the emperor and the King of Spain were married; the King of Hungary was betrothed to the Spanish Infanta; as for the Archduke, he would never be sovereign of the Low Countries;[52] I would not look at the rulers of Germany or Italy; in France, the king and Monsieur were too young to be married; and the prince de Condé had been ten years married, and his wife was in too good health. I answered, with a laugh: 'The empress is pregnant, and will die in childbirth.' At last, having argued for a long time and having expressed my misgivings, the matter being worth the trouble, I said to him: 'If Monsieur wants me to marry the King of England sooner or later, and if he is convinced that it is inevitable, I had rather marry him in misfortune, because, in that condition,

---

[52] Ferdinand IV, the son of Ferdinand III, Holy Roman Emperor, had been made King of Hungary in 1647. Archduke Leopold William, Governor of the Spanish Netherlands, was the Emperor's brother.

he will feel under an obligation to me, and when he returns to his states, he will respect me as the cause, because of the help he will have received from my house, out of consideration for me.'

Next day, we left for Amiens; I told my stepmother all about the matter, because I was well aware that she did not want it, and would use her influence with Monsieur to put a stop to it, as she did. Lord Jermyn came to see me at Amiens; he pressed me to tell him my feelings, and made me many fine protestations of devotion on behalf of the King of England. I knew, from what he said, that the queen and Monsieur, who did not want to quarrel with the Queen of England, had said of me: 'She is a creature who must be won over; she only does what she wants, and we have no control over her.' It is true that, as far as marriage goes, they had some grounds for having this opinion; for I have always thought that, since we have the power of reason, it should be used on this occasion, the most important in life, because all one's peace of mind is at stake, and so I should consider my interests rather than those of my kinsfolk. Seeing Jermyn going so deeply into the matter with me, which is rare with girls, I considered how to avoid offending the Queen of England: I told him that I honoured her infinitely, and, if I dared say so, loved her just as much (and I was speaking the truth); that, in this matter, consideration for her was stronger than anything else, and would make me overlook the state of the king, her son; but that, as for religion, that was something one could not overlook, and, if he had any affection for me, he must get over this difficulty, and I, on my side, was getting over many others.

He told me that, in the King of England's situation, he neither could, nor should, become a Catholic, and gave me many good reasons, too long to tell: becoming a Catholic would shut him out of his kingdoms for ever. We argued about that for a long time; then he took his leave of me, giving me to understand that he thought that what I had said to him gave him grounds for hoping that the difficulties I was raising would soon be overcome. Since Monsieur and the queen had spoken to me at Compiègne, I had been extremely worried, and my mind had been distracted, seeing myself on the point of deciding such an important and such an enduring matter; but that did not last long, for no one spoke to me about it again, or even of the King of England, till I returned to Compiègne a day before his arrival. [...]

When the King of England arrived at Péronne,[53] a courier was sent to inform Their Majesties. Then the queen said to me: 'Now your gallant is coming.' Abbé de la Rivière said the same thing to me. I said to him: 'I am longing to hear him say sweet nothings to me; for I do not know what they are, no one ever having dared to say any to me, not because of my rank, since they have been said to queens we know, but because of my humour, which is known to be far removed from coquetry; but, without being a flirt, I may well listen to them from a king whom I am expected to marry, so I should very much like him to.'

On the day of his arrival, we got up early; for, as he was only to dine at Compiègne, we had to go and meet him early. My hair was curled, which is rare with me. When I got into the queen's coach, she exclaimed: 'We know what girls expecting their lovers are like; how smart she is!' [...] We went to meet him a league from Compiègne. When we met, we alighted; he greeted Their Majesties, then me: I thought him very good-looking, more so than when he had left France. Had his intelligence seemed to me to match his looks, I might have liked him even then; but when he got into the coach, the king asked him about the Prince of Orange's dogs and horses and hunting in that country; he replied in French. The queen tried to find out about his affairs; he made no reply; and being questioned over and over again about serious matters of considerable importance to him, he apologized for being unable to speak our language. I confess that, at that moment, I resolved not to conclude the marriage, having formed a very poor opinion of a king of his age ignorant of his affairs. I ought to have recognized my blood in that, for the Bourbons care a great deal about trifles, and little about solid things; I, perhaps, as well as the others, who am a Bourbon on both sides. As soon as we arrived, we dined; he ate no ortolans, but fell on an enormous joint of beef and a shoulder of mutton, as if that were all there was; his taste did not strike me as refined, and I was very much ashamed that it was not so good in that as he showed it to be in his opinion of me. After dinner, the queen went off and left me with him; for a quarter of an hour, he said not a single word. I am willing to believe that his silence was due to respect rather than to lack of passion; I confess that, on this occasion, I should have wished him to be less respectful. I grew bored, and called to M. de Comminges to join us and try to

---

[53] Péronne, some thirty-five kilometres east of Amiens, is fifty kilometres north of Compiègne.

get him to talk; which was successful. M. de la Rivière came and said to me: 'He looked at you all through dinner, and still cannot take his eyes off you.' I replied: 'It is no use his looking before making himself agreeable, as long as he does not say a word.' He retorted: 'But you are ignoring the kind things he has said to you.' 'Pardon me,' I said to him, 'come to me when he is with me, and you will see how he sets about it.' The queen stood up; I went to him, and to get him to speak, I asked him about people I had seen with him; he answered, but said nothing affectionate.

The time for his departure came: we got into our coaches, and accompanied him to the middle of the forest, where we alighted, as on his arrival. He took leave of the king, and came up to me with Jermyn, and said: 'I think Lord Jermyn, who speaks better then I, has explained my intentions and my wish to you; I am your very obedient servant.' I replied that I was his very obedient servant. Jermyn paid me a lot of compliments, and then the king saluted me and departed.

[Louis XIV returned to Paris on 18 August 1649.]

Shortly afterwards, I had an illness which banished me from society, and which would have worried others more than it did me; it was smallpox. Although I am not a beauty, the effects of this disease are so unpleasant that one must be a little uneasy. I was not: for, as I no longer had a fever when the smallpox broke out, and I felt well enough not to be afraid of dying, I willingly sacrificed the little beauty I had to my life — and to prolong it for a moment I shall always be ready to sacrifice my looks. But the disease treated me so kindly that I did not remain red: before, my complexion was very blotched, which was surprising at my age and considering how healthy I am, and the disease cured me: few would be prepared to use such a remedy to have a clear complexion. The whole court sent to ask after me with the greatest assiduity, even people I did not know — to be precise, everyone except the prince de Condé, who did not enquire, which greatly increased my aversion to him. What made me notice it was that, not knowing how to pass the time, it amused me every day to ask for the notes of those who had called or sent to ask after me.

[Condé, his brother Conti, and the duc de Longueville (their brother-in-law), incurred the displeasure of the government and were arrested early in 1650. A year later, the parlement pressed for their release. Monsieur and the Cardinal quarrelled about this in the parlement in February 1651]

When I learned of this dispute, I ran to His Royal Highness's; he related the whole business to me, and told me that he would not go to the Palais-Royal again, as long as Mazarin was there. I was not sorry about this resolution; because, though I did not love the prince, I nevertheless loved Monsieur so much that I was delighted that he was undertaking two such great things as getting the prince out of prison and the Cardinal dismissed for having annoyed him. But my fear that he would tire of the difficulties of the matter and not carry it through gave me the greatest anxiety. All the prince de Condé's friends came to the Luxembourg at this juncture: I paid them a great many compliments, and at that moment I resolved to overcome my unreasonable aversion to him.[54] Guitaut, who is in his service, and in whom he has great confidence because he served him well during his imprisonment, came to see me.[55] I protested over and over again that I should be on good terms with the prince and all his house, and that I was sorry that I had not been in the past. He emphatically assured me of the respect and good will they all had for me, and their sorrow for the way I had treated them.

[Mazarin went to Le Havre, where the princes were, and set them free on 13 February 1651. He himself left France. The princes returned to Paris.]

The news that Condé had left Le Havre delighted everyone. It delighted me doubly, for I was pleased by the thing itself, and to know thereby what self-mastery I had, to have passed, as soon as I willed, from hatred to friendship. [...] He arrived in Paris the next day. Monsieur went to Saint-Denis to meet him; and, of all those at court, the only people who remained behind at the Palais-Royal were the ladies and the mazarins; that is the word that began to be applied around that time to the Cardinal's friends.[56] The entire route from Paris to Saint-Denis was lined with carriages; never has so much joy been demonstrated as that with which all the people greeted the prince de Condé.

[Condé, Conti, and Longueville went to pay their respects to the queen.]

---

[54] She says elsewhere that the original reason for her aversion to the prince de Condé and all his house was that, at his mother's balls, she was ignored and treated like a little girl (Chéruel, I, 45).

[55] This is not the well-known François de Comminges, comte de Guitaut, captain of the queen's guard, but his nephew Guillaume de Pechpeyrou de Comminges.

[56] The French word *mazarin*, with a small m, a term of abuse commonly used by the enemies of Mazarin to designate his supporters, is also found in contemporary English-language sources.

On leaving the queen, the princes went to supper with His Royal Highness in the Luxembourg. They came to Madame's room, where I was, and after greeting her, they came to me and paid me a great many compliments; and the prince, in particular [that is, Condé], told me that he was very glad when Guitaut assured him that I had repented of having had such an aversion to him. When the compliments were over, we confessed our mutual dislike: he admitted that he had been overjoyed when I had smallpox, that he had passionately wanted me to be marked and deformed by it, and that, in short, nothing could exceed his hatred for me. I admitted that nothing had ever given me greater joy than his imprisonment; that I had very much wanted it to happen; and that I could not think of him without wishing him ill. This mutual confession lasted a long time, delighted the whole company, and ended with many assurances of friendship on both sides. I asked him why he had not sent to ask after me when I had smallpox; he told me that I had sided with the Cardinal against him in a dispute that he had had with him in the year of the Paris war, after the return from Compiègne, when he wanted the Cardinal to keep the promise made to M. de Longueville that he would be given Pont-de-l'Arche.[57] That caused a great stir at court; he was given it eventually, and that is how the Cardinal always behaved. He would promise a thing lightly, and when the time came, he would raise difficulties so as to get out of it; and afterwards, under strong pressure, he would give in, but in such a way that one did not feel grateful to him. I confessed to the prince that I had been even more in the wrong than he thought, because I had almost gone on my knees to beg Monsieur to support the Cardinal and urge him not to give way. The prince de Conti came up next, and I assured him that his imprisonment had given me no joy, and that I had been sorry, for which he thanked me warmly. […]

Saujon[58] returned from Germany at that time, and I did not say a word to him about his journey, since I repented of having agreed to his going, and no longer cared about the purpose for which he had gone, the affair having come to nothing at all. As the emperor was betrothed to the princess of Mantua, I stopped thinking of it except with deep regret for having set my heart on it too much. This, as I have already said, is the shameful episode in my life; and I may say

---

[57] Pont-de-l'Arche is on the south bank of the Seine about 10 kilometres south-south-east of Rouen.

[58] The Empress had died, as Mademoiselle had predicted, and Saujon had gone to Austria to try to negotiate for the Emperor to marry Mademoiselle.

without vanity, that God, who is just, did not want to give a woman like me to a man who did not deserve me. [...]

The princesse de Condé fell seriously ill with erysipilas in the head, which turned inwards, and led many people to say that, if she died, I might well marry the prince. That reached my ears; I thought it over, and, that evening, walking about my room with Préfontaine, I discussed it with him.[59] I thought it feasible, because of the close union between Monsieur and him, and because of the queen's aversion to Monsieur, which put marriage with the king out of the question. Thus I reflected that the great qualities of the prince and the reputation he had won by his great exploits, made up for any other shortcomings; because, as regards birth, we are of the same blood. I reflected, too, that the court would not agree to the union of our two houses (I mean, of our two branches, for we have the same name), because from the high offices of Monsieur and of the prince, Monsieur, with his position in the state, supported and incited by the prince, would be very formidable. For the three days during which she lay at death's door, this was what I talked to Préfontaine about; I should not have spoken to anyone else about it. We discussed all these questions, and what gave me grounds for doing so, in addition to what I heard people saying, was that the prince came to see me every day; but her recovery immediately put an end to this episode, and no more thought was given to it.

I went on a trip, lasting two or three days, to Limours with His Royal Highness, and I took with me the most agreeable and the finest company, which was almost always with me. It consisted of Mme de Frontenac and Mlles de la Loupe,[60] all three pretty and witty; we did nothing but dance and walk and ride. That same year I went to Bois-le-Vicomte several times. Remenecourt, Madame's maid of honour, used to come there; she was amusing, and her mind was completely bent on banter; she was fond of society, and yet she soon left it, for, shortly afterwards, she went and became a Carmelite in the large convent in Paris.[61] Although she started from the same point as Mme

---

[59] Préfontaine was Mademoiselle's *intendant* or man of business.
[60] Mlles de la Loupe were the future wife of Marshal de la Ferté and the future comtesse d'Olonne.
[61] The main Carmelite convent in Paris, founded in 1604, was in the faubourg Saint-Jacques.

Saujon,[62] she did not behave in the same way; for she remained there, the best nun there could possibly be.

[Condé departed for the country on 6 September 1651, and there was further political unrest. News reached the court of Charles II's defeat at the Battle of Worcester.[63] Charles regained France in mid-October and, shortly afterwards, passed through Rouen and arrived in Paris. Mademoiselle had been unwell.]

I had not been out for some time, having a swollen face. I felt that, on this occasion, I could not get out of it, so, the following evening, I went to the Queen of England's without having my hair dressed. She said to me: 'You will find my son quite ridiculous; because, in order to escape, he cut his hair, and he has an extraordinary outfit.' At that moment, he came in. I thought him very handsome, and much better looking than before his departure, though he had short hair and a rich growth of beard, two things which alter men. I thought he spoke French very well.

He told us that, after losing the battle, he turned round, and with forty or fifty horse, passed through the enemy army and the town, on the far side of which the battle had been fought, and that he had then dismissed them all, and remained alone with Lord Wilmot. He had been in a tree for a long time, and then in a peasant's cottage, where he had cut his hair. A gentleman who had recognized him on the way had taken him to his house, where he had stayed. He had gone to London with this gentleman's sister behind him on his horse; he had spent a night there, and slept for ten hours with the utmost tranquillity. He had got into a boat in London to go to the docks, where he embarked, and the captain of the ship had recognized him. Thus he arrived at Dieppe.

He came and accompanied me back to my apartments by the gallery I mentioned at the beginning of these memoirs, from the Louvre to the Tuileries, and all the way he talked of nothing but the wretched life he had led in Scotland. There was not a single woman; the people were so backward that they thought it a sin to listen to violins; and he had been terribly bored. He had not felt the loss of the

---

[62] Saujon's half-sister, one of Madame's maids of honour, with whom Monsieur had been in love. She went into a Carmelite convent, but was persuaded to leave it and to become mistress of the wardrobe to Madame. As such, she acquired the courtesy title 'Madame'.

[63] It took place on 3 September according to the English (Julian) calendar, or 13 September according to the French calendar.

battle so much, in the hope of coming to France, where he found so much charm in people for whom he had a great liking. He asked me if we should not begin dancing soon. Everything he said gave me the impression that he was a shy and timid lover, who did not dare to tell me everything he thought about me, and who had rather I thought him insensible to his misfortunes than bore me by relating them; for he did not speak to other people about his joy at being in France, or his desire to dance. He did not displease me; and you may judge of that from the favourable account I have given of what he told me in pretty poor French.[64]

At the second visit he paid me, he asked me as a favour to let him hear a very good string orchestra I had. I sent for it, and we danced; and, as the swelling I have mentioned compelled me to stay in bed nearly all the winter, he came to see me every other day, and we would dance. All the pretty girls in Paris came, because there was no other court than mine, the queen not being in Paris, and Madame being in such delicate health that it stops her from liking to see society or any entertainments. Our assemblies — they were fine enough to be called so — began at five or six, and ended at nine. The Queen of England often came. One evening, she took me by surprise and came to supper with me, bringing the king, her son, and the Duke of York.[65] Although my table is as good as hers, for all the royal households are constituted in the same manner, I was sorry not to have given her better fare. After supper, we played for small stakes, which made us resolve to continue and to divide our time between dancing and cards.

The King of England simpered and smirked, as they say lovers do. He was very deferential to me, did not take his eyes off me, and spoke to me as long as he could. He said sweet nothings to me, so those who were listening told me, and spoke French so well while saying these things, that everyone must allow that love is French rather than a member of any other nation; for, when the king spoke the language of love, he forgot his own, and lost his English accent with me alone, for the others did not understand him so well.

[Henrietta Maria and Lord Jermyn, among others, urged Mademoiselle to marry Charles II. Henrietta Maria spoke to Monsieur at the Luxembourg,

---

[64] *Sic.* Mademoiselle flatly contradicts the remark made, just a few lines earlier, to the effect that his French was good. She is about to contradict herself again.

[65] James, Duke of York, the younger brother of Charles II and later king in his own right as James II.

where Mademoiselle was also present. When her father referred them to Louis XIV and the court for a decision, Mademoiselle was pleased that he had not given his unequivocal consent, since she did not wish to become queen of a country in which there was such unrest. Charles II did not seem fully to understand the implications of Monsieur's response.]

When I returned home, the King of England came, and, as he thought that the court would raise no difficulty, he regarded the matter as settled. He told me what joy Monsieur's favourable reply to the queen, his mother, had given him; which encouraged him to speak to me of his purpose; hitherto, he had contented himself with letting his mother speak. Hereupon, he said many fine things to me, and, amongst others, that he would more than ever wish to regain his kingdom, since he would share his good fortune with me, and that that would make it all the more pleasant to him. I replied that, unless he went there, he would find it difficult to regain it in the near future. He retorted: 'What? Do you want me to go away as soon as I have married you?' I said: 'Yes; because if you do, I shall be more obliged than I am at present to espouse your interests; if you stay here I should be grieved to see you dancing the tricotet[66] and enjoying yourself, when you should be in the act of having your head broken or putting your crown back on it: it would be unworthy of being on it if you did not go and seek it at the point of your sword and the peril of your life.' Mme d'Épernon, who was strongly in favour of the marriage, was delighted, because she could see that we were speaking to one another.

I had a slight indisposition: he came to see me and sent to ask after me most assiduously. Although I was in no hurry for the matter to be concluded, I nevertheless resumed the balls as usual when I recovered. The dowager comtesse de Fiesque expressed great affection for the King of England, and said I must make him a Catholic, and kept begging me to speak to him about it. I did once. He answered that he would do anything for me, but that if he were to sacrifice his conscience and his salvation to me, I must in return pledge myself in the matter about which he had so often spoken to me, and that, unless I did, he would do no such thing.

[Other people pressed Mademoiselle to agree to the marriage, but Goulas warned her that it would ruin her. She asked Lord Jermyn to tell the king to visit her less often.]

---

[66] A lively dance, said to be so called from the verb *tricoter* ('to knit'), because the feet move as nimbly as the hands in knitting.

After that, the King of England did not come to see me for three weeks. I think that annoyed and bored him; he had no entertainment. It was clear that mine did not consist in the honour of seeing him and talking with him, since my assemblies continued as frequent and as fine as when he was there, because many people who had not the honour of being known to him had not dared to come to them.

Mme d'Épernon took umbrage because I had spoken to Jermyn in that way without telling her, and as she did not know what made me do it, she thought I was wrong. She came and saw me less often; and on the days when there was dancing in my apartments, the King of England went to her house, where they played for jewels and tried to make people believe that they were enjoying themselves very much without me. I did not believe it, particularly of Mme d'Épernon, being very conscious that I was not seeing her so often; for I have always been so fond of her that the least coolness on her part worried me. So we soon made it up, and I told her that M. de Fienne was putting it about that I was passionately in love with the King of England and that I should marry him for love, and that that displeased me extremely. I also learned that, every evening at Mme Beringhen's,[67] Lord Jermyn was saying much the same, and adding: 'We shall trim her life-style; we shall sell her estates.' The kind of control they were claiming they would establish over me pleased me no more than the love; so, thereupon, I came to a decision. True, it was rather sudden, but such is my humour.

At the same time there was talk of marrying Mlle de Longueville to the Duke of York. He often went and visited her, and the match being almost arranged, I told the King and the Queen of England that I did not think it was to their advantage, an income of 50,000 écus not being enough to keep the Duke of York with a wife and children when they had some. They concluded, I think, that I was against it; I do not know whether that was the reason, or that of their own interests, which was considerable, that broke off the match. The first time I saw the Queen of England after my conversation with Jermyn, she reproached me over and over; and, when her son came in (he always used to sit on a stool in front of me), a large chair was brought for him, in which he sat. I think he thought this would greatly mortify me; it did nothing of the sort.

---

[67] Anne du Blé, who in 1646 married Henri de Beringhen, the king's master of the horse. She was the daughter of Jacques du Blé and the sister-in-law of Marie le Bailleul, marquise d'Huxelles, the great letter-writer and friend of Mme de Sévigné.

Chapter 3
The Fronde (2): Military Exploits (Orleans and Paris, 1652)

[In September 1651, the queen left Paris with an army. In December, Mazarin, with another army, returned to France. In February 1652, the government captured Angers. Gaston d'Orléans, in Paris, and Condé — in Bordeaux, in the province of Guyenne — had now thrown their lot in with the rebels.]

After the fall of Angers, the court turned back towards Paris; it remained for some time in Blois, whence the government sent to Orleans to enquire if the king would be received there with the Cardinal. This was not a matter of course, for the army of M. d'Hocquincourt had so ravaged all the lands of His Royal Highness, and, generally, all the country round Blois, that the people of Orleans were afraid of similar treatment. They had good reason to be afraid of being pillaged, for all the grain of the province and all the furniture of the whole district, that both of the nobility and of the rest, were stored in their city. Upon this first letter from the king, the inhabitants of Orleans sent to His Royal Highness to ask what they should do. He despatched the comte de Fiesque and M. de Gramont, who is one of his gentlemen, to the city; they calmed all the unrest to which fear and terror had given rise; and the eloquence with which the comte de Fiesque addressed the people made them submit to His Royal Highness, and so united the minds of all, that, thinking the intendant was the Cardinal's man, not the king's,[68] they very nearly did him to death, with shouts of 'Mazarin!', as he passed through a square known as the Martroy. [...]

The comte de Fiesque came back in great haste to urge His Royal Highness to go to Orleans, his presence there being altogether necessary to preserve that great city, such a considerable stronghold in time of civil war, and in peace-time so renowned for its trade; and that trade was all the more useful in our war, since we claimed to be waging it only for the public good. Communications with Guyenne were also of very considerable importance to our side, and to the interests of the prince [Condé], who always recommended that care should be taken not to antagonize Orleans. Thus, all Monsieur's friends urged him to go there; which he decided to do on the evening

---

[68] Intendants were officials, nominally appointed by the king, with wide-ranging legal and fiscal powers that often brought them into conflict with governors. The abolition of such posts was an early aspiration of the rebels of the Fronde.

of the Saturday before Palm Sunday. A few days previously, he had told me that the citizens of Orleans had sent to ask him to send me, should he be unable to go. I answered that he well knew that I was always ready to obey him. When, on the Sunday morning, I heard that Monsieur was leaving for Orleans next day, that it was quite settled, and that he had sent to the duc de Nemours and the duc de Beaufort to tell them to send an escort to meet him on the further side of Étampes, I said to Préfontaine: 'I wager I shall be going to Orleans.' He replied that he did not know what had put that idea into my head. I told him that, having committed himself to this journey, to which Cardinal de Retz would never agree,[69] Monsieur could only get out of it by sending me; and that I was not too sorry, because it was what mattered most to the prince. When one undertook to be a friend to people, I said, it was a fine thing to render them such a considerable service; it made them for ever formidable; and, since I should be doing a service to our side at the same time, everyone in it would be obliged to me.

I had intended that day to go and sleep at the Carmelite convent at Saint-Denis in order to spend Holy Week there, as I did at nearly all the major festivals; indeed, I had told Monsieur, and taken leave of him. But I put my journey off until next day, because of Monsieur's. M. de Beaufort, who had come, after the comte de Fiesque, to urge Monsieur to go to Orleans, came to see me and said: 'If Monsieur does not want to go, you must.' I went to the Capuchin convent in the rue Saint-Honoré, where Father Georges, a great Frondeur, was preaching. Monsieur was there; I told him that I had postponed my journey on learning of his. Then I went to the Luxembourg, where I found him very worried; he complained to me that the prince's friends were badgering him to go to Orleans; that if he were to abandon Paris, all would be lost, and that he would not go. All conversations with him when he was displeased with people who wanted to make him do something always ended with his longing to be able to live quietly in Blois and extolling the happiness of those who do not meddle with anything. Frankly, I did not like this. I concluded that eventually nothing would come of this business, and that we should be defeated, as we have been, and relegated each to his own estates. This ill becomes people of our station, and was even less likely to further my fortune, so remarks of this kind always made me shed tears, and

---

[69] The Parisians, led by Cardinal de Retz, mistrusted Gaston d'Orléans and Condé.

distressed me. I remained till quite late at Monsieur's; everyone came to me and said: 'You will certainly be going to Orleans.'

M. de Chavigny, a man of great intelligence and ability, trained in politics by Cardinal Richelieu, and known by him to be what I have just said, was a great friend both of mine and of the prince's;[70] he said to me: 'This is the finest thing you can possibly do, and it will be of great service to the prince.' Monsieur came in at this point; I bade him goodnight and went home. As I was having supper, the comte de Tavannes, lieutenant-general of the prince's army, came in and said softly to me: 'We are too happy, you are coming to Orleans; don't say anything about it, for M. de Rohan is coming to tell you on Monsieur's behalf.'

M. de Rohan came and brought me the order, which I received, as I have always received Monsieur's commands, with great joy in obeying him; but I felt an elation that heralded the extraordinary good luck that attended the execution of this venture. M. de Rohan told me that he would come with me; I asked the comte and comtesse de Fiesque and Mme de Frontenac to accompany me, which they were very glad to do. I gave orders about my baggage and everything I needed. I went to bed at two in the morning, and next day, which was the day of Our Lady in March [25 March], I went and made my devotions at seven o'clock, thinking it right to begin my journey by putting myself in such a state that God might be able to bestow on me the blessings I desired. Then I went back home to give some further orders, and dined at the Luxembourg, where Monsieur told me that he had sent the marquis de Flamarens to Orleans to say that I was coming, and had written to say that they were to do whatever I ordered, as if it were he himself. His Royal Highness told M. de Croissy and M. de Bermont, councillors in the parlement: 'You must go to Orleans with my daughter.' They answered that they would obey his orders. The former was entirely devoted to Condé's interests. I did not know him personally, but I had heard a great deal about him from some common friends. The other I knew very well.

After spending some hours at the Luxembourg talking to everyone, I knew what they all felt about my journey: the friends of Cardinal de Retz thought it ridiculous; those of the prince de Condé were delighted. As I still did not wholly trust the latter, what the others had said disturbed me a little. M. de Chavigny told me that he would

---

[70] Chavigny was the son of Mademoiselle's friend Marie de Bragelongne, comtesse de Bouthillier.

tell the prince how much he was indebted to me; that he was certain that, henceforth, he would pursue my interests as if they were his own — in other words, with the utmost vigour; and that, if a treaty were to be negotiated in my absence, I should see how the prince's friends would serve me.

To show what good intentions all the prince's friends had towards me, I shall tell you that Mme de Châtillon, while M. de Nemours was here, said to me: 'You know what obligations make me devoted to the prince's service, and my liking for you, which has always made me want you both to be on good terms. You are now; but I want you to be on even better terms — so much so that M. de Nemours (who — like me, as you know — has the greatest passion to serve you) and I talked for two hours yesterday about making you Queen of France. Do not doubt that the prince is wholeheartedly working for that; and, since peace will never be negotiated save by M. de Chavigny, as Monsieur has promised the prince, we have spoken to him about it. He thinks that nothing is so opportune, or so useful to France and the public good, as well as to your family and yourself, and that it is wholly to the advantage of the prince. So, when the comte de Fiesque leaves, which will be soon, get someone to say a word to him.' I did not tell her that the comte de Fiesque had spoken to me about it, nor that I had sent an answer to the prince on the subject. She called to M. de Nemours, who spoke to me at length about it, and made me a thousand protestations of service. He returned to the subject later, and so did Mme de Châtillon and M. de Chavigny. I had no reason to give any message to the comte de Fiesque, because he did not depart, and came to Orleans with me. [...]

After bidding everyone farewell, I took leave of His Royal Highness, who said to me: 'The Bishop of Orleans, who is of the house of Elbène, will inform you about the state of the city; consult the comte de Fiesque and the comte de Gramont, too; they have been there long enough to know what is to be done.' At all costs, I was to stop the army [Monsieur's army] from crossing the Loire on any pretext whatever; that was the only order he gave me.[71]

I got into my coach with the marquise de Bréauté (the comtesse de Fiesque's daughter),[72] the comtesse de Fiesque, and the comtesse de Frontenac. His Royal Highness remained at the window until he had seen me depart; a host of people in the courtyard and in all the streets

---
[71] Mademoiselle left Paris on 25 March 1652.
[72] She was a widow, her husband having died in 1640.

I passed through rained blessings down on me. His Royal Highness gave me a lieutenant of his guards called Pradine, two junior officers, six guards, and six Swiss. I had to pass the night at Châtres,[73] because I had been late in setting off. In the evening, M. de Rohan came to see me, and expressed his joy over and over again at being chosen to accompany me. I received his compliments graciously. Croissy complimented me too, and said: 'I know that, not having the honour of being known to Your Royal Highness, you will think me a surly fellow who will be a busybody and not obey your orders blindly; I can assure you that my conduct will prove the contrary.' He told me the truth; for I was very pleased with him. I left Châtres very early in the morning. [...] As I was leaving, M. de Beaufort arrived and rode at the door of my coach all the way. We dined at Étampes, and M. de Beaufort with me. Six miles further on, I met the escort, which consisted of five hundred horse, commanded by M. de Valon, a brigadier in Monsieur's army. The escort was composed of cavalry, light horse from the regiment of Monsieur and my brother,[74] and detachments of all corps, both French and foreign. They were drawn up in line and saluted me; then the light horse moved in front of my coach, the cavalry to the rear, and the guards and the rest, in squadrons, to the front, the rear and the sides.

When I reached the plains of Beauce, I mounted on horseback, because it was very fine, and something on my coach was broken; it gave the troops considerable joy to see me. I began to give orders at that point, for I had two or three couriers stopped, one of whom was a man from Orleans going to tell His Royal Highness that the king had informed them that he was spending that night at Cléry, that from there he was passing on without going to Orleans, but that he was sending the council there. I took this courier with me as far as Toury, so as to despatch him forthwith to His Royal Highness.[75]

On arriving at Toury, I found M. de Nemours and M. de Clinchamp[76] and a number of other officers, who expressed great joy

---

[73] Now Arpajon, south of Paris, just over half way to Étampes.
[74] The duc de Valois (1650–1652).
[75] Cléry is about ten kilometres south-west of Orleans, on the left bank of the Loire. Toury is 30 kilometres due north of Orleans. Mademoiselle has made good time since dining at Étampes.
[76] We know that Clinchamp, lieutenant-general in command of the foreign troops in Condé's army, was himself a foreigner, for Mademoiselle says so below; consequently, he could well have been a Lorrainer. Chéruel (I, 340, n. 2) identifies him as Bernardin de Bourqueville, baron de Clinchamp, but he was a member of the Norman branch of the family. Another branch was established in Lorraine and

at seeing me, more even than if it had been Monsieur. They told me that they would have to hold a council of war in my presence. That struck me as a novelty for me; I burst out laughing. M. de Nemours told me that I should have to get used to political and military talk, and that henceforth they would do nothing without my orders. M. de Rohan drew me aside, and said: 'You well know that Monsieur's intention is that the army shall not cross the river, and that he is afraid of being cut off in Paris. Tell these gentlemen this.' And then he told me that he was extremely eager that this journey should succeed to Monsieur's satisfaction, so that it would compel him to support my interests in essential matters; and that, as he was better informed of Monsieur's intentions than I, he would tell me what to do as things happened.

These remarks displeased me. From this assumption of superiority, I concluded that M. de Rohan thought me incompetent and unsuited to business. I said nothing. I left him, and returned to the rest of the company, and told M. de Nemours and the rest of the gentlemen in command of the troops that I was firmly convinced that, in all matters, they would act in concert with me, and that I was not afraid that they would want to cross the Loire to relieve Montrond and abandon Monsieur in Paris with no troops.[77] But Cardinal de Retz and his friends, I said, were aiming solely at dividing Monsieur and the prince, which is what I was afraid of most of all, and I begged them, in order to forestall mischief-makers, to give me their word that they would not cross the river without an order from Monsieur. They gave it, and wanted to sign an undertaking; but I did not think this necessary.

I at once wrote to Monsieur in their presence, telling him what they had said; then they protested that, henceforth, they would do nothing without my orders, and that they believed that in this way they were conforming to the prince's intentions. After that, it was decided that our army should march to Jargeau, and encamp in the suburb of Saint-Denis, which is at this end of the bridge;[78] that, if the town could be taken by storm, we should attack it, since it was vital

---

[a] Louis, sieur de Clinchamps (*sic*), living in this period, had a military career, but, while this is suggestive, we have not satisfactorily established the identification.
[77] The fortress of Saint-Amand-Montrond, some 130 kilometres to the south, loyal to Condé, had been holding out against the besieging royal forces since the previous October.
[78] Jargeau, on the south bank of the Loire, is 18 kilometres east of Orleans; Saint-Denis is on the opposite side of the river.

that we should be masters of a stronghold on the Loire [...] but that, if it were well defended, we should not, since we did not want to risk losing much infantry as fine as ours at the beginning of a campaign. [...]

M. de Nemours said that he would march next day at first light, and that he would come to Orleans in the evening in order to report to me about the state of Jargeau, and to receive my further orders before doing anything. I told M. de Beaufort to do the same; he replied: 'I have Monsieur's orders in my pocket, and I know what I have to do.' M. de Nemours urged him to show them, and told him that he ought to communicate them to me. As this behaviour of M. de Beaufort's vexed me, I told him that I did not believe Monsieur had changed his mind four hours after my departure, since he had set off no longer than that after me, and that I did not believe Monsieur had sent me to give orders of which I had no knowledge, so that they were useless and he could throw them in the fire. He spoke no more of them, and said that he would obey me. I ordered him and M. de Nemours, who was going to spend the night in his quarters, to march the armies away at the crack of dawn. I busied myself that evening with examining the letters of the courier from Orleans to Paris, to see what was going on there. I found nothing to my purpose; I only learned what a poor opinion they had of the marquis de Sourdis, their governor. When he had been arrested by a patrol two days earlier and had told them who he was, they had not allowed him to pass without calling out the guard. One night they had barricaded his door, and the next day he had been unable to leave. I did not know whether to be pleased or angry, since Monsieur, whom I had asked whether Sourdis supported him or not, had not been able to tell me.

I set out very early next morning, but it was of no use, for M. de Beaufort had forgotten to give orders about the escort in the evening. He did not remember until quite late in the morning, so that I had to ride at a walking pace for nine or ten miles, waiting for it. When I reached Artenay,[79] the marquis de Flamarens was coming to meet me, and he said that he had many things to tell me, in the light of which we should have to decide what was to be done. I alighted at an inn to hear him. He told me that the authorities in Orleans were unwilling to receive me. They had told him that, the king being on one side and I on the other, they were at a loss to know whom to admit. To avoid the difficulty, they had thought the best thing was to

---

[79] Artenay is 17 kilometres north of Orleans.

ask me to go to some house nearby and feign illness. They promised me not to let the king in, and that, as soon as he had gone by, I should be welcome; they begged me not to bring M. de Rohan; and they were very worried about what some of the councillors were going to do in the parlement. I said to M. de Rohan: 'You, Monsieur, are too important for me to take you against their will; but, as for M. de Bermont and M. de Croissy, no one knows them; when they are in the coaches of my equerries, they will be taken for servants of mine. For myself, there is no need for deliberation: I am going straight to Orleans. If, at first, they deny me entry, I shall not be discouraged; perseverance may carry the day. If I enter the city, my presence will fortify the minds of those who wish His Royal Highness well: it will win back those who do not. For seeing people of my rank taking risks greatly encourages the lower orders, and it is well nigh impossible for them not to submit, willy nilly, to people with a little determination. If the faction of the mazarins is the stronger, I shall hold out against it as long as I can: if eventually I have to leave, I shall go to the army, there being no safety for me anywhere else. If the worst comes to the worst, I shall be taken prisoner. If that happens, I shall fall into the hands of people who speak the same language as I, who know me, and who will pay me, in my captivity, all the respect due to my birth, and I dare even say that the occasion will fill them with veneration for me; for assuredly there would be no disgrace in my having run risks in this way in Monsieur's service.'

They were all amazed at my resolution, and gave me the impression of having less than I; for they were afraid of everything that might happen, and told me about it to deter me. But, paying no heed, I got into my coach, leaving my escort behind, so as to travel more rapidly, and taking with me only the companies of Monsieur and my brother, because this handful of troops could travel as fast as I.

I encountered a great many people from the court who were going to Paris with passports from Monsieur; for otherwise I should have had them taken prisoner. They told me that all my haste was in vain; that the king was in Orleans; and that my venture would not have the success I was expecting. That did not alarm me, for I am pretty resolute by nature, as will sufficiently appear in these memoirs in the most remarkable episodes in my life. I met Pradine, whom I had sent to Orleans in the morning to inform them of the hour at which I should arrive. He brought me a tolerably submissive letter; but, after writing it, they had changed their minds, and asked Pradine for it back, but he refused to return it. They told him that they urged me not to come to Orleans, because they would be compelled, with deep regret, to deny me entry. He left them in session, because the Keeper of the Seals and the king's council were at the gate, asking to be admitted.[80] At about eleven in the morning, I arrived at the Porte Bannière, which was shut and barricaded. Even after being told that I was there, they did not open it; I stayed there for three hours.[81] After waiting wearily all that time in my coach, I went to an upstairs room in an inn near the gate, called the Port-de-Salut [Port of Salvation]. I was indeed the salvation of that poor city; for, but for me, they would have been lost.

As it was a very fine day, after amusing myself by having the letters of the courier from Bordeaux opened — he had no amusing ones — I went for a walk. The governor sent me some candied fruits, which struck me as rather funny, since, by sending no message with them, he let me know that he was of no account. The marquis d'Alluye [the governor's son, Paul] was at the window of the gate-turret, watching me walking on the moat. All the gentlemen who were with me, and whom I called my ministers, opposed this walk, arguing that the joy of the populace on seeing me would alarm the wealthy citizens. Thus, in my desire to go, I consulted only my own inclinations. The rampart was lined with townsfolk, who, on seeing me, kept shouting: 'Long live the king and the princes, and down with Mazarin!' I could not help shouting to them: 'Go to the town hall and make them open the gate,' although my ministers had told me that it was inopportune.

Continuing on my way, I came to a gate; the guard took up its arms and formed up on the rampart to do me honour, but what honour! I shouted to the captain to open the gate for me. He made signs to show that he had no keys. I said: 'You must break it down,' and told him that he owed more obedience to me, as their master's daughter, than to the city council. In the end, I grew heated and threatened him; his only reply was to bow repeatedly. Everyone who was with me said: 'You are wrong to threaten people whose co-operation you

---

[80] The Keeper of the Seals was Mathieu Molé.
[81] The Porte Bannier (*sic*) was the northern gate of the city, on the Paris road. On the walk that she next relates, Mademoiselle must have circumnavigated the city rampart anti-clockwise, passing the Porte de la Madeleine and eventually reaching the north bank of the River Loire, a total distance of some 500 metres. It was there that she found herself close to the Porte Brûlée, which will be mentioned below. The Porte de la Faux, also to be mentioned, was further east along the quayside.

need.' I told them: 'We must see whether threats will make them do more than friendship.'

On the day I left Paris, the marquis de Vilaine, an intelligent and learned man, reputed to be one of the best astrologers of the age, drew me aside in Madame's closet, and said: 'Whatever you undertake between midday on Wednesday, 27 March, and the Friday will be successful; and, indeed, during this period, you will do some extraordinary things.' I had written this prediction down in my memorandum-book to see what would come of it, though I had not much faith in it. I remembered it, and turned to Mme de Fiesque and Mme de Frontenac on the moat to say to them: 'Something extraordinary will happen to me today; I have the prediction in my pocket. I shall have the gates broken down, or I shall scale the city walls.' They laughed at me, just as I was making fun of them by speaking to them like that; for when I said that, nothing seemed less likely. However, I eventually found myself at the water's edge, where all the boatmen, of whom there are a great number in Orleans, came and offered me their services. I gladly accepted, and said a host of fine things to them, of the kind one has to say to that sort of people to encourage them to do what one wants.

Seeing them well-disposed, I asked them if they could take me in a boat to the Porte de la Faux, because it opened on to the water; they told me that it was much easier to break down a gate that was on the quayside, nearer the place where I was, and that, if I wished, they would see what they could do. I said yes, and gave them money, and, in order to watch them at work and spur them on by my presence, I climbed up a moderately high knoll opposite the gate. Frankly, I did not bother to follow the path, for, without thinking, I clambered up as a cat would have done, catching on all the thorns and brambles, and leaping over all the hedges, without hurting myself. When I was at the top, many of my companions, fearing that I was taking excessive risks, did their best to make me go down again; but their entreaties annoyed me, and I bade them be quiet. Mme de Bréauté, who is the greatest coward in the world, started to rail at me and all those following me; indeed, I am not sure that, in her excitement, she did not swear. I was vastly amused.

I had at first been unwilling to send any of my people with the boatmen, so that, if the attempt failed, I could claim that I had not ordered it. There was only one of His Royal Highness's light horse with them; he was struck on the head by a stone and slightly injured.

He was a lad from the city who had asked me as a favour to let him follow me; for I had left the companies that had escorted me behind, about three-quarters of a mile from the city, in case the sight of troops should alarm the townsfolk, and they were waiting for me there, ready to accompany me to Jargeau, if I failed to get in.

Someone came and told me that the work was progressing; I sent one of Monsieur's junior officers who was with me, called de Visé,[82] and one of my equerries, called Vantelet. They did very well, and shortly afterwards I went down from the place where I was to see what was happening. But, as the quayside was revetted at this point, and there was a fort into which the river flowed and washed against the wall, although the water there was shallow, two boats were placed together to serve as a bridge for me, and, in the second, a ladder was placed, up which I climbed. It was quite high. I did not count the number of rungs; I recall only that one was broken and inconvenienced me as I climbed. But no trouble was too great in carrying out something so advantageous both to my party and, as I thought, to myself.

Having climbed up, then, I left my guards at the boats, ordering them to go back to my coaches, so as to show the city council that I was entering their city with every confidence, having no cavalry with me; although the number of guards was small, it nevertheless seemed to me that it would look better if I did not take them. My presence spurred the boatmen on; they worked harder to break the gate down. The citizens were doing likewise inside the city: Gramont was egging them on, and the guard at this gate was under arms, looking on without interfering. The council was still sitting, and all the officers of our troops who were then in Orleans had stirred up a revolt that would no doubt have decided them to come and open the Porte Bannière for me, had they not learnt that I had entered by the Porte Brûlée; for such is the name of this illustrious gate, which will be so renowned because of my entry. When I saw that it was broken through, and that two planks had been torn out of the middle (for it could not have been opened otherwise, there being two iron bars of excessive thickness across it), Gramont beckoned to me to come forward. As there was a great deal of mud, a footman took me in his arms and thrust me into the gap, and as soon as my head had passed through, the drums beat. I gave my hand to the captain, and said: 'You will be very glad to be able to boast of having let me in.'

---

[82] Antoine de Visé, an *exempt* ('junior officer') in Gaston's bodyguard and the father of the future author and journalist Jean Donneau de Visé.

The shouts of 'Long live the king and the princes, and down with Mazarin!' redoubled. Two men lifted me up, and placed me on a wooden chair. Whether I sat in it or on the arm, I do not know, so beside myself with joy was I: everyone kissed my hands, and I was helpless with laughter at seeing myself in such a comic position.

After being carried in triumph through several streets, I told them that I was able to walk, and begged them to put me down, which they did. I stopped, and waited for the ladies, who came up a moment later, very muddy, like me, and overjoyed, too. A company belonging to the city marched in front of me with its drums beating, causing the crowd to make way for me. Halfway between the gate and my lodging, I met the governor, who was rather embarrassed (as one may well be for less), with the corporation, who greeted me. I addressed them first. I told them that I thought they were surprised to see me come in like this, but that, being very impatient by nature, I had grown weary of waiting at the Porte Bannière, and that having found the Porte Brûlée open, I had entered; that they must be very pleased, because the court, which was at Cléry, could not resent their having admitted me; that my entry without them exonerated them; and that, for the future, they would no longer be responsible for anything, for I should be blamed for everything, since, when people of my degree are in a place, they are the masters of it, and with justice enough. 'I must be mistress here,' I added, 'since it is Monsieur's.'

They paid me their compliments, rather alarmed. I said in reply that I was quite convinced that, as they said, they were going to open the gate for me; but that, for the reasons I had given, I had not waited for them. I conversed with them all the way as if nothing had happened; I told them that I wanted to go to the town hall to be present at the debate about the entry of the council into the city; for they had told me in the letter that Pradine had brought me, that they were waiting for me for that. They told me that the decision was taken, and that they had refused; I expressed my satisfaction, that being what I wanted. I sent one of my junior officers to summon my baggage, and from that moment I commanded in the city as if they had begged me to. On arriving at my lodging, I received the harangues of all the municipal bodies and the honours due to me, as in normal times. The gentlemen who had remained at the inn arrived; they expressed exceeding joy at what I had done; though, in the midst of all this gladness, they did not conceal their regret at not having come with me on this venture. I was not a little tired that day; I ate nothing all day, though I had risen at five o'clock; and, instead of resting after my arrival, I had to despatch a courier to His Royal Highness and one to the army, so that I wrote till three in the afternoon. But my elation was such that I felt nothing; and when I had finished my despatches, I passed my time with the countesses [de Fiesque and de Frontenac] and Préfontaine, laughing at all the adventures that had befallen us. The governor gave me supper, my servants having arrived too late to prepare me any; but, to save me the trouble of going to his house, he had it brought to mine. His wife, who was very plain, but very intelligent, came to see me; she was the daughter of the comte de Cramail. I asked if the intendant was in the city, with a view to enabling him to leave it in safety; but I was told that he had left it that morning. [...]

The day after my arrival, which was Maundy Thursday, I was awakened at seven, so as to walk about the streets and forestall the attempt of the Keeper of the Seals to enter with the council. I dressed in great haste, and sent for the mayor of the city and the governor to go with me. All the chains were stretched across the streets; I did not want them to be lowered. I walked to mass in St Catherine's, which is a church near the bridge.[83] After hearing it, I went and walked on the bridge, and climbed the turrets at the end which look over Le Portereau, the part of the town on that side; then I saw M. de Champlâtreux[84] walking about in front of the Augustins with a large number of men of the court. As I had a great many officers of our troops with me, it amused me to make them show themselves, so that their blue sashes could be seen, announcing that I was mistress in Orleans. All the people on the bridge shouted: *Long live the king and the princes! and down with Mazarin!* Those in Le Portereau said the same in reply; so these shouts went on and on, and I think they were heard even by the Keeper of the Seals, who was three-quarters of a mile away. The guard on the bridge fired a volley, after which the shouts increased, and I ordered the guard to be reinforced, thinking it too weak; thus the mazarins knew they had nothing left to hope for. [...]

I dined with the bishop,[85] a worthy man, for whose conduct I had good reason to be thankful during this journey. While I was with

---

[83] St Catherine's church was demolished during the Revolution. It occupied a site in the rue Sainte-Catherine, a street that still exists, a hundred metres or so north of the rebuilt George V bridge,
[84] Jean-Édouard Molé de Champlâtreux, son of the Keeper of the Seals.
[85] Alphonse d'Elbène, Bishop of Orleans.

him, the lieutenant-general, a staunch supporter of Mazarin, brought me a letter he had received from the Keeper of the Seals, because he knew that I had learnt that he had received it;[86] I burnt it, and forbade him to make any reply to it. I seized some horses in an inn, that the agent of the enemy army had bought; in short, I acted with absolute authority. I went to the town hall, where I had ordered the council to meet. [...] Once I was in the town hall, seated in a great chair, and saw that everyone was waiting in profound silence to hear me, I confess that I was highly embarrassed — I, who had never spoken in public, and who was very ignorant; but necessity and Monsieur's orders gave me both confidence and the power to express myself clearly. So I began to speak.

[She told them that her father and Condé, not Mazarin, represented the king; she stated that she had sent for Nemours and Beaufort to ask them to move the army further away from Orleans, and that she would sign an order to tell officers to leave the city; and she asked the assembly to do nothing without her participation, and assured them that she would do nothing without them.]

As I left, I saw the windows of the prisons of the town hall crowded with our soldiers, asking me for their freedom. I asked the councillors who were escorting me what they had done; they told me that they were accused of several things. I offered to have them all hanged in the public squares of the city; they refused, and handed them all over to me. I sent them to the army that same evening, and the councillors had their arms and their horses restored to them (for some of them were cavalrymen); there were some two or three score of them.

When I was back at my lodging, I asked the councillors if they were pleased with me; for before I had gone to the town hall, they had told me that it would be wise to think out what I was to say. I told them: 'I know what I have to talk about; if I thought about it, I should make a mess of it; I must say whatever comes into my head, and, above all, stand behind me; for if you look at me, I shall not know what I am saying.' They told me that it had been quite clear that I did not see them, and that I had spoken very well.

[She met Beaufort and Nemours outside the city 'in a wretched, unfurnished hovel', and a council of war was held, to decide where the army should go.]

---

[86] In Orleans, as in most jurisdictions, a lieutenant-general nominally appointed by the king exercised the governor's powers when, as often happened, the governor was absent.

M. de Beaufort, M. de Nemours, and I were leaning against an old wooden chest, and Clinchamp, who could not remain standing for long, on account of an old wound, was sitting on a bedstead.

After everyone had given his opinion, I asked the councillors what they thought. They refused at first, saying that it was not their trade; I rejoined that it was not mine; so they gave in to my persuasions, and supported the view of the majority, which was mine; for I gave my opinion. You may well think that this was wrong, for young ladies do not usually talk sensibly about war; but, I assure you that in this, as in everything else, common sense prevails, and, with it, any lady would command armies successfully. I came down in favour of Montargis, the best choice, because the army would be going into a very good district, in which the troops would have adequate food; if we arrived there soon enough, men could be sent to Montereau;[87] thus we should control the rivers Loire and Yonne, and in that way cut the court off, and stop it from going to Fontainebleau. Blois seemed a bad choice to me, because we should be going to a district where the enemy army had been for three weeks and pillaged everything; and to let the enemy march for ten days when we could cut them off seemed to me a wrong decision. Everyone had spoken in favour of Montargis, and we must absolutely go there.

M. de Nemours began to curse and swear, saying that we were abandoning the prince, and that, if he had any sense, he would abandon Monsieur. I told him that I thought the prince would disagree with what he was saying, and that he ought not to be so furious about something that was not contrary to the prince's interests, which mattered as much to me as to him. I said everything I could to bring him round: he threatened to go away; I begged him to let me know if he meant to, because the enemy was close at hand and in strength, and it would be as well to know soon if he intended to abandon Monsieur's troops. I said that I did not want them to cross the river, and that I should take pains to put them in a place of safety. He was so angry that he did not know what he was saying; he started to curse and swear again, saying that the prince was being betrayed, and that he well knew by whom. M. de Beaufort asked: 'By whom?' He replied: 'You.' Whereupon they both struck each other. But, as I was looking the other way, talking to Clinchamp, I did not see who

---

[87] Montargis is 70 kilometres east-north-east of Orleans and Montereau a further 50 kilometres north-north-east beyond Montargis, at the confluence of the Yonne and the Seine. These were ambitious plans.

struck the first blow. I have been told by those who were there that it was M. de Beaufort, and that is what brought about what happened afterwards.[88] They drew their swords, and the bystanders rushed to separate them.

Immediately, all those who were outside ran in; a terrible uproar and utter confusion broke out, which astounded M. de Clinchamp, for foreigners have more respect for those to whom respect is due. M. de Nemours refused to give his sword to anyone but me — and then reluctantly. I handed it to the lieutenant of Monsieur's guards [Pradine], who was with me, as well as that of M. de Beaufort, whom I took into a garden; he knelt down before me, and asked my forgiveness, with all possible regrets for having been wanting in respect to me. M. de Nemours did not behave likewise; for he remained for an hour in an unparalleled rage. I reprimanded him, and said that this action was the worst possible thing in the world for our side, and the enemy would welcome it, as if they had won a great victory over us; and that, at this juncture, he should show his zeal for the prince's service by sacrificing his passion to his interests. He paid no heed. [...]

On the morning of Easter Saturday. I was told that at Saint-Mesmin there were guns that had come up the river from Blois,[89] waiting to be taken and escorted to the army. Straight away, I sent for the councillors, and said: 'Here is an opportunity: I must go to Saint-Mesmin; I shall ride, and all my carriage horses will be available to bring the guns here. All my men will ride; there will be a hundred good men on horseback; I shall take two hundred musketeers from the city, so the escort will be strong enough, and we shall capture their guns.' They all burst out laughing at my keenness to do something; I thought nothing impossible. They told me that if I had troops, it could be done, but that, as I had none, it was difficult, which vexed me. [...]

On my arrival at Orleans, I received a great many complaints from the noblemen and gentry of the district about the misbehaviour of the soldiers, who were carrying away the cattle and the horses of the ploughmen, beating people, treating them with all possible brutality, so it was said, and burning the feet of peasants to extract money; in short, all the fables that old peasant women tell one another. As I

---

[88] At the end of July, they fought a duel, in which Beaufort killed Nemours.
[89] Saint-Mesmin is about three kilometres down river from Orleans; the guns were intended for the royal army, the court being nearby at Cléry.

am very sensitive to the sufferings of the poor, I felt sorry, and I very much love justice; for both reasons, I instituted a thorough enquiry to put matters right. The cattle and horses were found in the soldiers' quarters, and restored, and the ploughmen went back to their ploughs twenty-four hours after my arrival, as if it were peace time; they went to market, too. As for all the other disorders, they turned out to be baseless, and I had everything restored, down to the last chicken, so that I was blessed as much in the country as in the city.

[Condé joined the army. Mademoiselle wanted him to come to Orleans. To overcome the opposition of the authorities, she showed them a warrant given her by her father.]

As I had shown my warrant to the city, it had to be registered by the présidial. As soon as this was mentioned to the company, some objected, on the grounds that the marquis de Sourdis being appointed by the king, Monsieur might well give him orders, but not delegate this power to another, and there had never been any precedent for a king's son behaving in this way in his apanage. I conferred with the councillors of the parlement of Paris who were with me, and told them that I thought that, in my position in Orleans, nothing ought to be out of my power, and that, even if there were no precedent for such a thing, I should be very glad to set one for the future; and that it was glorious to set a precedent for something so beneficial as this would be in future for all kings' sons, to be able to make appointments on occasions when hitherto only the king had done. As the thing was not unjust, they agreed with me. I sent for the royalists in the présidial, and handed them the said warrant for them to give their conclusions; I also sent for the lieutenant-general, a staunch supporter of Mazarin, with whom I was thoroughly dissatisfied.

While all this was being dealt with, Saujon, the captain of Monsieur's guards, arrived. I was not on good terms with him, because of some intrigues of his with Mme de Fouquerolles, with which I was displeased, because I do not like people to interfere in my household unless I order them to. He came to my house; I put up with him; but, when one has reached that point, relations are far from satisfactory.[90] Having been a party to some confidence or other, he put it into the marquis de Sourdis's head that he could wind me round his little finger; and the marquis, being convinced of that and

---

[90] In 1650, she had bestowed on Saujon the governorship of Dombes, but if she was hoping to improve her relations with him, she failed. He was very much her father's man.

of his influence with Monsieur, took it into his head that he would do better to stop seeing me, on the pretext that the warrant was incompatible with his own even though he had approved it, and to oppose its registration. All the councillors came to see me to say that I ought not to commit myself, since, as M. de Sourdis opposed the registration, I should be obliged either to pursue a course of action of which the outcome was doubtful, or give in to him; and, in order to persuade me that it did not matter, they kept telling me — what I had said all along — that the thing was so far beneath me that that is how it should be treated. I agreed, but I felt that, for men of ability, they had got me into difficulties, since I had been reluctant; that, at this juncture, the matter was so trivial that I had to carry it through; and that, even in trifles, it was hard for people like me to give up.

I lost my temper, and spoke for four hours, looking at it from all sides, and never letting them lose sight of the aim, from whatever side I was looking at it. I do not know if I was right, but I defended my case so well that they were all very satisfied, and said I was right; but still they did not give in. As my wrath did not diminish, it brought me to tears, I protesting that anyone would think that M. de Sourdis and I were implacably opposed, and that he would get the better of me. At last, after many pressing lamentations, what made me wild was that they had all got me into this scrape, and had then changed their minds; the councillors of the parlement had stood out till the end, for they had even gone as far as to tell me that the parlement of Paris would have made no bones about registering it so as to set the precedent I have mentioned. The city councillors told me that I had little influence in the présidial; that they were all staunch supporters of Mazarin; and that I should take that into consideration. I considered nothing, being stubborn in my opinions. The whole day passed in this way, and the whole evening; and, as I could not sleep, I even sent and woke them up, one by one, making them come and talk to me, and trying to win them over separately, so as to find them all on my side when I should see them together.

In the morning, they came and told me that I was the mistress; that I should do whatever I wished, but that one must give in to reason, which, and not their humble prayers, was what I should give in to; and that it was very important for Monsieur's service that I should behave in this way. At last I gave in, and I sent Préfontaine to tell the members of the présidial to come and see me when I returned from mass.

When I arrived, and learned that they were in my house, I burst into tears once more. I had the windows of my room shut; I dried my tears, bade them enter, and told them that I knew they had pronounced judgement on the matter I had put to them; and that I begged them to stop at that point and go no further — and that with a cheerful expression, as if it had been the most agreeable thing in the world for me. That is the compromise the councillors had devised, and I agreed to it. I leave you to judge whether I should not have done better to follow my original feelings in the matter, as I had done in others. M. de Sourdis came to see me, and we made it up. He was in the habit of giving me a packet of sweetmeats every day, having some excellent ones, and during our dispute I had not had any; so that I told the Bishop of Orleans, who reconciled us, that he should restore to me everything that was mine; which he did, for I did not lose one of my packets, and had a great many when we made it up.

[On 6 April 1652, Condé defeated the royal army under Hocquincourt at Bléneau, east of Gien and not far from Saint-Fargeau. On 2 May, Mademoiselle left Orleans, and returned to Paris. Condé decided to move his headquarters to Charenton. After that, things went less well for the anti-government party. Turenne's royal army won a number of skirmishes and, on 29 June, the court, gaining in confidence, took up residence at Saint-Denis, just north of Paris. A contingent of troops was encamped in the Cours-la-Reine, and it was decided that they should march to Charenton, on the other side of the city.]

The next night [that of 1 July], all the troops passed along the moat,[91] and as only the Tuileries [gardens], which are on the edge of it, stood between my apartments and the moat, I distinctly heard the drums and the trumpets, and made out the different marches. I leant out of my window till two o'clock, listening to them file past, sorrowfully thinking of what might happen; but, withal, I had some instinct that I might help to save them, and I even said to Préfontaine in the evening: 'I shall not purge myself tomorrow; for I have an idea that I shall do something unexpected, as at Orleans.' He answered that he

---

[91] The unseen troops were moving around the perimeter of the city, starting from a point seven hundred metres west of the Tuileries palace, beyond the old city rampart. Their route can be traced by taking a modern map and following the rue Royale, the boulevard des Capucines, and the Grands Boulevards as far as the place de la République, and thence along the boulevard du Temple and the boulevard Beaumarchais — none of which existed, of course, in Mademoiselle's time.

hoped so, but that he was very much afraid that it would not happen. […]

At six o'clock on the morning of 2 July 1652, I heard someone knocking on the door of my room. I awoke with a start, and called to my women to open the door. The comte de Fiesque came in, and told me that the prince [de Condé] had sent him to see Monsieur and tell him that he had been attacked at daybreak between Montmartre and La Chapelle; that, on the way to report the state of affairs to him and take his orders, he had been turned back at the Porte Saint-Denis;[92] and that he begged Monsieur to take horse, and he would continue his march, being unable to wait for him where he was. Monsieur had replied that he was unwell. The prince had also told the comte de Fiesque to come to me and beg me not to abandon him.

I immediately got up, dressed as quickly as possible, and went to the Luxembourg, where I found Monsieur at the head of the stairs. I said: 'I thought I should find you in bed; the comte de Fiesque told me you were unwell.' He replied: 'I am not ill enough to be in bed, but I am too ill to go out.' I urged him, as strongly as I could, to ride out and help the prince; but in vain, for none of the reasons I put forward had any effect on his state of mind; and seeing that I could achieve nothing, I begged him to go to bed, thinking that he should either feign illness, or act, and that, behaving as he was, his interests were as much at stake as the prince's. He did nothing, and my tears affected him as little as what I said. It was difficult not to shed any in this situation; even without the interests of the prince and of a great many friends of mine with him, I felt great pity for a large number of officers in Monsieur's troops, decent, well-bred men, all of whom I kept remembering in turn. The sight of Mme de Nemours, in a pitiful state, due to her anxiety for her husband and for M. de Beaufort, her brother, further aggravated my worries.

In the midst of my grief, it angered me to see some of Monsieur's people very merry, hoping that the prince would perish. They said: 'On occasions like these, every man for himself.' They were friends of Cardinal de Retz, which is why they spoke in this way. Monsieur was walking up and down; I spoke to him as he went by. To persuade him, I went as far as to say: 'Unless you have a treaty with the court in your pocket, I do not understand how you can be so calm; but have

---

[92] In 1652, the Porte Saint-Denis, at the northern extremity of the rue Saint-Denis in what is now the second arrondissement of Paris, was still a fortified barrier. It was replaced by the current triumphal arch in 1672.

you really made one in order to sacrifice the prince to Mazarin?' He did not reply. What I have described lasted an hour, during which all our friends might have been killed, and the prince like anyone else, without anyone minding; that seemed very hardhearted to me.

At last, M. de Rohan and M. de Chavigny came, those in whom the prince at that time had most confidence. After speaking to His Royal Highness for some time, they persuaded him to send me to the Hôtel-de-Ville on his behalf to ask for the things that were necessary. For that purpose, he gave me a letter to M. de Rohan for the city council, in which he said he relied on me to tell them his intentions.[93]
[...]

When I arrived at the Hôtel-de-Ville, Marshal de l'Hôpital, the Governor of Paris, and the provost of the merchants, who, at that time, was M. le Fèvre, a councillor in the parlement, came to the top of the staircase to meet me, and apologized for not having come further, not having been informed.[94] I told him that I was sure that my coming must have greatly taken them by surprise, but that Monsieur's indisposition was the cause. When we reached the great hall, I asked: 'Is everyone here?' They said yes.

I said to them: 'Monsieur, feeling rather unwell, and having to give orders constantly, has not been able to come; the duc de Rohan is commanded to give you a letter from him.' He handed it over, and the town clerk read it aloud; it was very flattering to me, expressing his confidence in my behaviour from his recent experience of it. After that, I told them that Monsieur had ordered me to tell them that he wanted arms to be taken up in all districts of the city — they told me that was done; and that 2000 men were to be detached from the regiments of all the districts, and sent to the prince. They replied that civilians could not be detached like soldiers, but that they would not fail to send the 2000 men ordered by His Royal Highness.

I told them that I should not doubt, as soon as they had given the order, that it would be carried out, since I knew what affection all the citizens had for us, and that they would be delighted to extricate the prince from his perilous situation. His person ought to be dear to all good Frenchmen, and I believed there was not one who would

---

[93] On the authority of the provost of the merchants, the gates of Paris had been closed and it had been decided that no army should be permitted to enter the city. Only Gaston d'Orléans, nominally representing the authority of the king himself, had the power to order that the decision be rescinded.

[94] The correct etiquette when meeting someone of Mademoiselle's standing was to come to the foot of the staircase.

not risk his life to save his. I asked them for 400 men to station in the Place Royale,⁹⁵ which they granted. I saved the big request up for the end — which was to allow our army to pass through. At that, they all looked at one another. I said to them: 'I do not think much deliberation is needed. Monsieur has always shown so much kindness towards the city of Paris that it is quite fair that, at this juncture, when the salvation of both is at stake, that you should show him gratitude; for you must not allow yourselves to believe that, if the worst came to the worst, and the enemy troops defeated the prince, they would show any more mercy to Paris than to the military. Cardinal Mazarin is convinced that he is unpopular, and, indeed, he has been given many signs of it; consequently, if he can take his revenge, it cannot be doubted that he will. It is up to us to avoid it by our efforts; and we cannot do the king a greater service than to save for him the largest and fairest city in his realm, and the one that has always served him most faithfully.'

Marshal de l'Hôpital spoke first: 'You well know, Mademoiselle, that if your troops had not come near this city, the king's would not have come, and they were only coming to drive them away.' Mme de Nemours disagreed, and started to argue with him. I interrupted, saying: 'The question is not whether Cardinal Mazarin has it in for those inside or outside Paris. We may believe that he means neither well; but consider, gentlemen, that while we are wasting time arguing about trifles, the prince is in peril in your suburbs, and what grief and what shame it would for ever be for Paris, if he perished there from lack of help! You can give it to him; so do it quickly.'

At that, they went out and deliberated in a room at the end of the hall; and all the while I prayed to God, looking out of a window on to the Hospital of the Saint-Esprit.⁹⁶ Mass was being said, but I did not hear it continuously, walking about and sending people to hurry up the councillors and ask them for an answer, the matter about which they were assembled being urgent, and to say that if they did not grant what we were asking, we should have to see about other measures, and I had so much confidence in the people of Paris that I did not think they would abandon us. Shortly after that message had been delivered, they came out and gave all the orders I was asking for. I hastily sent word to the prince that I had obtained permission for

---

⁹⁵ The Place Royale is the modern-day place des Vosges, renamed in 1800.
⁹⁶ The hospital of the Saint-Esprit (*Holy Ghost*) was an orphanage in the place de Grève by the north end of the Hôtel-de-Ville. (The place de Grève is the modern-day place de l'Hôtel-de-Ville, renamed in 1830.)

our troops to enter Paris whenever he wanted, and that I had sent the marquis de la Boulaye to the Porte Saint-Honoré to let in the troops [who had come] from Poissy.[97]

On leaving the Hôtel-de-Ville, I found the citizens gathered in the place de Grève, shouting insults at Marshal de l'Hôpital. One said to me, looking at him closely (because he was escorting me): 'How can you stand this mazarin? If you are not satisfied with him, we shall drown him.' He tried to beat him; I stopped him, and shouted: 'I am satisfied with him.' None the less, to place the Marshal in safety, I made him go back into the town hall before my coach set off. In the rue de la Tixeranderie I saw the most horrible sight: it was the duc de la Rochefoucauld.[98] A musket shot had gone through the corner of one eye, and come out on the other side between the eye and the nose, so that both eyes were affected; so much blood was pouring out of them that they both seemed to be dropping out. His face was covered with it, and he was puffing and blowing as if he were afraid that the blood going into his mouth might suffocate him. His son was holding him by one arm, and Gourville by the other, for he could see nothing; he was on horseback and wore a white jerkin like those who were with him, and theirs were all covered with blood like his; they were weeping: for, seeing him in that plight, I should never have thought he could have survived. I stopped to speak to him, but he did not answer; it was all he could do to hear.

One of M. de Nemours's gentlemen came to tell his wife that he had been sent to warn her that he had been slightly wounded in the hand, that it would be nothing, and that he had gone another way so as not to alarm her if she saw him all bloody; she left me immediately to go to him. Many said of the wounds of these gentlemen that God had punished them, and that their negotiations, having caused everything to be neglected, had been the cause of this battle, in which they had been trounced;[99] and, although this idea had occurred to

---

[97] Poissy is 15 kilometres from Paris, to the north-west of Saint-Germain. The Porte Saint-Honoré lay at the western end of the rue Saint-Honoré, a few metres east of the present-day rue Royale.
[98] The author of the *Maximes*. The rue de la Tixeranderie (or Tisseranderie) has since disappeared under the rue de Rivoli as it passes the north side of the Hôtel-de-Ville.
[99] Mademoiselle had complained to Flamarens that negotiations with Mazarin had been an unwise diversion because, while they had been going on, too little had been done to strengthen the army. Previously, she had condemned Mme de Châtillon and Nemours for hoping that the Cardinal would reward them for their part. We shall shortly see her berating Condé, whom she also held responsible.

me as well as to others, I nevertheless felt very sorry for M. de la Rochefoucauld.

After leaving him, I met, at the end of the rue Saint-Antoine, Guitaut on horseback, bare-headed and all unbuttoned, propped up by a man, because he could not otherwise have stayed upright; he was as pale as death. I shouted to him: 'Are you dying?' He shook his head, but he had a bad musket wound in his body. Then I saw Valon in a sedan-chair which came up to my coach; he merely had a bruise in his back. As he is very fat, it had to be dressed promptly. He said: 'Well, my good mistress, we are all lost.' I assured him of the contrary. He said: 'You are giving me life, in the hope that our troops will be able to withdraw.' At every step I took in the rue Saint-Antoine, I saw men wounded — some in the head, the others in the body, the arms, the legs, on horseback, on foot, on ladders, planks, and stretchers — and corpses.

When I got near the gate, I sent M. de Rohan to order the captain on duty to allow our people to come and go, so that he should do whatever I should tell him to, the orders of the Hôtel-de-Ville being that everything that I ordered was to be done. I went into the house of a maître des comptes,[100] named M. de la Croix, who came and offered it to me; it is the nearest to the Bastille, and the windows look on to the street. As soon as I went in, the prince came to see me; he was in a pitiful state: the dust on his face was an inch thick and his hair was all tangled; his collar and his shirt were soaked with blood, though he had not been wounded; his breastplate was battered, and he held his sword in his hand, having lost the sheath; he handed it to my equerry. He told me: 'You see a man in despair; I have lost all my friends: Nemours, La Rochefoucauld, and Clinchamp are mortally wounded.' I assured him that they were all three rather better, that the surgeons did not believe them dangerously wounded, that I had just had news of Clinchamp, who was only two doors away; Préfontaine had seen him, and he was in no danger. That cheered him a little: he was deeply afflicted, for, when he came in, he threw himself on to a chair, weeping, and saying: 'Excuse my grief'; and then let them say that he loves no one! As for me, I have always known him to be affectionate towards those whom he loves.

He stood up and begged me to see that the baggage outside the gate was allowed in, and not to stir from the spot, so that they could come to me for everything that had to be done. He said he was in

---

[100] A member of the Chambre des Comptes or Audit Chamber.

such a hurry that he could not stay any longer. I urged him to come into the city with his army. He answered that he would not; that I was not to worry; that, henceforth, he would only skirmish; that I need no longer fear for my friends; that he undertook to bring Monsieur's troops back safe and sound; and that, for his part, no one would reproach him with having retreated before the mazarins at high noon.

After he had gone, the marquis de la Roche-Giffard went by, wounded in the head, but unconscious, and stretched out on a ladder like a dead man. I felt very sorry; he was a handsome, good-looking man, and even in that plight was still good-looking; what is worse, he was a heretic. I spent the whole day seeing nothing but dead bodies and wounded men, and I realized at last what soldiers say, that the number one sees inures one to such an extent that one has less pity for the last than for the first, particularly for the ones one does not know. There were some Germans who did not know what to do, nor how to complain, being unable to speak our language; I sent them to hospitals or surgeons' houses, according to their rank.

The colonels of all the districts sent to me for orders to call out their men. It was like being in Orleans again, to see myself commanding and being obeyed. I had the baggage brought in, as the prince had asked me, and ordered it to be taken to the Place Royale, considering that it would do very well there, that it would be stacked in the middle, and that the horses would be unharnessed, and fed in the arcades; for the prince had forgotten to tell me where they were to be sent. There, they were in a place from which they could conveniently go wherever they were wanted; for at that time no one knew where the army would encamp that evening.

Of the four hundred musketeers who had been given me as a reserve to send to the prince as he needed them, I sent half on to the rampart of the Porte Saint-Antoine, and the other half on to that of the Arsenal,[101] where the men of the Grand Master of Artillery raised objections to receiving them; but the second time, they were allowed in. I thought that would have a good effect, showing that the citizens were defending us and themselves; and that the mazarins would judge from that that they were entirely on our side; for I attached no importance to the help they might have given us. But anything that

---

[101] That is, to the north and the south of the Bastille, the fortress that dominated the Porte Sainte-Antoine on its south side. The Grand Master of the Artillery (Charles, Marshal de La Meilleraye), had his quarters in the Arsenal.

made Paris appear to have declared itself for us was advantageous. I worried a great deal that day; but I had no cause to regret my worries, since they were so fruitful.

The dire straits in which I had seen our affairs in the morning had left me with a good deal of anxiety, although we were out of them. Monsieur's behaviour to the prince, which was so detrimental to himself, drove me to despair, so that my mind was quite distracted, and I do not understand how, in my agitation, I was able to do everything that I did; but it was one of the effects of the miracle God worked for us that day; for, if heaven had not intervened, things would not have gone as they did.

The prince was attacked near the faubourg Saint-Denis; he sent cavalry to distract the enemy, while he hastily marched to the faubourg Saint-Antoine, where he was attacked by the whole of M. de Turenne's army, which came up at the same time as he. He barricaded himself in the main street in sight of the enemy as best he could, and sent troops to guard the other avenues. It should be said (and it is pretty well known) that this suburb is open on all sides, and that it would have taken twice as many troops as the prince had to guard a single avenue. The enemy had over 12,000 men, and the prince only 5000, and he withstood them for seven or eight hours, during which the fighting was horrible; he was ubiquitous. The enemy said that, unless he had been a demon, he could not humanly have done all he did; he was in every attack.

The enemy forced the main barricade, which blocked the crossroads from Picpus to Vincennes. Our infantry did well; but the cavalry was so terrified that it fled, and carried all it encountered on its way right up to the market, in front of the abbey of Saint-Antoine. But the prince, enraged by that, went back, sword in hand, with a hundred musketeers of Monsieur's regiment and such cavalry or infantry officers as he found to hand, thirty or forty of them, recaptured the barricade, and drove away the enemy. It was defended by the regiment of guards, and those of the navy, Picardy, and Turenne, which were certainly their best regiments and the strongest they had. In short, he performed feats beyond the bounds of imagination, by his great valour, by his generalship, and by a coolness at which everyone wondered. I was still watching the baggage, the dead, and the wounded going by; a horseman was killed, and remained on his horse, which was following the baggage with its poor master; that was pitiful.

[She was joined by Mme de Châtillon, President Viole, the comte de Fiesque, and the comte de Béthune.]

The Governor of the Bastille, called Louvière, the son of M. de Broussel, sent word that, providing he had a written order from Monsieur, he was at his service, and would do whatever he ordered.[102] I asked the comte de Béthune to tell Monsieur, and he sent the message to him by the prince de Guéméné. Abbé d'Effiat, who, like many others, had come to see me, seeing that it was late, and that I had not dined, rightly assumed, from the haste with which I had left my house, and the time, that I had not eaten, that I was in need of sustenance, and even that I should not think of it, having other things on my mind. He offered me food; his house being close by, I accepted his offer, and he had some brought, very quickly and very opportunely, for I was very hungry. Mme de Châtillon dined with me, and made the most ridiculous grimaces, at which I should have laughed, had I been in the mood for it.

At about two o'clock, the comte de Béthune sent word that Monsieur was coming. I immediately sent the comte de Fiesque to tell the prince. The comte made dozens of journeys that day, coming and going endlessly. M. de Rohan, who had been bled in the morning, nearly fainted from fatigue; his wife stayed with me and him all day. The prince came; I saw him coming from the window. I went to the staircase to meet him. He seemed to me quite different from what he was in the morning, though he had not changed in any way; but he was smiling and cheerful. He greeted me with a host of compliments and thanks for having been of some service to him. I said: 'I have a favour to ask of you: it is, to say nothing to Monsieur about the way he has treated you.' He answered: 'I owe him nothing but thanks; but for him, I should not be here.' I laughed and said: 'Stop joking; I know what reason you have to complain of him. I am in despair about it; but, for my sake, do not mention it.' He promised seriously, being convinced that Monsieur was indeed his friend, that it was the friends of Cardinal de Retz who had stopped him from doing what he had wanted, and that he well knew the respect he owed him; but he had, too, been long well aware of the truth.

We went into the room where the comtesse de Fiesque was, with Mme de Châtillon and M. de Rohan. He went up to them, but glared horribly at Mme de Châtillon, and looked at her with the utmost

---

[102] Strictly speaking, Broussel himself was Governor of the Bastille. His son, Louvière, was the captain of the fortress and acted in his father's name.

contempt. I was delighted, and she was so affected that she nearly fainted; she had to be given water; then she left. When Monsieur arrived, he embraced the prince as cheerfully as if he had failed him in nothing. He expressed his joy at seeing him out of such danger, and made him talk of the battle; he admitted that he had never been in such a dangerous situation. They expressed regrets for the wounded and the dead. [...] Monsieur and the prince resolved that the army should enter the city in the evening; then Monsieur went to the Hôtel-de-Ville to thank the council, and the prince returned to his army. M. de Beaufort strutted about, and thought he had done it all.

When they had gone, I went to the Bastille, where I had never been; I walked round the towers for a long time. I had the guns, which were all pointing towards the city, turned round; and I had some placed on the side of the river and the suburb, to defend the bastion. I looked through a telescope: I saw a lot of people on the heights of Charonne, and even some coaches, which made me think it was the king, and I have since learned that I was not mistaken. I also saw all the enemy army in the distance, towards Bagnolet; it seemed strong in cavalry. I could see the generals without knowing their faces; but they could be recognized by their retinue. I saw them splitting up their cavalry so as to cut us off between the faubourg and the moat, some going towards Popincourt, and the others via Reuilly, along the river; had they done it earlier, we should have been lost. I sent a page post-haste to tell the prince; at the same time, he was on top of the steeple of the abbey of Saint-Antoine; and when I confirmed exactly what he was seeing, he ordered the army to march into the city.[103]

I went back to the house where I had spent the day, in order to watch the army march past; for I well knew that all the officers would be delighted to see me. I must not forget to say that, in the morning, all the officers and men were full of consternation, for they thought there would be no quarter for them. As soon as they learned that I was at the gate, they shouted with exceeding joy, and said: 'Let us do

---

[103] From the Bastille, Mademoiselle could see the high ground at Charonne, where the king was. Beyond Charonne, troops were advancing from the direction of Bagnolet. Popincourt and Reuilly — nowadays in the eleventh and twelfth arrondissements of Paris — were to the north and the south of her position and much closer. The abbey of Saint-Antoine-des-Champs, 800 metres or so to the east of Mademoiselle's position, stood on the site of the present-day hôpital Saint-Antoine. Turenne had lured Condé and his troops into a trap in the streets outside the city wall and could pound them with his artillery until they died or surrendered.

wonders; we have an assured retreat; Mademoiselle is at the gate, and will have it opened if we are hard pressed.' The prince sent to ask me to send them wine, which I very speedily did, and, as they marched past my windows, they shouted: 'We have drunk your health; you are our liberator.' There were no decent people who would not have said the same thing, if they had dared. [...]

The prince came to see me on his way back into the city; and, as I wanted to reproach him with everything that had happened, I said: 'These are fine troops; they have not degenerated since I saw them at Étampes, and yet they have sustained a siege, and fought two battles; God preserve them from negotiations!' He turned red, and said nothing. I went on: 'At least, cousin, promise me that there will not be any more.' He said: 'No!' 'I cannot help telling you that this day must make you distinguish between your real friends and those who are only concerned with their own interests, and who have exposed your person in the hope of gaining 50,000 écus. For my part, I am only speaking out of friendship, to make you reflect; for others will not dare to tell you.' Tears of wrath stood in his eyes; I put an end to the conversation by saying: 'I have said enough; I hope you will mend your ways.' He departed, and I stayed until the last of the troops had filed past.

The troops that Marshal de Turenne and Marshal de la Ferté had sent to drive ours back advanced close to the city, but the guns of the Bastille fired two or three volleys, as I had ordered when I left. That frightened them by mowing down a row of horsemen; had it not been for that, all the foreign infantry, the gendarmerie, and some cavalry, which were in the rearguard, would have been destroyed, because they had been obliged to wait for some guns that were to be brought back from near the church of Sainte-Marguerite.[104] It worried me that they were taking so long to go past; I despatched the comte de Hollac, who had come to see me, to hurry them up; and when they had all passed, I went to rest for a while in the hôtel de Chavigny.[105]

I strolled in the garden with M. de Chavigny to refresh myself, for it was terribly hot that day. We talked a great deal about all that had happened; then I went to the Luxembourg, where everyone

---

[104] The guns were in an exposed forward position about 1 kilometre to the east. The church of Sainte-Marguerite still stands in what is now the rue Saint-Bernard in the eleventh arrondissement of Paris.

[105] The hôtel de Chavigny, rebuilt in the 1640s, was 500 metres north-west of the Bastille, roughly at the north end of what is today called the rue de Sévigné, in the third arrondissement.

regaled me with what had happened. The prince paid me a host of compliments, and told Monsieur that I had done well enough for him to be able to praise me. He [Monsieur] came and told me that he was satisfied with me, but not as affectionately as he should have done. I attributed this to his regret that I had done what he ought to have done; so his indifference, which I find so hard to bear, consoled me that day, since I believed that he felt what I wished he always felt.

When I reflected that evening — and when I still reflect — that I had saved that army, I confess that it was a source at the same time of great satisfaction and great wonderment to me to think that I had also caused the guns of the King of Spain to rumble through Paris, and the red flags to pass by with the Saint Andrew's crosses. My joy at having done such yeoman service for our side and at having, on this occasion, performed such an extraordinary feat as has never, perhaps, fallen to the lot of a person of my quality, prevented me from thinking the thoughts to which it may now give rise, and which might have disturbed my joy. The marquis of Flamarens was killed, which caused me considerable grief, for he had been a particular friend of mine since the journey to Orleans, on which he had followed me and served me very well. It had been foretold that he would die with a rope round his neck, and, during that journey, he had often recalled this prediction, laughing at it and mentioning it as something ridiculous, being unable to convince himself that he would be hanged. When they went to look for his body, they found him with a rope round his neck, on the very spot where, some years before, he had killed Canillac in a duel.

I did not sleep all night; I had all these poor dead men on my mind. Next day, I did not leave my house, to which a great many people came, particularly army officers; they spoke of nothing but the daring of the prince, and all his noble exploits; they were all full of admiration. He came to see me, and asked me to explain everything that had happened before the battle. He ended by saying that he wanted our side to be successful for the sole purpose of being able to help me to be married as advantageously as he wished, and that that was the thing of all others he most passionately desired.

The good will shown by the people on the day of the battle was quite extraordinary. They fetched the dead to have them buried, they gave drinks to the wounded and the whole as they went by, did whatever was in their power, and shouted: 'Long live the king, and down with Mazarin!' [...]

I learned from a man who was with the king that, when His Majesty heard the guns of the Bastille firing, the Cardinal said: 'Good, they are firing at the enemy!' [...] When the guns fired several times more, someone said: 'I am afraid it is at us.' Others said: 'Perhaps Mademoiselle has gone to the Bastille, and they have fired a salute.' Marshal de Villeroy said: 'If it is Mademoiselle, it will be she who has made them fire at us.' It was some time before they learned the truth.

[On 4 July, on her way to the Hôtel-de-Ville, the scene of serious rioting, she had an unpleasant experience.]

An incident occurred on the Petit-Pont, which would have given me a good fright on any other day, when I had less on my mind: my coach caught against the cart of the dead that is taken every night from the Hôtel-de-Dieu to the Trinité.[106] I merely moved over to the other door, lest any of the feet or hands sticking out should strike me on the nose.

---

[106] The Hôtel-de-Dieu or Hôtel-Dieu was the poor hospital; the Trinité was a burial ground.

Chapter 4
Exile and Country Life (1652–1657)

[The Battle of the Faubourg Saint-Antoine was virtually the end of the Fronde.[107] On Saturday 19 October 1652, the king sent an order to Mademoiselle to vacate her home in the Tuileries by noon on the 20th. On the 21st, the court returned to Paris.]

In the morning, Monsieur went to the Palais de Justice to assure the members of the parlement that he had made no treaty, that he would not desert the company, and that he would perish with them. He spoke to them in these terms, or even stronger ones; the company thanked him. It was Monday morning. We heard, at Mme de Choisy's, that His Royal Highness had orders to leave. I ran to the Luxembourg. As I went in, I met the duc de Rohan, who was accused, rightly enough, of being on good terms with the court and of having abandoned the interests of the prince, to whom he owed a great deal. I told him what I thought, pretty roundly; then I went into Madame's closet, where I found Monsieur. I asked him if he had orders to leave. He told me that he was not obliged to report to me. I said: 'What! you are deserting the prince and the Duke of Lorraine!' He repeated his retort. I begged him to tell me if I should be sent away; he said he was not meddling in my affairs; and that I had behaved so badly towards the court that he declared he would not meddle with my affairs, since I had disregarded his advice.[108]

I took the liberty of saying: 'When I went to Orleans, it was by your order; I do not have it in writing, because you gave me the order yourself; but I have your written orders for everything that was to be done there, and even letters, more flattering than need be, from Your Royal Highness, in which you express feelings of kindness and affection, which would not have led me to believe that Your Royal

---

[107] In August, the king summoned the parlement to Pontoise, and enough councillors attended for the rump in Paris to be deprived of any semblance of legitimacy; by September, the people of Paris were beginning to call upon their leaders to recognize the king's authority. The rebels fell out; Condé left the capital on 13 October and eventually went to fight for Spain against his own country. He was not to return to France until 1660. The last act of the Fronde is generally taken to be Candale's recapture of Bordeaux, where Mme de Longueville had long been holding out against royal authority.

[108] The king, tutored by Mazarin, had almost certainly required Gaston to abandon his daughter to her fate since, were she to have remained with him, she might have stiffened his resolve to resist and perhaps even to make common cause with the (by now) fugitive Condé.

Highness would treat me as you are doing now.' 'And the Saint-Antoine affair,' said he, 'do you not think, Mademoiselle, that that has harmed you in the eyes of the court? You were so pleased to play the heroine, and to be told that you were the heroine of our party, and had saved it twice, that, whatever becomes of you now, you will not fail to be comforted when you remember all the praise lavished on you.'

I was extremely astonished to see him in such a mood. I retorted: 'I do not think I served you worse at the Porte Saint-Antoine than in Orleans. I did both these damnable things by your order; and if it were to been done all over again, I should do it, because it was my duty to obey and serve you. If you are unfortunate, it is fair that I should share in your misfortune; and, even had I not served you, I should nevertheless have shared in it. It is better, therefore, according to my fancy, to have done what I have done, than to suffer for nothing. I do not know what being a heroine is: I am of such birth as never to do but what is great and lofty in whatever I undertake, and you may call it what you will; I call it following my inclination and going my way; I was born not to go any other.'

When this outburst of Monsieur's was over, he came back; I begged him to allow me to stay in the Luxembourg, thinking it wrong to be so near the Louvre without going there. He answered: 'I have no rooms.' I said: 'There is no one here who will not give his up to me, and I think no one has a better right to stay here than I.' He retorted angrily: 'I need everyone who is lodging here, and none of them shall move out.' I said: 'Since Your Royal Highness does not wish it, I shall go and stay in the hôtel de Condé, where there is no one.' 'I do not wish it.' 'Where do you want me to go, Monsieur?' 'Where you will'; and went off.[109]

[She stayed for a short time with Mme de Montmort, sister-in-law of Mme de Frontenac, and then, accompanied by the latter, travelled to Mme de Bouthillier's at Pont. There, news reached her that she was being pursued, and she decided to go to her castle at Saint-Fargeau.]

We arrived at Saint-Fargeau at two o'clock in the morning; we had to alight, the bridge being broken down. I went into an old house with neither doors nor windows, and grass knee-high in the courtyard; I

---

[109] The hôtel de Condé was a stone's throw from the Luxembourg in what was then a southerly continuation of the rue Dauphine, nowadays the northern end of the rue de Condé, roughly on the site of the Odéon. Gaston himself was about to flee to Limours, and thence to Blois.

was horrified. I was taken to a horrid room with a post in the middle. Fear, horror, and grief overcame me to such an extent that I burst into tears. I felt wretched, since I was away from the court, had no better residence than that, and reflected that this was the finest of my mansions, having built no house for myself.

[Afraid of being arrested, she took refuge at Dannery, the house of one of her agents five kilometres to the north-east, while La Guérinière, her majordomo, inspected Saint-Fargeau to establish whether she could put up there in safety. He reported back that the premises were sufficiently secure.]

My people urged me to go to Saint-Fargeau; it took me two days to make up my mind. I was not bored in that little house at Dannery; I found books in it; I walked; I went early to bed, and got up late. I received a piece of news that shocked me, that of the death of Mlle de Chevreuse, who had been ill for only three days. I was extremely sorry; she was a good and pretty woman; she was not very bright.

At last, after three days, I went one fine morning to Saint-Fargeau; I was taken to a set of rooms I had not seen, which I found more comfortable. The duc de Bellegarde had fitted it up, Monsieur having given him the use of that house to compensate for the losses he had suffered in his service. This apartment consisted of part of a gallery, blocked off by the thickness of a wall. That very day, I decided to change round the fireplaces and the doors, and to make an alcove. I enquired whether there was not an architect in the district, which was a blunder; for the workmen of Paris are always better and more hardworking; but people who have not built, and have not been in the provinces, do not know this; and I should have chided anyone who had told me, since I liked anything provincial a hundred times better than anything Parisian.

I began, therefore, to fit up the inside of the apartment where I was, and for that I had to move out; I went and lodged in the attic above. In addition to the discomfort of this lodging, I had nothing to sleep on, for [...] my bed did not come until ten days after I arrived in Saint-Fargeau. [...] Fortunately for me, the bailli[110] of Saint-Fargeau was newly married; so he had a brand new bed.

The duchesse de Sully and Mme de Laval[111] came to see me shortly after my arrival. I was deeply ashamed to be unable to put them up in my house; every evening, they had to go and sleep in the bailli's

---

[110] President of a *bailliage*, a court of first instance, below a *présidial*.
[111] The duchesse de Sully and the duchesse de Laval were sisters.

house, where the bed was, in which I had slept before my own came. A great many other ladies came, all of whom lodged in the town. I sent to Bois-le-Vicomte for some furniture I had there, so as to get rid of this feeling of shame.

While I was in the little house [at Dannery], I had a great fright. I woke up, hearing the curtain of Mme de Frontenac, who was sleeping in a bed close to mine, being pulled back. Immediately, I heard it closed again. I asked her: 'Are you mad to open your bed-curtain at this time of night?' She replied: 'It is the wind.' We were in a room on the ground floor, with windows on one side only, and there was no wind that day. I was frightened; I said: 'Come and sleep with me.' She did not wait to be asked twice, and as she was passing from her bed to mine, I heard the curtain being pulled open again. Until daybreak, neither of us spoke. When daylight had come, she confessed to me that, seeing her curtain being opened (for there is always a light in my room), her first impulse had been to rush to my bed; but she had retained enough presence of mind to be afraid of being disrespectful, and of frightening me, and had seen her curtain opened and closed twice. We racked our brains to think what it could be, in vain. A few days later, I learned that a lad in my service, my foster brother, who had gone with the comte de Hollac in my company of gendarmes, had been killed. I did not doubt that it was he who had come to bid me farewell. I had a great many masses said for him.

[In December 1652, visiting her father in Blois and Chambord, she found his welcome somewhat strained. She returned to Saint-Fargeau.]

I returned via Sully, where I spent a day, and then settled in at Saint-Fargeau for good; I changed my room on arriving. Fireplaces had had to be installed in the one in which I was; so I took Préfontaine's, which he had already been occupying, and which had a lovely view, which is not unusual in an attic.

I worked at my embroidery from morning to evening, leaving my room only to dine downstairs and to go to mass. That winter was so severe that one could not go out; so, as soon as there was a moment's fine weather, I went out on horseback, and when the frost was too hard, on foot, to see my workmen. First I had a mall laid out; trees were already planted, but there were so many brambles and holes that one would never have thought it possible to make an avenue there. But, by dint of cutting down the undergrowth and bringing earth, a fine avenue was revealed; but, not judging it long enough to make a mall, I had it extended by a terrace a hundred paces long, which created a very fine effect; for, from the terrace, one can see the castle, a suburb, woods, vineyards, and a meadow with a river running through it, which in summer turns into a pool; this is not an unpleasant landscape. Saint-Fargeau, when I arrived, was such a wilderness that one could not find any vegetables for cooking.

While I worked at my embroidery, I got someone to read aloud; and it was at this time that I began to be fond of reading, which I have always loved since. As I was arranging my caskets and my papers, I remembered the *Life of Mme de Fouquerolle*, which I had written, and which Préfontaine was keeping for me. He gave it back to me, and I completed it; and, as I very much wanted to say something about everything that had happened, I contrived to put a little of it in. Finally, I wanted to have this work printed, with a manifesto to clear myself of her complaints about me, one that she had composed in reply, a letter by Mme de Frontenac about the *Kingdom of the Moon*, and one that I had also written with verses by her; for I am very bad at verse — and if many people are to be believed, the verse in this little book, though very pretty, is not all by her; they say a certain M. du Châtelet wrote it. In short, I had all these bits and pieces printed. I sent to Auxerre for a printer, gave him a room, and amused myself by going and watching him printing. It was a great secret; only Mme de Frontenac, Préfontaine, his clerk, and I were in it.

[Condé, d'Escars, and Hollac kept in touch by letter, and she was visited by a number of noble ladies of her acquaintance.]

We led a pleasant life free from boredom; I am the person least liable to be bored, always occupying myself, and even enjoying day-dreaming. I am bored only with people I do not like, or under constraint.

When the *Life of Mme de Fouquerolle* was printed, I realized that this occupation had amused me; and I had read the memoirs of Queen Marguerite; all that, together with a suggestion from the comtesse de Fiesque, Mme de Frontenac, and her husband, that I should write memoirs, made me resolve to begin these. Préfontaine told me that, if it gave me pleasure, I ought to write them. I soon wrote from the beginning up to the business of the Hôtel-de-Ville; and as my handwriting is bad, I gave them, bit by bit, to Préfontaine to make a fair copy.

[Towards the end of January 1653, Madame left Paris to join Monsieur in Orleans. A few days later, Mademoiselle went to visit them there.]

Monsieur and Madame gave me a warm welcome. [...] I found some actors there; it was a very good company that had been with the court all the previous winter at Poitiers and Saumur.[112] I had them perform one evening in my apartment; His Royal Highness came. All the talk at that time was of Cardinal Mazarin's return to court, the idea of which displeased Monsieur.[113]

A certain Jesuit father, called Jean-François, formerly of Blois and now of Orleans,[114] came to propose to Monsieur that I should marry the Duke of Neuburg. [...] His Royal Highness summoned me to his closet one day, with Madame there, and put this proposal to me. I answered that I thought that he was making fun of me, or that, during his absence from court, he had forgotten who he was, to think of marrying me to a petty German sovereign. Madame said that they had married princesses of Austria and Lorraine. I answered that others married as they liked, but that, for my part, I was determined not to marry in such a way. We spoke no more about it.

Monsieur and Madame went to Blois, and I to Saint-Fargeau. I passed through Sully, where I spent a day. On my arrival, I gave all my mind to fitting a theatre up in haste. At Saint-Fargeau, there is a large hall which is very suitable for the purpose; I attended plays with more enjoyment than ever before. The theatre was well lit and well decorated; the audience, indeed, was not large, but there were some quite good-looking women. We, the ladies and I, had bonnets trimmed with feathers; I had got this idea from one that Mme de Sully wore while hunting. The number had been increased or diminished, so that the effect was very pretty. M. de Bellegarde, who lives only thirty or forty miles from Saint-Fargeau, often came. When Lent put an end to the pleasure of the theatre, the game of shuttlecock took its place. As I like active games, I played for two hours in the morning,

---

[112] Traces of a company of actors who went by the name of the 'troupe du duc d'Orléans' are found in provincial cities from 1643 onwards, and some of the individual actors afterwards made names for themselves on the Paris stage. They had acted in Poitiers and Saumur from November 1651 to February 1652, and it was they whom Mademoiselle was later to invite to Saint-Fargeau. By 1655, they had begun calling themselves the 'troupe du duc d'Orléans et de Mademoiselle'. They acted in Lyon in 1658, when the court of Savoy was there and Mademoiselle no longer lived in exile. After 1658, they toured mostly in Savoy itself and the Low Countries, the last-known mention of them in contemporary documents occurring as late as 1678.

[113] Mazarin returned to court, nominally summoned by the King, on 9 February 1653.

[114] In correspondence with Mademoiselle, the Duke of Neuburg calls this man Jean-Antoine (Chéruel, II, 261), but Mademoiselle writes 'Jean-François'.

and as much in the afternoon. My mall was completed, and I played that game with Mme de Frontenac, who constantly found fault with me, though she always beat me; because, though I played with greater skill, her strength got the better of it.[115]

[She rebuffed a further attempt to make her marry the duke of Neuburg. On another visit to Orleans, at the request of the abbess of Fontevrault,[116] she urged her father to put one of her half-sisters into that convent. He referred her to his wife.]

So I spoke to Madame about it. She said that, for her part, she would be delighted, but that Monsieur was one of those indecisive people; and that Mlle de Valois was the one to go. I offered to take her there; she answered that there was no hurry. I took the liberty of saying that, when they were grown up, it would be difficult to put them there, and, as for marrying them, suitable partners were not found every day; and that their condition was very different from mine, although we were sisters. For my part, I could wait patiently for an establishment, and I did not even know if I wanted to change my state; as for them, if Monsieur were to die, which was not impossible, they would be in a sorry plight; Madame would be hard put to it to support four daughters, and it was very easy to take them from a convent to marry them, but very difficult to put them into one when they were grown up. After listening to me carefully, she said: 'I have such good reason to trust Providence that I do not doubt that it will treat my daughters as it did me; so I shall not worry about them at all.' I made so bold as to say that she was right, and that she herself had done some quite extraordinary things, but that the house of Bourbon was not so lucky as that of Lorraine.

On arriving at Saint-Fargeau, I experienced one of those joys that one does in the country; the apartment that I was having fitted up was, I found, ready; I had it furnished, and moved in. There was an anteroom, in which I had always eaten, and a gallery in front of my bedroom, in which I hung portraits of my nearest relatives — the late king, my grandfather [Henry IV], and the queen, my grandmother [Maria de' Medici]; the King [Philip IV] and Queen of Spain, the

---

[115] In the game of 'mall', a heavy ball is propelled along the ground and through a metal arch. The balls are of boxwood and can be up to 30 centimetres in diameter, while the mallets resemble croquet mallets, but with curved heads. The word is also used for the alley, often between trees, in which the game is played.

[116] Jeanne-Baptiste de Bourbon, Mademoiselle's aunt, a legitimized daughter of Henry IV and half-sister of Gaston d'Orléans.

King of England [Charles I] and the Queen, his wife [Henrietta Maria]; the king [Louis XIII], the queen [Anne of Austria], His Royal Highness and my mother and my stepmother and Monsieur; the King of England [Charles II] and the Duke of York, the prince and princesse de Condé, and M. de Montpensier — his was in the best place, though he was not the greatest lord: he is the master of the house, and I learnt from experience that, if he had left me none, I should have no place.[117] Mme de Guise is there with her children, the prince de Joinville, the duc de Joyeuse, the chevalier de Guise, and Mlle de Guise. The Duchess of Savoy sent me hers and those of her husband, her son, and her three daughters — the eldest married to Prince Maurice of Savoy, her uncle; the second, to the Elector of Bavaria; and Princess Marguerite.

There are still some blank spaces, and I still have sufficient cousins to fill them.[118] I had a billiard table put in this gallery, for I love active games. My bedroom is quite pretty, with a closet at the end, and a wardrobe, and a little closet in which there is room only for me. After eight months in an attic, it was like living in an enchanted palace. I adorned the closet with a great many pictures and mirrors; in short, I was delighted, and thought I had created the most beautiful thing in the world. I showed my rooms to all who came to see me with as much satisfaction in my work as the queen, my grandmother, might have done when she showed her Luxembourg.

[At the end of September 1653, she went to stay with the recently widowed Mme de Bouthillier at Pont, and stopped at Fontainebleau on the way back.]

At Fontainebleau, I found some English horses I had sent for. I was very glad, having long wanted some; for it is a country pastime to love horses, to see them, to exercise them, and to show them to people who come to see them. These were handsome and good; out of four, two were suitable for me. I had never cared for dogs; I began to like them. The comtesse de Fiesque had a large, but beautiful, black hound, which had a litter; she gave me a very beautiful bitch, which I still have and like very much.

---

[117] 'M. de Montpensier' is Mademoiselle's maternal grandfather, Henri de Bourbon, duc de Montpensier; Mme de Guise, whom she mentions next, is her maternal grandmother.
[118] Mademoiselle's switch to the present tense at this juncture reminds us that she has her current situation very much in mind even as she writes her text.

At Fontainebleau, we heard that the comtesse de Fiesque had had fever; but my doctor, who wrote, said: 'The previous day, she had gone to Champinelle to see M. and Mme de Langlée (he is a gentleman in my neighbourhood), and had eaten a great deal.[119] That, therefore, may have been the cause of her fever, and it is to be hoped that her indisposition will have no consequences.' I would not let anyone tell Mme de Bréauté, for that would have made her worry. I merely told her at Châtillon, which is where one dines between Saint-Fargeau and Montargis: 'Your mother has been a little out of sorts, but it is nothing.' I mounted my horse and galloped to Saint-Fargeau. When I arrived, I went straight to the room of the comtesse de Fiesque, whom I found rather low; I did not stay long, because the room smelt bad, and this reason stopped me from going next day.

At ten o'clock in the evening, as I was at cards, someone came and said: 'The comtesse is dying; she is unconscious.' Her daughter-in-law, who was playing with me, abandoned the game, and ran to her; I went, too, but, as I am timid, I hesitated for some time to enter her room; however, I got over my fear. I saw extreme unction being administered; she was in a pitiable state, but I was not much affected. She was given antimony; she came to herself, and was capable of having the sacred host given to her. When this was proposed to her, she asked: 'Am I ill enough for that?' She was told that she had received extreme unction that night, and had been at death's door. She was greatly alarmed. I went to the church for the last sacraments, and accompanied them to her room. Her daughter-in-law and I were very much afraid that she would preach long sermons to us, but the fear of death prevented her; she was so frightened that she did not say a word. She did not ask anyone's forgiveness, though it is usual enough, when one is dying, to ask those with whom one has lived to forgive one. All that day, she remained tranquil.

On the Tuesday, the day of her bout of fever, as soon as it began, she fell into the same delirium as on the Sunday, did not recover from it, and died on the Wednesday [15 October], at eleven in the morning. I had wept a good deal on the day when she received the host — people reproached me, saying it was because she was better; but it was because I was reflecting on one's state at such a moment, and thinking of myself.

---

[119] Champinelle is Champignelles, 12 kilometres north of Saint-Fargeau. Châtillon, on the Loire, is about 25 kilometres to the west.

As soon as she had died, after seeing Mme de Bréauté in her room, I went to Ratilly, a house only thirteen miles from Saint-Fargeau, belonging to Menou, the Governor of Saint-Fargeau.[120] As it was small, I did not take many people with me, and did not even keep a coach there. I walked, every morning, to the parish church, which is three-quarters of a mile away; I hunted the hare with greyhounds belonging to some of the gentlemen of the neighbourhood. That made me want hounds, and I sent to England for a pack. I remained five or six days in this secluded spot to allow time for the body to be opened and removed, and the room aired; for I am afraid of the stench of death in a house, and I find it hard to sleep in one when there is any.

[She made further visits to Orleans, principally to discuss with her father who should be her lady-in-waiting in succession to the dowager comtesse de Fiesque.]

Then I returned to my Saint-Fargeau, where I built in real earnest. I brought an architect called Le Vau from Paris. The work lasted until I went away; and I left the building in a state to be lived in. It now only needs painting. It was certainly not a waste of my time, because the work amused me very much, and those who see it will think it rather magnificent and worthy of me. I was not able to do more to it, for I merely adapted an old house, which, nevertheless, had something grandiose about it, even though it had been built by a private citizen. He was, it is true, a Surintendant des Finances under Charles VII, but at that time they were not so magnificent as they are now. I wish he had been, and that my house were as fine as theirs; I should not have spent so much money — 200,000 francs is a great deal to me, and not much to these gentlemen.[121]

[Here she begins a lengthy account of her life at Saint-Fargeau from 1654 to July 1655; the correspondence she exchanged with Condé and others; visits

---

[120] Menou, who lived at Ratilly, was the Governor of the duchy of Saint-Fargeau, not of Mademoiselle's château of the same name. His house still stands, south-south-east of Saint-Fargeau.

[121] Mademoiselle's ancestor Antoine de Chabannes built the château, but folk tradition held that it was built by Jacques Cœur, Charles VII's *surintendant*. The Surintendant des Finances was the king's chief gatherer of tax revenues, the last and most notorious holder of the office being Nicolas Fouquet. When Mademoiselle talks of the magnificence of the *surintendants* of her own day, she is thinking of Servien and, particularly, Fouquet and his magnificent mansion at Vaux-le-Vicomte. Mademoiselle's architect, François Le Vau, was the brother of the man who built Vaux-le-Vicomte.

to Blois and Orleans; news of the continuing war, particularly on France's northern borders; the difficulties she had resolving her financial affairs with her father; and the advice and support given her in that connection by her intendant, Préfontaine.]

I was at my castle at Saint-Fargeau, where, after putting my affairs in order (which I usually did twice a week), I was concerned only with enjoying myself. The comtesse de Maure and Mlle de Vandy came to see me on their way back from Bourbon;[122] this was a most enjoyable visit for me, as they are women of great intelligence and excellent qualities, of whom I have a high opinion. Mme de Montglat, Mme Lavardin, and Mme de Sévigné came specially from Paris: the first had already been twice. Mme de Sully came while they were there, and the comte and comtesse de Béthune, on their way to the waters of Pougues.[123] They all constituted a very pleasant court. M. de Matha was there, too, beginning to fall in love with Mme de Frontenac; her husband, [and] Saujon, and others were there. We went and walked in the grounds of the prettiest houses in the neighbourhood of Saint-Fargeau, where I was given collations; I gave some in beauty spots in the woods, with my violins; in short, we endeavoured to enjoy ourselves.

[Other visitors came and went. She continued to have trouble with her father over his stewardship of her affairs. He made her dismiss Préfontaine.]

When the comte de Béthune was gone, I spoke to no one but the comte d'Escars; for I was convinced, and with good reason, that the ladies around me[124] were not sorry about all that had happened to me; so I had little to do with them. That autumn, from the end of September to Christmas, when d'Escars went to Paris, I spoke to no one but him, unless visitors came from outside.

In the morning, as soon as I awoke, while I was being dressed, someone would read aloud till mass. After dinner, I worked at my embroidery. Then there was more reading aloud, until it was quite dark. I would go and walk in the gallery for half an hour by candlelight; then I would come and work again till supper, after which I would

---

[122] The comtesse de Maure was Anne Doni d'Attichy, wife of Louis de Rochechouart, comte de Maure, Mme de Montespan's uncle. Bourbon is about 50 kilometres south of Nevers and 120 kilometres from Saint-Fargeau.
[123] The comtesse de Béthune was the sister of the comte de Saint-Aignan. Pougues is just to the north of Nevers.
[124] The (younger) comtesse de Fiesque and the comtesse de Frontenac, who were at Saint-Fargeau with her. She considered them to be in her father's pocket.

walk with the comte d'Escars once more, and speak to Préfontaine's clerk, whom I had asked him to leave behind, to settle accounts every week with my workmen, and to write to my estates and engross the necessary documents; so, every day, he reported what he was doing. As we wrote to Paris twice a week, I did no embroidery on those days; I shut myself up and wrote. We often noticed, d'Escars and I, that, while I was at dinner or supper, I often felt like weeping; tears would come into my eyes; the countesses looked at me, and laughed in my face.

[Her father objected even to the clerk.]

As soon as I heard that, I dismissed him, and remained without anyone to act as my secretary. I received all the letters from all the officials on my estates and from all the farmers, and I answered them. As for contracts, I had them engrossed by all and sundry; I would draft them, and they would be copied. I wrote to my lawyers in Paris about all my business. It is no fault of His Royal Highness's people if I am not a good business woman, for they set me on the way to becoming one. I realized then that Préfontaine had been right to want me to be acquainted with my affairs, and to pester me to look into them when I did not feel like it; because, if I had not understood them, they would have got into a worse mess than they did. Whatever one's rank, one is fortunate if one has faithful servants; they are not only useful while one has them, but one is always conscious that one has had them. Had anyone told me, when I was at court, that I should have known the price of bricks, lime, plaster, carts, and a workman's daily wage — in fact, all the details of building — and that, every Saturday, I should have settled their accounts, I should have been most surprised; and yet I did that job for a year and more, having no one on whom I was willing to rely.

When Préfontaine entered my service, it was the first year that Monsieur allowed me to spend my own money. I was so pleased to have any, to spend it, and to add to it, that I exceeded my income by over 300,000 francs. I did not reduce my ordinary expenditure in the years that followed, nor even during my exile; I increased it, having more hounds and horses than usual. A great many people came to see me; I built; and if, with all that, my treasurer, when he left my service, had not anticipated my income — or by very little — all that is to be attributed to his good management.

[She continues to describe life at Saint-Fargeau. In August 1656, her father made his peace with the court. Mme de Fiesque and Mme de Frontenac chided her for being on bad terms with him, for if she were not (they said), she could have expected leave to return to Paris. She recalls earlier events, not in their correct chronological places, including the death, on 25 February 1656, of her grandmother, Mme de Guise. Further disputes with her father occurred. Then she went to Forges, deliberately choosing a route that meant a wide detour around Paris in order to spite Mme de Fiesque and Mme de Frontenac. After a stop at Montargis, she went to Fontainebleau and then on to Corbeil in time for dinner.]

That same day, the Queen of England sent to ask me to appoint a day and a place where she could come and see me, bringing with her her daughter, the Princess Royal,[125] who was longing to see me. I thought Chilly a more suitable place to receive her than Corbeil, where I was badly lodged. I spent a day there, however; the Duke of York came to see me — he had grown a good deal, and filled out. A host of people came, and amongst others Mme d'Olonne, whose beauty was beginning to create a stir.

[She stayed a little longer at Corbeil, where she entertained a number of guests.]

After the departure of Mme de Lixein[126] and Mlle de Guise, I got into my coach and went to Chilly to sleep.[127] I found a great crowd of people waiting for me. After they had paid their court to me, only Mme de Thiange remained to spend the night. She is a very entertaining creature, and I was very pleased to see her again; she was Mlle de Mortemart.[128] She had come to see me at Saint-Fargeau the year she was married, on her way to Burgundy, her husband's home.

---

[125] Mary Stuart, Princess Royal and sister of the currently throneless Charles II, was the widow of William II, Prince of Orange, who had died in October 1650 shortly before the birth of their son, William, the future King of England. She had come to France to visit her mother.

[126] Mme de Lixein was the sister of Marguerite de Lorraine, Mademoiselle's stepmother, and of Charles IV, Duke of Lorraine.

[127] Chilly, nowadays Chilly-Mazarin, is 17 kilometres south of Paris, at the southwestern corner of Orly airport. The château was built by the marquis d'Effiat, the father of Cinq-Mars. His daughter became the first wife of the marquis de la Meilleraye, who was the owner of the property when Mademoiselle stayed there. As she observes below, Effiat was both a Surintendant des Finances (1626) and a Marshal of France (1631).

[128] Mme de Thiange was the elder sister of the future Mme de Montespan, Louis XIV's mistress.

Next day, the Queen of England arrived at midday; I went to her coach to meet her. She said: 'Here is someone who was very keen to meet you; I present her to you,' indicating the Princess Royal, who embraced me very affectionately for someone I had never seen. The princess of England [Henrietta Anne] was with her, too, the Duke of York, and Mme d'Épernon, whom I had not seen since I left Paris (it was a great joy for both of us), and the duchesse de Roquelaure, of whose beauty I had heard a good deal, but whom I had not seen since she was a little girl.[129] The Queen of England's court was large, there being in her coach, in addition to those I have named, her lady-in-waiting and the Princess Royal's, and many ladies and maids of honour, and a host of English and Dutch.

I was in a most suitable place for receiving such company, for Chilly is a very fine, large, and magnificent mansion; there were a great many men and women from Paris. I showed the Queen of England into a large room, anteroom, and closet, and then into a gallery, the whole furnished like the house of a man who was both a Marshal of France and a Surintendant; all full of people. The Queen of England sat down on a couch, and her assembly was larger than it had ever been, all the princesses and duchesses of Paris being there; she dined in a room downstairs. You may believe that I gave her the most magnificent dinner possible. No one ate with her save those who had come in her coach, and Mme de Béthune and Mme de Thiange.

It was when we went back upstairs that the fine assembly I have mentioned was held. The Princess Royal talked to me incessantly, and told me how she had longed to see me, how sorry she would have been to leave France before managing it, and that the king, her brother, had spoken of me so affectionately that she loved me on that account, without knowing me. I asked her if she was satisfied with France; she told me that she liked it very much, that she disliked Holland intensely, and that as soon as the king, her brother, was restored, she would go and live with him.

The Queen of England told me: 'I have not seen my daughter talk so much, since she came to France, as she has talked to you; you have great influence over her, and I can see that, if you were long together, she would do whatever you told her.' She said: 'Notice that my daughter is dressed in black, and has a fichu, because, since she

---

[129] The duchesse de Roquelaure, newly married, was the younger sister of Mademoiselle's childhood friend, Mlle [Françoise] du Lude.

is a widow, and has never seen you, I wanted her first visit to be very correct.' I replied that I thought there was no need of formality with me. She had the most beautiful ear-rings in the world, fine pearls, bracelet clasps of large diamonds, and rings of the same kind. The Queen of England kept saying: 'My daughter is not like me; she is magnificent, has jewellery and silver, and likes spending money. I tell her every day that one must be economical, that I was like her, even more so, and that she can see in what a state I now am.'

After some time in this assembly, the Queen of England said: 'It is agreed that I should go and talk with my niece.' She told me how distressed she was by all Monsieur's persecution of me, and how glad she would be to see concord restored; all most affectionately. Then she said: 'And the poor King of England! You are so ungrateful as not to ask after him.' I replied: 'It behoves me to listen to Your Majesty when you are speaking, and not to interrupt; so I was waiting for a convenient moment to ask you about him.' 'Alas!' she said, 'he is so stupid that he still loves you; and when he went away, he begged me to let you know that he was in despair at leaving France without saying goodbye to you. I did not want to let you know, for fear of making you too conceited. But when I see you, I cannot keep my good resolutions. Consider that, if you had married him, you would not be on such bad terms with your father; you would be able to do as you pleased; you would employ whomsoever you liked; and you would, perhaps, be restored in England; for I am convinced that the wretched man can have no luck without you. If you had married him, we should be on better terms than we are; you would have helped to make him be on good terms with me.'

I replied: 'Since he is not on good terms with you, can one think that he would be on good terms with another woman?' Her reply to that was full of affection for him. She said: 'Have you not noticed that Mme de Châtillon is giving me black looks?' I said that I had not noticed, and that it hardly crossed one's mind that such things were possible. She replied: 'Crofts had a little cottage near Marlou, where the king, my son, often went hunting, and he used to go and see Mme de Châtillon.[130] She took it into her head that he wanted to marry her, and that I was stopping him; so she gave up seeing me, and has given everyone this grievance as the reason.' I told the

---

[130] Marlou, nowadays Mello, lay at the edge of the forest of Chantilly, some 30 kilometres south-east of Beauvais. Crofts had taken up residence in 1652, and Charles II visited at least twice in 1654.

Queen of England that I had certainly heard that Mme de Ricousse, doing her hair and seeing her in her looking-glass, would say to her, 'You would be a lovely queen!', but I did not think it was anything more than a wish. After this conversation, the Queen of England left. The Princess Royal said many kind things to me, and told me that she would be staying long enough in Paris to see me on my way back from Forges.

[Next day, Mademoiselle left Chilly for Forges, spending one night at Poissy, and another at Pontoise.]

M. de Flavacourt, who is Governor of Gisors, received me there the following day with all the citizens under arms, and the day after, I went to dine at his house, called Sérifontaine, which is only about six miles from Gisors. I was told that it was not twenty-five miles from Forges; I reckoned that, if I left at four, I should arrive at eight; but I miscalculated. Although I had taken a guide, I went astray in the woods, where I saw the sun set, and the moon rise and set, without any pleasure.

At last, at dawn, after having travelled a long way, we heard dogs, and I found myself in a hamlet near Forges, where I arrived at four in the morning. I thought it better to hear mass than to get up at midday. I thought they would open the church specially; on the way, I met the Father Superior of the Capuchins, who came and harangued me.[131] I was most surprised; I thought that no one had ever harangued anyone at that hour. After hearing mass, I went to the spring, where I found a great many residents, whom the news of my arrival had awakened earlier than usual, though it is usual in Forges to get up very early. I tasted the water, which I did not find bad; then I went to catch up on the sleep I had lost.

Next day, I received visits from everyone at Forges; there were a great many people. The ladies I saw most of were the comtesse de Noailles and Mme d'Estrades, the abbess of Caen, Mme de Montbazon's daughter, who was there, and many other nuns.[132]

Life at Forges is very pleasant, but very different from ordinary life. One rises at six, at the latest; one goes to the spring; for I, for my part, do not like taking the waters at home. One walks about as one takes them; there are a great many people, and one speaks

---

[131] In other words, he made a formal speech of welcome.
[132] Louise Boyer, the wife of Anne de Noailles, comte d'Ayen (they were later the duc and duchesse de Noailles); Marie du Pin, the wife of Godefroi d'Estrades; and Marie-Eléonore de Rohan-Guéméné, abbess of La Trinité at Caen.

to everyone. Diet and the effects of the waters are often discussed, as well as the diseases that bring people to them and the progress being made in combating them. One learns exactly who arrived in the evening, and, when there is a newcomer, one accosts him or her, because it is the easiest place in the world to get to know people.

When one has finished drinking (usually about eight o'clock), one goes to the Capuchins' garden, which is not enclosed by walls, because it is the only place where one can walk, and, if it were enclosed, women could only enter with people of my quality, and there are so few of us that there are not always any at Forges. The garden is small, but the avenues are quite shady; there are arbours with seats to rest on, but, for my part, I kept on walking, because, as soon as I sat down, the vapours of the water made me feel sleepy. No one could bear walking for four hours, so they took it in turns.

I often spoke to two gentlemen who were there: one called Berville, a man of great intelligence and discrimination, through whose hands a great many important matters had passed; but his speech was slurred as the result of a slight stroke, and he stammered, and his memory, even, was a little affected; nevertheless, on his good days, he was good company. The other, called Brays, was a lieutenant-colonel in Holland, and served there for thirty years; he is a soldier, with intelligence, but less polish than the other.[133]

These two gentlemen and the ladies I have named were my usual companions. I walked with the others, nevertheless; there was plenty of time for that. It is a place where there are all sorts of people, monks of every colour, nuns likewise, priests, Huguenot ministers, and people of all countries and professions; the diversity is very entertaining.

After walking, one goes to mass; then everyone goes and dresses, morning and afternoon dress being very different; for, in the morning, one wears ratteen[134] and fur, and, in the afternoon, taffeta. The best season for taking the waters is the dog-days, when it is generally rather hot; but, when one has a lot of water inside one, one feels very cold. One dines heartily at midday — which is new to me, because, except at the waters, or when I go without food for a long time, I am almost never hungry.

In the afternoon, people would come to see me; at three o'clock, I would go to the theatre. One of the Paris companies was at Rouen,

---

[133] Berville died a few weeks later. She took Brays into her service.
[134] A thick twill-like woollen cloth.

and I brought it to Forges, which was a great help.[135] At six, one sups; after supper, one walks in the Capuchins', where litanies are said; nearly everyone goes and hears them before going walking; then, at nine o'clock, everyone retires.

I had a great many visits; M. de Longueville came, his wife, and all the people of quality in the province, many ladies from Rouen, and members of the parlement; so my court was always large.

[On her way back from Forges, she decided to take a route that passed closer to Paris.]

As it was late, I resolved to sleep at Saint-Cloud; and, as I had dined at Des Noyer's, a decent eating-house, I went to spend the night at Mme de Launay-Gravé's.[136] I learned that the Queen of Sweden was at Fontainebleau, and, as I was to pass near her on the way back, I sent to the court, then at La Fère,[137] to ask if the king would approve of my seeing her, because I owed it to my dignity, even in exile, not to see a foreign princess without his permission. Mme de Launay's house is beautifully situated; there was a moon; and, at the sight of Paris, the comtesse de Fiesque and Mme de Frontenac broke into loud lamentations. For my part, I beheld Paris without nostalgia, and as if I were more detached from everything than anyone else in the world.

Next day [...], I went to Chilly, where I found Mme d'Épernon and the comtesse de Béthune; I spent a day there. I heard that the Queen of Sweden was to leave Fontainebleau; I waited very impatiently for the return of my envoy to the court, afraid that she would depart. He arrived at the very moment I was feeling uneasy, and told me that the king agreed to my seeing the Queen of Sweden.

I immediately sent a gentleman to Fontainebleau to pay her my respects, find out where I could have the honour of seeing her, and get someone to enquire how she would treat me. The comte de Béthune, who was at Chilly, said: 'You must say what you want.' I answered that I wanted an armchair; he exclaimed that I was jesting. I laughed at his reply, and said: 'Since I have no orders from the king about the terms I am to be on with her, I cannot ask for too much; it is better to go too far in that direction than to ask for too little, and assuredly she

---

[135] The company of the Marais Theatre, which often in this period spent part of the summer in Rouen.
[136] Françoise Godet des Marais, Mme de Launay-Gravé, whose husband had died in 1655.
[137] La Fère is 20 kilometres south of Saint-Quentin.

will not be surprised.' M. de Guise was told this, in order to put it to her. He was with her representing the king, and had gone to receive her at Lyon.

When she was asked how she would treat me, she answered: 'As she will; for, much as is due to her rank, there is no honour that I am not willing to do to her person.' The armchair was suggested; she made no difficulty. Then she asked: 'Will she want to pass in front of me? For, from what I have heard about her, it is as well to know; because, if she were at the door, she would not give way.' She was told that I had no intention of claiming precedence, and that I was in duty bound to treat her as the guest of France.

I had left Chilly and gone to Petit-Bourg, a house belonging to the Bishop of Langres, formerly abbé de la Rivière, only three miles or so from Essonne.[138] The reply was brought to me at seven in the evening [of 6 September 1656]. I dressed and set off. I had with me the comtesse de Béthune, Mme de Bouthillier, Mme de Frontenac, Mlle de Vandy, and Mlle de Ségur (the sister of the comte d'Escars). The comtesse de Fiesque, who had gone to Paris the day before, had not returned, which was rather naughty of her. When I arrived, M. de Guise, Comminges, who was there representing the queen, and all the king's officers who were serving the Queen of Sweden, came to meet me.

She was in a fine room in the Italian style, in Esselin's apartments.[139] As she was about to see a ballet, she was surrounded by an enormous crowd of people, and there were benches around her seat, so that she could only come two paces towards me. I had so often heard of the oddity of her costume that I was mortally afraid of laughing on seeing her. When cries of 'Mind out!' warned people to make way for me, I saw her; she surprised me, but not so as to make me laugh. She had a skirt of grey silk material with gold and silver lace, a tunic of flame-coloured camlet with lace like the skirt and a small strip of gold, silver, and black braid; similarly, there was also on the skirt a knotted handkerchief of Genoese lace with a flame-coloured ribbon; a blond wig, and at the back a padded ring such as women wear; a hat with black plumes in her hand.

---

[138] Petit-Bourg, a sizeable château on the left bank of the Seine at Evry, was gutted by fire in 1944 and later demolished.
[139] Louis Esselin (or Hesselin), master of the king's pleasures since the reign of Louis XIII, was responsible for organizing court ballets.

She is white;[140] blue eyes, at times gentle, at others very harsh; her mouth quite attractive, though large; beautiful teeth; a large aquiline nose; she is very short, her tunic conceals her bad figure. In a word, all in all, she struck me as being like a pretty little boy. She embraced me, and said: 'It gives me the greatest joy in the world to have the honour of seeing you; I have been eagerly looking forward to it.' She gave me her hand to help me step over the bench, and said: 'You would really like to jump over.' I sat down in the armchair. There was a door through which we could see a recess for watching a ballet. She said: 'I have been waiting for you.' I tried to excuse myself on the grounds that I was in mourning for one of my sisters, who had died only a fortnight before;[141] she begged me to remain, which I did. The ballet was very pretty.

I amused myself quite well by talking to the people around me. Among them were Comminges, whom I was very pleased to see and converse with, M. de Servien and Marshal d'Albret. She asked how many sisters I had, about my father, and where he was; she said: 'He is the only person in France who has not done me the honour of sending someone to call on me.' She enquired to what house my stepmother belonged; she asked me several questions and said all kinds of flattering things to me, praising me above all things; then, apropos of the ballet, to which she saw that I was not paying much attention, she said: 'What! after not seeing one for so long, you care so little about it. I find that very surprising.' The comtesse de Fiesque and Mme de Montglat arrived; I presented them to her, as I had the other ladies who were with me; she said: 'Considering all the stir she has made, the comtesse de Fiesque is not very beautiful. Is the chevalier de Gramont still in love with her?' When I presented the comte de Béthune to her, she spoke to him about his manuscripts.[142] She gave the impression of liking to show that she knew everybody and all about them.

After the ballet, we went to see a play; there she astounded me, for, praising the passages she liked, she blasphemed; she lay back in her chair, and threw her legs this way and that, and over the arms;

---

[140] This is a compliment; a pale complexion was considered attractive. Mademoiselle has already mentioned that her white skin was admired at the ball that followed the performance of Cavalli's *Egisto* in 1646.
[141] Marie-Anne d'Orléans, her father's youngest legitimate child, had died very recently at the age of four.
[142] The comte de Béthune was a celebrated collector of manuscripts, many concerning the history of France. He bequeathed his collection to the royal library, and it now forms part of the Bibliothèque nationale de France.

in short, she struck attitudes which I have seen no one else in, save Trivelin and Jodelet, two clowns, one Italian and the other French. She repeated the lines she liked; she talked of many things. What she said, she said agreeably enough. She is seized by fits of deep reverie, and heaves deep sighs; then, all of a sudden, she comes to herself, like someone waking up with a start; she is altogether extraordinary.

After the play, a collation of fruit, fresh and candied, was brought; then we went to watch a firework display on the water. She held my hand during the display, in which some rockets came very close to us; I was afraid of them; she laughed at me, and said: 'What! a young lady afraid, who has seen fighting and done such fine and great things?' I answered that I was brave only in battles, and that that was enough for me.

She spoke softly to M. de Guise, who said: 'You must tell Mademoiselle.' She said that what she most wanted above all else was to be at a battle, that she would not be satisfied till then, and that she was madly envious of the prince de Condé for all he had done. She said: 'Is he a good friend of yours?' 'Yes, madam,' I answered, 'and a near kinsman.' 'He is the greatest man in the world,' said she; 'no one can take that from him.' I replied that he was very fortunate to be so highly esteemed by her.

When the fireworks were over, we went to her room. Then she said: 'Let us go through; I want to talk to you.' She took me into a little gallery nearby, and closed the door. We remained there together; she asked me what were the matters of disagreement between me and His Royal Highness. I told her; she thought I was quite in the right, and he very much in the wrong; she said that she would like to see him to talk to him about it, and that she would be very happy to reconcile us; that it was unjust to have taken away from me people [Préfontaine and his clerk] who were serving me well; that she would leave no stone unturned to have them restored to me, and to make my peace with the court and His Royal Highness; that I was not made to live in the country; that I was born to be a queen, that she passionately wished I were Queen of France; that that would be in the interests and to the advantage of the state; that I was the most beautiful, the most charming, the richest, and the greatest princess in Europe; that it was politically desirable; and that she would speak to the Cardinal about it.

I thanked her for all the honour she was doing me, and for the obliging way in which she spoke; but, as regards this last point,

I entreated her very humbly not to mention it. After this, she complained to me of a gentleman whom I had sent to Auxerre to pay her my respects, and who, in a drunken bout in an inn, had spoken most disrespectfully of her. I was most surprised by his impertinence; I made her every conceivable apology, and said I should send him packing. She answered: 'You will do well, and I shall be very glad.' She said: 'You know how favourably I have spoken of the prince, and the affection I have always had for him; now I am in despair at having a grievance against him. I have been told that, when I was in Brussels and after I had left, he mocked and insulted me in the most outrageous way possible; I like to think that it was his people and not he, so as to palliate his offence, though it is still a serious enough one to have allowed me to be abused — me, who have always esteemed and honoured him more than any man in the world, to treat me so!' I did my best to exonerate the prince; she appeared to be much affected by what I said.

Her supper was announced; I took leave of her, and went back to Petit-Bourg. It was two o'clock in the morning, and by the time I had supped and gone to bed, it was broad daylight. Next day, I sent to ask after her; she sent word that she would come and see me. However, as she was going to the other side of the river, and she would have had to come back to cross the bridge at Corbeil, she sent her apologies, and told me that the king's officers who were conducting her had stopped her from coming to see me, which she deeply regretted.

[Passing via Pont and Jouarre — about 25 kilometres east of Meaux — Mademoiselle slowly made her way back to Saint-Fargeau. In 1657, the prospect of returning to court came nearer. In the course of a journey to Orleans, Blois, and Limours, she visited Port-Royal-des-Champs.]

One day, I was told that Port-Royal-des-Champs was only about six miles from Limours; that made me long to go there. I should explain the reason for my curiosity; for an abbey of the Order of St Bernard is not an unusual sight. Jansenius, Bishop of Ypres (who, when he died, was believed to be a saint because of the life he had lived, according to my stepmother, who heard a great deal about him when she was in Flanders, both during his lifetime and after his death; I think she had even seen him), had written about grace in the same way as St Augustine. The abbot of Saint-Cyran, a very learned man, who also lived a very good life, adopted the same opinion, and Cardinal Richelieu, whether he feared that these propositions would be harmful to religion, or whether he was afraid of people whose knowledge and virtue provided new light, or revealed light that had been hidden, put him in prison, where he remained until the Regency, when the queen set him free. The abbot frequented the convent of Port-Royal, which is in the faubourg Saint-Jacques — for, at a particular period, many abbeys that were outside towns, particularly near Paris, were transferred within. The Val-de-Grâce did the same thing.

M. d'Andilly had a number of daughters and sisters in this convent, and, as he devoted himself to piety, together with M. Arnauld, his brother, and M. Le Maître, his nephew, they were all often in this house, where they served God with great zeal, and their fellow men with great charity. Many doctors of the Sorbonne went and visited them there; so, through them, there were always good preachers in the church of Port-Royal. As France was very quiet, and as nuns, as well as the laity, could live in the country, the nuns of Port-Royal in Paris sent some back to Port-Royal-des-Champs. The gentlemen I have named moved out; following their example, many who wanted to leave the world went there. They began to write, and made admirable translations, worked in their gardens, assisted the poor of the neighbourhood — in short, lived lives that were far from ordinary. In their works, they carried penitence further for the laity than religious usually do, who have more to do with it than the gentlemen of Port-Royal, and who thereby sometimes consider their own interests more than the consciences of their neighbours. That, above all, set the Jesuits against them; they called them *Jansenists*, as who should say *Calvinists*, so that this name, which suggests the other, should make people afraid of them and think they were heretics.

All these are questions of theology, and it does not behove women — nor even many men — to talk about them; they are to be settled by those to whom God has given the power and the authority to understand them. But, as regards morals, they are admirable men; they preach and write with the finest eloquence, and compose wonderful works to the glory of the Church and the saints. This year, they have made a translation of the Church's Office of the Holy Sacrament, of which it is said that nothing is more likely to convince the Huguenots, and to prove by strong and conclusive arguments the truths of our religion to those unhappy enough to lack faith. Their piety is sincere; they are cut off from society, indifferent to wealth and honours, and charitable in the last degree. If their doctrine is mistaken, it is to be hoped that, with such good morals, they will obtain, by their prayers, the illumination necessary to realize that, and to change it.

This doctrine, then, caused a great stir in the Sorbonne, where the propositions of Jansenius were condemned. They subscribed to that, and submitted most respectfully to the Church and the Holy Father. The dispute was exploited by the Huguenots, because the Jesuits wrote letters attacking the severity of the Jansenists, and the Jansenists others attacking the laxity of the Jesuits; there is little of the spirit of charity in that.[143] Those who dislike the Jesuits say that every day they eat bread kneaded with hatred for M. Arnauld and M. Le Maître, because their grandfather, a famous barrister in the time of the king, my grandfather, called Marion, spoke against them in one of two matters of which they were accused when an attempt was made to assassinate the king, my grandfather. But, for my part, I cannot believe that of such an illustrious congregation, in which there have been so many able, and even holy, men.

At Port-Royal-des-Champs, there was a little school, where boarders were taken in, and not only perfectly brought up in the fear of God and in study, but taught a great many things essential to social life and gentlemanly behaviour. Thus, unlike those schoolboys who, when they leave school, are normally stupid and pedantic, and need time before they can enter polite society, these, on leaving their studies, had as much polish as if they had been brought up at court and in high society. Those who ran this school were forbidden to receive any more boys, and these orders were brought by one of the king's junior officers, and, on this occasion, everyone recognized the hand of the Jesuits. It was thought, too, that Cardinal de Retz had something to do with it, since some Jansenists were thought to be friends of his — and that may be, since it is not unlikely that an archbishop should be acquainted with doctors of the Sorbonne; but, certainly, those who are called Jansenists never did anything contrary to the king's service.

I went, then, to this place; on arriving, I asked for M. d'Andilly. I know him, because he was secretary to His Royal Highness; but it was several years since I had seen him. I was told that he was in his room. I asked to see it. I looked first on his table; he said, 'You are curious; you want to know how I am spending my time at the moment: I am

---

[143] This is a reference to the polemic that, on the Jansenist side, included the celebrated *Provincial Letters*, by Blaise Pascal, published between January 1656 and March 1657.

translating something by St Theresa.' I thanked him, saying: 'I am so fond of this saint that I am very glad to see what she wrote, in good French; for hitherto her works have been badly translated.'[144]

I went into the convent, where I found a very numerous community, and nuns looking devout, ingenuous, simple, and unaffected. Their church gave an impression of great piety. I walked round the whole convent, looking at everything, expecting not to see anything in this house that I had seen in the others; I found it exactly like all the reformed abbeys of the Order of St Bernard. The nuns were very much surprised: when I saw images of saints in their cells, I exclaimed: 'Ah! there are some saints.' They dared not ask me questions.

As I left, M. d'Andilly said to me: 'Well, you have seen that there are images of saints here, that we pray to them and revere them, and that our sisters have rosaries, and relics on them.' I said: 'It is true that I had heard that no one here cared about them, and I am glad to know the truth.' M. d'Andilly said: 'You are going to court; you will be able to report what you have seen to the queen.' I assured him that I should be very happy to do it, and he assured me of the prayers of the whole community and himself, and he adjured me most eloquently to be pious. In short, I departed highly satisfied with what I had seen and heard.

---

[144] Arnauld d'Andilly's translation of *Les Œuvres de Sainte-Thérèse* was eventually published in two folio volumes (Paris: Le Petit, 1670).

Chapter 5
Return to Court (1657–1659)

[At Port-Royal, Mademoiselle received letters instructing her to go to Saint-Cloud. There, she was told that she could join the court, which was then at Sedan. At Reims, she was provided with an escort of gendarmes and light horse, together with other troops. Four carts carrying money for the king went with her.]

When we reached the outskirts of Sedan [on 1 August], Damville went ahead to the meadow where we were told that the queen was, to find out if she was willing for me to go to her there. He came back and said she agreed. I went; I galloped into the meadow with my gendarmes and light horse, their trumpets sounding triumphantly.

When I came near to the queen's coach, they halted and formed up between her coach and mine, for I alighted twenty paces from hers. I kissed her dress and her hands. She did me the honour to embrace me, and to tell me that she was very glad to see me; that she had always been fond of me; that there had been times when she was angry with me; that she did not mind about the Orleans affair, but that, as for the Porte Saint-Antoine business, if she had had me in her hands, she would have strangled me. I told her that I deserved it, since I had displeased her; but that it was an effect of my misfortune to have been with people who had involved me in matters in which my duty obliged me to behave as I had. She said: 'I wanted to speak to you about that first, and get it all off my chest; but I have forgotten everything; we must not talk about it again, and believe me, I shall love you more than I have ever done.' I kissed her hands; she embraced me. […]

The queen looked at me and said: 'I do not think you have changed at all, even though I have not seen you for six years; you have improved; you are plumper and your complexion is better.' I asked her: 'Has Your Majesty not heard that I have some grey hairs?' She said: 'Yes.' I said: 'As I do not want to deceive Your Majesty at all, I have put no powder on today, in order to show them to you.' She looked at them straight away, and expressed surprise to see so many at my age. I told her that Mme de Guise had been as grey at twenty as when she died, and that, on my father's side, we turned grey at an early age. […]

When I reached my lodging, I found a gentleman from the king, one from Monsieur, and another from the Cardinal, come to say how sorry they were (I may put it like that, because all three said the same thing) not to have been at Sedan when I arrived, but the siege of Montmédy, now in its last stages, prevented them from leaving it, and that they were most impatient to see me. I replied appropriately. [...]

In the afternoon, when I went back to the queen's, she played cards, but did not stop talking to me as she played. She told me that I should find the king greatly changed, that he was tall and broad and plainer, but she thought I should think him good-looking; that, as for Monsieur, he had not grown much, but he had a fine head, and was like me. As we partook of a collation, she said: 'My niece eats just like my son; she reminds me of him.' In the morning, Mme de Beauvais said to the queen at her toilet: 'Madam, does not Mademoiselle remind you of Monsieur? Jesus! What ideas come into my head as I look at her!' The queen was laughing. All these remarks, together with what everyone said, suggested to me that they were thinking of our marriage. [...]

The king arrived on Tuesday at two in the afternoon.[145] The queen expected him for dinner. He galloped in, and arrived so wet and muddy that the queen said to me as she saw him through the window in this state: 'I do not want you to see him till he has changed.' I replied that I did not care. He came in, and, disordered as he was, I thought him good-looking. The queen said to him: 'I present to you a young lady, who is very sorry to have been naughty; she will be very good in future.' He laughed, and then she asked him: 'Where is your brother?' The king answered: 'He is coming in my coach, for he did not want to ride, being unwilling to appear untidy; he is dressed up to the nines.' He said that, laughing and looking at the queen, as if to imply that it was for my benefit.

The king began to relate what had happened at Montmédy. [...] We heard a coach; the king said: 'Here is my brother arriving.' He entered, dressed in a plain grey suit with smart flame-coloured ribbons. After greeting the queen, he came to me, drew me to the window, embraced me, and expressed great joy at seeing me; he said that he thought my looks much improved. I told him that I thought he had grown; we sang each other's praises. The queen said to me:

---

[145] The king arrived in Sedan on 7 August 1657. Montmédy, 40 kilometres to the south-east, had capitulated the day before.

'Go and dine, and this evening you must come for a family supper.' I curtseyed low, and went to my lodging, where I received a great many visitors. I was told that the Cardinal had arrived. I went to him; the queen and he were in a closet overlooking the square, at a window. When they saw me, they came into the large room. The queen told me: 'The Cardinal was going to your house.' I curtseyed to the Cardinal; then I said to the queen: 'I think, madam, at this moment, after all that has passed, Your Majesty should make us embrace each other. For my part, I shall do so cordially.' The queen went to the window, and the Cardinal came to me and embraced my knees. I raised him and embraced him. He told me that it gave him the greatest joy in the world to see me; that he had long wanted to, but that the obstacles in the way were beyond his control. I laughed with him at what he had been told about the will and the passports,[146] and said that they had served me well, and that I ought not to be blamed, since I had brought the king's money safely. His reply was most complimentary, and then he congratulated me on my good health, and we went back to talk to Their Majesties and Monsieur.

In the evening, the queen went to benediction to thank God for the capture of Montmédy. Monsieur came and accompanied me most civilly. I noticed that the queen had taken to gaming, for she never played when I left her. I said to her: 'There is no change greater than seeing Your Majesty playing cards every day, while my father has given them up.' She said that it was true. When she went to prayers, she said to the king and Monsieur: 'Entertain your cousin'; and, turning to me: 'I leave you in good company.' The king chatted freely, and did not seem embarrassed by me.

At supper, the comtesse de Fleix gave me the napkin, which I handed to the queen; the king refused to wash his hands, and the queen said: 'He will not.' He tried to get me to wash mine with him; you will readily believe that I would not. The queen told him: 'It is no use; my niece will not.' I even stood on ceremony with Monsieur, but at last the queen told me not to. The queen was in the middle of the table; we ate in private, that is to say, served by her women; for there were a great many people there. The king was at the end, on the right, and Monsieur and I at the other. The queen told Monsieur that it was uncivil of him not to have had me placed above him. He

---

[146] Mademoiselle's enemies had accused her of making a will leaving all her possessions to Condé, and making him promise that he would not attack her on the way to Sedan.

replied that such formality was unnecessary between close relatives, and that, in fact, it had not occurred to him. The comtesse de Fleix poured wine for me as for them; in short, I was treated with every possible honour. The violins played during supper, and afterwards we danced. The queen never ceased praising me, and saying that I danced well, that I looked well, that I appreciated who I was, that she was delighted when she turned round and saw me behind her, and a thousand things of the kind. I was between the king and Monsieur; the king chatted with Mlle de Mancini, and sometimes with me; but I was afraid of asking questions, and he did not say much about himself.

Next day, I went to the queen's mass. The Cardinal was there, too, and said to me: 'I am grief-stricken to find you here; I was going to your house.' When it was over, he told me that he was coming. I said: 'Get into my coach.' He sat down at the door beside me, and said: 'If anyone had told you in 1652 that Mazarin would be opposite you at the door of a coach, you would not have believed it, and yet here he is, this Mazarin who did so much harm.' I laughed and said: 'For my part, I never thought him so bad, and I always expected things to turn out as they have.' 'You even said so; for I know that the prince and you often laughed at Monsieur's diatribes against me, and that you said to each other: "He will come back; he is a decent fellow. For my part, I shall be very glad, providing he treats me well, and that we do not lose by it." Is it not true that you said that?' I admitted it, and that I was glad that he knew from that that I had never disliked him.

As we entered my lodging, he saw the comte d'Escars; he said to me: 'He reminds me of the comte de Hollac and the prince's ill-treatment of him;[147] it is a cruel thing that he had so little consideration for a man you gave him, and with his rank and qualities.' I laughed and said: 'You will not make me fall into the trap: you would like me to complain of the prince, so that you can say: "As soon as she got to court, she deserted her friends in disgrace." The prince, from what I know of the Hollac affair, is in the wrong; but, as I do not know the details, not having dared to write to him, I shall suspend judgement until I see him; and if he is in the wrong, and I should know it, I shall not complain as long as he is in his present state; but when he is back, I shall give him a good scolding.' He said: 'His obligations to you must have given you enough authority over him for you to scold him

---

[147] Hollac had gone to join Condé in the Spanish Netherlands. Condé had clapped him in prison.

as much as you like; for no man has ever had so many obligations. You saved his life. You would have married him if his wife had died; he was in love with Mme de Châtillon all the while, and she says she would have married him; and, in confirmation, abbé Fouquet brought me some of your letters that the prince had sent him.' I said: 'This is another trap, into which I am not going to fall, any more than into the first. The princess was never at death's door, and no one ever spoke of marrying me to the prince. I do not say that, if his wife had died, it might not have happened, and I do not even think that Mme de Châtillon could have been a hindrance; but God has left me in such a position that I shall not be married save through you, and I shall leave the glory of it to you. For my part, I am convinced that it will be very advantageous for me, and that, expressing so much affection for me as you do, you will marry me off very well.'

Thereupon, he said the finest things in the world to convince me of his zeal for my service, and said that, if my father had wanted, I should be Queen of France, but that his misconduct had got the better of his [Mazarin's] zeal to serve me; that, now that these things were over, they must not be spoken of any more, and that all the possible evil consequences were locked in his heart. Then he spoke of the way my father had treated him, blaming him severely, and praising my conduct. I wanted to show him out; he said: 'You must not stand on ceremony with me, who am your servant, and to whom you have promised your friendship; if you did, I should think that you were still treating me as a mazarin.' I laughed, and so did he, and I went back to my room.

In the afternoon, the king came to see me, and conversed with the greatest possible civility. I wanted to accompany him out; he refused, bandying compliments just like anyone else; however, I went as far as his coach. I said: 'If Your Majesty will not let me go with you for your sake, let me for that of others, who would think me ignorant of my duty.' 'And it is my duty,' said he, 'not to allow you to come.' When he reached his coach, he said: 'Do you order me to get in? For otherwise I should not dare in your presence.' In short, nothing could have seemed more civil to me. […]

Monsieur came as soon as the king had left. After staying some time, he said: 'You want to go to the queen's; let us go together.' I asked him: 'Are you not summoning Marshal du Plessis?', because, when I left, he always came with him. He said: 'No; I no longer have a governor; I go about by myself.' He had a new suit, and wore a different one every day. As long as I remained at Sedan, I played at *bête* [a card game] with the queen; we went halves, Monsieur and I; but she thought I paid so little attention to the game that she made me stop. Monsieur insisted on taking my place, but did not keep it any longer, and gave it to Mme de Fiennes, and we went and talked together. He asked me how much longer I should remain at court. I said that I did not know on what day I should leave, but it would be soon, because I wanted to go to Forges. He told me that I was joking, and that that was all right when I did not know what to do, but that now I ought not to leave the court. I said: 'This year I shall go to Forges again, and in subsequent years I shall stay with the court; it would be too much for the first time.' I had announced this journey to everyone on arriving, so that it should not be thought that I did not want to leave the court.

Monsieur took me to his room to see his jewellery. The comte de Béthune took it amiss that I did not call his wife, who was watching the queen at cards. I did not think it necessary; there were two or three of the queen's maids of honour with me, and Monsieur's room was next to the queen's. [...]

I told the comte de Béthune to ask the Cardinal when he would like me to leave. The Cardinal answered that that was for me to decide, and that I could stay as long as I pleased. I went to see him in the upper castle,[148] where he was lodging. He did not want me to go; when I sent to ask him for an audience, he sent word that, if I had orders to give him, he would come to me. At last, I was so insistent that he said that, since I was giving him an order, he would expect me. The queen's sedan-chair was sent for me, because it is not easy for coaches to go up to the castle. He came to meet me; then we went to the alcove by his bed.[149] I told him that I had come to receive his orders, and to find out if he did not want me to leave the next day. He said that that was my affair; that if I wanted to remain and follow the court for the rest of its journey, I could; and that the king and the queen would agree. I told him that it was too much for the first time, that His Royal Highness, who had only been there for three days, might not approve, and that I had to go to the waters. He protested

---

[148] The *château-haut* or *château d'en-haut* was the name commonly given to the medieval fortress of Sedan, built on a promontory above the River Meuse. It was the birthplace, in 1611, of Turenne.

[149] In seventeenth-century France, hosts and hostesses often remained in bed to receive their guests. The space between the bed and the wall, used for conversation, was called the *ruelle* ('alcove').

that I was healthy enough to be able to do without them, and that the court would do me more good. I told him that I had made up my mind; that, when one had taken them one year, one had to take them for a second for them to do any good; and that I had to go to Champigny. [...]

We spoke of the prince de Condé, of the mistakes that had been made on both sides during the war, and of Cardinal de Retz. He told me that he had been made a cardinal by the queen alone; that he had constantly written asking her to refuse her consent, and telling her that he was untrustworthy, but the queen did not believe him, and had since seen what he had done. He was an evil man; the prince, on the contrary, was good, and the government would be reconciled with him. He spoke of the comtesse de Fiesque with the same contempt as the queen; as for Mme de Frontenac, he said he did not know her. I said: 'All these topics take up a good deal of time, and, as yours is precious, I must not encroach on it.' I departed; he wanted to walk down to the queen's beside my sedan-chair; I got out, in order to walk with him. At last, we agreed that he should stay behind, and that I should go in the chair. I told the queen that I should leave next day. The king asked me at what time, so as to arrange for my escort. I said, at whatever time he wished. I was told that I should sleep at Charleville, of which the duc de Noirmoutier is governor. He was delighted, and so was I, for it is a noble fortress.

Since the king's return, there had been dancing every evening, as on the first day, and, although Monsieur had told me to go, I did not, until the king sent to invite me; he said to me himself, 'I beg you to come every evening, as long as you are here.' He came to be at ease with me; he spoke to me of his musketeers, and apologized for not having sent any to meet me, because one part of them was at the siege of Montmédy, and the other was his bodyguard. I asked a great many questions about this company; he told me that he had been very sorry that my father would not let the chevalier de Charny join it.[150] I told him he was in the guards. He asked me in which company; I told him, in Pradelle's. He spoke about the strength of the regiment of guards; I asked him how many battalions he was making. He told me that his bodyguard was going to the army, and how many of them; he asked me how I liked their tabards; I said they were very fine. He said: 'Nothing is so fine as the two blue squadrons; you will

---

[150] Louis, chevalier de Charny, was the son of Gaston d'Orléans and Louison Roger. Mademoiselle had taken him under her wing.

see them, for they are to escort you. I am sorry I cannot give you any musketeers, but as the regiment of guards is with the army, they are on guard here.' He spoke to me of his companies of gendarmes and light horse, which consisted of two hundred men, and of his cavalry regiment, in which he took an interest. He said that, in all those, he had a great many of the best trumpeters in the world; I might have seen some, and they were smartly dressed. He asked me if I had never heard kettle drums (I had been told, when speaking to him, to make some allusion to what had happened during the war. It would have been unseemly to drag one in out of season; these kettle drums seemed a good opportunity); I answered: 'Yes, Sire, I have heard some.' 'Where?' I smiled, and said respectfully: 'In the foreign troops who were with us during the war. The memory cannot be very agreeable to me, because it was at the time when I displeased Your Majesty. I ask your forgiveness; I ought to do it on my knees.' He blushed, and said: 'I ought to kneel down myself, hearing you talk so.' I went on: 'It is an effect of my misfortune that my duty compelled me to do things that displeased Your Majesty; I beseech you to forget it, and to believe that I desire nothing so passionately as to find opportunities of doing as much in your service as I have done against you.' He answered most obligingly: 'I am firmly convinced of what you say; we must not talk any more about the past.' We talked of the war again. He told me about all his campaigns and everything he had done; I said: 'The king, your grandfather, did not go to war so young.' He answered: 'Nevertheless, he did more than I; hitherto, I have not been allowed to go as far as I should have liked, but, in future, I hope to make a great noise in the world.' I said, he would do well to; and that kings must want to have achieved as much as anyone else. In short, I thought he had the best feelings in the world, and I was altogether satisfied with him.

On the Friday evening, when I went to the queen's, Monsieur came running to meet me, and said: ' You are not going tomorrow; not till Sunday.' I went into the closet, where were the queen, the king, and Montaigu, a cornet[151] in the king's light horse, who was to escort me on the way back. The queen said: 'We have decided that you shall not leave tomorrow for Charleville; it is a long day's journey; you would have to leave early. Your carts are outside the town; they cannot come in till the gates are opened. The road is not

---

[151] A junior cavalry officer, so called after his duties as cornet- or standard-bearer; the equivalent of an ensign in the infantry.

too safe, according to Montaigu; you had better not leave till after dinner on Sunday. You will sleep at La Cassine, which is a very fine house belonging to the Duke of Mantua, not fourteen miles from here, and I take it that you will not be sorry to spend another day with us.' You may imagine my answer, for they expressed the greatest possible joy at this postponement. I sent the news to my lodging and to the comte de Béthune, who told me next day that the alteration was due to the fact that Montaigu was not on very good terms with Noirmoutier, and would not be too happy to go to Charleville, and that Noirmoutier was deeply disappointed.

On Saturday afternoon, I was told that the enemy had sent out a large detachment from Rocroi, so that it would be imprudent for me to sleep at La Cassine, a house in the middle of the woods, from which I and all my escort could easily be carried off.[152] It was thought safer for me to go back the way I had come; and, in fact, in the evening, as we were walking in the meadow, gendarmes and light horse came from the guards' quarters to say that they had been warned that an attempt was to be made to carry them off from their quarters. They were ordered to come and sleep in the meadow, which is protected by the culverins[153] of Sedan. That evening, the king went riding: he did so every evening, but he made me ride, and the queen's maids of honour with me. He showed me his horses in turn, and I thought them very handsome. There was dancing as usual, and afterwards I went and took leave of the queen, who treated me, as she had done, most kindly. I wanted to go to the king's room, but he bade me farewell in the queen's, and so did Monsieur. On my way down, I did await the king in his room; the comte de Béthune felt that it was proper, even though the king had told me not to; of course, the king did not come.

Next day, Monsieur came, between seven and eight, to say goodbye to me; which is a great deal for him, for he never gets up before eleven. He stayed a long time with me, and did not go until the Cardinal came. I told the Cardinal that I might not go via Paris, unless I needed to go to a bathing establishment.[154] He begged me to

---

[152] Rocroi, in 1643 the site of a famous victory won by Condé when still duc d'Enghien, is about 60 kilometres north-west of Sedan, beyond Charleville, now Charleville-Mézières. The château of la Cassine, some 10 kilometres to the south of Sedan near the village of Vendresse, burned down in the 1920s.
[153] Long-barrelled artillery pieces.
[154] Mademoiselle writes 'si je n'avois besoin de me baigner'. Her meaning is unclear; she may mean to seek accommodation in Paris at the establishment of a *baigneur* while on her journey — although, as we shall see, she stayed in the Luxembourg.

go, so that everyone should know that I was free to do as I pleased; he made me a thousand protestations of friendship and service. I left Sedan [on 12 August] very satisfied; many people left with me, the Grand Master, the Grand Provost,[155] Froulai, La Salle, Colbert, abbé de Bonzy, Matha, and many others; the duc de Navailles, who commands the king's light horse (on leaving the town, he placed himself at their head just as I went by, and then got back on his horse); the comte and comtesse de Saint-Aignan and their children. She refused to travel in my coach, being unwilling to leave her husband. The king's bodyguard slept in the room outside the door of my bedroom, followed me, went to fetch my meals, and marched in front of my dishes; treated me, in short, just like the king; and La Lande, the ensign in command of them, told me that he had been given orders to treat me in the same way.

[Mademoiselle went to Forges, and then to Paris.]

When I arrived in Paris, I found such a multitude of people waiting for me at the Luxembourg that I had to prolong my stay. I had decided to remain for only seven or eight days, but I was compelled to spend nearly three weeks there. At Forges, I had got some painful patches of shingles on my arms, and I had to bathe and be purged and bled to make them go away quickly. Mme d'Aiguillon came to see me; I had been bled an hour before; I had got up to go to mass. After greeting her, I smelt her Spanish gloves, which were very strong; I recoiled, holding my nose, telling her that I could not go near her without fainting. Some were stupid enough to say that I did not want to speak to her, and that I had played this trick to offend her. I am not capable of devising such silly tricks, and, if I want to quarrel with someone, I do it openly.

[She bought the estate of Eu — just inland from Le Tréport in Normandy — and set out for Blois.]

At Toury, I learned that the Queen of Sweden was at Orleans, and was to leave for Fontainebleau the following day.[156] I was tempted to

---

She cannot have anticipated having to cure her shingles, as she was not suffering from that infection while in Sedan.

[155] The Grand Master of the Artillery was La Meilleraye. The Grand Provost, responsible for justice in the king's household, was the marquis de Sourches.

[156] She had returned from Italy, against Mazarin's wishes. He was determined to keep her away from Paris and the court. As we shall see, she eventually reached Paris, but not before Mazarin had decided that she had to be sent away definitively.

hurry on to meet her; then I thought that three or four hours' sleep would do me more good than seeing her. However, I sent someone to pay my respects. She was getting into her coach when my emissary arrived; she asked whether she would not meet me on the way; she was told that she would, providing she took the Paris road, and that it would not take her much more than three miles out of her way. I found one of her gentlemen come to pay her respects and tell me that she had gone out of her way on purpose to see me. I sent her my compliments. I found her in a rickety coach with the chevalier Sentinelli and Monaldeschi, her master of the horse. She was wearing a disreputable yellow skirt, a threadbare, black tunic, and a cap; I thought her as ugly as I had thought her pretty the first time. It was so muddy that I could not get out. Our coaches came together; her people got out, and I climbed into her coach. She did not tell me anything special or worthy of note. I was taking Prince Charles of Lorraine, the second son of Duke Francis, to Blois, and I presented him to her. That led us to talk about the Duke of Lorraine.[157] We travelled a mile and a half together, and then we parted. She presented the chevalier Sentinelli to me, and said: 'He is the captain of my guards.' She was followed by a coach and only a few horsemen; her retinue looked more like a public coach than the retinue of a queen.

[From Blois, Mademoiselle went to Champigny, where she considered what repairs and improvements might be done, and had the property valued.][158]

As soon as I heard that the court had returned to Paris, I dispatched a gentleman to make my excuses for not going there myself at once, for my affairs obliged me to remain at Champigny. The princesse de Tarente and Mlle de la Trémouille came twice or thrice, and stayed a long time on each occasion.[159] They showed me their portraits, which they had had written in Holland. I had never seen any; I thought this

---

[157] The three members of the Lorraine family just mentioned are, respectively, Charles, second son of Francis of Lorraine, who later succeeded (though never reigned) as Charles V; Francis himself, Count of Vaudémont; and Francis's older brother, Charles IV, nominally the current reigning Duke. Francis and Charles IV were the brothers of Marguerite de Lorraine, Mademoiselle's stepmother.
[158] Champigny had been restored to the Orléans family two years earlier, in exchange for Bois-le-Vicomte, after a protracted lawsuit against the duc de Richelieu. More recently, Mademoiselle had won a secondary dispute concerning the cost of repairs to the property. Thouars, to be mentioned in a moment, is about 40 kilometres west of Champigny, beyond Loudun.
[159] They were sisters-in-law.

style of writing very elegant, and wrote my own. Mlle de la Trémouille sent me hers from Thouars.

[Then she set out for Paris, but stopped en route in Blois.]

My father was told that I had written my portrait at Champigny; he asked to see it, told me that he thought it well done, and then advised me not to show it to anyone, in case portraits should become fashionable and libellous, and people should say: 'It was Mademoiselle who started them.' I assured him that no one should see it. I confess that I thought that his advice was not disinterested, and that he was afraid his own might be written.

[She spent Christmas 1657 at Saint-Fargeau, and then went to Paris.]

I passed through Fontainebleau, where the Queen of Sweden was. I went straight to her; I was told that she was still asleep. I went to the inn, where she sent a gentleman to say that she was getting dressed quickly so as to see me. When she was ready, I was sent for. In her courtyard, I found twenty Swiss clad in grey with gilded halberds, a great many footmen and pages, also in grey, and a large number of gentlemen in the hall and the anteroom. She wore a black velvet tunic, a flame-coloured skirt, and a velvet bonnet with black feathers, and a great many flame-coloured ribbons. She seemed to me as pretty then as the first time I saw her. I asked her if she was coming to court; she said that she did not know, and would do whatever she was ordered. [...] Speaking to her, I thought so much of what she had done, and the baton of her captain of guards, which was in her alcove, made me think of him I had seen carrying it, and the blow he had struck, which it is meet to tell of here before proceeding further.

Count Sentinelli was the man who seemed on the best of terms with the Queen of Sweden; she had sent him to Italy. It is said that Marquis Monaldeschi, her master of the horse, had tried to take advantage of his absence to turn her against him, and that, with this purpose, he had seized some of his letters, and had opened them, and even some of those of the queen, his mistress. No more is known of the details of this affair; but what is known is that, one day when he was dining in the town, she sent for him, and said: 'Go into the gallery' — that is, the Galerie des Cerfs at Fontainebleau — and there he found the chevalier Sentinelli, the captain of the guards, who said: 'Make your confession; here is a Mathurin father.' The queen had told him what she had against Monaldeschi, to make him understand that cutting his throat in Sweden or executing him in the gallery at Fontainebleau was one and the same to her. Monaldeschi did not resign himself easily to his fate; he sent the father to ask the queen to forgive him and spare his life. She refused; he tried to throw himself out of a window, but they were shut. Sentinelli had difficulty in despatching him, since he was wearing a coat of chainmail; he struck him several times, so that the gallery was full of blood, and though it has been well scrubbed, there are still some marks.[160]

When he was dead, he was taken in a coach to the parish church and buried at a time when no one was about; which is easy enough, Fontainebleau parish church being three-quarters of a mile from the town and the château. It has been said that she went and looked on while he was being killed; but I do not know if that is altogether certain. This act, and the fact that she dared to commit it in the king's house, were condemned. She claimed, as I have said, that it was doing justice, and that, as kings have the power of life and death, that power extends to the places to which they go, as well as to those that belong to them. This manner of execution is barbarous and cruel inflicted by anyone, let alone a woman. She treated me very civilly, as she had done every time I had seen her. [...]

I reached Paris late[161] because I had a bad cold; and, as I had not slept that night, I made up in the morning for the time I had lost. [...] My cold obliged me to spend three or four days in bed, which prevented me from going to the Louvre. Monsieur [that is, Philippe] came to see me on the very day after my arrival, and I learned that he had waited a long time for me at Mme de Choisy's on the day I arrived. He did me the honour of saying so; he spoke to me of the death of Mme de Roquelaure, and told me how sorry he had been, and that he had not put on coloured clothes until that day. He was very smart; he told me everything he knew in the friendliest way, and gave me oranges from Portugal; in short, he behaved in the best possible way towards me. He talked about lotteries; as I had never heard of them, I enquired what they were. I was soon well informed, because no one spoke of anything else. [...]

It will readily be believed that for the first days after my arrival, my house was never empty; for, if duty and my popularity had not brought people, the grace of novelty is a fine thing for the French. Monsieur came a second time, and I was told that no one spoke

---

[160] This event had taken place on 10 November 1657.
[161] On 31 December. She took up residence in the Luxembourg.

of anything else but his attentions to me. I noticed that he and his companions were very attentive; that did not displease me. A young prince, good-looking, personable, and the king's brother, I regarded as a good match for me. [...]

The whole month of January [1658] went by without any other amusements than the plays in the Louvre, to which I did not always go, because I had a cold and was cossetting myself, and also because I was not bored at home, where I always had good company. I put my money into several lotteries, in which I was unlucky; I got one up in my house on 2 February. Marshal de l'Hôpital's wife gave a ball; we went to it masked, that is to say, clad in gold and silver cloth, with bonnets with feathers, very smartly dressed, and the men had silk stockings and embroidered suits. When we went in, our hands were on our masks, which we whipped off straight away. After dancing, we went into a magnificently decorated room for a collation; there was only one place set and one armchair. The king said: 'Cousin, you sit there; that is your place.' I protested, thinking he was joking; he said to me, 'But who will sit there?' The comtesse de Soissons laughed and said: 'I shall', and was going to it. Monsieur said to her: 'Don't!' This familiarity with the king surprised me; there was more formality when I left.

Everyone sat down at table; the king sat down last, saying: 'Since this is the only place left, I shall have to take it.' He did not touch a dish without asking if anyone wanted any of it, and ordered us to eat with him. That surprised me, who was brought up to be very respectful, and it took me a long time to get used to behaving like this. But when I saw that the others did, and when the queen had told me one day that the king disliked ceremony and wanted people to eat from his dish, then I did; but for that, the faults of others would not have made me commit any. When I was ready to go, the king said to the comtesse de Soissons, 'Go and take my cousin home'; she agreed. We had come in separate coaches, because I had the queen's maids of honour with me. The king said to them, as he got into his coach: 'Ladies, my cousin dispenses you from accompanying her; go back to the Louvre.' That was particularly noticed, because it was Mlle de La Mothe whom he addressed. They departed, and only Gourdon and Fouilloux remained to accompany the comtesse de Soissons. We galloped away, so fast that the king's guards, who were on horseback, had great difficulty in following us, and the king said: 'How glad I should be if the thieves were to attack us!' The king's coach fell behind; so that, while we were waiting for him, we strolled about the terrace in the court of the Luxembourg, on 3 February, at three in the morning, as we might have done in the month of July. Monsieur asked me if I should like to go to the fair next day [at Saint-Germain-des-Prés]; I said I should be delighted. He had me awakened at six in the evening, for which I was very glad, because I am extremely fond of the fair. We often went, particularly during Lent, because we had other things to do during the carnival. I was very lucky; I won a large number of cabinets and mirrors, which I needed to adorn my apartments.

I gave a very pretty party for the king: the Luxembourg is the most suitable place in the world for giving parties, both large and small. [...]

There was a large reception at the chancellor's, to which the queen and the Cardinal went; the queen took the Princess of England [Henrietta Anne], who was delighted to be there, for she never goes to balls, except those in the Louvre, or to which the queen goes. I was bedecked with pearls; I had no bouquet, being in mourning for M. de Candale,[162] who had died in Lyon three weeks before. [...]

Three or four days after the chancellor's reception, I was told that it was being rumoured that the Queen of England complained that I had tried to pass before her daughter, and that Monsieur and I had made up our minds that I should do so. I went to see the Cardinal, whom I had not yet been able to find in his room since my return: either he was going downstairs to the queen's when I wanted to go, or he was engaged. At last, I found him; I asked him what this rumour was, and told him how, at the chancellor's, after supper, the Princess of England had remained at play with Mlles de Nemours,[163] and that I had followed the queen; but, when I reached the end of the gallery, I had called to her before going in, and we had taken each other's hands, as we usually did, and I did not think anyone could see anything wrong in that. Thereupon, the Cardinal said: 'The fact is that, the other day, in the queen's apartments, it was said that you had tried to pass in front of the princess in the chancellor's house, and Monsieur replied: "Well, if she had, would she not have been right? What business have these people, to whom we give bread, to come and pass before us? Why don't they go elsewhere?" This was

---

[162] The duc de Candale, lieutenant-general of the king's forces, renowned for his handsomeness and his bravery, was the son of the duc d'Épernon and the brother of Mademoiselle's childhood friend Mlle d'Épernon.

[163] Marie-Jeanne Baptiste de Nemours and her sister Marie-Françoise.

repeated to the Queen of England, who wept bitterly. The queen, on hearing this, rebuked Monsieur, saying: "Related to you as they are, it ill becomes you to speak of them like that!" That is all I have heard.' I blamed Monsieur, and told the Cardinal that the Queen of England was in such a situation as to oblige her kinsfolk to do her every possible honour; that, perhaps, at another time, I might have thought of contesting her daughter's right of precedence,[164] but that was a thing I had never contemplated, having lived on the friendliest of terms with the queen and her daughter, and they had always evinced a great deal of friendship to me, and no one was more civil than the Queen of England. The Cardinal said: 'The Kings of Scotland used formerly to give way to the sons of the King of France, and therefore you would be justified in passing before the Princess of England.' I begged him not to speak of that, and said that, in the situation of the queen, my aunt, I should be sorry to be a source of mortification to her.

The king was practising a ballet, which I went with the queen to see rehearsed;[165] and, on the day it was performed [14 February], we were bedecked with jewellery, and placed in a stand on the right of the stage, so as to be able to go down on to it easily, in order to dance after the ballet. The Princess of England was there, and Mlles de Nemours and the rest of the usual people. As ballets are danced in a great hall, and everyone comes uninvited, there are all kinds of people. [...]

A day or two afterwards, at the fair, Monsieur gave me a message from the queen: I was not to put my jewels away, and she wanted people to wear their jewellery once again at the ballet. I suspected that this was for the Queen of Sweden; he admitted it, and told me not to tell anyone. She arrived next day; the queen said she was coming incognita, and that she would stay only one day in Paris; that everything had been done to deter her, but it had proved impossible; however, to make it clear that she must not stay long, the Cardinal had put her into his apartments in the Louvre, and had moved into his little room, so that she could judge, from the inconvenience to which she was putting him, that it was incumbent on her to go away promptly. The queen told Monsieur and me to be careful not to tell her that there were masked balls, and that we were greatly enjoying

---

[164] Henrietta Anne, the daughter of a monarch, had precedence over Mademoiselle, the granddaughter of a monarch; but the matter of precedence was complicated because the Stuart monarchy was currently throneless.
[165] *Le Ballet d'Alcidiane*.

ourselves; on the contrary, we were to say that no winter had ever passed so drearily, that there were no entertainments, and that we were all thoroughly bored. Then she said: 'The fact is that my niece and my son think that it is to the honour of France to tell the queen all sorts of things.' It was announced that she had arrived; the queen departed, and told Mme de Carignan and me to stay behind, for which I was very sorry. I told her, petulantly: 'You will send for me, because the Queen of Sweden will want to see me.' She did not go all the way upstairs, for she found Nogent in her closet, who told her, on behalf of the Cardinal, to bring me. She sent for me. The Queen of Sweden, after greeting her, asked her: 'Where is Mademoiselle?' I went forward and greeted her.

Next day, the ballet was performed. I wore jewellery, as on the previous occasion; the Queen of Sweden was dressed like the others, and it suited her well. [...]

Next day, though tired after a late night, I got up and dressed expeditiously to go and see the Queen of Sweden, who, I thought, was to depart the next day. I sent to her to ask for an audience; she sent word that I was to go early, and that I should go to the theatre with her. I did not go to the Louvre till very late, not meaning to go with her, and knowing full well that I should have been laughed at. When I arrived, I asked the queen: 'Is the Queen of Sweden leaving tomorrow?' She said: 'I think not, and I am very sorry; she is going to the fair this evening; my son and you will have to go with her.' I answered that I should go if Monsieur went, not otherwise. She came back from the theatre very late. When I heard that she was in her room, I went up and dissuaded her from going to the fair; she asked me if she could go to the queen's; I told her that the queen was playing cards, but that she would be welcome. We went to her; the king and Monsieur, who were afraid she would want to take them to the fair, hid when she arrived, and did not come back until I went and assured them that she was not going to the fair.

Mme de la Bazinière[166] gave a reception, to which the Queen of Sweden came, and a most magnificent supper; the Queen of Sweden danced, in a quite ridiculous manner, and made the audience laugh. The account we gave the queen of the Queen of Sweden's dancing made her want to see her; and, so as to be able to laugh all the more freely, it was decided not to give a large party; so the king sent one evening to ask her if she would come down, for he danced every

---

[166] The former Mlle Chemerault, who had married the financier La Bazinière.

evening, and the queen ordered me to go. But she missed the pleasure to which she had been looking forward, for M. de Brégis, with misplaced zeal, warned the Queen of Sweden that she had been laughed at, and that she must not dance; for which reason she merely curtseyed, and the ball ended early.

Next day, a play was performed for her in the great hall,[167] and we went to Damville's, where there was supper after midnight, and where we even heard mass. We were mortally afraid lest the Queen of Sweden should take it into her head to come during the ball. We had a great many maskers, for there was no reception to which a large number did not go. On Shrove Monday [March 4], the queen gave a party in her large closet, where there were only the usual people I have named, and, in addition, the wives of a few of the officials of the king's household. The Queen and the Princess of England were there, whereupon the Queen of Sweden said she could not be present unless she placed herself above the Queen of England; and, as this poor princess has no joy in this world, and as she can see the princess, her daughter, dancing scarcely once a year, the queen intimated to the Queen of Sweden that she should come masked, which she did. She came dressed as a gipsy in a most ridiculous fashion; she had with her Marianne,[168] the little Nogent girl, who is of the same age,[169] and Bonneuil. I forget who the others were.

At this ball, I had a serious disagreement with Monsieur. Mlle de Gourdon, who is a very thoughtless young woman, as you will see from what I am about to say, having no partner to lead her out to dance a brawl,[170] called to Frontenac, who was hiding behind her; for, out of respect to me, he did not often appear, though I had not, at that time, forbidden him to appear before me. I said to Monsieur, who was my partner: 'Your Gourdon is a fool,' and one thing led to another, and we bickered, so much so that I did not dance a second courante with him; everyone noticed. At supper, he sulked a good deal, I was told.

Next day, it was agreed that we should go masked; it was Shrovetide. When I arrived at the Louvre, Monsieur was dressed as a girl, with fair hair; the queen said he looked like me; she had great difficulty

---

[167] Possibly *Le Feint Alcibiade*, by Quinault, then in its first flush of success.
[168] Marie Mancini, one of Mazarin's nieces, *not* her much younger sister Marie-Anne Mancini.
[169] Charlotte Bautru, daughter of Nicolas Bautru, comte de Nogent. She later married Nicolas d'Argouges, marquis de Ranes.
[170] A French dance resembling a cotillon.

in persuading him to take off his mask and let me see him. As there were a great number of us, the king said we must split up; I begged him to allow me to go with him. Monsieur went with the queen's maids of honour. That day, maskers had not been forbidden to go where the king was, because he was masked himself; and, though he was elaborately dressed, as were we, too, we had decided before leaving the Louvre that we should not unmask. We first went to M. de Sully's, where a large number of maskers came, and, amongst others, a group of women disguised as pilgrims, amongst whom were the comtesse de Fiesque and Mme de Frontenac, who did not unmask. When we had gone out, Monsieur spoke to them ostentatiously, so that I should hear about it.

Two or three days before, we had met them on the stairs at Mme Sanguin's house, where they had gone masked, and when they heard that I was going, they left; but we met them, as I said. I took the comtesse de Fiesque's hand and squeezed it; she told everyone, assuming that I was relenting towards her. When I heard this, I said: 'I did it in order to disguise myself, not being able to do anything more unlike myself than to appear to be on familiar terms with the comtesse de Fiesque.' At several balls we met the pilgrims, who never dared to take off their masks. Everywhere, we were asked if we had not encountered a group of Capuchin monks and nuns; they always left a moment before we entered. At Marshal d'Albret's, we were told that one Capuchin had a beautiful arm and hand, and that he had touched M. de Turenne's hand as he passed.

During the first days of Lent, nothing was spoken of but the scandal to which this masquerade had given rise. The preachers denounced it. The king and the queen talked of it very angrily; no one boasted of having taken part in it. At last it transpired that it was Olonne, his wife, abbé de Villarceaux, Thury, Lord Crofts, and a young lady of Mme d'Olonne's, and that it had been her husband who had insisted on her dressing up like that. She had not appeared in society during the whole of the carnival season, she remained at home, having a sore foot, from which a few bones had come out,[171] so she was bedridden. M. de Candale had long been very much in love with her, and had been extremely upset when he left her. But since his departure, it had been rumoured that Jeannin, the Trésorier de

---

[171] This is, indeed, what Mademoiselle says.

l'Épargne,[172] often visited her. Her behaviour on M. de Candale's death caused comment. She appeared very distressed, and it was even said that she wept all night, and confessed to her husband, asking him to forgive her, that she had loved him dearly.

The coolness between Monsieur and me lasted for eight or ten days, but the queen made us embrace, and we were as good friends as ever. [...] On Shrove Tuesday, the Queen of Sweden also went masked, dressed as a Turk. When she went home at four o'clock in the morning, she went to see the Cardinal, who had gout, and was complaining loudly, and talked affairs with him in fancy dress. On the first Sunday in Lent, she wanted to see a little ballet devised by Montbrun. The queen begged her not to use the Louvre; she proposed that I should let it be danced in the Luxembourg; I entreated her to excuse me. In the end, it took place in Marshal de l'Hôpital's house, where the king, Monsieur, and I went with her. We were incredibly eager for her to depart, and the day she left, the Cardinal went to the Bois de Vincennes.[173] [...]

The king and Monsieur had a violent quarrel. Monsieur had broken Lent, and was eating in his room. He came one day as the king and the queen were about to dine; he found a casserole of boiled meat; he put some on a plate, and took it to show the king, who told him not to eat it. Monsieur said he would; the king said, 'I bet you won't.' They grew heated; the king tried to snatch it from him. As he seized the plate, a few drops flew on to Monsieur's hair. Monsieur has a very fine head, and is extremely proud of his hair, and that riled him, and he lost control of himself. He threw the plate in the face of the king, who did not immediately grow angry. But some of the queen's women in waiting, who were present, began to shout at Monsieur, so that the king lost his temper, and said that, were it not for respect for the queen, he would kick him to bits. Monsieur shut himself up in his room, where he remained all day alone; the queen and the Cardinal made them make it up next day. Fortunately, I had not gone out that day. I stayed at home the day after, too, and did not go to the Louvre till it had all blown over: my actions would have been closely observed, since it was known that Monsieur's feelings for me put me very much on his side. As soon as he saw me, he said: 'Do not talk to me, because people would think we were talking about what has

---

[172] Nicolas Jeannin de Castile, one of three Trésoriers de l'Épargne, appointed by the king, who served for one year in every three as head of the Royal Treasury. His cousin was the wife of Nicolas Fouquet.
[173] That is, the château of Vincennes.

happened.' He related it to me afterwards, very bitter and resentful about the way the king had treated him. […]

One day, the chevalier de Béthune abducted Mlle des Marais as she was coming out of mass in the Temple, where her father and mother were living.[174] Mme des Marais sent one of her friends to tell me, and say how sorry she was.[175] I sent a message to say that I advised her to go to her country house as soon as she could, that everybody thought she had connived at it, and that she would, perhaps, be compelled to admit it eventually. The comte de Béthune was very much upset, and reasonably enough; but he would have done better not to say that the thing had been done on my advice, since no one had tried harder than I to prevent it; for I had given him all the warnings I had thought necessary. M. des Marais, on his side, was in despair, and wanted the provosts to pursue them, which compelled Mme des Marais to tell him that they were married with her consent, that Béthune had promised her not to see his wife when he was married lest she should become pregnant, and that she hoped in time to persuade M. des Marais to give her enough money to satisfy the comte de Béthune. M. des Marais sent his wife to a convent in which she has daughters, and has seen her only once since, when she went to see him, and he received her formally, and accompanied her to her coach, as he would have done a strange lady.

The wretched couple remained for a long time hidden in attics in Paris, as poor as church mice, but very contented, living like perfect lovers in novels; and, knowing Béthune's disposition, I do not doubt that he will write his with pleasure.

[Mademoiselle remained in Paris, living at the Luxembourg. In the campaign of 1658, Turenne defeated the Spaniards on 14 June at the Battle of the Dunes.]

Joy for the capture of Dunkirk and the Battle of the Dunes did not last long. The king returned from the army, sick with a very dangerous continuous fever. When the news reached Paris, the sacred host was exhibited to ask for his recovery. I was ready to leave for Forges, but

---

[174] The Temple — a medieval fortress built by the Knights Templar, the site of which is marked today by the Temple metro station, just south-west of the place de la République in the third arrondissement of Paris — gave its name to the complex of streets in the immediate vicinity. The keep of the fortress is notorious for having been the final prison of the French royal family during the Revolution. Napoleon caused it to be demolished in the early years of the nineteenth century.

[175] Mme des Marais, the niece of Mademoiselle's late governess, Mme de Saint-Georges, had herself been in Mademoiselle's service before her marriage.

this news delayed my journey. For five or six days, nothing but bad news came; amongst other things, a courier sent by Saint-Quentin to His Royal Highness, on whose behalf he had gone to ask after him, brought me a letter, in which he informed me that antimony had done no good, that the doctors had given up hope, and that he was very much afraid that, by the time I received the letter, the king would no longer be alive. I was very much affected, as will readily be believed: the king is my cousin; he treats me kindly; and, above all that, to see a young king dying is terrifying, and reflections on the future affliction of the queen worried me a great deal. I was fond of Monsieur, but I did not think that, as he was at present, it would be a good thing for him, since he was too much of a child to rule, and even to know what was good for him. For, as for me, I think that the defects of the great are more apparent than those of others; so I shall never wish my kinsfolk to gain anything unless I know them to be worthy of it. Not that Monsieur lacks intelligence; but there is nothing solid about it as yet; and if one has neither knowledge nor experience, a state is not well governed. His companions and particular friends were more calculated to ruin him than to serve the state. I admit that that vastly increased my worries about the king; there was not much self-interest in this: for I knew very well that he would never marry me, and I had good reason to believe that kingship would not change Monsieur; but I am so attached to my house and its glory, that I should like all who belong to it to maintain its dignity as nobly as the king, my grandfather, and not to succeed to the throne otherwise.

In Paris, everyone was very alert. [...] A message came from the court one day to the effect that the king had received the holy sacrament at midnight, and that the queen and the Cardinal had left his room in despair. Monsieur did not see him after the first few days of his illness. For subsequently purpura broke out on him, so it was decided not to put him at risk. After all this bad news, we heard that the second dose of antimony had had some effect. Next day, we learnt that a purgative had worked wonders; so, from day to day, we learned that he was getting better, and was quite out of danger, which gave everyone, and me in particular, great joy.

[In the autumn, the court went to Fontainebleau, where Mademoiselle, having been in Forges, joined it.]

When I had finished bathing, I went to Fontainebleau, where they were very glad to see me. Next day, Monsieur gave a collation at a hermitage, called Franchart,[176] at which the twenty-four violins were present. We rode on horseback, gaily dressed. The comtesse de Soissons, who was pregnant, went in a coach. When we arrived, she took it into her head to climb about the most inconvenient rocks in the world, where, I think, no one but goats had ever been. For my part, I remained in an arbour in the hermit's garden, watching them climb up and down, and Monsieur and many ladies who were there stayed with me. The king sent for the violins, and then sent word to us to go and join him. We had to obey, but it was not without difficulty; it was hard enough to make one's mind up and go, and then, a moment later, we had to turn back. I am amazed that no one was hurt, for we ran the greatest risk in the world of breaking our arms and legs, and even our heads. I think that the good hermit's prayers saved us.

After supper, we returned in calashes with a great many torches, and, on arriving, went to the play. The forest caught fire, and three or four acres were burnt down. The court was very fine; there were a great many people; the French and Italian players were there;[177] people went sailing with the violins and the singers, but the prediction I have mentioned[178] prevented me from taking part in this amusement, and I remained in the queen's coach. The king rode in a calash with the comtesse de Soissons and Mlles de Mancini and Fouilloux; Monsieur with Mlle de Villeroy,[179] Mmes de Créqui and Vivonne, and the queen's maids of honour. For I would not leave the queen. In the evenings, after the queen's supper, there was dancing till midnight and sometimes one o'clock in the morning, to which I always went; for if I had not, they would have sent for me. Mme de Montausier came, and brought with her a précieuse, Mlle d'Aumale;[180] and, though she did not dance, she adorned the ball. Mme de Châtillon also came to Fontainebleau; in short, there was a great quantity of high society.

One incident was much talked of. The king's nurse, on her way back from mass, found a letter in the great hall; she picked it up, and took it to the queen, who was at her toilet. The king read it; it was a

---

[176] About 5 kilometres west of the château.
[177] The French actors of the Hôtel de Bourgogne in Paris, whose rivals (the company of the Marais Theatre) we met earlier, and the Italian actors who normally played in the Salle du Petit-Bourbon at the eastern end of the Louvre. In this period, both companies were frequently summoned to court.
[178] That she was to meet with a dangerous accident on water that year.
[179] Younger daughter of Marshal Villeroy.
[180] *Précieuse*: a lady with intellectual interests and, often, what we might today term feminist leanings.

very affectionate letter from a lady to a gentleman. No one talked of anything else all day: Fouilloux said it was from La Mothe to the marquis de Richelieu, who was her gallant, now that the king had given her up. The poor girl wept and protested, and disclaimed the whole thing. Anyway, to get to the bottom of it, the queen insisted on seeing the handwriting of all her maids, and fortunately it was found that none resembled that of the note. [...]

His Royal Highness came to Fontainebleau; I went to meet him; he received me kindly: he alighted in the forest as soon as he saw me, and talked to me for a quarter of an hour; then he got back into his coach, and I into mine. I drove on in front, being curious to see how he would be received. When they said: 'Here is the duc d'Orléans,' the king and the queen were playing cards; they scarcely got up to greet him, and went on with their game. Everyone was surprised that they thought so little of him. Their Majesties drove out as usual; His Royal Highness did not go with them. I went to see him in the evening; he treated me quite well. [...]

His Royal Highness went out with Their Majesties; and, as the king scarcely ever wears a hat, His Royal Highness, who was older than the king and very much afraid of the evening damp, was embarrassed. The king and the queen left him for a long time without telling him to put his hat on, although he had his gloves on his head, to show how much he feared that the evening dew might injure his health. That was talked of; and, when the Cardinal had come, as they were walking in the little garden, His Royal Highness waited a long time before telling him to put his hat on. It was said that he wanted to pay him out for what Their Majesties had done to him. Nearly every day, His Royal Highness came to my room, or I went to his; but we talked only of the most indifferent things, like people who care little for each other. In connection with my fear of the arrival of those women,[181] His Royal Highness gave me a kind of reprimand for having worried the queen with my complaints on the subject, which happened whenever the opportunity arose. I rebuked him for his behaviour to me, both as regards that and as regards his neglect of my fortune and his concern for that of my sister. Instead of taking that in good part and like a father fond of his daughter, he took it like a man who hated me and from whose heart the affection that I trust he naturally had for me — that he ought to have had for me, at least — had been eradicated. We separated on bad terms. He went

---

[181] Mmes de Fiesque and Frontenac.

away very angry, and left me in tears, very much upset to see myself so ill-treated by a father, from whom I ought, for all kinds of reasons, to have expected nothing but affection. The princesse de Guémené came to see me, and found me in this pitiful state.

[The Cardinal joined the court on 7 September 1658; Gravelines, west of Dunkirk, had fallen on 30 August after a short siege.]

The Cardinal returned; the king, Monsieur, and I went to meet him; he returned in excellent health and very satisfied, Marshal de la Ferté having captured Gravelines a few days before he left. The marquis d'Huxelles, lieutenant-general, was killed in that battle. […] The whole court was pleased to see the Cardinal, for everyone had things to discuss with him; it is always thus when he is not with Their Majesties. At least it provides a pretext for him to put off those people whose affairs he does not want to deal with. After he had paid his compliment to Their Majesties, they took him off to a private room, and everyone went away. […] I was not born ever to receive joy or contentment from His Royal Highness. He stayed at Fontainebleau only two or three days after the Cardinal's arrival. He came to say goodbye to me, and we separated on fairly good terms, but coldly. I was quite glad when he went, because, when one does not receive from one's kinsfolk the affection and kindness one has a right to expect, they are better far off than near. […] The Cardinal did not remain long at Fontainebleau after the departure of His Royal Highness; he went to Paris to see the princesse de Conti,[182] who had given birth to a son who lived for only nine days, having come into the world all covered with ulcers from head to foot. Cromwell died at the same time. The death of little Conti spared the court the shame of going into mourning for the destroyer of the English monarchy. I should not have worn it without an express order from the king, owing that respect to the Queen of England, to whom I am so closely related. For this reason, the queen dispensed me from going to the Louvre whenever the English ambassadors were there.[183] Once the ambassador came to the Val-de-Grâce when I was there: I hid.

[The court returned to Paris.]

---

[182] His niece, née Anne-Marie Martinozzi.
[183] Sir William Lockhart and Viscount Fauconberg. We do not know which of them went to the Val-de-Grâce.

The journey to Lyon began to be talked of; the Duchess of Savoy [Mademoiselle's aunt, Christine de France] was to go there with her daughter [Marguerite], and, if the king found her to his fancy, he would marry her. Nothing was talked of at the Louvre but this journey. The queen was to remain in Paris, as was Monsieur, who was still on good terms with me, but less attentive than during the first three months after my arrival at the court. To be frank, I did not mind too much; for, knowing him better, I regarded him as a man more likely to think of his good looks and his dress than to distinguish himself by great deeds and to become famous, so that I was very fond of him as a cousin, but I should never have loved him as a husband.

[On 26 October, Mademoiselle set out for Lyon with the court. They stayed a while in Dijon, and later, they passed by her principality of Dombes.]

We travelled for a long time along the Saône, so that, for a long time, we saw the country of Dombes, which is on the other side,[184] and all the peasants, and even some minims, had crossed the river, and asked all those who were following the queen's coach: 'Where is Madame?' And the king enjoyed pointing me out. They shouted: 'Long live the king and Madame!' We travelled for quite a long way on my estates and in sight of them; for, while we were looking at the country of Dombes, we were in Beaujolais. We lay at Villefranche, which is its capital, and may be called a very pretty town.

[In Lyon, the court entertained the Duchess of Savoy, and later the Duke of Savoy, who had travelled there from Turin.]

It occurred to me that the parlement of Dombes had not paid its respects to Their Majesties, and that they ought to come in red robes. I spoke to the Cardinal about this; I told him that those of Orange and Geneva had come and greeted Their Majesties booted, as having come from afar; but that, since His Majesty allowed them to do justice to my subjects in Lyon,[185] he ought, having conferred that privilege on them, to confer another, which seemed to me inseparable from the first — that they should be dressed as the sovereign judges they

---

[184] Dombes, nowadays the southernmost constituent part of the département of the Ain, was nominally an internally autonomous principality recognizing the suzerainty of the King of France, and remained so until being fully incorporated into France in 1762. Its capital was Trévoux; Villefranche, to be mentioned in a moment, is about 10 kilometres up river from Trévoux.

[185] Until 1696, the parlement of Dombes sat in Lyon.

were, and that, therefore, they should have red robes. This matter was negotiated as if it had been most important. I sent for M. Le Tellier;[186] I wrote several letters to him. I also wrote to the Cardinal, and spoke to him about it every evening. At last, I got what I wanted, and, though it was only a trifle, I was delighted, being fond of matters of honour.

My parlement, therefore, went and paid its respects to the king in a body and in red robes. They did not kneel, and addressed the king as not being subjects of his.

[She reproduces the texts of five separate harangues and briefly recounts some of the entertainments enjoyed by the court in Lyon.]

As the sovereignty of Dombes is only sixteen miles from Lyon, and as my subjects wanted to see me, I also wished to visit that country. I asked the Cardinal if I should have enough time to go there; he said yes, provided I did not stay very long; so, after Christmas, I went. The weather seemed to have been designed on purpose to make my journey enjoyable. There was a sharp frost, and the sun shone as in spring; on the way I rode on horseback. For, besides the beauty of the weather which tempted me to, the river had overflowed, and as I do not like water and my coach had to travel a very long way in it, I rode on horseback so as to take the upper road. I called at Vimy, which belongs to the Archbishop of Lyon,[187] and which is quite a pretty house, with a very beautiful terraced garden overlooking the river, fountains and grottoes, in short a house highly thought of in the district: I thought it very pretty. One of his gentlemen asked me if I wished to partake of the pleasure of the chase: his hounds were ready. I was delighted; the pack is handsome and good, for the Archbishop of Lyon is very fond of hunting. As we left Vimy, a hare was started at the right moment, on my road, and the hunt did not swerve aside, so I had the pleasure without prolonging my journey.

It is true that the country of Dombes, from the side on which I arrived, is the most beautiful in the world; one keeps along the edge of the Saône, and on the other side are great expanses, the corn on which was already tall enough to turn them green as if they were meadows, and they are bounded by hills, nearly covered with villas

---

[186] Michel Le Tellier, Secretary of State for War since 1643.
[187] Camille de Neufville de Villeroy, Archbishop of Lyon, the brother of Marshal Villeroy and the Bishop of Chartres. In 1630, he built a residence in Vimy, a riverside town, since renamed Neuville-sur-Saône, that lies roughly half way between Lyon and Trévoux.

belonging to citizens of Lyon, not so pretty as those around Paris, but very pretty for Dombes. In the sovereignty, there are several very fine, well-built mansions; but they are not on that side.

I had asked Monsieur to lend me his guards for the journey. He had given me fourteen, a trumpeter, and a junior officer. When I was near Trévoux, I got into my coach. I found the militia of the country under arms, in sufficiently good order and sufficiently numerous for the short notice they had had; for I had not said until the day before I left that I wanted to make this journey. Thus they could only come together from the places around Trévoux, for there are some a long way off. At the gate of the town, I found the lieutenant-general with the consuls,[188] who harangued me on their knees and brought me the keys of the town. I went straight to the church, which is very fine, where I received another harangue from the dean; then the Te Deum was sung; the guns were fired; and all the militia fired salvo after salvo. Then I went to my house, which is only a middle-class villa I bought, but which is very pretty. The courtyard is a terrace above the river; there is a fountain in the middle; and the view from it is admirable. Beaujolais is on the other side of the river, so, however good one's eyesight, one can only look at my estates. The landscape is the pleasantest in the world; no painter can depict a more beautiful one. This dwelling is composed of a hall, a bedroom with an alcove and a closet and wardrobes behind, and at the end of the hall two more bedrooms; all those have the same view I have mentioned. [...]

I had brought Mme de Courtenay with me. My court was swollen by the officers of the parlement and a few noblemen — not many, because the finest estates in the land are owned by the officers of the parlement and the présidial of Lyon. The most considerable of the nobles is the marquis du Breuil. He is of the house of Damas and has a lot of property in Burgundy and in Bresse as well as in Dombes, of which he is now the governor, having purchased [the governorship] from Saujon. For the same reason, I did not see many ladies and those who are there were unwell. The common people there are very fine; the women are nearly all pretty and have the finest teeth in the world. The peasant women are dressed in the costume of Bresse; the men are well-dressed. One sees none who are poverty-stricken; indeed,

---

[188] Members of the town council. The lieutenant-general was the marquis du Breuil, a distant cousin of the marquis de Thiange. He did not purchase the governorship of Dombes (to be mentioned below) until 1660.

they have not paid any tailles to this day, and perhaps it would be better if they did.[189] For they are idle, and apply themselves to no labour or trade, which would be easy for them, since they are near the river and thriving towns. They eat meat four times a day. At least, they did before they had had the soldiers, but as they have made a good recovery from that, I expect they have gone back to their good customs.

There is a certain knight of honour in the parlement of Dombes: this is a very unusual office, but my late father's people were very good at creating all kinds of offices to raise money. They followed the example of the parlement of Dijon. The knight is a very comic fellow who amused me, having some wonderful disputes with his company. The day before I left for Dombes, I told him that I was being offered an island for sale, of which I wanted to make him governor. He thanked me warmly, and asked me its name. I told him that I did not know, but that it was to be sent to me by the first post, together with a description of the island. On the evening I arrived in Trévoux, I went into my closet and began the description.[190]

Next day I went to mass in the church; then I dined in public, so as to show myself to my subjects. I received a great many harangues from all the towns, and presents from Trévoux, namely sweet lemons, instead of candied fruit (that is less common and more agreeable), and muscat wine. I ordered the consuls to give harangues and gifts to Mme de Courtenay and Mlle de Vandy. After my dinner, the parlement came and harangued me in red robes, for I had not wanted them to come to me in Lyon like that, lest anyone from the court should be in my house, and I should be accused of being very pleased to be harangued like the queen and to have people kneeling before me. They knelt down at Trévoux, as all parlements do before their sovereigns, and I told them to get up. The First President spoke very well.[191] I thanked them for their good will; I assured them of mine; then I recommended them to serve me well, and said that they could not give me any mark of their affection more acceptable to

---

[189] The *taille* was the main tax. In some parts of France it was levied on income; in others, on land.
[190] The knight of honour in this anecdote, Bussillet de Messimieux, was as well known for his gullibility as for his vanity. It was, at first, in furtherance of this jape that Mademoiselle began to compose the text that became La Relation de l'isle imaginaire.
[191] In other words, Mademoiselle had required the parlement of Dombes, albeit normally convened in Lyon, to repair to Trévoux to pay homage on this occasion. Its First President from 1653 to 1675 was Guillaume de Sève de Laval.

me than to render justice fairly to my subjects; that I felt obliged by my conscience to recommend that to them; and that, if I allowed them to fail in their duty, I should be responsible before God for their injustice. Thus, I virtually harangued them on the obligation of sovereigns to have justice done in their states. I spoke as best I could, and I believe I spoke well.

As there is no play, however serious, after which ludicrous farces are not performed, when the serious part was over I smiled at Messimieux, the knight of honour, who was with the parlement, and said to him: 'You ought to give me a harangue all by yourself, since I know you love me so much.' He replied lightheartedly and made me laugh. As it was a Sunday and one must set a good example to one's subjects, I went to vespers, and, on my return, found the letters from Paris. Messimieux was at pains to come and ask me for news of the island; but, as I had not had leisure to complete it, I replied that half my letters were still in Lyon, but that I should certainly have it next day. I finished it in the evening, and it was copied all day Monday, for it takes longer to transcribe what I compose than I take to write it.

On Monday, I went to mass at the Observant Fathers, who have a monastery in Trévoux. Next, I went to see the chapel of the Penitents. These are confraternities that are ubiquitous in those parts. Those of Trévoux are white. In the afternoon, I went to the Ursulines, and in the evening, the description of the island was read to the knight, who, henceforth, was known as Governor. This account appeared very pretty to those who heard it. The fireplace caught fire under the hearth, and, had it not been noticed, there would have been an accident. But, fortunately, when I got up, I became aware of a smell of burning. A beam underneath was already almost burnt away; it was made good. Previously, on the way [to Lyon], my lodging at Beaune had caught fire. Next day, the same beautiful weather which had brought me and which had continued during my stay, took me back. It is most unusual, during the last days of the year, to drive by moonlight until six in the evening. On arriving in Lyon, I changed my clothes and went to the queen's, where I was given a warm welcome.

I was forgetting to say, what will readily be believed, that in Dombes prayers were said for me, and not for the king; but, before setting out in the morning, after my mass, I had the *exaudiat* sung, and a prayer said for him. I set free a great many prisoners; I gave free pardons; and those guilty of irremissible crimes, who could not be pardoned, but who had come and given themselves up in the hope of being pardoned when I arrived, were allowed to escape: for they had come and gone to prison of their own accord; it is a severe enough punishment not to dare to return to one's own country without fearing to be hanged. This is the custom wherever the king passes, that is to say in places where he has never been.

When I went to the Cardinal's with the queen, he said to me: 'Well, Mademoiselle, you are quite rich: your country has given you a present, and you have created new offices in your parlement.' I replied: 'On all the king's journeys, I should like to have a sovereignty sixteen miles from the town where we are staying; at least that would pay for my journey.' It is true that I had created a president and some councillors and other officers in my parlement. The office of councillor for the Church was purchased by a comte de Saint-Jean-de-Lyon, of the house of Albon.[192] He was given it cheap, because I was very glad to have men like that in my parlement, where there had always been some.

[The proposed marriage between Louis XIV and Princess Marguerite came to nothing, the King of Spain offering the king his daughter. The Duchess of Savoy and her daughter left Lyon on 8 December 1658. The court remained until January before returning to Paris. On the way, Mademoiselle left it at Cosne, spending a week or so at Saint-Fargeau before returning to Paris herself.]

---

[192] In each of the several branches of the house of Albon, the second son was commonly installed as comte de Lyon and canon (*chanoine*) of the cathedral of Saint-Jean (Saint John). At certain times, there was more than one *chanoine-comte*, but the only one we have identified as being in office in this period was François d'Albon, the brother-in-law of Mademoiselle's childhood friend Charlotte de Rancé.

Part II
1659–1671

Chapter 1
The Treaty of the Pyrenees and the King's Marriage (1659–1660)

My great fondness for pleasure, from having been deprived of it for so long, the high society I saw, much travelling, an exile, and many other things, one in particular, which occupied me pleasantly for a time, during which I was not free from anxiety, fearing the outcome, which cost me (and still costs me) a great deal of suffering — all these things had made me forget my memoirs and the desire to continue them. But since I have been here, having amused myself with reading them, the desire to work at them has come back to me. A break of seventeen years, and all that has happened during this break, may have made me forget many things; but, as I write for myself alone, it does not matter. I am, therefore, going to begin them today, 18 August 1677, at Eu.

[The marriage having been arranged between Louis XIV and Maria Theresa, Infanta of Spain, the court set off for the Pyrenees.]

We left Paris amidst the cries of joy of the populace and the blessings they were asking God for the king, the success of his journey, and the object for which he was undertaking it. The princesse de Conti accompanied the queen, as well as the princesse palatine [Anne de Gonzague], the comtesse de Fleix, her lady-in-waiting, and the duchesse d'Uzès, her knight of honour's wife. Mme de Noailles was pregnant or unwell. We went to Fontainebleau, where we stayed some time.[193] We slept at Jargeau, so as to avoid going through Orleans. Since Monsieur was at Chambord, Madame having had a miscarriage, the court slept there instead of going to Blois. The day we arrived, the king said in the coach: 'I did not want to change my clothes nor unloose my hair, because, if I had dressed up, I should have made your father, your stepmother, and your sister too sorry not to have me; I have made myself as plain as possible to put them off.' He jested in this way very merrily.

---

[193] In fact, for over a month. The court left Fontainebleau, in the first instance for Bordeaux, at the end of July. Mazarin had departed for Saint-Jean-de-Luz just over four weeks earlier.

Monsieur came to meet the king outside the park of Chambord. We went straight to the château to see Madame. Then the king went out riding and shooting pheasants with my father. As we had arrived early, the king had time to go riding. The queen remained in the château, for there are no walks at Chambord. My sisters were not there. My father told the queen, who asked about them, that he had sent them to Blois, so that they should not take up any room; he had even sent his officials to Blois, so no meals were provided. He supped with the king and the queen. I had my staff, and wanted to do the honours of the house: I gave supper to all the ladies who were with the queen and her maids of honour.

Next day, we went and dined at Blois; my father entertained Their Majesties in the château. My sisters came down to the bottom of the steps to receive them. Unfortunately, some flies, known as mosquitoes, had bitten my sister in the night; as her chief attraction is her complexion, it was so marred — and she is flat-chested as most girls of thirteen are — that she was a pitiful sight, even without her chagrin at having believed she was to marry the king: for no one talked to her about anything else; she was always called the little queen; and to see him on his way to marry another — none of that makes a girl attractive. Little Valois was very pretty. They were made to dance. The queen asked Mme de Raré to make them, because my sister's dancing was highly prized; she danced very badly. The little one, who, according to my father, was a thorough chatterbox and entertained him greatly, would not say a word.

As my father's officials were out of touch with fashion, the repast, however splendid, failed to please, and Their Majesties ate very little. All the ladies of the court of Blois, who were numerous, were dressed like the dishes of the meal — unfashionably. The queen and the king were in such a hurry to leave that I never saw anything like it. It did not look polite, but I think my father felt the same, and was delighted to be rid of us.

The day we left Chambord, he came and woke me at four in the morning; he sat on my bed, and said: 'I do not think you will be sorry that I have woken you up. I should not have had the time to see you later. You are setting out on a long and protracted journey; for, whatever may be said, it is not so easy to make peace as people think, and perhaps it will not be made; so your journey may take longer than is expected. I am old and worn out, so I may die during your absence. If I die, I commend your sisters to you. I know that you do not care for Madame, and that she has not treated you as well as she might have done; it is not the fault of her children; for my sake, look after them. They will badly need you; for Madame will not be much use to them.' He kissed me three or four times. I was greatly moved by all that, for I have a kind heart, and, if people mend their ways towards me, they easily touch it. I told Monsieur my feelings about that, saying things respectful, tender, and full of gratitude for the sincerity with which he spoke to me. We parted on good terms, and I went to sleep again. Had I not had a vivid memory of that, I should think I had dreamed it, in view of what had gone before.

As soon as we were in the coach leaving Blois, we talked a lot about what had happened there, and laughed about it. My father was fond of his pheasants, and took great pleasure in preserving them. The king said: 'Your father was very sorry that I killed fourteen pheasants.' In short, everything amused him.

[The court arrived in Bordeaux on 19 August and stayed there for seven weeks.]

During our stay in Bordeaux, the queen led her ordinary life. She visited the convents, went walking, and, in the evenings, played *bête* for high stakes. Although my father, whom I might be expected to take after, was very fond of it, I do not naturally like it; however, either because I had not much to do, or to be like the others, I had joined the queen's game, but so as to be able to get out of it I went halves with the comte de Roye, so that I did not need to play when I found a more congenial occupation. The king often had the regiment of guards drilled. News frequently came from Saint-Jean-de-Luz, where the Cardinal was negotiating terms with Don Luis de Haro. You may judge how pleased the queen was when progress was made. Marshal Gramont went to Madrid as ambassador extraordinary to ask for the Infanta. I sent the comte de Charny,[194] whom I had brought with me on this journey, with him. As nothing was being done in Flanders, he would have been quite useless to his company. I had obtained one of cavalry for him.

Mme de Montausier came to Bordeaux. M. de Montausier is Governor of Angoulême and Saintonge, not far from Bordeaux; and she was at Saintes when we passed through. The princesse de Conti and I had supper with her. She often came to see me; she is a very intelligent and excellent woman. She kept trying to reconcile Vandy

---

[194] Formerly the chevalier de Charny.

and the countesses, in order to put them on good terms with me again afterwards. One day, when she was talking of Saint-Fargeau and all their squabbles, she said to Vandy: 'You are very proud, Princess of Paphlagonie!' Mlle de Scudery had given her that name in one of her novels, for she was loved by all the wits who frequented the comtesse de Maure. Thereupon I said: 'The Princess of Paphlagonie is at war with Queen Gilette!' The comtesse de Fiesque is called Gilone, and at the beginning of her widowhood, after the death of her first husband, lived on a magnificent scale and saw a great many people; she was given that nickname. I said to Mme de Montausier, therefore: 'You will make peace between these two crowns, when the treaty between France and Spain is concluded.' This conversation lasted for a whole evening. When she had gone, I said to Vandy: 'I feel like drawing up a memorandum of your interests to present to Mme de Montausier.' She said: 'That would be very entertaining.' I meant to do no more than that; but, as I had time and enjoyed it, I wrote a little story which I finished in three days, writing for an hour or two in the evening when I came back from the queen's. I showed it to Mme de Montausier, who liked it; it was a trifle. I showed her *L'Isle imaginaire*, which I had written in Dombes. It occurred to Mme de Pontac to have it printed, and a little volume was made of it, which was seen only by a few people.[195]

[The court went to Toulouse, where Mazarin joined it on 21 November, having negotiated the Peace of the Pyrenees (signed on the 7th). From there, it went to Montpellier and thence to Nîmes.]

We went on to Nîmes; I begged the queen to allow me to go to Avignon, because I had heard a great deal about the beauty of the town, and because I was afraid of the crossing from Beaucaire to Tarascon, where the Rhône is very broad. I preferred to cross by the bridge at Avignon. I sent to say that I wanted to be incognita, and requested that no honour should be paid me. Mlle de Vandy had remained at Toulouse, ill; so, having only Mme de Montglat, I asked the duchesse d'Orval, the wife of the queen's master of the horse, who had travelled with us, to come with me. I also took Mlle d'Armentières, her cousin, who was living with her at Nîmes. The queen remained there. We

---

[195] The first recognized edition of this work is *La Relation de l'isle imaginaire et l'Histoire de la princesse de Paphlagonie*, published in 1659 without name of place or publisher and containing an engraved portrait of Mademoiselle. Mme de Pontac, the wife of the First President of the parlement of Bordeaux, was the sister of François de Thou, whose execution had so distressed Mademoiselle.

went to see the arena and some aqueducts, built in Roman times, over which a river passes.

I left for Avignon on the day the court left for Arles, intending to be there next day, not meaning to spend more than one in Avignon. I went over the Pont du Gard. It is a curious thing, and worth seeing: three bridges on top of one another, built as one. They are supported only on one side. You have to see to understand. I walked over; such large coaches as mine had never crossed; only one of my coachmen had the skill to cross all three. I did not go up to the top two bridges, having a sore foot, for which I was very sorry. At the end of the bridge of Avignon, I reached a little town, which belongs to France, though formerly it all did: the Pope [Alexander VII], perhaps wrongfully, owns it now.[196] This town, called Villeneuve, has a fort above it, known as Saint-André. The governor had the guns fired. They came and harangued me, for a dual reason — because of what I am, and because Monsieur was Governor of Languedoc. I did not welcome these honours and harangues. I said to them: 'I am not I; I am incognita.' That was all the reply they got. At the end of the bridge, I found the vice-legate's sedan-chair, and many others. I got in; I saw the bridge and the Rhône by moonlight; they both seemed very fine to me, and frightened me enormously; for the Rhône is very rapid and very broad, and the bridge is very narrow, very high, and in a bad state of repair.[197] When I reached the end of the bridge on the town side, I saw a lot of people and a great many torches; I heard drums and trumpets; it struck me as terrible. My only idea was to be incognita.

When I saw all that, I got out of my chair, and rushed into a house, which was one of the king's offices, and I had no other idea than to close the door. Mme d'Orval and all my retinue were laughing to see how afraid I was, that day, of having honours paid to me. That is not my custom, since I was born, and am accustomed, to be honoured everywhere. At last, the vice-legate,[198] carried away by zeal to do me

---

[196] Avignon — and the Comtat Venaissin, in which the city is situated — had passed to the Kingdom of Naples and then, in the fourteenth century, to the Pope. Mademoiselle arrived on 12 January 1660 and left again on the 14th. Villeneuve is on the opposite (right) bank of the Rhône.

[197] The famous 'pont d'Avignon' of the song had been in poor repair for many years, and crossing it was dangerous. Several of its arches were swept away only ten years after Mademoiselle describes it here, and it was then left in the state in which it is known today.

[198] Gaspard de Lascaris, newly installed as vice-legate, the effective Governor of Avignon. One of his predecessors was Mazarin, vice-legate from 1634 to 1636.

honour, and helped by his great strength (for he was a very big man), struck the door with his fist, and broke it down. I ought to have recognized the Pope's authority and revered it, but it did not occur to me. He paid me a great many compliments in Italian. I replied, most uncivilly: 'I want to be incognita.' He had with him the commander of the Pope's arms, called Commander Lomelino, as well as the Grand Prior of England and the consuls.[199] In short, in spite of myself, they did me every conceivable honour. All the citizens and the garrison were under arms; in addition, torches, and ladies in the windows. They fired like mad; the guns of Saint-André answered those of the town.

I arrived at the house of the marquis de Grillon, a nobleman of the district, whom I knew.[200] I had refused to lodge in the Pope's palace. Grillon's house is very fine, built and painted in the Italian style. When I entered this mansion, in which was a vast number of people, I felt reassured, and was then willing to be what I was. I became civil, stopped scolding, and received people in my usual manner. The vice-legate stayed a long time. When everybody had left, one of my people told me about an incident that made me laugh heartily. There is a company of cavalry, neither very warlike, nor often on horseback; the chevalier Rospigliosi commanded it. I think he is now a cardinal. They tried to form it up in a part of the town I passed through. The commander, unaccustomed to such matters, as was his horse, fell into a cellar. This episode is still remembered.

As I had travelled a long way, and as my officials had not arrived, the marquis de Valavoir, who was in the Cardinal's service, and whom I knew, said to me: 'If I dared, I should give you supper.' It was late; I was sleepy; I joyfully accepted the offer. I supped with his wife's aunt, who was Mme de Grillon's sister-in-law. One could pass from one house into the other. During supper, I talked to one of the chief wits of the town, who was head of the Academy.[201] After, there was a marionette show; but I was so sleepy that better entertainments would not have kept me awake.

---

[199] The Grand Prior, the chief officer of the Knights of St John, had been expelled from England in 1540 by Henry VIII. We have been unable to ascertain who aspired to the title in 1660.
[200] Mademoiselle writes *Grillon* but she must surely mean 'Crillon', the name of an Avignon family that had for generations provided military officers to the king's armies.
[201] This academy, modelled on the Académie-Française, had been founded in Avignon about fifteen months before Mademoiselle's visit. We have not identified the 'wit' who was its principal in 1659.

Next day, I resolved to see the curiosities of the town. I was told to begin with the palace. I went there; I found the whole garrison in the square, under arms. From the outside, the palace is admirable; the rooms are large; but it is an old building, shabby, furnished in the Italian style. In one of the finest rooms, there was a portrait of the king, under a canopy. In the vice-legate's closet, there was a book about his genealogy on the table, to show me that he was related to the house of Joyeuse. He did not say anything; but I read straight away, for the book was open at that place. I made some polite remark to him about it. Then I went to the Corso, where everyone was; it is on the bank of the Rhône, along the walls of the city, which are the finest in the world. Then I went to the synagogue to see the Jews. They sang; I have never seen such an ugly place or such ugly people. After that I went to a Notre-Dame which is at the end of the town, a very fine chapel, where they said many miracles were worked. I also went to the Carmelites, which are not like those here, and to another convent, to which Mme de Grillon asked me to go; then to the ball. They are held at the houses of all the ladies in turn. If I remember aright, this one was in that of the marquise de Châteauneuf, whose husband belongs to the house of Simiane. Mme d'Orval and Mme de Montglat were in the best place. As I was incognita, I was on a chair with the vice-legate next to me. I was told that vice-legates usually danced, but I think that the size of this one would have made it difficult; but there is another custom, which was not observed that day — namely that, at every courante, the lady should come and kiss him. That struck me as rather ludicrous for an elderly bishop and priest. I told him I thought it ludicrous; he told me that he was very glad, and would abolish it. That was all.

Next day, before leaving, I went to the Célestins to hear mass in the chapel of St Peter of Luxemburg, who is much worshipped in this town; he has not been canonized, because he was made a cardinal by one of the anti-popes who lived in Avignon; but because of the large number of miracles he has worked, having brought back a great many people from the dead, he is so much worshipped there that the Church tolerates it.[202] In the last few years, they have begun to worship him in Amiens, in the church of St Martin, where the Célestins are.

---

[202] Mademoiselle is only partly correct. St Peter of Luxemburg (1369–1387), Bishop of Metz at the age of fifteen, was made Cardinal of Avignon in 1386, by Clement VII, the first of the Anti-Popes whose reign after the election of Urban VI in Rome marked the beginning of the Great Schism of 1378–1415. Following a number of miracles associated with his tomb in Avignon, he was canonized in 1527.

Last time the court was there, I went to it. We need the help of saints so much that we cannot too much seek them out. If we could form a close friendship by doing their will, those friends would be more staunch and useful than those of this world. We are connected with this house by several marriages.

I wanted to cross by a ferry to join Their Majesties by land; but it was broken; I was compelled to set out on the Rhône. The vice-legate, who was going to see the king, had a very pretty boat; he gave it to me, and took another. If I had insisted on avoiding the water, of which I was very much afraid, I should have had to wait some days. I had told Their Majesties the day on which I should join them, so necessity got the better of my fear. On entering the boat, I prayed God wholeheartedly; I commended myself to him, and set off. A thaw had set in, and the frost had been severe, so, on the Rhône, there were blocks of ice of a frightful size. It runs with a speed that, to my mind, is more pleasurable than alarming. The weather was very fine; the country is admirable. I felt so reassured that I fell asleep in the boat, so I found the trip to Arles very short.

When I arrived at Arles, as I went into the queen's room, she exclaimed: 'What! you have come by water?' I told her that the desire to join her had overcome all my fears, and that I should never have any which would make me fail in the least of my duties. Everyone said to me: 'What! you were not afraid?' For, at court, it does not take much to set people talking for a long time, so idle and clever are people there! That was the talk of the whole evening. There was such a horrible frost, and it had lasted for so long, that the lieutenant-colonel of the guards, Fourilles, a reliable man, told the king and the queen that the regiment of guards had crossed from Tarascon to Beaucaire on the ice, and that they had been covered all over by the dust there was.

We were only one day at Arles; the next we stayed overnight in Salon.

[The court went to Aix, where it arrived on 17 January 1660. Condé joined the court ten days later and peace was celebrated by a Te Deum on 2 February. The king decided to go to Toulon, and Condé departed for Paris, but Mademoiselle and Mazarin, both of whom were indisposed, remained in Aix. There, Mademoiselle heard that her father was unwell, and later, that he had died on 2 February.]

I went into my closet, weeping with all my heart; as it is very tender and very kind, I felt in it at that moment all the affection that nature makes one feel at such times, and I forgot all the occasions that might have driven it out. After my first emotions, I remembered that it was my duty to inform the king. It is a matter of honour that one behaves in such a manner, and it is also right and proper within one's own family. I wrote to the Cardinal, saying that, as my present state did not allow me to write to the king, and as my duty required me to inform him of Monsieur's death, I entreated him to tell him of it, and that I was sending this gentleman for the purpose. It was Colombier; I charged him to see the queen and Monsieur. I arranged for everything needed for my mourning; then I went to bed, with a feeling of regret that Monsieur had died with all the bitterness he had been made to feel towards me about the business of Savoy, without having known the truth.[203]

Everything that had passed between us came back to me, not making me feel resentment towards him, but making me worry whether, at those times, I might have failed in the respect I owed him. All these thoughts distressed me, and redoubled my grief. For, although I realized, the more I searched my heart, how little I was at fault in all that, nevertheless I was mortally grieved that Monsieur had not known, before he died, my tender and respectful feelings for him, and the malice of those who had told him the contrary. That occupied me during some sleepless nights. [...]

The court was at Toulon when it learned of Monsieur's death; it was the last days of the carnival, the pleasures of which ceased. The king finished the journey he had decided on, and then returned to Aix. All the time I remained there in their absence, the weather was fairly good; I drove out of the town, it being most unpleasant to be always in rooms hung with black. I had a set of grey mourning clothes made, the first made for a single woman; until then only wives had had them for their husbands. But, as I wanted to wear the strictest and the greatest mourning there had ever been, that came to my mind. Everyone was clad in mourning, even the scullions and the valets of all my dependants, the trappings of mules, and the housings of all my horses and beasts of burden. Nothing was so fine, the first time we

---

[203] The three references to 'Monsieur' in this paragraph are to, respectively, her father, her cousin Philippe, and her father. Her father had complained to Mazarin that Mademoiselle had tried to prevent her half-sister from marrying the Duke of Savoy by writing a derogatory letter to him (Chéruel, III, 391–92). She had dispatched Brays to Turin, where he obtained a letter from Christine of Savoy exculpating her, but her father died before she could communicate its contents to him.

went out, as to see all this great mourning procession. It had an air of magnificence and real greatness. They say that I have it adequately in everything. While I was in Aix, then, I drove out, but our expeditions always ended at some convent. I often went to the Carmelites and it was there that I had a service held for Monsieur.

[She recounts what she has heard of the Christian death of her father. Her stepmother, she says, was not with him when he died. In Aix, many people came to pay their respects.]

The court left Aix to go to Marseille, which we entered [on 2 March] by the breach made by knocking the walls down to punish them for their revolt.[204] The troops had entered that way, and there were a great many of them. While we were there, there were guard posts of cavalry and infantry in every square, as in an occupied town. We stayed there for three or four days, but I was in bed with migraine. I thought it pitiful to see the galley-slaves in chains passing through the streets. It seemed frightful to me. One day we walked round the port, where, too, we had these objects continually before our eyes. There were a great many ships and a few galleys, but they were not all fitted out. There were shops round the port, in which I found nothing as fine and as rare as I had heard was to be found there. I bought scarcely anything.

[People think the countryside around Marseille is attractive, she says, but she liked neither the countryside nor the food, and much preferred Paris.]

We sailed in the galleys; guards and even some of the king's musketeers were stationed on them; they are painted and gilded; there are some pretty staterooms; but it is dreadful to see all these men, without shirts, naked except for a kind of slip, shaven, and blackened by the sun; they are chained, and that puts one in mind of Hell; one feels horror and pity. Then, when one reflects that they are wicked men, one feels less. There were many friars. This trip was not too pleasant; everyone was sick and faint. Only the royal party was not affected by the sea air. We got into little boats; a great many fish, unknown to me, were caught — I had not seen the like in the Atlantic. The fish, which, there, is very good, is very bad at Marseille, and as I do not know the kinds they admire there, I do not eat them.

---

[204] Unrest in Marseille following an outbreak of plague had deteriorated by the late 1650s into a state of rebellion, and the king was determined to put a stop to it.

The king wanted to go to the château d'If; it is eight miles from Marseille.[205] We had to go in a very little vessel. The queen refused to go; she allowed me to follow the king. As we came alongside, a wave came and covered us all with water. One has to choose the right moment to jump on to the rock; and if one missed it and hesitated a moment, one would fall into the sea. It is a castle built on a rock, with a little courtyard and some terraces on one side. It is strong because of its situation; I do not think guns would be effective, and, if it were attacked, it would be taken by starvation rather than anything else. The outside is very fine; the inside neither beautiful nor ugly. It was quite handsomely furnished. A substantial collation was provided, but, as it was Lent, few partook of it. I was anxious to be away, because the castle looks like a prison, and I have hated them all my life. I think this was due to one of those remote presentiments, the cause of which one does not discover until one is unfortunate enough to know it and feel it.[206] It was a great pleasure to me to be back with the queen,[207] who was waiting for us on the galley.

On the way back from Marseille, we did not stay long in Aix.[208] People there were very shocked because I did not go to the Sainte-Baume, where St Mary Magdalen is particularly worshipped; but there was a good deal of smallpox, and as I am very much afraid of it, I did not go. From Aix, we went to Avignon; the king and the queen took different roads, because the queen wanted to go to Apt, where St Anne's body was reputed to be; my mules followed the king's and did not arrive at Malmore,[209] where the queen went. I slept in a chair, and at midnight, Comminges sent me his bed; I threw myself on to it. The lodging is wretched. There was an old man of sixty, paralytic, chairbound; I did not want him to be moved from the room with a fireplace, lest it should harm him; I took the closet. The queen was little better off; for they had to pass through her anteroom to go to

---

[205] It is barely one-third of this distance; on the other hand, we cannot be sure where the king's party embarked.
[206] By the time that Mademoiselle was writing this part of her memoirs, six years of Lauzun's imprisonment in Pinerolo had already elapsed. However, she must also have had in mind that when the chevalier de Lorraine was arrested, in 1669, he was imprisoned in the château d'If.
[207] Mademoiselle, who completed this part of her memoirs after the king's marriage, writes 'reine-mère' ('queen mother'). Both here and at the beginning of the paragraph, where she writes 'la reine', she means Anne of Austria.
[208] The court left Marseille on 8 March, stayed a few days in Aix, and left for Avignon on the 16th.
[209] Mallemort on the River Durance, 30 kilometres north-west of Aix on the route the queen would have taken to reach Apt.

the loft to fetch hay and oats for our horses, there being only one hostelry in the place. At Apt, we were excellently lodged. In Provence, all the people of rank live in the towns, so the houses are habitable and well furnished. The queen made her devotions there. Although St Anne is much worshipped here, and although people come from far and wide, I did not think the relics were carefully preserved — they were in a wretched wooden shrine, like a chest falling apart. It is constantly being opened. Some were presented to the queen, and the canon broke the boards with his hands, took handfuls of dust, and gave everybody some. [...]

From Avignon, we went to Perpignan [where the court arrived on 10 April]. Perpignan seemed to me a very ugly town; its avenues are fine; the country is beautiful; a pretty river. When we arrived, it was very fine, but it rained so horribly that we had to stay there, the rivers, or rather the torrents, having overflowed their banks and swollen. The queen went to see all the convents. The nuns of the same order who, here, are very austere, are very coquettish there; they have wimples of pleated quintin,[210] wear rouge and make-up, and boast of having lovers. One asked Comminges to introduce her to me, and to tell me that she was M. de Saint-Aunais's mistress.[211] I was very frightened by this remark. She told me that she hoped, because of the good will he had often told her I had for him, that I should have a little for her; and that she had been his devotee (for so they call it) for ten years. I did not know what to say to her. [...]

When the waters went down, we left. I was very frightened, for we forded rivers, and the water seeped through the doors of the coach. One of my men was nearly drowned where my jewellery and my dogs were, and one of my women, who was not afraid and did everything that was necessary, had to be rescued shouting: 'I have Mademoiselle's jewels here.'

[The court went on to Toulouse, Dax, and Bayonne, where it arrived on 1 May and stayed until the 8th. On that day it went to Saint-Jean-de-Luz.]

I did not like it when Madame [her stepmother] said she wanted my sisters to lodge with the queen, because, if they had, they would have

---

[210] A kind of lawn or fine woven cotton used in ecclesiastical dress. Although its English name comes from the town of Laon, it is a Breton version, named for the town of Quintin, that Mademoiselle has in mind.
[211] Saint-Aunais is either Henri de Bourcier de Barry or his son Charles, both of whom were living at this time. Henri was the Governor of Leucate, a small town about twenty kilometres north of Perpignan.

been with her at all times of the day when I was not there, since I was not living there; they would always have eaten with her, morning and evening, which I did not at that time. I confess that I thought this suggestion cunning on my stepmother's part — trying to obtain distinctions by poverty, of which my opulence deprived me; for, had I not had the means to maintain a house, and had I had to live with the queen from childhood on, I should always have eaten with her, for I have heard her say that the duchesse d'Elbeuf, Henry IV's bastard, who was known as Mlle de Vendôme, had lived with her for some years after the queen's marriage and before her own, and always ate with her. Not that, even then, I did not go and eat with her when I wanted, but as I had not got into that habit, as I have since, I rarely went. All my life I have been jealous about all the marks of greatness that distinguish one from the others, and yet I have neglected them from a certain spirit of independence and loftiness of feeling which led me to live in my own house without bothering about anything, seeing that I needed no one. And when others, more pliable and more single-minded, and lacking many things, thought of them, I was in despair. In what I am saying about myself, there is much nobility of feeling, but there are also defects in my temperament. I do not, therefore, need to be afraid of praising myself too much, because, at the same moment, I admit the faults in what might appear a praiseworthy act on my part.

My sisters came, then. A lodging had been provided for them, which greatly pleased me, because I had not dared to express my fear to anyone. [...]

One day, looking out of the Cardinal's window, from which we could see the river and the Pyrenees, we — Mme de Motteville was with me — began to talk of solitude, the country, and how one could lead a happy life there, of the worry and the fatigue of court life, and the injustice of fortune; how few are satisfied with it, and how many complain of the injustice of its distribution. All these things were an ample field for moralizing, particularly if one threw in a dose of Christianity. The queen came out and put an end to our conversation. I took her to the theatre, and left her there to go walking by the sea shore. The reason why I did not go to the theatre was that I did not understand much Spanish. The king and Monsieur had learnt it before leaving Paris. I had tried, too, deeming it necessary because of the queen who was coming; but however much I tried, I could not manage it.

Walking by the sea shore, then, a great many things went through my head about the project of a solitary life for people who withdrew from the court without being driven from it. I ran home; I took a pen and ink, and I filled two or three sheets of paper with a letter to Mme de Motteville, which I caused to be copied, and sent to her by someone she did not know. I wanted no love affairs in this rural retreat; I did not even want anyone to marry. She guessed that it was I who had written it. She replied; I wrote a second letter to her, and the correspondence lasted a year or two, on and off. Enough was written on both sides to make a little volume. As she is very learned, what she wrote is admirable, because, in it, there is Italian and Spanish, and quotations from the Holy Scriptures, the Fathers, the poets, and the historians. In short, many things gathered together; for my part, I only write trifles. The first two letters were taken from her (for I know that I did not give them to anyone) and printed in one of those miscellanies called *Œuvres galantes*. But her name is their only merit. They were mutilated and all spoilt. I confess that I was sorry to see them in this state.

[The wedding of Louis XIV and Maria Theresa took place on 9 June 1660. The court returned to Fontainebleau; and thence to Paris, where the king and his bride made their ceremonial entry on 26 August.]

Chapter 2
Mademoiselle's Second Exile (1662–1664)

[In 1662, Turenne came and proposed that Mademoiselle should marry the King of Portugal.]

M. and Mme de Navailles said to me: 'Do not think that this affair is a fancy of M. de Turenne's. The king knows of it; but, as he does not want to talk to you about it yet, he is leaving it to M. de Turenne.'

It occurred to me to write a letter to the king, in which I said that, fearing he would have a poor opinion of me if he thought that I had nothing in mind but amusing myself like a little girl and gave no thought to being married, I was very glad, from my trust in his kindness, to beg him to remember it, but to consider, too, that at my age not everything was suitable for me, and to put me in places where I could serve him usefully and pleasantly. In the meantime, if, as a mark of his consideration, he would do me the honour of giving me a pension, he would give me great pleasure. The letter was rather long, but that is the gist. I thought that would compel him to speak. I gave it to the duc de Saint-Aignan, the first gentleman of the bedchamber on duty that year,[212] and told him, when I gave him the letter, everything that M. de Turenne had said to me; that that was what was making me write to the king, to see if he had heard of it. M. de Saint-Aignan told me that I had done right; that he thought M. de Turenne had spoken on his own account; and that the king was not a man to force me. Some days later, he told me that he had given the letter to the king, and that he had said nothing. I tried to get him to ask for a reply; he said that I must leave it to the king without saying anything to him; that he would do what I liked; but that, if I took his advice, that is what I should do; I followed it. [...]

On taking leave of the king to go to Forges, I said to him: 'Sire, if Your Majesty wanted to think of marrying me, there is M. de Béziers who is going to Venice and will pass through Turin; he could negotiate my marriage with the Duke of Savoy.' He answered: 'Who has told you that he is going to Venice and will pass through Savoy on his journey?' 'Sire, everyone is saying so, and it seems to me that Turin is on the way.' 'You are wrong; one does not go through it. I

---

[212] Many of the officers of royal households served for a quarter or six months at a time. Mademoiselle writes 'duc', a title that Saint-Aignan had possessed for many years, but at the time of this event, he was the comte de Saint-Aignan.

shall think of you when it suits me, and I shall marry you where it will be useful for my service' — in a cutting tone, which frightened me very much.

Thereupon he saluted me coldly, and I departed; I took my waters [at Forges].

[From Forges, she went to Eu, where she received a visit from the marquis de Gesvres.]

He arrived very late. I was in my closet with several people, whom I dismissed as soon as he entered. He said to me: 'The king has commanded me to come and tell you that he commands you to go to Saint-Fargeau until further orders. You may believe, Mademoiselle, that I am very sorry to be entrusted with an errand that is disagreeable to you.' I said: 'I shall obey; when must I leave?' 'When you wish.' 'Have you orders to take me?' 'No.' 'Which way does the king want me to go?' 'Whichever way you like.' 'Tell the king that I shall leave on such and such a day (which I named); that I shall take the road the furthest away from Paris; and that, as it is nearly All Saints' Day, he will allow me to stop at Jouarre, and spend the holy days there, and not in a village.' He said: 'I do not doubt that the king will approve.' Then I made my compliments, and said: 'Being well aware that I have done nothing to bring this treatment upon myself, I might be in doubt about the cause, but I am not, because M. de Turenne threatened me with it this winter. I beg you to tell the king.' He replied: 'I most humbly entreat you not to charge me with anything.' We talked about many indifferent matters. He saw me have supper and then went to sleep at the inn; he absolutely refused to stay or to sup here. I put my affairs in order and departed.

[On her journey, she passed a few days in Jouarre, as she had intended, before going to Saint-Fargeau. A monk and a M. de la Richardière were sent to try to persuade her to marry the King of Portugal, the latter bringing a letter from Turenne with him.]

I asked him what the King of Portugal was like. As regards his person, he described him as I had already heard him to be, neither exaggerating nor attenuating anything; but, as regards his character, he described him differently, more truthfully and more unfavourably. He told me that he had intelligence but was malicious and ignorant, and that his mother could now see, from his behaviour towards her, how wrong she had been to have had him taught nothing;

debauched; cruel, taking delight in killing; no politeness — which the people of those countries usually have. 'They lack judgement, but they have lively, polished minds; his is uncultivated and not like that of a nobleman; he likes wine and tobacco, and is bored by the society of well-bred people; but, as he is only nineteen or twenty, he will change. His favourite is a young man, a libertine like him, but gentler in character; so, when care is taken to surround him with decent people, and he sees how you support him, and how useful you are to him, you will make a gentleman of him. The country is beautiful, but it is not cultivated. There is money, so you will do whatever you wish. You will set free the women, who are like slaves; they dare not walk in their own gardens. If a woman is seen at her window, she is said to be no better than she should be. In short, it is the most horrible country in the world, but you will transform it as you will.' I assured him that I should please him if I could, but that in Portugal he would not have my protection, and that I should never go. I gave him the answer for M. de Turenne, and I begged him to tell him to get the idea of sending me to Portugal out of his head, and that my opinion and my feelings had not changed since the first time I had seen him.

[Mademoiselle was allowed to spend the winter of 1663–1664 at Eu.]

Then I came here [to Eu], resolved to spend my winter without being despondent. I had begun altering the interior of a pavilion before I left; I had the pleasure of watching the joiners and painters working at it: and although this part of the country is colder because of the sea, the winter is less severe; that year, it was the finest in the world. I had no garden, and no intention of trying to make one. I would walk along the moats outside the town, where it is not muddy. I used to go to the house of a gentleman called Matomenis, whose house is in a suburb, and who has a rather pretty garden and fine avenues; taking a good deal of exercise was very good for my health, for I did not suffer from my sore throats; I merely had a slight cold. Mme de Rambures, who was in residence, often came to see me; there were a lot of tolerable ladies in the district, and many noblemen and women; my court was large. Actors came and offered themselves, but I no longer had a mind for that; I was beginning to lose my taste for it. I read; I embroidered; letter-writing days took up time; all these things made it go by imperceptibly. I went to compline nearly every day; I began to go to high mass on saints' days and Sundays. There are two convents here — the Ursulines and the Hospitallers — to which I went. At that time, I did not visit the hospital. I was afraid of catching the fever. I had a general hospital established for the poor children of the town; in short, I spent the winter quietly.

[In 1664, she was allowed to return to court. Her memoirs rapidly recount the next five-and-a-half years up to the beginning of 1670. Needing a residence in Paris, she settled a dispute with her stepmother and acquired the right to share the Luxembourg. She writes of the final illness of Anne of Austria, the court's sojourns in Versailles, Fontainebleau, and other places, her own visits to Forges, and she makes the first reference to a 'M. de Péguilin', to whom the king gave the command of a regiment of dragoons. Her half-sister married the young duc de Guise and, she adds — in a passage that has some bearing on what was to follow — that the king denied that it had been his idea, claiming only to have permitted it. The conquest of Flanders — in which Péguilin distinguished himself — and that of Franche-Comté are briefly mentioned, as are various births, marriages, and deaths and the arrest of the chevalier de Lorraine, Monsieur's favourite. Gradually, Péguilin starts to be referred to by the name she will use for him during the rest of her memoirs: Lauzun.]

Chapter 3
Lauzun and the Journey to Flanders (1670)

As man cannot leave well alone and has a fickle mind, I began to be weary of my condition, though a happy one, and to wish to be married. I turned it over in my mind (for I spoke to no one about it), saying to myself: 'It is not a vague idea; it must have some object'; and I could not find out who it was. I thought and thought, all to no purpose. At last, after racking my brains for some days, I became aware that it was M. de Lauzun whom I loved, who had stolen into my heart. I regarded him as the most gentlemanly man in the world, and the most agreeable, and I felt that nothing was lacking to my happiness but to have a husband like him, whom I should dearly love, and who would love me in return; that no one had ever shown me affection; and that it was necessary, once in one's life, to enjoy the sweetness of being loved by someone who was worth being loved. I realized that I found more pleasure in seeing him and conversing with him than usual, and that I found the days on which I did not see him irksome. I believed that the same idea had occurred to him, and that he did not dare tell me so; but that the frequency of his visits to the queen, and of our encounters in the courtyard when she went out, and in the galleries, in short, wherever one could meet by chance, were a sufficient indication of it.

I was delighted to be alone in my room [at Saint-Germain]; I planned what I could do for him to give him a lofty station; but I felt that the qualities that fitted him to occupy it worthily exceeded anything I could do. I indulged myself with these thoughts, and I was delighted to see, from the esteem he enjoyed in society, that it was not bias that made me see all I am saying, but that it was the truth. I convinced myself of it, and I remembered some lines of Corneille's that I had formerly seen in one of his plays and had never forgotten, but for which I sent to Paris in great haste, and which I have often reread since. Here they are:

> Quand les ordres du ciel nous ont faits l'un pour l'autre,
> Lyse, c'est un accord bientôt fait que le nôtre:
> Sa main entre les cœurs, par un secret pouvoir,
> Sème l'intelligence avant que de se voir;
> Il prépare si bien l'amant et la maîtresse
> Que leur âme au seul nom s'émeut et s'intéresse.
> On s'estime, on se cherche, on s'aime en un moment.

> Tout ce qu'on s'entre-dit persuade aisément;
> Et sans s'inquiéter d'aucunes peurs frivoles,
> La foi semble courir au-devant des paroles:
> La langue en peu de mots en explique beaucoup,
> Les yeux, plus éloquents, font tout voir tout d'un coup,
> Et de quoi qu'à l'envi tous les deux nous instruisent,
> Le cœur en entend plus que tous les deux n'en disent.[213]

[When for each other God's will has made us, | Union between us, Lyse, is soon achieved. | God's hand, with secret power, attunes two hearts | E'en before they meet. He so well prepares | Mistress and lover that their very names | Arouse their souls and kindle sympathy. | At once they feel esteem, affection, love. | Whatever one says, persuades the other; | And, heedless of imaginary fears, | Trust appears to haste to bid speech welcome. | The tongue explains a great deal in few words; | The eyes, more eloquent, reveal the whole all at once; | And yet, let tongue and eyes vie as they may, | The heart divines far more than they can say.]

These verses appeared to suit me admirably, so they often occupied my memory and my mind, and they are engraved in my heart. They can be turned in all ways. They are Christian, though from a play. Nothing better can be said about the predestination of marriages or God's foreknowledge than they say, and one can find a good moral in them and meditate upon them; I have certainly often thought of them in church. They are the most elegant and touching in the world; but one turns everything as one wants, and we view everything through the preoccupations of our heart. I owe thanks to God for the inclinations He has given mine, and the way He has made it. I reflected how much he [Lauzun] would owe me; how glorious that would be for me; who would praise me and who would blame me; the pleasure of remaining in my native land, where there were so few above me, which must cure me of the regret I might have at not being a queen in foreign countries, the kings of which were not like M. de Lauzun. As for sovereigns, I thought that being the subject of such a great king as ours outweighed sovereigns. In short, one day I would consider everything that, in my purpose, could give me all conceivable satisfaction: I would find great pleasure in depriving my heirs of the expectation of having my property and wishing for my death. Another day, I would look for all the drawbacks I could and everything that would be said to condemn what I wanted to do. I

---

[213] Corneille, *La Suite du Menteur*, Act IV, scene 1, lines 1221–34.

would speak to him only in the presence of a third person, of very indifferent things; never two consecutive remarks. But the sight of him would persuade me and destroy the resolutions of the day on which I was out of love.

As I was often with Madame [Henrietta Anne] and she liked him very much, I longed to speak to her of my intention, being convinced that she would approve of it; but I did not dare; I prepared her indirectly for it as much as I could. At last, after I had frequently turned the pros and cons over in my mind, my heart decided the matter, and it was at the Recollects' monastery that I finally made my mind up. A novena was being held at the Recollects' for the canonization of St Peter of Alcantara. The queen went every day; the sacred host was exhibited. Never have I gone to church with so much devoutness, and those who observed me found me very much absorbed; for assuredly I was quite engrossed, and I think God inspired me to do what He wanted me to do.

Next day, 2 March, I was very merry; I chatted a good deal with him when we met; he appeared very merry to me; I do not know if he saw what was in my heart. I was dying to give him an opportunity to tell me what his felt for me. I did not know how to do it. At last, a rumour reached me that the king was giving Lorraine back, and that he wanted to marry me to Prince Charles. I said to myself: 'Here is a lucky chance to give M de Lauzun an opportunity to speak to me.' I sent to his room for him; I was told that he was not there. As he was very friendly with M de Guitry, he was often in his room. Guitry had recently furnished it in an extraordinary manner, for he was extraordinary in everything he possessed, and I had told him that I should go and see it. I left my room, saying: 'The queen is at prayer; I shall have time to see Guitry's room.' I went; he was not there. Going downstairs, I went to the queen's apartments. I found M. de Lauzun talking to the comtesse de Guiche; I said to him: 'I am delighted to have found you; I had sent for you; I have something important to tell you.' The comtesse de Guiche said to me: 'You shall have him when you wish; but for my part, while I have him, I entreat you to leave him with me.' He said to me: 'It will only take a moment.' My heart beat, and I think that his beat fast, too, and that he divined from my expression that I had nothing but what was agreeable to say to him. He looked at me constantly as he was talking to the comtesse de Guiche. So it seemed to me, at least.

When he left her, I went up to him, and took him to a window. His haughtiness and his air made him look like the emperor of the whole world to me. I began: 'For some time you have been showing me such friendship that it has given me the utmost confidence in you, and I will no longer do anything without your opinion.' He told me that he was much obliged to me for the honour I was doing him; that he felt the utmost gratitude for it; and that he wished I could see into his heart, and I should see that I was not mistaken in the good opinion I was doing him the honour to have of him. We exchanged a great many, most affectionate, remarks; then I began: 'It is rumoured that the king wants to marry me to the Prince of Lorraine; have you heard about it?' He said no, and that he was sure the king would want only what I wanted; he would not compel me. I said to him: 'At my age, people are very rarely married against their will. Hitherto, many matches have been suggested for me; I have always listened to everything; but, when it came to the point, I should have been in despair if they had come off. I love my country, I am such a great lady in it that my ambition can be restricted to it, and when one has reason, one must be satisfied with it, and seek happiness in life; one cannot have any with a man one does not know. Unless he is well-bred, one does not esteem him; for my part, I cannot love anyone I do not esteem.' He said: 'You have very reasonable feelings, of which one can only approve; but you are so happy! Would you think of marrying?' I said: 'I am truly happy; but it drives me mad when I hear people enumerating the prospective heirs of my property.' 'Ah!' said he, 'that would make me despair, and nothing would make me want to be married so much as that.' The queen came. He said to me: 'I want to take advantage of the honour you are doing me in trusting me, and there are too many things to say on such an important subject for us not to take it up again where we left off.' I thought to myself: that is a great step forward, and he can no longer be in doubt about my feelings; at the first opportunity, I shall know his. I was very pleased with myself and what I had done.

Next day, when the queen had dined, he came up to me and said: 'Everything that has passed through my head since I had the honour of seeing you would make a book: I have been building many castles in the air.' 'So have I,' said I, 'but everything we have been considering might come true.' He said: 'Oh! I do not think so!' 'But let us talk seriously,' said I, 'because all this matters a great deal to me.' He laughed and said: 'I shall be very vain if I am your counsellor in chief; I shall think highly of myself.' 'And all the more so,' said I, 'since your advice will be followed and not contested; for I shall speak to no one about all this. I mistrust everyone, and I am convinced that you alone will advise me truly and without any interests save my own. Let us come to the point.' 'Your last remark,' said he, 'was that what first gave you the idea of marrying was the annoyance you feel on hearing: *so and so will have this estate; someone else another*. I consider this very just; for we must live as long as we can and not love those who wish for our deaths. For the idea that you had thought: *I shall get married because I have found someone I like*, can occur to nobody, since there is nobody in the world who could deserve you. So I find you in a quandary, and I pity your state of mind, and I think you are very lucky to have found in me someone with whom you can sometimes give vent to your feelings; for I can see clearly that you have long been looking in vain for someone worthy of the honour of your confidence. I esteem myself the happiest of all men for this choice, and I make so bold as to tell you that you will be very satisfied, and that I shall make it my pleasure and my only joy after the king's service; it shall be my study. You must quit the state that worries you. You have nothing to wish for as regards rank, estates, or position; in these respects, you are highly favoured. You are esteemed and honoured for your virtue and your good qualities as much as for your rank; how pleasant to be indebted to oneself for that. The king treats you admirably; he loves you; I can see that he enjoys your company. What have you to wish for? If you had been a queen or empress, you would have been very bored; these positions are not much above you, and offer more trouble and less enjoyment. Remain here, then, all your life, with all the pleasures and all the advantages you enjoy here. If you want to be married, you have the means of making a man equal in greatness and power to sovereigns. He will know, in addition, that you will have the pleasure of having done it, and that he will be indebted to you for it; he will depend on the king, who has a liking for you, and will hold his greatness from him as from you; which is another pleasure for you, from the affection you have for the king and the connection between his greatness and yours, which touches you so deeply. I need not say what a man must be like to possess such an honour; for one who pleases you and is chosen by you, will be an admirable man. He will have no shortcomings; but where is he? All this is fine; but I am afraid, as I have said, that it is a castle in the air, from the impossibility of finding anyone who can please you.' I laughed. I think that the joy with which I was listening to him was a great joy to him. I said: 'All this is feasible, and I shall take your advice.'

This conversation lasted a good two hours, and, if the queen had not come out of her oratory, I think it would have lasted a good deal longer. I was very glad; I think he was, too. We spoke to each other in passing nearly every day; but he rarely came up to me; it was I who went up to him. A few days later, I said to him 'Well?' He said: 'I have thought of a host of difficulties.' Our conversation completely ruined the thing; that day he pointed out nothing but drawbacks and difficulties. It displeased me; but it had no effect. It was clear to me that he did not believe what he was saying, and that it was to see what I should say.

Our subsequent conversations were few and far between. We spoke to each other only once a week or fortnight; afterwards, they became even rarer. I said to him: 'I have given a good deal of thought to what you said; but I can find remedies for everything,' and I told him what they were. We would keep coming back to the subject, and he would say: 'If I do not always agree with you and argue with you, do not let that put you off me; the fact is, I am speaking sincerely to you, and I do not want to flatter you in a matter in which your salvation and the peace of your life are at stake. I am going to say things to you that are disagreeable and may displease you: I think you are right to come to some decision, since nothing in the world is so ridiculous as to see a spinster of forty, whatever her rank, dressed for entertainments and in society like a giddy fifteen-year-old. When a woman is that age, she must become a nun, or turn devout, or dress modestly, and go to nothing. Because of your rank, you might, once in a while, in order to do your duty as a courtier, go to an opera, and even then it would not have to be all the time, and you should wait to be asked insistently, not show that you were pleased or enjoy it, praise nothing, to show that you were not paying attention; and you might go to vespers, to sermons, to benediction, to meetings of the poor, and to hospitals, and only do your duty to the queen, which your rank obliges you to, on such occasions; or you might get married. For, being married, a woman at all ages goes everywhere; she dresses like everyone else, to please her husband. She goes to entertainments because he wants her to behave like other women; but this husband seems to me very hard to find; and perhaps, if you were to find one to your fancy, he would have faults that would make you miserable. That is why I do not know what to say.'

We broke off at that point, for someone would always come and interrupt us, or the queen would come out. He did not come to my room, and I did not dare to tell him to come, being quite sure that he knew what he was doing. I was not in doubt which course to choose: I considered that he was right in what he said, and that I had to choose one of the three, and I realized that, knowing my intentions, it was not for him to say directly: 'Take me', that it was up to me to understand him, that I did understand very well, and that he was giving me great pleasure. I should have liked him to speak more plainly, being rather eager to settle the matter; but I have since learned what consideration he had for me, and how grateful I should be to him for the moderation which no one but he would have had in a situation in which the stake was a great future, of a kind one does not usually risk losing by dilly-dallying. [...]

A journey to Flanders was talked of, and though it was peace time, the king was not going without a body of troops. He announced that M. de Lauzun was to be in command. I was in Paris; I heard the news, which gave me great pleasure, and when I congratulated him, he said: 'I rather thought that would give you genuine pleasure.' I was accustomed to come here in Holy Week, and to stay for a fortnight or three weeks. That year I said nothing about coming to Paris, and all my people kept asking: 'When are we leaving?' They gave me accounts of what I was having done here. I cared nothing at all about it; they were amazed. In Holy Week, however, I made up my mind to set out for Paris on Good Friday after tenebrae, to spend Easter there; and as the king and queen were to come on Easter Tuesday, since the dauphin was to be godfather — and I godmother — to Mlle de Valois,[214] I stayed till then. On Friday, before I left, while we were waiting for tenebrae, we had a long conversation. We spoke of nothing but religious matters; he spoke about them admirably, as he did of everything when he wanted, for he is eloquent naturally, being no scholar. He said to me: 'Confess that you are going to be bored in Paris.' I admitted it. I said goodbye to him.

I left on Easter Saturday; I went to see about a lawsuit; Mme de Rambures came with me and talked incessantly about him; that gave me great pleasure. On Easter Monday, I met him in the street; you

---

[214] The younger daughter of Philippe d'Orléans (Monsieur) and Henrietta Anne.

cannot know what joy I felt, and he seemed to feel, as our two coaches passed each other.

Their Majesties came to the christening on the Tuesday; they dined with Monsieur, and I went back with them. I told M. de Lauzun how bored I had been in Paris, and he said: 'But you used not to be bored there; how comes that? Let us look for the reason. You used to have nothing on your mind; now you have something, and you would not dare to talk about that something to anyone but me; so you are bored because you are not seeing me. That would be a great honour for me, if it were known without the reason; for as soon as that were known, it would be obvious that it has nothing to do with me.' Such was his playful talk.

[She returned to Paris for medical treatment.]

I stayed as little as possible in Paris, where I was terribly bored; I now understood the reason, and I was mortally afraid that someone would guess it. I made only one more brief visit to Paris before the journey [to Flanders]. On the way back, I met M. de Lauzun's baggage train, which was setting off. It filled the whole of the rue Saint-Honoré; it was very handsome and magnificent. I thought to myself: 'Next year, it will be even finer.' I told him that I had seen it and what I thought of it; he smiled.

After leaving [on 28 April], we spent the first night at Senlis and the next at Compiègne, where I chatted with him a little; but Guitry was with us the whole time. I asked him: 'When you are at the head of your army, will you not come here any more?' He told me that he would come as often as he could. Next day, at Noyon [half way between Compiègne and Saint-Quentin], I spoke to him a little alone; I said: 'Are my affairs to remain in abeyance? Shall I not know what my decision is to be until I am back from the country? Will you leave me in the quandary that you told me you pitied so?' He said: 'We must think of nothing but the journey.' While the queen was at play, the king was walking in the garden; I was at the window; the king said to me: 'Are you not coming out for a stroll?' I was dying to go, but the queen would have complained. I contented myself with speaking to him every time he turned round, saying a casual word to M. de Lauzun, who looked towards the window more than at those to whom he was speaking. He came up to the queen's apartments with the king and told me that he was setting out very early in the morning to go and assemble the troops that were due to arrive. He came to meet the king nearly a mile from Saint-Quentin, splendidly attired, with a large number of officers following him. I turned my head right round to look at him, for he was on the king's side, and I on the queen's. The day we spent at Saint-Quentin, I went to mass with the queen. [...] On entering, I found M. de Lauzun in the anteroom, elegantly and splendidly dressed. Rochefort was there, too, dying with jealousy of him. I curtseyed to them and called to Rochefort, and said: 'One does not dare to approach the general of an army.' He came up to me, laughing, and we chatted for a moment quite normally, Rochefort, he, and I. The king went to the camp in the afternoon. I was at the queen's window. M. de Lauzun left a little earlier. I saw with pleasure M. de Soubise come and take an order from him; he doffed and donned his hat, while M. de Soubise held his in his hand. This air of authority became him very well. If he had seen that I was watching him, I think it would have given him pleasure; but he had the pleasure of hearing about it in the evening; I did not fail to tell him.

The next day, we left Saint-Quentin at seven in the morning in frightful weather. We dined badly, it being a Saturday when there was no fish or even fresh butter or eggs, and the bread was not baked; and yet we were very merry. For my part, everything pleased me: this journey seemed made for me; I thought that everyone was bent only on pleasing me, counting M. de Lauzun as everyone and all the rest as nothing, save the king, who has always been more than everything to me. And if I had not had these feelings, born with me, he would have instilled them into me, so strong are they in his heart.

We encountered frightful roads, dead horses, mules that had fallen into the mud and lost their loads, carts stuck in the mire, in short, all the mishaps that befall vehicles in bad weather. What greatly displeased me was that he was on horseback and drenched. At the end of the day, the king complained of the distance and the bad roads. I was afraid that M. de Lauzun might be blamed and accused of lack of foresight, but the king said that M. de Louvois had planned the route.

When we approached Landrecies an hour after dark, the son of Roncherolles, its governor, came and said that the river was so swollen that it could not be forded safely; and that Bouligneux had nearly been drowned there, and had climbed on to the roof of his coach.²¹⁵ He related many other incidents of this kind to show how dangerous it was to think of using the ford. It was said that there was another one, three miles away, very safe. We had scarcely any torches. Two or three were given out. Before going to the river, the king mounted on horseback. The queen was very much afraid; so was I. As I am afraid of water, I go out of my wits as soon as I see it; I screamed loudly. The queen was worried about her women, and I about mine and my maids of honour, who were in my coach with my jewels. In short, there was a good deal of noise, which upset the king. When we saw that we could not cross, we went back to the main road; we found a wretched cottage in a meadow; the queen alighted. It was ten o'clock. We had a wax candle. The queen insisted on going into another room (there were two); Mme de Béthune, holding the light, helped her. I followed, holding her train. I sank knee-deep into the ground. The queen said: 'Cousin, you are pulling me.' I said: 'Madam, I have sunk into a hole; wait till I have pulled myself out.' I was all wet, and it all dried on me. The queen was very uneasy. The king said: 'We must wait till daylight and rest in the coaches.' They were unyoked; I had mine furnished with the cushions from the others. I put a bonnet and mobcaps on my head, and my dressing gown over my dress. I unlaced myself a little. I could not sleep, for there was a frightful din.

I heard Monsieur's voice; I sent someone to see where he was. I was told that his coach was quite close, and that Madame and Mme de Thiange were with him and asking me to go and visit them. I had myself carried to them. Madame, who was delicate and in poor health, was in low spirits. Mme de Thiange was chatting. Monsieur was talking to the marquis de Villeroy,²¹⁶ saying: 'Nothing would induce me to make such an exhibition of myself as M. de Lauzun did just now. He looked dreadful with his wet hair; I have never seen such a horrible man.' The marquis de Villeroy answered in the same vein, and I thought to myself: 'And I find him handsome in whatever state he is in, and he does not care about pleasing you, and I think he is well aware that he pleases me.' Monsieur did not like him. The marquis de Villeroy had once had a quarrel with him; I think it was over Mme de Monaco, and M. de Lauzun had treated him very haughtily. They had had nothing to do with each other since.

---

²¹⁵ Landrecies is about 45 kilometres north-east of Saint-Quentin, on the River Sambre.
²¹⁶ Son of Marshal Villeroy.

I got bored there and went back to my coach. Someone came and said: 'The king and queen are about to eat.' We were dying of hunger. I had myself carried there, for it was impossible to walk through the mud without boots. I found the queen very querulous, saying that she would be ill if she did not sleep; what pleasure was there in such journeys? The king said to her: 'Mattresses have just been brought; Remenecourt has a brand new bed on which you will be able to sleep.' She said: 'That would be horrible! What? All sleep together!' The king said: 'What? Fully dressed on mattresses, is there any harm in that? I see none. Ask my cousin; we can put it to her and do as she says.' I could see no objection to ten or twelve women being in a room with the king and Monsieur. The queen agreed.

The king went down to see to everything; food was brought. The meal came from Landrecies; there was soup without any meat in it. The queen said it looked unappetizing, and she did not want any. It was so cold that it would have congealed if it had been cooked enough; but the broth was very thin. The king commanded us to eat with him, so Monsieur, Madame, and I set to with a will, with the greed that comes from great hunger. When nothing was left, the queen said: 'I wanted some, and it is all gone'; and was rather cross. We felt like laughing; but a dish was brought, on which there were all sorts of highly unappetizing roast meats, so tough that two of us would take hold of a chicken by the legs and, pulling with all our might and main, find it hard to tear it apart. The meal went off in this way. Then we went into the bedroom, in which a fire had been lit. The queen lay down on the bed by the fireside, and turned herself so that she could see the whole room. The king said to her: 'You have only to keep your curtains open, and you will see us all.' Mme de Thiange and Mme de Béthune were on a mattress beside the queen's bed; then there were three close together, for there was no room for them to be apart: Monsieur was first, then Madame, the king, I, Mlle de la Vallière,[217] and Mme de Montespan; and another at right angles, on which were the duchesse de Créqui, the marquise de la Vallière, and one of the queen's maids of honour, La Marck. The king and Monsieur, like us, put on their dressing gowns over their clothes and

---

[217] Mademoiselle uses a number of styles to refer to Louise de la Vallière. They include 'mademoiselle de la Vallière', 'la duchesse de la Vallière', 'madame la duchesse de la Vallière', and just 'La Vallière'. Here (and elsewhere), she writes 'madame de la Vallière', a style that is correct for both Louise and her sister-in-law Gabrielle, the marquise. In order to avoid confusion, we always call Louise 'Mlle de la Vallière', irrespective of Mademoiselle's choice of style.

their nightcaps, and we had a few blankets and coats. In the room behind were the principal officials of the king, and M. de Lauzun. People kept coming and asking for him the whole time. At last, the king said: 'Make a hole through to the other room, so that you can give your orders without coming through here.' Once, as he passed through, he had to leap over the corner of one of the beds; he caught one of his spurs in the head-dress of the marquise de la Vallière; that made everyone laugh, except the queen. Then, all of a sudden, hearing cows and asses in a cowshed behind us, Mme de Thiange said: 'This makes me feel religious, because it reminds me of the birth of Our Lord.' Seeing the king in a cowshed like Him might, indeed, have made one feel religious, and the comparison was appropriate enough; but she expressed the idea comically. At that, the queen laughed; that pleased the king, who was sorry to see her grumbling. We fell asleep.

At four o'clock, M. de Louvois came to the door and went and awoke an adjutant: 'The bridge is ready,' he told him. 'Day is breaking; the king should be told.' He answered that we were asleep. I heard him and thought it better to get to the town and sleep in a bed, since that was possible. I said to the king: 'Sire, here is M. de Louvois.' The king called him in; we got up. One can imagine how we all looked, for ladies who wear a good deal of rouge are paler than the others in the morning and when they have not slept. I was the least disfigured. I am strong, and almost always ruddy when I wake up. We got into our coaches and went straight to the church. After hearing mass, the queen went to bed; she had some broth. There was some left in the pot, which I swallowed. I had no one with me; I was quite at a loss to know where to go. Someone came and told me: 'A coach is here waiting for you.' I was very glad. I asked whose it was. I was told: 'Mme de Chetrupe, the wife of a Swiss captain who is here, has sent it for you.' I got in. It took me to my lodging, where I found dinner ready, and my bedroom hung with tapestries, but I had no women or clothes to go to bed. [...] My women arrived; I went to bed at seven. When I awoke at three or four o'clock, I found myself in the ugliest room in the world, which I had been far too sleepy to notice in the morning. My maids of honour told me: 'We are very angry with M. de Lauzun: he let your women over the bridge an hour before he let troops march past; he sent for them.' I said: 'He was quite right; he thought that I needed them to go to bed, and that I should go to sleep sooner. I am grateful to him for this attention.' He never let slip any opportunity of showing his attentiveness to me. As soon as I was dressed, I went to the queen's apartments, into which he was coming. He chided me severely for having shown fear; he said that it had distressed the king, and that, for his part, it had distressed him greatly; and he told me to watch myself in future. In short, he gave me a thousand lessons, from which I have tried to profit, the better to please the king. I told him how worried I had been by those bad roads, and by his worry. You may judge how he received all that.

[The court remained in Landrecies from 4 to 6 May, and then went to Avesnes,[218] where, on the evening of its arrival, the following conversation took place, just as Lauzun was about to go and see the Venetian ambassador, Morosini.]

I said to him: 'I can think of nothing more enjoyable than commanding an army. In peace time, no one can be in command of a larger one, and I, who am afraid for my friends, would rather see you at the head of this one than of a larger one.' As that did not tally with his own inclinations, he said: 'What you are saying is pitiful; you should pity me for not playing a different part. Not that this command, such as it is, is not above me, because of the manner in which the king gave it to me; but as I have to go to my troops, and to be with them morning and evening, and as that robs me of a great many moments I should like to employ better, I am furious at being with them.' I said: 'But how could they be better employed? Tell me how.' He said nothing.

He said: 'In my present state, I feel more like going and throwing myself into a hermitage than remaining in the world; I catch glimpses of such fine and great prospects here! and if they come to nothing, I shall die of disappointment; I should do better to turn my back on them by some such retreat. Everyone would say that I was mad, but I should know very well that I am not.' I said: 'I confide all my affairs in you; tell me something about yours.' He replied: 'I have none.' I asked him: 'Will you never think of getting married? And have you never in your life had any ideas on the subject?' He said: 'When people have tried to suggest any to me, I have always turned away, and the only thing I should consider if I wanted to marry would be the lady's virtue: for if there were the least blemish, I should not want her, even you, who are above everything. If I could marry you, and anyone had said anything against your reputation, and your person

---

[218] Avesnes-les-Aubert, about 20 kilometres west of Landrecies in the direction of Cambrai.

did not appeal to me, I should refuse you.' I said: 'Are you speaking the truth? For if that were so, I should love you even more.' 'Yes, I am and nothing would shock me more than to hear it said that I would take a woman whose life was not what an honest girl's should be. I had rather marry your chambermaid, if I loved her; I should give up society; I should shut myself up in my house, and live there honourably.' I said: 'But you would accept me, for I am good, and I have nothing that displeases you.' 'Let us not tell Ass's Skin stories,[219] when we are talking seriously.' 'But to come back to me: when will you allow me to come to a decision and quit the state which, as you tell me every day, fills you with pity?' 'You forget that my ambassador is waiting for me.'

Rochefort came in as we were at the door; he said to him: 'You come at the right time to talk to Mademoiselle; you will do it more agreeably than I.' I told him [Lauzun] that I had heard him passing by my windows with the troops in Landrecies at two in the morning; that when the trumpets had woken me up, I had cursed them roundly; but that when I had heard him speaking, I had felt sorry for him for being out in the rain, and had thought: 'I am luckier than he, although I am awake; I must not complain. He is more to be pitied than I; he has the rain to put up with as well.' He seemed to me to be satisfied both with himself and with me when he saw that I was so taken up with him. For all his impatience to go, he stayed another hour talking to Rochefort. He had been talking to me for two or three hours. [...]

The morning we left Avesnes, as the troops were in the town before marching off, they had to be assembled in the square. I was lodging in a house with balconies that looked on to this square. When the order to mount was sounded, I woke up; I got up quickly and went to see the troops march past. [...] M. de Lauzun kept going to and fro; he looked to see if I was there; he even spoke to me. 'You are awake early,' he said. It was only five o'clock.

[The court went to Le Quesnoy, east-north-east of Avesnes, and then turned south-west to Cateau-Cambrésis and Le Catelet, each leg of its journey constituting a distance of about 20 kilometres.]

There he came to the queen's, where we had a long conversation. I said: 'I have quite decided to be married; I have got over, in my mind,

---

[219] Clearly, Lauzun knew this fairy-tale, in French *Peau d'Âne*, long before Perrault told it in 1694.

all the difficulties you pointed out to me, and I have almost found this happy man (at least the one you call so); he lacks nothing but your approbation.' 'You make me tremble, wanting to move so quickly in such a matter; you need centuries to think it over.' 'Alas!' said I, 'when one is forty[220] and wants to do a foolish thing, one must not think so long about it; one need only see that the man one is taking is not being foolish; at least, he makes up for the woman who is committing the folly, and I am so determined that, at the next prolonged stop, I mean to speak to the king and to be married in Flanders; that will cause less of a stir than in Paris.' 'Oh! Do not! I, who am the head of your council, do not agree; I oppose it.' We talked about it for a long time; then I said: 'It is ironical that you, who do not want to be married, should prevent others.' 'If I were willing to believe in horoscopes, I might think of it; for a woman I knew told me that she had cast my horoscope, and that I should make the greatest fortune any man has ever made by marriage; she was in despair.' 'Was she not a friend of yours, then?' 'She was quite fond of me, but she was sorry not to be the woman who would make it. It is not a sign that she did not love me.' In the evening, I asked him who she was; he refused to tell me, and then said: 'Let us talk of something else.'[221]

I resumed the conversation after we had remained silent a few moments. 'But I am your friend and follow your advice so faithfully, you must follow mine. In God's name, think of what you were told; imagine the greatest ambition you can have, and pursue this match. Without being an astrologer, I am convinced that you may aim at anything, so think of something, and do not waste time; take my word for it.' He listened, with an occasional interjection, in such a way as to allow me to believe that he might end up following my advice. The king came to supper. We separated. [...]

We went to Bapaume and Arras, where we stayed; it was the rogation days; he was very strict: the fast was observed in his household. When we were staying somewhere, no one could be better dressed than he. Going to the king's mass, I met him coming out of church, followed by a large court; he came up to me, and warmly praised a new habit I had on, and a skirt. I said to him: 'What a miracle! You never seem to me to notice anything.' We went to Douai, where Madame, being present while the queen was being harangued, sat down,[222] and so did

---

[220] Almost forty-three, in fact.
[221] He told her later that it was the younger Mlle de Nemours [Marie-Françoise], who in 1666 married the King of Portugal.
[222] She was in poor health.

I; the queen noticed, and told the king. Monsieur said to me: 'The king did not approve of your sitting down; you know very well that it is wrong.' I thanked him. On arriving at Tournai, I wanted to speak to M. de Lauzun about it. As I got out of my coach, I tried to lean on him; he walked away; I nearly fell over. He sometimes did things that appeared ridiculous to those who witnessed them; but I was so confident that he had his reasons when he shunned me that I was not vexed. [...] Every evening, when he left the king, and the queen's room looked on to either the courtyard or the street, after he had mounted his horse he would look at the window, having once seen me at it, to see if I was there. He seldom failed to see me.

[They went on to Courtrai, Lille (whence Madame departed to meet her brother, Charles II, at Dover, for the signature of the treaty), Saint-Venant, Bergues,[223] and Dunkirk.]

We returned from Dunkirk to Calais, where M. Colbert, the king's ambassador in England,[224] came to see the king. In the morning, as we were setting off, someone came and said to me in the queen's apartment: 'You have not heard the news; there are a great many Englishmen here, who are saying that the King of England is getting a divorce, because his wife cannot have children, that she is being sent back to Portugal,[225] and that they are talking openly in England of your marrying the king.' This news upset me. When we were in the coach, Monsieur said: 'If I wanted, I should tell a piece of news I have heard.' The king laughed and said to Monsieur: 'I was surprised that you had not told it already.' We looked at one another. The king said: 'From the face my cousin is making, I wager she knows it.' I did not answer. Monsieur retorted: 'Nothing else has been talked of since yesterday evening.' The king said: 'I must tell her, but not as a certainty, nor as a thing anyone has had orders to tell me; but Colbert, my ambassador in England, who arrived yesterday evening, says it is public knowledge in England, and even that all the most important people of rank are saying, that the king is going to have a divorce, that the queen agrees, that she is going back to a convent, and that the King of England will marry my cousin. That is what I have heard.'

---

[223] Saint-Venant is 13 kilometres south of Hazebrouck, Bergues 9 kilometres southeast of Dunkirk.
[224] Charles Colbert, marquis de Croissy (often called Colbert-Croissy), the brother of the Controller General.
[225] In fact, Charles II did not divorce his wife, Catherine of Braganza, and she remained in England until 1692, seven years after her husband's death.

The queen said: 'But it would be horrible! What! cousin, would you accept him?' I did not answer. The king said to me: 'Answer; what do you think about it?' 'I have no will but Your Majesty's; but I do not think you would want me to do anything contrary to my conscience.' The queen said: 'What! you would leave it to the king?' The king said: 'She could; I should not want to be damned for the sake of others.' I began to weep heartily. Monsieur said: 'For my part, I think it would be excellent: the King of England is such a gentleman!' Mme de Montespan said: 'You know each other so well; he was so much in love with you! It would be charming; you would write to the king; you would give each other a host of pretty and novel presents.' The more they talked about it, the more I wept. The king said: 'But to weep about a rumour!' I said to him: 'The mere rumour of leaving Your Majesty moves me to tears.' I think there was something in it, and it was true.

[They went to Boulogne.]

Going out [of the queen's room], I met M. de Lauzun, whom I told of this rumour. He told me that he had heard of it, and even of my weeping, that I was right to feel so much affection for the king, and that he was delighted. I think he was as delighted at the part he thought he played in it.

We went to Hesdin [on 3 June; around 60 kilometres south-east of Boulogne], where the troops were all in battle order. The day the king left, M. de Lauzun saluted him at their head, and then all the troops were sent back to their garrisons, and he went and got into his coach. I met him in the evening at the queen's; he said: 'You see a man extremely glad to have taken his boots off and to have come in a coach.' I scolded him for being so lazy, and said that if he knew how well he looked at the head of his troops, he would never stir from them. Afterwards, he went to the apartments of the queen, who was at cards; I said to him, 'Now that you have no camp to go and see to, you will stay here till the king's supper.' 'I do not know.' We were at the window when he arrived. I was talking to Maulévrier, who went away when M. de Lauzun came up. He said to me: 'You were asking him if his brother, the ambassador, had told him the news from England; for at the moment you are overjoyed at it:[226] you like novelties, and this one must be pleasing to you. For my part, I very much approve of your inclination to be a great queen in a country

---
[226] Maulévrier was the brother of Colbert-Croissy and Jean-Baptiste Colbert.

in which you can serve the king, and there is nothing in my power that I would not do to help. I greatly honour the King of England: he is a perfect gentleman, and a friend of the king's. After that, can you doubt that I passionately hope for this marriage?'

He did not mean what he was saying; but although he says he does not like talking, he is, of all men, the one who says the most seemingly futile things when he wants to get people to talk; but he does not mean them to be. I replied: 'If I wanted it so much, I should not have done what I did yesterday, but you know so well that what you are saying is the opposite of the truth, that I shall not bother to answer you.'

I think that all the noblemen at court went by as we were at that window. We fell to examining them, their figure, their air, their looks, and their intelligence: in short, we said what we felt about them all. After that, he said: 'So far as I can see, you will not choose one of them.' 'Certainly not. I should like him to go by and to be able to show him to you. Let us consider everybody who is left here and has not gone by.' He said: 'Charost, who is beside the king.' The comte d'Ayen[227] came in; I said: 'There is another who will not go past. You must look round: there are still one or two others.' At that, he smiled, and we changed the subject.

---

[227] Son of the duc de Noailles.

Chapter 4
The Death of Madame and its Aftermath (1670)

[The court returned to Saint-Germain on 7 June, and then went to Versailles. On the late afternoon of 29 June, Madame, who had returned from Dover, fell ill after drinking a glass of chicory water. She thought she had been poisoned. The news was brought to Versailles, and the king and the queen, accompanied by Mademoiselle and the comtesse de Soissons, went to Saint-Cloud to see her.]

On the way, we met M. Vallot [first physician to the king], who told us that it was only colic, and that the indisposition would not last and was not dangerous. That showed on the faces of everyone we saw when we arrived; for there were few mournful ones. Monsieur was upset; Madame was on a little bed that had been made up for her in her alcove, almost dishevelled (for there had not been time to do her hair for bed), her nightgown loose at the neck and on the arms, so that, thin as she was, with her pale face and her pinched nose, one would almost have taken her for a corpse, but for her cries. She said to us: 'You see what a plight I am in.' Everyone burst out weeping, at least those who were with the queen. Mme de Montespan and Mlle de la Vallière arrived. She was trying to vomit, but could not. Monsieur said to her: 'Be sick, madam, so that the bile does not suffocate you.' She was distressed to see everybody's calmness, for I have never seen anything so pitiful as her state and that in which she could see the others. She spoke softly to the king for a while. I went up to her, and took her hand; she pressed it, and said to me: 'You are losing a good friend; I was beginning to love you and know you.' I made no reply; I was weeping. She asked insistently for an emetic; the doctors, whom I told several times, said: 'It would be useless. Her complaint can only get better; these colics sometimes last for nine, ten, twenty, or twenty-four hours, not more.' The king tried to remonstrate with them. They did not know what to say, and I said to them: 'No one has ever let a woman die without trying some remedy.' They looked at one another and said nothing. People chatted in the room, and walked about; they were all but laughing.

[Madame asked for a confessor. The local priest being thought insufficiently important, it was decided to send for abbé Bossuet, who had recently been appointed Bishop of Condom.]

She asked to be put back into her bed while we were there. The king bade her farewell; he embraced her. She said many affectionate things to him, which he told us about; but I think she said some he did not tell. She embraced the queen. I said goodbye to her from the foot of the bed; I was weeping so much that I did not want to go near her.

We went back to Versailles; the queen went for supper. M. de Lauzun came at the end, and, as I rose from the table, I said to him: 'This throws us out.' He said: 'Very much so, and I am afraid that it ruins all our projects.' I said: 'Oh! No, whatever may happen.' I went to bed; the queen had said that she would go to Paris next day, and that we should see Madame on the way; but Madame died at three o'clock and the king heard at six; he decided to stop drinking his waters, and to take a purgative. I was told of her death, about which I was very sorry. I had not slept all night; I reflected: if Monsieur takes it into his head to marry me, I shall not change my mind, but it will take time to break it off decently. If the king wants it, what shall I do? In short, I was in a serious, unhappy, and painful quandary. [...]

After dinner, the king got up; he came into the queen's room as soon as he was dressed, and said to me: 'Cousin, come and let us talk of what is to be done about Madame; I must give my orders to Saintôt' (who was present).[228] The king took me into the alcove of the queen's bed, and after talking about that, he said to me: 'Cousin, there is a vacant place: do you want to fill it?' I turned as pale as death, and said: 'You are the master. I shall never have any will but yours.' He pressed me; I said to him: 'That is all I have to say.' 'But do you feel any aversion?' I said nothing. He said: 'I shall see about it and let you know what happens.' I drove out with the queen and all the while no one spoke of anything but Madame's death, of suspicions she had had about her sudden death, and of the relations between Monsieur and her; he would soon be consoled, and if he were to marry — who would it be? They looked at me. I said nothing. [...]

I saw M. de Lauzun in the evening at the queen's. I said: 'Well, are you not distressed by Madame's death? I am even sorrier, because I know she was a friend to you.' He replied: 'I am losing more by this than anyone; I am in despair.' 'And, as for me, I was very fond of her, but at this juncture I am even sorrier, because it holds up my affairs; for, as for altering them, I assure you that nothing will.' He would not

---

[228] Saintôt was the master of ceremonies.

speak to me any longer. The next day, which was the first day of July, he took up his command in the usual manner.[229]

[On the same day, Mademoiselle visited Monsieur.]

When the queen had left Mme de Montausier's room, I went to see Monsieur; he did not seem too distressed: he told me that he had sent to ask Mme d'Aiguillon to lend him her house at Ruel, and that in his present state, he could not stay in Paris. Next day, I went back in a mourning veil to see Mademoiselle.[230] At that time, one of the Duke of York's daughters,[231] who had very bad eyes, was staying there; she had been sent to the Queen of England to be cured, and since her death,[232] Madame had kept her. She was with Mademoiselle, both with veils; they were rather young,[233] but Monsieur is a stickler for etiquette and attaches importance to such things. Mlle de Valois, though not yet weaned, also received visitors, but had no veil.[234] I went to Saint-Germain in mine, it being respectful to see Their Majesties in these trappings of mourning. I supped; I told the king what I had done, and about the veils of Mademoiselle and the Princess of England, and that Mlle de Valois had none. He said: 'Stop mocking my brother because, if you marry him, you will have to get out of the habit.' After supper, he said: 'I have spoken to my brother; he said he welcomed the proposition I put to him, but that it was not yet time to think of getting married.'

Next day, at mass, M. de Lauzun said to me: 'So, you are marrying Monsieur.' I answered: 'I am not counting on it.' He said: 'You must; for the king wants it. At least, I shall always be the friend of a Madame: the last one did me the honour of liking me; I beg you to do the same.' 'Ah! it will not happen.' 'Yes, it will, and I shall be very glad, because I put your greatness before my joy and my fortune: I owe you too much to feel otherwise.' These words surprised me; he had never said so much; but the situation was so critical that he could not help speaking. He said: 'I request an audience of you; shall it be in your apartments or in the queen's?' I said: 'In the queen's.'

---

[229] Four captains of the guard each served for three months of the year. Lauzun's tour of duty began on 1 July.
[230] That is, Mlle d'Orléans, the elder daughter of Monsieur and the late Madame.
[231] Princess Anne, the younger daughter of James, Duke of York, and his first wife, Anne Hyde. In 1702, she would become Queen Anne.
[232] That is, the death of Henrietta Maria, in September 1669.
[233] Mlle d'Orléans was then eight years old, and Princess Anne five.
[234] Mlle d'Orléans's younger sister, born on 27 August 1669, and aged ten months.

After dinner, as soon as the king went to council, he came. He said to me: 'The king wants you to marry Monsieur; you must obey. You have done me the honour of trusting me; you must trust me even further: obey the king without reserve, without argument; only do your duty blindly; you will be the better for it. Reflect what Monsieur is; he has only the king and the dauphin above him; you will only have the queen; you will be the most esteemed woman in the world. The king and all the court would go to your house every day. There will be plays and balls, all the pleasures in short.' 'Reflect,' said I, 'that I am over fifteen, and that you are offering things suitable for children. I am convinced that the king wishes me well, that I shall always deserve his kindness by my behaviour, and that it is enough for me to be his cousin. I have my own ideas about what to do to be happy; I shall not change, say what you will.' 'You must forget the past,' said he. 'For my part, I know nothing now of what you told me; I forgot it all some time ago; I am now thinking of nothing but the pleasure it will give me to see you Madame; when you walk along this path to go to the Château-Neuf, followed by your guards, and I am at the window, I shall be delighted to see you go by. That is what fills my mind every day, and I take pleasure in thinking of your greatness, as I used to in thinking of all you had told me about the difficulties of your marriage.' The conversation lasted half an hour; he had a gay, detached air, which I thought assumed, being convinced that he could not be glad; and I, who could not always repress my feelings, I went and wept in my room.

I went to Saint-Cloud to fetch Madame's body; I took it to Saint-Denis; the princesse de Condé and Mme de Longueville came with me.

I went and slept in Paris that evening, or rather that morning, and then I returned to Saint-Germain. M. de Lauzun came and spoke to me again in the queen's apartment. He said: 'I come to entreat you most humbly not to speak to me any more. I am unlucky enough to be disliked by Monsieur, because I was the very obedient servant of the late Madame. He would think that all the objections you might raise about whatever is proposed, came from me. So, unless you have anything to say to the king in person and he can say that he knows what you are going to say to me, I shall no longer have the honour of speaking to you. Do not summon me anywhere, for I should not reply. Do not write or send anyone to me. I am in despair to have to behave like this; but it is what I must do for love of you. You must approve, therefore.' I told him that I was in despair; that I absolutely did not want to marry Monsieur; that, if I did, I should not be a greater lady than I was — the only advantage would be that I should be followed by guards; that for several years I should not sit on the folding-seat on journeys, because when the dauphin was married and Madame, the king's daughter,[235] grown up, she would sit on it; that no one would be seated in my presence; and that I should be given a place at the king's table. Apart from these four things, I said, one of which, the most comfortable, would not last, I did not care about all that; Monsieur was younger than I; I should not be any more willing than the late Madame to submit to the chevalier de Lorraine or any other favourite who took his place; I wanted to be happy and was convinced that I could not be with Monsieur.

He kept telling me that I was wrong, that I must obey, that I should be the happiest woman in the world, and that he would not speak to me any more. 'But at least give me a time when, if my marriage with Monsieur comes to nothing, you will speak to me again; for I am sure that I shall break it and I should be in despair not to talk to you.' 'Goodbye,' said he; 'it will go on as long as it pleases the king, and no one shall reproach me with having failed you in any way by my imprudence.' I said: 'But do not go. What! I shall not speak to you any more!' 'I have one more thing to say to you,' said he. 'This is the season when you usually go to Forges; I advise you to go as soon as you can. At least, if you have something in your mind, you must get rid of it now; and if the sight of someone keeps it there, and if you do not see or speak to that person, health will make you forget it; and if he knows it, he will be wise enough to do everything possible to make you forget him.' Thereupon we parted. I went and wept, and a day or two later I set out for Forges.

The king spoke to me before I left, and said: 'My brother has spoken to me; he said that he would very much like the marriage, but that it would not be seemly to be married so soon; that he must wait till the winter; but that he would be very glad if everything were signed before you went to Forges.' I said to the king: 'Sire, Monsieur will not get married without the agreement of the chevalier de Lorraine; if he does not want it, I should be sorry that a marriage signed should be broken off, and, even more, that Your Majesty, having brought it about, should be obliged to uphold it; and if Monsieur no longer wanted it, he would be at loggerheads with Your Majesty, and I should

---

[235] Marie-Thérèse de France, called 'the little Madame', born in 1667.

be the cause. I am so equal in rank to Monsieur, and he will find it so advantageous to marry me in comparison with all the princesses in Europe, that, unless Your Majesty wishes to arrange this marriage, there is no advance that Monsieur ought not to make, but he does not appear to be making any. So I hope Your Majesty will give me time to go to Forges. On my return, I shall see how Monsieur behaves, and Your Majesty's will shall be my rule in all things. I am about to go to Forges, where I shall stay for no more than the exact time needed for taking the waters.'

I do not know how they did me good, for I was very worried.

[She returned from Forges.]

I was two days at Saint-Germain without the king's mentioning the marriage with Monsieur to me. On my return, Monsieur was very polite to me; but, since Madame's death, because of everything people were saying, we had been treating each other more frigidly; for we have always lived on very familiar terms together. He went off to Paris, and the day I went there, I said to the king in the queen's oratory before dinner: 'Well, Sire, how is my marriage going?' He laughed and said: 'You are not very concerned about it.' 'I assure you, Sire, that I am, and that I am very eager for it; but the fear of boring everyone, and of being bored by it myself, makes me beg Your Majesty most humbly to hasten it on.' [...]

When I had gone back to Saint-Germain, one morning (as Monsieur was always with the king, he only spoke to me when Monsieur had gone to Paris, or in the evening when he came back to the queen's apartment; but he was usually so late that that only happened once), one morning, then, when Monsieur had gone to Paris, the king said to me: 'My brother has spoken to me; he wants you, if you have no children, to give all your property to his daughter, and he says that he very much wishes not to have any, providing he is sure that his daughter will marry my son. I told him that I advised him to have children, because that was not certain.' I laughed, and said: 'No one getting married has ever said he did not want any children. I do not know if this remark is flattering; what does Your Majesty say?' The king laughed, and said: 'He said many more ridiculous things in this connection, which I advised him, for his honour's sake, to keep to himself.' The queen said: 'Your brother is ridiculous; that is very disgusting.' The king said: 'Do you want me to say this?' He was mocking me a little. I said to the king: 'As for giving my property to bring about a marriage with the dauphin, I do not think the dauphin will marry for property, and I do not think Your Majesty would want this article inserted in the contract. Although I am not young, I am not too old to have children. Propositions of that kind are made to very inferior creatures; so Your Majesty will allow me to say that they are not agreeable to me.'

The king said to me: 'At least, before you marry my brother, I shall tell you (for I do not want to deceive you) that I shall never give him a governorship, so that, if one were to fall vacant, you should not tell him to ask for it, and that I shall not give one to persons attached to him or at his request. All the favours I shall grant him will go through you, in order that he shall esteem you — for example, occasional gifts of money, jewellery, and furniture, but nothing else.' I said: 'Knowing how eager I am for this marriage, Your Majesty is adding all conceivable inducements to make me want it even more; so I shall certainly follow my inclination and conclude it.'[236]

'By the way,' said the king, 'is it true that, when Madame died, you were to tell me next day that you wanted to get married and to ask for my approval?' 'If Your Majesty was told that, it is true; if not, not.' The queen asked: 'What does that mean?' The king laughed, and said: 'I do not know. Is it M. de Longueville?'[237] I said: 'No.' 'Who could it be? for you would only marry a prince.' The king said nothing. I said to the queen: 'I have the means to make a greater lord, if I wish, than a younger son of the house of Lorraine, and should give a better gentleman and one who would serve the king better than M. de Guise;[238] and since he consented to that marriage, I dare to hope that I shall do what I want, and that he will not force me.' The king said: 'No, indeed; I shall let you do whatever you want, and I shall never force anyone.' The queen said: 'But what is the point of all this? And the marriage with Monsieur?' I said: 'Your Majesty knows very well that the king is amusing himself and telling Your Majesty and me incomprehensible stories to puzzle us; for I genuinely want, Sire, to marry Monsieur, and if Your Majesty does not bring it about, I shall have reason to complain. I beseech you to give your mind to it.' 'Let us dine,' replied he.

---

[236] These sentiments may appear somewhat surprising. In fact, alarmed at the apparent cooling of Lauzun's ardour, Mademoiselle was making a pretence of wishing for the marriage to Monsieur. It does not seem to have fooled anyone.

[237] Charles-Paris, comte de Saint-Pol, duc de Longueville. His biological father was La Rochefoucauld.

[238] Louis-Joseph de Lorraine, the husband of her half-sister, Mlle d'Alençon.

Seven or eight days later, the king went to Colombes,[239] a house that Madame had inherited from the Queen of England, where he dined, and, on the way back, in the evening, he said: 'My brother is very keen on this match; he would like the contract to be drawn up. I told him that he must wait till we got back from Chambord; do you not agree?' 'Certainly, Sire; the later, the better, as always.' [...]

On St Francis's day, I was coming back from confession; I was going to the queen's apartments to go to mass with her. M. de Lauzun was coming out of his room to attend the king's *levée*.[240] When he saw that no one was about, he followed me, for we were going the same way. I said: 'You are very bold to dare to speak to me; true, no one can see us.' 'Where are you going so early?' said he. 'You can see very well,' said I. 'Tell me about my match; shall I soon marry Monsieur?' He said: 'I hear nothing about it, but I think so. Everybody says you are very eager and importune the king every day.' ' I want it,' I said, 'as much as on the first day.' 'But you are talking to me when you are coming from confession and about to take communion; is that right?' 'Oh, there is no time when I do not speak to *you*; I shall never have any qualms, you being to me what you are.' He said: 'I do not understand.' 'I understand very well, and I hope that soon you will understand better; because I am sick and tired of all this.' He said no more, and we went our different ways.

We left for Chambord. [...] We enjoyed ourselves very much at Chambord: there was a play every day,[241] we went hunting, and there were cards; but I was very sorry that there are no walks, because I like walking. Usually I only played for jewels; one day we played for watches, Mme de Montespan, Mlle de la Vallière, M. de Lauzun, and I; he never looked in my direction. A ribbon on my wristband came loose; I told him to tie it. He answered that he was not deft enough. Mlle de la Vallière did it; nothing was so amusing, and I am astounded that no one noticed the affectations by means of which he avoided speaking to me or looking at me.

News came that the dauphin had fever again — he had had it long before we went to Chambord; that made the king resolve to return, and to set off two days later. I did not waste time. In the evening, I

---

[239] Colombes lies in a loop of the Seine east of Saint-Germain. Henrietta Maria had died there. The king gave her property to her daughter Henrietta Anne, after whose death it passed to her husband, Monsieur.
[240] The ceremony of the king's getting up in the morning.
[241] By no means every day; but Molière and his company gave the premiere of *Le Bourgeois gentilhomme* at Chambord.

waited for the king in the queen's apartment; I drew him aside and said: 'Your Majesty said that the question of Monsieur and me would be postponed till we got back from this journey; I should be very glad to have it settled; I honour Monsieur as I should; and I am deeply grateful for the honour Your Majesty has done me in trying to arrange this marriage. But I should not be happy, for a host of reasons known to Your Majesty; so I beg you to let it be spoken of no more.' 'What! do you want me to tell my brother?' 'Yes, Sire.' 'What! do you want me to tell him that you never want to get married?' 'No, Sire, but that I do not want to marry him, that we shall be on good terms with each other like cousins, as God willed us to be born; but that we must stop there.' 'I shall tell him,' said the king, and said nothing more, and did not appear to be annoyed. [...]

Next day [...] he called to me, and said: 'I told my brother what you said to me; he was quite taken aback, and said: "So she said she would never get married?" "No, she did not say that; but to you." That annoyed him.' [...]

We set off for Saint-Germain. In the coach I was beside him. He simpered and made wonderful remarks, as a child would have done. I said nothing, and smiled at the king. The queen was disappointed, for she wants people to be married and have children, and does not consider whether the marriages are suitable or not. On the road, M. de Lauzun shunned me.

On arriving at Saint-Germain, he went on doing so.

Chapter 5
The Match Made (1670)

We went for a couple of days to Versailles, where M. de Lauzun shunned me as usual. That displeased me. Finally, one day when he was at his door as I went by, I stopped and said: 'The marriage with Monsieur is off, thank God; I may speak to you, and I want to talk to you.' He said: 'Whenever you like.' 'I will see you tomorrow in the queen's apartments.' He did not fail to come; I related everything that had happened, though he seemed to know about it already. He very much approved of my behaviour, and thought everything I had done was right. I told him that I must go back to my original plan, pursue it, and carry it out; that it was something so firmly fixed in my mind that I could not doubt that it was the repose of my life and the state in which God wanted me to achieve my salvation. He advised me strongly not to hurry, and to examine everything carefully. We talked about it once more; then I told him that I wanted to tell him the name of the man I had chosen. He said: 'This choice makes me tremble; for, if I do not approve of it, determined as I see you are, you will never want to see me, and it would be the hardest thing in the world for me to lose the honour of your good graces. Equally, betraying my heart, and not telling you what I think, is something I cannot do; but, perhaps, without meaning it, I shall do a bad turn to the best of your friends by delaying his very great happiness. In short, I am so disturbed by all this that I almost feel like entreating you not to speak to me any more about it.' The more he resisted, the more I begged him to advise me.

At last, one day he came to the queen's apartments; it was a Thursday, after supper; he was passing through the anteroom on his way to the king. I called to him, and said: 'I want to tell you definitely who it is.' He said: 'Wait till tomorrow.' 'That cannot be, because it would be Friday.' 'Ah! I cannot tell you to your face what I think.' 'If I had a writing-desk, I should write it down for you. I am going to breathe on the looking-glass and write it.' We trifled like this for half an hour. As midnight was striking, I said: 'It cannot be told now, for it would be Friday.'

Next day, I wrote on a sheet of paper, right at the top: 'It is you', and sealed it, and put it in my pocket. That day, I did not see him till I went to supper. I said: 'I have the name in my pocket, but I do not want to give it to you on a Friday.' He said: 'Give it to me; I promise you that I shall put it under my pillow and not open it till midnight has struck; you may believe that I shall not sleep, and that I shall await that hour with great impatience. Tomorrow, I am going to Paris, and shall not get back till very late.' 'Very well, I shall wait till Sunday.'

On Sunday, I saw him at mass. He came to the queen's apartments after dinner; he chatted with me at the assembly. When the queen went away to pray, I remained with him by the fireplace. I pulled out the sheet of paper on which there was only one word that told a great deal; I showed it to him; I put it back in my pocket; I put it in my muff. He strongly urged me to give it to him, saying that his heart was beating, and that he did not know what that meant. We had half an hour's very embarrassed conversation, and, before giving it to him, I said: 'Reply as you think fit on the same sheet, and we shall talk this evening at the queen's.' [...]

In the evening, after supper, he appeared before me twice or thrice, but I had not the strength to go to him, nor he to come to me. He returned my letter; I leaned on him as I stood up. I put it in my muff. Then the queen went to M. d'Anjou,[242] and, in the meantime, I went into a closet of Marshal de La Mothe's widow to read the letter. I do not recall the exact words; but, in a few words, he complained that his zeal in my service should be rewarded by such an outrageous jest as that, that he could not flatter himself that I was thinking of that seriously, and so he dared not reply otherwise; but he was so devoted to my wishes that I should always find him very submissive. The letter was very prudent, but through it all I could see what I wanted to see, and he expressed great respect, not wanting in affection. [...]

The next day, the Monday, we went to Versailles; in the morning, before setting off, I was at the door of the queen's room; Charost and the comte d'Ayen came and spoke to me. He was by the looking-glass and did not come over. I called to him, and said: 'But you are very unsociable not to come near people.' He answered: 'I did not know but what you had business with these gentlemen.' I walked up and down; the others went away. He remained behind. I said: 'Shall we have a talk at Versailles?' 'How can one talk to people who poke fun at others?' I said: 'It is you who are poking fun at me; you can see clearly that I am serious.' We went to mass. I was a whole day at Versailles without seeing him. [...]

---

[242] Philippe-Charles, two-year-old brother of the dauphin. He died the following year.

Next day, on leaving the table, I said to him: 'Your reluctance to speak to me astounds me; I am not like you: I am most impatient to talk to you.' 'Whenever you will.' 'Straight away, if you wish, when the king has gone out.' As soon as he had, he [Lauzun] went up to the queen's apartments and into the drawing-room, and a moment later my maids of honour stationed themselves in a window, and he and I walked about for nearly three hours. I said: 'Who is to begin?' 'It is for you to give orders.' I said: 'I have told you the reasons that have made me want to be married; but I think that, of them all, the real one is my esteem for you; and, as I have told you in other connections, one easily loves what one esteems. You may have the same feelings for me; if so, we shall be happy.' He said: 'I am not conceited enough to believe or to flatter myself that what you are doing me the honour of telling me, can be possible; but since, to amuse yourself, you want me to reply, I must obey you, from the respect due to you. I shall speak, therefore, as if I believed what I am unwilling to believe. What! Would you marry a retainer of your cousin? For nothing in the world could compel me to relinquish my office: I love the king so much and am so much attached to him from inclination, that I shall not leave him for the honour you wish to do me.' I answered: 'My cousin is my master as well as yours, so I think nothing is so glorious as to serve him, and I love you the more for having this honour and these feelings; if you had them not, I should instil them into you, and if you had no office, I should purchase one for you, since I love no one more than the king.' 'I am not a prince. I am sure that I am a nobleman, but that is not enough for you.' 'I am satisfied; you are everything that is needed for me to make the greatest lord in the kingdom; I have wealth and dignities to give you.' 'When one gets married, one must know people's characters. I want to tell you about mine: of all men, I am the one who least likes talking, and it seems to me that you are very fond of conversation. I shut myself in my room for three or four hours at a time; and if my valet came in, I think I should kill him, and I feel that it would be impossible for me to talk for the rest of the time. My duties to the king are so onerous that I should have little time left to see my wife, if I had one. I should thus be a husband who would rarely be seen, and who, when seen, would not be amusing. She would not have cause to be jealous, if she were so inclined; for I hate women as much as I have loved them, and I no longer understand how one can enjoy oneself with them, and I should have enormous difficulty in getting into the way of it again. You might think that I should like a greater office, and that my lofty position would give me ambition. I have none; I want no other office than mine; it appeals to me particularly for what would put others off, its onerous duties. I wish they were more so. If I were offered a governorship, I should not want it. After all that, would you want me?' 'Yes, I want you, and all these ways of yours appeal to me.' 'Do you not find anything distasteful in my person? For that must be considered too.' I said: 'When you are afraid of not being attractive, you are joking; you have been only too attractive in your life; but, as for me, do you not find anything displeasing in my face? I think I have no outward defect but my teeth, which are not good; but that is a defect of my race, and that race can carry off some defects.' 'Yes, indeed!' said he. 'But answer.' 'I shall talk of nothing but my own failings, to show that I know myself.' 'You have none.' 'I shall say nothing about the other things; they would give you grounds for laughing at me all my life. I regard all this as so many fairy stories; I am sorry you are fond of them, and I wish I were not the butt of them; but since you like them, I have nothing to say; but I am neither a madman nor a day-dreamer: the more you say, the less I believe.'

I strove hard to persuade him that he did not mean it. We spoke like this all the time I said. At last I was so chilled that I felt it, and my maids of honour, whose conversation was less heated and less absorbing, were numb with cold. As he went out, he asked them most benignly: 'Ladies, are you warm?' I think they thought it a bad joke; but he had many other things on his mind.

After supper, he came back to the queen's apartments and talked to me, and said: 'There are moments when I think that it is not an illusion. I give way to joy; then I come to myself, and I reflect that it cannot be.' Our conversations for some days took this form. One day, he said to me: 'I have been thinking a governorship over. If you really wanted one to please me, I should accept it for love of you, provided the king were willing to give me one, and I might even ask for one.' I enumerated my great estates. I spoke to him of the beauty of the situation of this house [Eu], of everything I was having done here, and of the pleasure I thought it would give him to come here. He asked: 'Is it not somewhere near Gisors?' 'Yes, one has to go through it to get there.' 'It will be easier for me to go there, then; for this Lent I have to inspect one of the billets of my company, which is stationed there, and I shall be able to go on to Eu.' It was impossible to propose to do anything without his finding something in it connected with the king's service. No man has ever loved another so much.

We went to Paris to settle in there for the winter, and to hear the first Advent sermon. He came to the queen's every evening, and, before she left, we had long and frequent conversations, and we concerted measures for our marriage; but there was no day on which he did not tell me to think seriously about it, adding that I might repent of it, and that nothing was definite, since we had not yet spoken to the king. He alarmed me when he said: 'But perhaps the king will not agree?' I would say to him: 'He knows.' When I was talking to him and the king came, he would say: 'Let us stop talking; if the king asks what we are up to, what are we to say?' For he insisted that he had not spoken to him about it; I would answer: 'I am not asking you to. For heaven's sake, take your punctiliousness about the king elsewhere; but do not talk about it to me.'

Almost all our conversations turned on the king. He was afraid that he would go out without him, or need him for cards. I would say: 'If anyone could see how you are endeavouring to make your fortune (for marrying me was a great enough one for him to pay me some attentions), he would be astonished.' He would say: 'I think nothing appealed to you in me save my great affection, my great respect, and, if I dare say so, my great love for the king, and, as that is the only good thing about me, I pay my court to you better by paying it to him than by paying it to you. One does not treat people, not only of your rank, but also of your character, like other ladies, and, if I were not able to restrain myself, I should not have the honour of seeing you, and I should not forget myself and talk nonsense: I should regret it too much if our marriage came to nothing, as I still believe, and as I am beginning to fear; that is as far as I shall let myself go now.'

We spoke of his company. He said: 'If it happens, my company will be splendid at the March review. The four brigades must be mounted on Spanish horses, barbs, geldings, and Croatian horses; all the guards must have new buff-coats with sleeves spangled with gold and silver.' I said: 'They must all have green and white feathers and flame-coloured ribbons.' He was delighted to see that I was taking such an interest. Then he said: 'The king will say: "My cousin enjoys it as much as you."' I said: 'Next year, your baggage train will be much finer than this year: for the trappings of your mules and the housings will be covered with fleurs de lys. You will not be like my sister, who took M. de Guise's liveries and did not put her arms on them; you will be very glad to take mine and to have my liveries, which are my father's.'

[At last, she wrote a letter to the king, asking him to allow her to marry Lauzun.]

I sent it to M. de Lauzun, who replied that it was good. You may judge whether the letter in which he gave me his approbation was submissive and grateful. He writes well and sensibly; I should like to have his letters now; they would have been a great comfort to me in his absence;[243] but I burnt them all.

I sent it to Bontemps,[244] who gave it to the king. He replied instantly; I stupidly burnt his letter, which I have very much regretted, as well as those of M. de Lauzun. It was very fair. He expressed his astonishment; he begged me not to act lightly, and to think it over carefully; he said that he would never force me, that he loved me, and that he would always show me that he did at every opportunity. I had said at the end of my letter that I entreated him to answer me in writing and not to speak to me about it unless I began.

That day I was receiving ambassadors from Holland, who had just arrived. There was a horrible throng of people at the Luxembourg. I was in the middle of a large cluster of people. I had said to M. de Lauzun the day before: 'It is ridiculous that, though you often converse with me, you never come to see me; come tomorrow in the crowd.' He did not fail; he was behind everybody. When the ambassadors had gone, I went near the fire. M. de Longueville was there; I believe they had come together, and I even think that he told me that he had said to him: 'I am going to Mademoiselle's. Will you come?' I went into my little room, and said to him: 'You have not seen it. Come and see it.' I read the king's reply to him; I was sorry he had not consented straight away. M. de Lauzun said: 'What better could he have said? You want to do something you ought not; he points that out to you, begs you to think it over, and then assures you of his friendship, and says he will not compel you at all. I think that admirable.' I wanted to show him my closet. He said: 'I shall have time to see it, and I must go; I do not want to be seen staying so long with you.'

M. de Longueville came to the queen's apartments every evening, as she sat down to cards; no one was there. When he found me in

---

[243] We should recall that, at the time when she was writing this, Lauzun was in prison.
[244] The king's valet de chambre, a powerful figure in the king's household.

conversation with M. de Lauzun, he did not come near, and M. de Lauzun, when he went away, would say: 'Go and talk to him; that works wonders.' And when he came and I was with M. de Longueville and there was no one, he would say to him: 'Monsieur, I beg your pardon for interrupting you, but I have business with Mademoiselle, and I must go back to the card-table.'

The day after my letter, the king took a purgative. I went and dined at the Tuileries; I looked at him fixedly the whole time, without daring to say a word to him. I spoke to M. de Lauzun in front of him; I thought he watched us indulgently and in a way with which we ought to be satisfied. He [Lauzun] said to me: 'He has not said a word to me about your letter, and I did not mention it to him.' I said: 'But will you always keep saying such things to me? I am sure he has spoken to you about it; I am very glad; but I should be even more so if you said nothing to me before.'

Mme de Nogent[245] accompanied me to the Luxembourg every evening when I came back from the Louvre, and, as I often remembered many things I had forgotten to tell M. de Lauzun, I would write to him; she would send his reply in the morning. He also wrote to me without having a letter to answer. We had enough business for that. M. de Guitry, who was a good friend of his, knew nothing about it all. He forbade me to talk about it so strictly that I thought no one at all knew of it, and I spoke to no one about it. The matter was too important not to be kept secret; I even shunned society. I was more attentive than ever to the queen; I went and dined with her, and did not come home till late; and as soon as I had supped, I went to bed. I no longer spoke to anyone in my house, all my people being suspect to me, since I was sure that they would be in despair about the marriage. M. de Lauzun thought so, too, and I said to him: 'If any of my staff are stupid enough not to speak of you as they should when the marriage becomes public, I shall dismiss them and start afresh if you want.' He said to me: 'We must forgive their first impulse, for they will be right to be annoyed. If they serve you well, we shall be good friends; as for those who serve you badly, no mercy.'

On the feast of Our Lady [8 December], as I was coming away from the sermon in the Tuileries, he said to my equerry: 'I want a word with Mademoiselle.' He fell back, and he [Lauzun] gave me

---

[245] Lauzun's sister, the wife of Armand de Bautru, comte de Nogent. Bautru was the brother of Charlotte, 'the little Nogent girl', and Mme de Rambures, whom we met earlier.

his hand and said: 'Guilloire has found out about the marriage and has gone and told M. de Louvois.[246] I shall tell you more; where are you going?' I said: 'I am following the queen, who is going to the Carmelites in the rue du Bouloi;[247] but I shall go wherever you like.' He said: 'It will be soon enough if I talk to you when the queen comes back; I shall be here.' You may imagine my impatience. I found him in M. d'Anjou's apartments, whither the queen always went.

On arriving, he said: 'Guilloire has gone and said to M. de Louvois: "I do not know if it is with the king's agreement that Mademoiselle wants to marry M. de Lauzun; but I have come to warn you, in case you do not know about it, so that you can take action."' I said: 'If you wish, I shall dismiss him forthwith.' 'By no means, but I am telling you, so that you may beware of him.' I said: 'I have mistrusted him for a long time — indeed, I know him to be incompetent; but I did not want to make any change in my household or my affairs until it was all over, so that you might appoint people you liked and arrange everything similarly.' He said: 'You must not put off speaking to the king any longer. Stay behind this evening for the queen's *coucher*[248] for the purpose.' 'If you will tell me what to say to him.' 'If you take my advice, you will say: "Sire, the shorter the folly, the better; so I have thought over what Your Majesty did me the honour to say to me, and I have changed my mind."' 'What! Would you have me say that?' 'Do not make me say anything; for I do not want to speak; but, as for you, speak as your heart dictates.'

That day the king played very late; he did not return till nearly two o'clock. The queen was preparing for bed, and kept saying: 'You must have important business with the king to wait for him so late.' 'Madam, tomorrow a matter of the utmost importance to me is to be discussed in council.' The king came; he found me in the queen's alcove. He said: 'You are very late, cousin.' I replied: 'I have to speak to Your Majesty.' He went out hastily; he said: 'I must lean against something, for I have vapours this evening.' I said: 'Let us go and sit down.' 'No. I am all right like this.' 'Sire, I want to say to Your Majesty (my heart is beating) what I wrote to you. I am not changing

---

[246] Guilloire, who had been in her service since 1657, was eventually dismissed for disloyalty. Later, when the marriage came to nothing, Segrais, her secretary since 1648, was dismissed, purportedly for urging Harlay de Champvallon, the new Archbishop of Paris, to advise her to stop seeing Lauzun.

[247] The rue du Bouloi is nowadays in the first arrondissement of Paris. A Carmelite convent had been founded there about five years before the events in this narrative took place.

[248] The ceremony of the queen's going to bed.

my mind: the more I think it over, the more I look into it, the more I think I should be happy. I esteem, Sire, and I love M. de Lauzun; the honour Your Majesty does him gave rise to these feelings in me. I have the means to raise him higher than a foreign prince.[249] The honour of being your subject makes him greater in my eyes than a sovereign. It is Your Majesty who is raising him up, not I; for everything I have, and I myself, depend on you. I am doing nothing for him; it is you, Sire, who are doing everything, and who will also determine the repose and the joy of my life. I should not have thought so formerly in such a matter; everything changes. I am doing nothing in this matter contrary to my honour or my conscience. One can give an unfavourable interpretation to anything when one wants to. The approbation of Your Majesty and the conduct of my whole life make me think that an unfavourable one cannot be given to this. I think nothing suffers in this affair but my ambition. But there is ambition in doing extraordinary things; and the raising up of a man as extraordinary as M. de Lauzun appears to me a noble thing.'

The king said: 'After seeing you condemn your sister's marriage so severely, I was surprised by your letter. Not that I think that there is any difference between a great lord of my kingdom, as M. de Lauzun will be, who is one already by his birth, and who will be one by the benefits you want to confer on him, and a foreign prince.' 'Sire, Spanish grandees are not inferior to sovereigns. From M. de Lauzun's courage and worth and what Your Majesty will allow me to do for him, I think he will be equal to anything.' 'Well, cousin, think it over carefully; it is not a thing to be done lightly. I give you no advice; because people would think it was I who was making you do it. You are old enough to know what is right for you; I should be very sorry to force you in anything. I should not want either to contribute to M. de Lauzun's fortune, since your interests are at stake, or to injure him. In any case, whatever your state, I shall love you, I shall always respect you as usual, and I shall never change towards you. But I do not advise you to do it; I do not forbid you; but I beg you to think it over. The only suggestion I have to make to you is to let no one know; many suspect; the ministers have spoken to me about it. Many people do not like M. de Lauzun. Take your measures accordingly.' 'Sire, if Your Majesty is for us, no one can harm us.' I tried to kiss

---

[249] This is a sly dig at her half-sister, Mme de Guise, whose husband was of the house of Lorraine.

his hands; he embraced me; we separated thus. No one witnessed or heard our conversation.

Two days later, we went to Versailles. [...] Mme de Nogent said to me: 'M. de Lauzun has charged me to entreat you to agree to his keeping his room in the Louvre when you are married. He did not dare to tell you.' I told her that I agreed, and that same evening I said to him: 'Why did you get Mme de Nogent to tell me that?' 'Because I did not dare tell you myself. It would look odd in the case of another woman; but, as for you Mademoiselle, I am convinced that you would like me always to be at the king's feet if I could, and, as I am at his *coucher* every day and do not come away till two in the morning, as I have to be up at eight to be at his *levée*, and as it is a long way from the Tuileries to the Luxembourg, I should have very little time there. It will be better for me, therefore, to go on living in the Tuileries, and I shall have the honour to see you as often as I can.' I said: 'I go to the Tuileries every day; when the queen is at prayers, I shall visit you in your room.' He replied: 'But will that be all right? Would no one object?' I reassured him, for he was always afraid of being at fault.

On this last journey to Versailles, I often stood behind him to watch him at play: the king would laugh, and, on seeing the interest I took in him, make faces at him and at me. [...] Next day, Saturday, we were to return to Paris for the sermon; I remembered in the evening that I had forgotten to say something to him. I wrote to him; he came to my room. It was the first time. We talked at length about our affairs: he told me that on the Monday, the duc de Créqui, the duc de Montausier, Marshal d'Albret, and Guitry were to go to the king on my behalf to beg him to allow the marriage to take place and to thank him, too, for the honour he was doing him. So many things happened at that time that I do not recall exactly what they said; but I know that I asked M. de Lauzun why it should not be he and I to speak to the king. He said that they were friends of his, who, by playing a part in the matter, would silence the objectors, and give it their authority by their way of talking about it as something right and proper.

[Almost as though to delay the climax of the account, Mademoiselle now devotes a number of pages to other matters, including a brief report of the marriage, on 15 December 1670, of Mlle de Thiange and the duc de Nevers which, she says, Lauzun had helped to bring about.]

M. de Lauzun had told me that, on the Monday, the peers would speak to the king, and that I should come to the Tuileries early. The queen, after staying a moment with her assembly, went into her closet, and I remained in her room. M. de Lauzun came and said: 'I should like to have a word with you.' I went over to the window. He said: 'The gentlemen have gone in; the king is in council, and has sent for Monsieur.'

The queen came out, and went to the Recollects. While I was at the sermon, I was told: 'The duc de Montausier is waiting for you.' I went to the parlour. He said: 'I have come to give you my most humble thanks for the honour you have done me, and to report what happened. The king listened to what we said, and replied that you had already spoken to him; that he had said to you what was to be said about this marriage and what he could have said if he had been your father; that, seeing that you wanted it, he had only to give his consent; and that, since he had consented to the marriage of your sister to M. de Guise, he could not refuse this one.' At that, Monsieur had heatedly pointed out the difference. The king had told him that he did not see any, and that he [Monsieur], for his part, liked foreign princes,[250] whereas he [the king] was obliged to uphold the great noblemen of his kingdom. Thereupon, Monsieur had said to him: 'Say that you are obliged to uphold what you have done, for it is you who wanted this marriage.' The king had spoken with great kindness and equity of M. de Lauzun and me, and the great lords of his kingdom. The ministers had not said a word, and the gentlemen had all thanked the king in the name of the whole aristocracy of his kingdom. M. de Montausier said: 'The matter is settled; I advise you not to let it drag on any more than you can help, and, if you take my advice, you will get married tonight.' I thought he was right, and I asked him to tell M. de Lauzun if he saw him before I did.

Guitry came next, related the same things, and said that M. de Lauzun asked me to speak to the queen. After benediction, the queen went into a room. I told her that I had something to say to her. I knelt down before her, and began: 'I think Your Majesty will be surprised at my having decided to get married.' 'Indeed,' said she, very tartly, 'what are you thinking of? Are you not well off as you are?' 'I am not the first woman, madam, to get married, and Your Majesty thinks it right and proper for others. Why should I be the only one you do not want to be married?' 'To whom?' 'To M. de Lauzun, madam, and, if he is not a prince of the blood, madam, there is no greater lord in the

---

[250] Monsieur's favourite, the chevalier de Lorraine, was technically a foreign prince.

kingdom, and, when Your Majesty knows our customs,[251] you will learn that he is not inferior to foreign princes, who have no standing in ceremonies, unless the king does them the honour of giving them dignities.' 'I strongly disapprove, cousin, and the king will never approve, cousin.' 'He does approve, madam, and it is all settled.' 'You would do better not to get married, and to keep all your property for my son, d'Anjou.' 'Ah! madam, what feelings you are letting me see! I am ashamed for you! I shall not say anything more.'

She got up; so did I; we went to the Louvre, to the dauphin's apartment.

[Later, Mademoiselle returned to the queen's apartment, having sent a message to Lauzun to say she intended to do so.]

I found M. de Lauzun, who gave me his hand. We went and talked in a corner; I told him how the queen had treated me. He said: 'It does not signify; Monsieur and the queen do not control the king.' [...] I told him what M. de Montausier advised us to do — get married straight away. He said: 'I will not do that. I am going to thank the king for the honour he is doing me, play cards with him as usual, and show myself worthy of the honour you are doing me by the moderation with which I am receiving it. I shall have the honour of seeing you tomorrow; but at what time can I see you without finding people there?' 'It would be wrong for you not to want to be seen; you must behave like other people.' [...] He went off to the gaming-table.

At my house, I found a crowd of people, some astonished, others glad (his friends), others sorry. Guilloire was like a madman; he displayed his want of judgement. A woman came in a manto,[252] and threw herself at my feet. I did not know who she was. At last she raised her head: it was Mme de Gesvres, who thanked me as if he had been her son. She was very fond of him. That cheered me. As she is very witty, she spoke most eloquently. There were people with me all that evening.

You may believe that I got up early and scarcely slept. Another host of people came to see me. He came in as I was doing my hair,

---

[251] The queen having been in France for ten years, this remark was impertinent, to say the least. On the other hand, it was probably valid.

[252] A 'manto' was a flowing dress of richly ornamented material, split at the waist with the sides held in place by pins or ties. Lacking the bones and stays of formal court dress, it was more comfortable. Mantos were not ordinarily worn in formal situations — at least, not in this period. Mademoiselle may be indicating momentary disapproval, but it seems more likely that she means that Mme de Gesvres's failure to spend time donning suitable attire betrayed her eagerness.

hiding behind everybody; I went to him. He bowed so low as almost to prostrate himself. The Archbishop of Reims, M. Le Tellier's son,[253] who was there, said to us: 'Would you be so unkind as to choose somebody else to marry you?' I said: 'The Archbishop of Paris[254] has said he would like it to be he.' I called to M. de Lauzun, and we thanked him. I went to hear mass. [...]

I learnt that the queen had spoken acrimoniously to the king about M. de Lauzun and me, that the king had been very angry with her, and that she had wept all night. Monsieur had upbraided Marshal de Bellefonds and even M. de Montausier. The king had disapproved. Marshal de Bellefonds came to see me, and almost knelt before me, and said that all the nobility of the kingdom ought to kiss my footsteps where I walked, that there had been a coolness between M. de Lauzun and him, but that he hoped he would deserve his good graces. He [Lauzun] was present; he bowed low to him several times, and said: 'Since Mademoiselle answers for me, I have nothing to say; she is a good guarantor; you may believe that I shall not disavow her.' [...]

Everything that happened during these three days,[255] and everything that was said about the marriage, made it such a delightful period for me that, if I could always think of it and imagine myself back in it, I should be very glad. I am remembering and spinning these moments out as the happiest in my life, having known some very cruel ones since, as you will see in what follows.

[Mademoiselle went to the queen's apartments, where she met Lauzun.]

The queen came out of her oratory with a face that made us draw apart, and went to the novena in the Theatines. I followed her; she said nothing to me. My sister, who was with her, did not speak to me. Coming back in the evening, I found the whole house of Lorraine in force, for now they only marched as a single body to make war on me.[256]

---

[253] Claude-Maurice Le Tellier, Archbishop of Reims, was the son of Michel Le Tellier and the brother of Louvois.
[254] Hardouin de Péréfixe, who died suddenly two weeks later.
[255] Tuesday, 16 December to Thursday, 18 December 1670.
[256] Many members of the house of Lorraine were members of the French court and very jealous of the rights and privileges that they enjoyed as foreign princes and were always trying to extend. They were not willing to give way to a mere nobleman like Lauzun.

[Mademoiselle went to her room, where Lauzun and Mme de Thiange joined her.]

When Mme de Thiange had gone, we went and talked to Guitry and someone else — I forget whom. I told him that my stepmother had written to the king, opposing the marriage; that the prince and M. le Duc[257] had come to see her; that Mlle de Guise was marshalling all her forces; that Madame[258] was sending Mme du Deffant all over; and that in short we must get married at the earliest moment. [...]

I felt unwell that night; I had vapours: I was upset enough for that. I woke up late. I was told: 'M. de Montausier and Lauzun are out there.' I confess that I did not want to show myself to him, dishevelled as I was; I put on an elegant mobcap; then they came in. [They decided that Mademoiselle and Lauzun should be married at the duc de Richelieu's house at Conflans.][259] He [Lauzun] came back at five o'clock. When he came in, I said: 'I have seen the crescent moon on the right.' 'So have I,' said he. We both had great faith in that. I have been rather disillusioned since this terrible experience.

[A document was drawn up, donating the duchy of Montpensier and the principality of Dombes to Lauzun.]

We left these people [the lawyers] and went into the closet, where were Mme de Nogent, Mme de Gesvres, Mme de Rambures, Mme de Guitry, and Mme de la Hillière, and I said to them: 'Here is the duc de Montpensier, whom I am presenting to you; I beg you not to call him anything else henceforth.' We chatted, and Mme de Rambures, who is very amusing, told a story — a true one: she said she had noticed in the last two days that the whole of France had come to see me, including many women and girls with whom M. de Lauzun had been in love; or, rather, pretended to be; for he was never in love with anyone but Mme de Monaco, from what he has told me or I have gathered. I have often asked him about his love affairs; but so as not to answer, to stop me questioning him, and to silence me more quickly, he would say: 'That is a topic about which such a virtuous girl as you must not speak.' [...]

---

[257] Just as the prince de Condé was called Monsieur le Prince, his son, the duc d'Enghien, was called Monsieur le Duc.

[258] That is to say, Mademoiselle's stepmother. (Monsieur's wife having died in June, he did not remarry until November of the following year.)

[259] The château of Conflans was at Charenton, on the south-eastern edge of Paris. It was largely demolished during the twentieth century.

We resolved to be married next day at noon, and to go to Conflans. He departed at eight o'clock; at ten, he sent Barail, whom I had not yet seen.[260] [...] He brought a note in which M. de Lauzun told me that M. de Richelieu had come to see him and told him that, as Mme de Richelieu needed to keep in the good books of the queen, who was furious about the marriage, she could not lend him her house. He had been very glad because I had made it clear that I did not like it; M. de Créqui had offered him Épône; but, as it was twenty or twenty-five miles from Paris, he thought it too far away.[261] I said to Barail: 'There is another difficulty: it is in the diocese of Chartres; the Bishop of Chartres[262] is not in Paris, and would need time to obtain the dispensations (we needed one for advent and one for the banns); but Marshal de Créqui's wife has one in Charenton; that would do admirably.'[263] After a long talk, Barail left. Our titles were written down for the banns, and he took them away with him.

We were very gay and happy. [...] On the Thursday, I got up very early in the morning; at ten, Mme de Nogent came and said that they had been unable to complete the contract, and it could not be ready that morning. I said: 'Let it be done for tomorrow evening, then, for I will not be married on a Friday.' This was a bitter blow to me; it seemed to presage what happened.

[Lauzun came to see her, and they discussed their plans for the morrow.]

He departed at seven. We talked by the fire with the ladies who were there, Mme de Nogent, the comtesse de Fiesque, Mme de Rambures, and Mme de Guitry. He had very sore eyes. I said: 'Your eyes are very red.' He answered: 'Do they make you uncomfortable?' 'No, because they are in no way offensive.' The ladies laughed at us. We were very merry. And yet I had a kind of premonition. I wept on seeing him go; he was downcast; they laughed at us. The ladies all went, too; Mme de Nogent alone remained.

---

[260] Henri de Barail, previously a soldier, was Lauzun's confidant. He was married to the former Mlle de La Mothe.
[261] The château of Épône was in fact around thirty miles (48 kilometres) from Paris, a few kilometres east of Mantes-la-Jolie. It was destroyed in 1944.
[262] Ferdinand de Neuville de Villeroy, brother of Marshal Villeroy and of the Archbishop of Lyon.
[263] The house in Charenton, known as the hôtel de Créqui, was much less grand than the similarly named hôtel de Créqui in the rue des Poulies in Paris (between the present-day rue du Louvre and rue de l'Oratoire).

Chapter 6
The Match Unmade (1670–1671)

At eight o'clock I was told that a gentleman in ordinary of the king was asking to speak to me. I went into my closet; it was a man called Montsoreau;[264] he said: 'The king has ordered me to tell you to go and see him immediately.' I asked: 'Is he at cards?' 'No, he is with Mme de Montespan.' 'I am going straight away.' I told Mme de Nogent: 'I am in despair; my marriage is off.' She said: 'Ah! M. de Lauzun should know.' I did not think of anything; I sent for my coach, and, at the Croix-du-Trahoir,[265] I met the gentleman, coming to tell me that the king wanted me to go straight to his room, and to go there through the wardrobe.[266] This precaution struck me as a bad omen. Mme de Nogent remained in the coach.

When I entered the wardrobe, Rochefort came and said: 'Wait a moment.' It was clear that someone was in the king's room whom he did not want me to see; then he said: 'Go on in.' The door was closed behind me. I found the king all alone, upset and downcast. He said: 'I am in despair at what I have to say to you. I have been told that it was being said in society that I was sacrificing you to make M. de Lauzun's fortune, which would be detrimental to me abroad, and that I must not allow your marriage to be concluded. You are justified in feeling aggrieved towards me; beat me if you like. However unbounded your wrath, I will suffer it and I deserve it.' 'Ah!' I exclaimed, 'what are you saying, Sire? What cruelty! But whatever you do, I shall never fail in the respect I owe you; it is too firmly rooted in my heart, and M. de Lauzun has instilled it too much in me since I have known him,

---

[264] Mademoiselle writes 'Monthonot' or 'Montsorot'; 'Montsoreau' is Chéruel's suggested reading (IV, 233). If he is right, the individual may well be Louis-François du Bouchet, better known to posterity as the marquis de Sourches, the memorialist. In 1644, his father, Jean, marquis de Sourches, had purchased the lands and title of Bernard de Combes, comte de Montsoreau. Twenty years later, Louis-François married Mlle de Montsoreau, Combes's eldest daughter.

[265] The Croix-du-Trahoir, a commemorative cross that had been removed in the 1630s, gave its name to the junction of the rue de l'Arbre-Sec and the rue Saint-Honoré, nowadays in the first arrondissement of Paris. Pierre de Broussel had been arrested there, and the junction acquired symbolic status as the place where the Fronde began. Mademoiselle's coach would have turned into the rue Saint-Honoré at the Croix-du-Trahoir after crossing the Pont-Neuf on the way to the Louvre.

[266] Unlike a *closet*, which was normally accessible only from within a person's private apartment, a *wardrobe* was often, though not always, provided with a second door and could be used as an ante-room in which visitors could be kept waiting.

and even if these feelings had not always been in my heart, he would have put them there, and one cannot love him without having them.' I threw myself at his feet and said: 'Sire, it would be better to kill me than to distress me as you are doing. When I told Your Majesty about the thing, if you had forbidden it, I should never have thought of it; but the matter having gone so far as it has, to break it off — how can that be? What is to become of me? Where is he, Sire — M. de Lauzun?' 'Do not worry; nothing will be done to him.' 'Ah! Sire, I have everything to fear for him and me, since our enemies have got the better of your kindness towards him.'

He threw himself on his knees at the same moment as I did, and embraced me. We remained in an embrace for three-quarters of an hour, his cheek to mine; he was weeping as copiously as I: 'Ah! why did you give me time for second thoughts? Why did you not make haste?' 'Alas! Sire, who would have doubted Your Majesty's word? You have never broken it to anyone, and you are beginning with me and M. de Lauzun! I shall die, and I shall be only too happy to die. I had never loved anyone in my life; I love, and I love passionately and honourably, the finest gentleman in your kingdom. Raising him up was the delight and the joy of my life. I was looking forward to spending the remainder of it pleasantly with him, honouring you and loving you as much as him. You had given him to me; you are taking him away from me, tearing my heart out. And yet,' I shrieked, 'that will not make me love you less; but it will make my suffering all the more cruel, coming from him I love best on earth.'

I said to the king all that was most passionate and most favourable for M. de Lauzun, and most tender and most respectful for him. I heard a cough at the door on the queen's side. I said: 'To whom are you sacrificing me there, Sire? Would it be to the prince?[267] I do not believe, after all his obligations to me, that he would be willing to witness a scene so cruel for me, and you would not think well of him if, after I saved his life, he should attack mine out of hatred for a man whose only faults for all those who bear him a grudge spring from the fact that he depends on you alone. What! Sire, would the prince belong to the cabal of the house of Lorraine? They are in the ascendant now, and M. de Lauzun is doing them a great service. After this, what will Mlle de Guise not do against you?' 'Ah! cousin, this will only help to make you happier. Your obedience to me in a situation which is so painful to you puts me in a position never to be able to refuse

---

[267] She means Condé, who was, indeed, the person listening in the next room.

you anything.' 'Ah! Sire, what is mine? I ask you for only one thing, in which your greatness is at stake — to keep your word. What will be said abroad? If this marriage is shameful to you, that you did not know what you were doing, and have been reprimanded, whereas great kings should stand by what they have done. It is much more shameful to stop me from doing a good action than to have allowed me to do it. What! Sire, will you not give in to my tears?'

He raised his voice so that it could be heard: 'Kings must satisfy the public.' 'Certainly, you are indeed sacrificing yourself to it, for those who are making you do this will laugh at you. I beg Your Majesty's pardon for saying that, but it is very true.' He replied: 'It is very late. I should not say anything more or different if you were to stay here longer.' He embraced me and took me to the door where I met someone — I forget whom — I went home as quickly as I could, where I broke into bitter lamentations.

I saw M. de Montausier, M. de Créqui, M. de Guitry, and M. de Lauzun come in. On seeing him, I lamented bitterly, and he refrained from tears only with great difficulty. [...] M. de Montausier said to me: 'The king has ordered us to bring M. de Lauzun to thank you most humbly for the honour you wanted to do him, and to tell you that he is highly satisfied with you and him, that the way you spoke to him, without anger, and preserving, in your grief, a great deal of respect, will oblige him to think more highly of you in the future than he has ever done, and that, as for M. de Lauzun, he will do such remarkable things for him that you will have reason to be satisfied.' I wept abundantly, and said to them: 'Whatever he may do, I shall never be satisfied separated from him [Lauzun]. And you [Lauzun], you have such strength of mind that everyone will think you do not care for me. What do you say?' And I sobbed at every word. He said to me, very coolly: 'If you take my advice, you will go and dine at the Tuileries tomorrow, and thank the king for the honour he has done you in stopping something that you would have rued all your life.' 'I shall not take your advice; I shall weep all my life, but I hope it will not last long, and I shall never repent.' I said to them: 'Will you allow me to speak to him?' I took him into my alcove; he pleased me, for he wept. He could not say a word, nor could I. I merely said to him: 'What! Shall I never see you again? If that be so, I shall die.' Then we came back out.

The gentlemen, to whom I could say nothing, departed. I went to bed; I remained for twenty-four hours without speaking, almost without consciousness. When M. de Lauzun's name was mentioned, I would ask: 'Where is he? What does he say?' When one of his friends came (for I did not want to see anyone), I would say: 'Look after him.'

[The king, the queen, Monsieur, and others called on her.]

At last I saw everyone; but I did not speak. I was thin, with hollow cheeks, like one who neither ate nor slept, and I wept as soon as I was alone, or saw friends of M. de Lauzun and we spoke of things connected with him. The saying 'There is a remedy for everything except death' came into my mind; it was a kind of consolation to me; but this consolation seemed so remote that it only enhanced my grief. It had only removed from my mind the longing for death, which, in some sort, gave me more tranquillity from the hope of a speedy end, than the expectation of a happy and remote one could. I was in a pitiable state, and one must have experienced it to understand it, for these are the kind of things that cannot be expressed. One would have to know them oneself to appreciate them, and no one can have felt a grief like mine; there is nothing to which it can be compared. Throughout all this, God alone could have given me comfort; but as He wanted suffering to make me His, He was not willing to give me any.

[She wrote a letter to Mlle d'Épernon, who in 1649 had become a Carmelite nun. Later, she asked that it be returned to her.]

I wrote this letter in the first twenty-four hours, when I did not know what I was saying; if I had had to reread it, I do not even know if I could have; which is what made me ask to see it. I wanted to see what one says when one is in the state I remembered having been in, which seemed to me very terrible, for, from feeling too much, I felt nothing. [...]

I was told that I must go to court; that it was very wrong to let a week go by without seeing the king. I thought it more respectful not to show him an object who reminded him of what he had done, and what, it seemed to me, he had disliked doing. I told him [Lauzun], in the first moments, that I wanted to go away, and should never set foot in the court. He urged me to remain; he was afraid I should go; he sent me repeated requests not to. After hesitating for a long time, I went to the Tuileries on the morning of Christmas Eve. I arrived while they were at mass. The queen came back, and asked me how I was. I said: 'Very well.' We went into the gallery. Passing the room in which the cruel sentence had been pronounced wrung my heart. When we reached the gallery where the king was, he started to walk about. During the first turn, I burst into tears, and stopped in a window, very unwilling to be a figure of fun to many who were delighted to see me in that state.

The king, after completing his turn, came back alone and said to me: 'I am more sorry than you to see you in this state. I am well aware that I am the cause of all these tears, and they are so justified that I do not know what to say to you.' He went away. I realized that it was because he felt as much like weeping as I. [...] While we were in the gallery, the king was summoned to dinner. He said to me: 'Will your health allow you to come to Versailles with us tomorrow?' I replied: 'I am in no fit state' and I went out through his apartments, because no one was there, shedding copious tears. Going into the guardroom, I found a great many officers, who wept as they saw me. When I got home, I had to be unlaced; I was bursting. I had it announced that I would see no one. M. de Lauzun came towards evening, rather smart, and looking cheerful. I burst out screaming. Only Marshal de Créqui's wife and my maids of honour were present; after these first tears (he wept a little, for all his cheerful looks), we went and talked by a window. I was delighted to see him; but when I recalled the cruel way in which we had been treated, I wept again and said to him: 'We must hope, everything changes.' 'What! Can you believe that, and can we think of it if the king is unwilling?' And he restrained himself. We talked for about two hours. When he left, I started to weep again for all the rest of the evening. I did not go to midnight mass; I was not calm enough to make my devotions. He exhorted me to, preaching to me about society; but I was so affected by him at that moment, that he could not move me by what he was saying. I asked him: 'But will you not come here again soon?' 'Not if you behave like this. The way to see me is to stop weeping.' He treated me like a child.

I spent the Christmas feast days in convents. I went to the Carmelites in the rue du Bouloi; I complained loudly to them about the way the queen had treated me. They were ashamed, and did not know what to say; they said many kind things; that they were in despair; that they were sorry for me. Mme de Noailles was there. She said to me: 'I have never seen M. de Lauzun; tell me what he is like.' Through my tears and my grief, I joked a little with her. I said: 'But you will not believe what I say about him; it is better that M.

de Noailles should tell you than I.' 'No; I want you to.' I began: 'He is a little man; no one can say that he has not the most upright, the prettiest, and the most attractive figure. His legs are shapely; he does everything handsomely; fair hair, but scanty, and with a good deal of grey in it, unkempt and often greasy; beautiful blue eyes, but nearly always red; a shrewd look; a pretty expression. His smile is pleasing. The end of his nose is pointed and red; there is something lofty in his face; he is very untidy; when he has a mind to dress up, he is very fine. As for his character and his manners, I defy anyone to know them, to describe them or to imitate them. In short, he appealed to me; I love him passionately. At present I am to him as the king pleases; let us talk no more of him, for I have wept enough. Let us change the subject.'

I took mourning for a child of the Elector of Bavaria, for whom no one else did; but I did not want to wear anything bright. I was at the Tuileries when the king and queen arrived. The king said a few words to me as he passed, and went away; the queen did likewise, and I went away myself. People asked for whom I was in mourning, for no one else was. I said I was a friend of the Electress of Bavaria, as well as a relative of hers,[268] and that I wanted to be in mourning.

On New Year's Day Their Majesties always go to the Jesuits. I went to the Tuileries to go with them. The king was about to sit down at table; he asked me if I had dined. I said yes; and as the violins were there, and I did not want to hear them, I went to the queen's room; Mme de Rambures was with me. Looking towards the door, I saw M. de Lauzun and M. de Guitry come in; I closed the door; they came over to us. Mme de Rambures told M. de Lauzun that she had some business to talk to him about. When she had told me about it, I said to her: 'I do not think he will undertake it; for I am on the side of your adversaries, and obviously M. de Lauzun will never take sides against me.' As I said that, I burst into tears and ran away. He followed me and said: 'If you behave like this, I shall never come where you are; you will drive me out of society.' As he exhorted me not to weep, he wept himself and ran off. When the king came back from dinner, I did what I could to cheer up; but my eyes were red and as big as my fist. In short, I wept incessantly; but whenever I saw him, I could not help bemoaning my lot. […]

---

[268] In fact, they were first cousins.

There was an admirable opera that year; I did not miss a single performance.[269] The place where the queen sat was dimly lit, all the lights being on the stage; so I could weep to my heart's content. I had the pleasure of day-dreaming for four hours without being interrupted by anyone. M. de Lauzun always came in towards the end, and went into a box, and I would look at him. My attentions to the queen did not decrease, however much I had had to complain of her; but I saw M. de Lauzun, and I was glad to see him, even more so when I could speak to him, although I frequently wept; but he looked so hard at me that I dared no longer weep, and his influence over me restrained my tears; his influence was great, for one cannot control oneself.

[The court went to Flanders in April 1671.]

He had a bad billet in Dunkirk; he was very angry with the billeting officer. He said to me: 'Alas! I am aware every day that I am a poor wretch; formerly I was used to being one and did not mind; but after what I have nearly been, I miss everything.' You may imagine how we both wept. […] A rumour got about that we had been married before we left Paris; the *Gazette de Hollande* reported it. It was brought for me to see. He laughed; I said nothing; I sent it to him.

[The Duchess of York having died on 31 March, Lauzun took it into his head to offer to negotiate her marriage with the Duke. She replied as follows:]

'I think of nothing but you; I am occupied with nothing else; I think of nothing but waiting for a chance to speak to the king and to tell him that no one will say he has sacrificed me to you when he allows me to marry you; that if he stops me, he will be blamed for his cruelty, and people will say he is keeping me like a slave to get my property; and that he owes it to his equity and his justice to leave me at liberty. That, Monsieur, is what I am thinking of.' He threw himself at my feet and remained there a long time without speaking; I was strongly tempted to raise him; but I stepped swiftly backwards and left him in the middle of the closet. He said: 'This is where I should like to spend my life; but I am not fortunate enough. We must not think of anything displeasing to the king. As for me, I have nothing to wish for but death.' I wept copiously, and he went away.

---

[269] *Psyché*, with music by Lully and words by Molière and Quinault, was premiered on 17 January 1671 at the Tuileries and performed two or three times every week until 9 February.

[The court went to Tournai. While they were there, Lauzun left for Holland without saying goodbye to Mademoiselle. The court went on to Ath, about 25 kilometres east of Tournai, and Mademoiselle and others visited Enghien, some 20 kilometres beyond Ath.]

When we got back from Enghien, M. de Lauzun came to the queen's and told me about his trip to Holland; I was annoyed that he had left without saying goodbye to me. I should have liked, therefore, to show him my displeasure, but as soon as he saw that I felt like scolding him, he had ways of bringing me round and putting me in a good humour, the like of which never were seen; he is just like the garden of Enghien; in some respects, you must see him, for he cannot be described or imitated.

[After further travels around Flanders during the summer of 1671, in the course of which, on 1 July, Lauzun resumed his duties as captain of the guard, the court slowly returned to Versailles. When it then removed to Saint-Germain, Mademoiselle went to Forges.]

I wept copiously when I left: my grief was frequently revived. As there was much talk of a visit to Fontainebleau, I told M. de Lauzun, 'Be sure to wear a skull cap when you are there: the evening damp there is dreadful for teeth, and you are subject to sore eyes and colds; the air there makes hair fall out.' He said: 'As for teeth, I have some to preserve. I am afraid of colds; for, as regards the red eyes you complain of, it is because of late nights that they are sometimes sore. As for my hair, I have so little that it is not worth bothering about.' 'It is not the powder that makes it thin, for you do not put much on, and if you had put it on, you would not have been accused of wasting your powder on sparrows.' He smiled, and I wept; for nothing made me smile for a moment without my weeping afterwards.[270]

[In November 1671, plans to marry Monsieur to the daughter of the Elector Palatine came to fruition. The court went to Versailles and returned to Saint-Germain.]

The comte d'Ayen said to me one evening: 'I am just back from Paris, where I was asked if M. de Lauzun had been arrested. I did not like the sound of it.' I sent for him [Lauzun] to tell him, but he was in Paris. I told Barail, so as to let him know. I often went to Paris; people went on saying that we were married. Neither he nor I said anything,

---

[270] *Tirer sa poudre aux moineaux*, literally, 'to use one's gunpowder on sparrows', is used figuratively in the sense of 'to waste money on something unobtainable or not worth having'.

since only our particular friends dared to speak to us about it, and we laughed in their faces, saying no more than: 'The king knows the truth.'

I had arrived at Saint-Germain one evening very late. As the king was to take a purgative that day, I spent the whole morning in his room. M. de Lauzun was very glum; so was I. After dinner with the queen, I said to him: 'I am going to Paris.' He said: 'What a whim! You came back yesterday; stay here.' I said: 'I do not know what is wrong with me; I am so horribly depressed that I cannot abide it here.' I did not see him again. I departed; I wept all the way. It was Monday. He came on the Tuesday, in the morning, and went back on the Wednesday. I was to go on the Thursday.

As I was at table on the Wednesday, someone came and said something softly to Mme de Nogent, who was having supper with me. She left the table with the others. I lingered a short while. When I returned to my room, the comtesse de Fiesque said: 'M. de Lauzun...' I thought he had gone into my little room by way of the wardrobe. I hurried in, saying to her: 'How like him! I thought he was at Saint-Germain.' I was going out, laughing. The comtesse de Fiesque said: 'The fact is, he has been arrested.' 'What?' said I. 'M. de Lauzun has been arrested!' I was thunderstruck. I found Mme de Nogent almost swooning; I was speechless for a long time; then I asked how. Rollinde[271] told me he had been arrested an hour after arriving at Saint-Germain, and that Rochefort had found him in his room. You may imagine what a state that put me in. I could not go to Saint-Germain the next day. You may judge what a state I was in. I was advised to go on the Friday; I went. When the king came in to supper, he looked at me with a very downcast and embarrassed air. I looked at him with tears in my eyes; I said nothing. I heard that, on going back to the ladies, he had said: 'My cousin has treated me very well: she said nothing to me.' It would have been most imprudent of me to speak, because he was ready for anything I could have said.

It was the 25th of November, the feast day of Saint Catherine; it is an unforgettable day for me, as well as the 18th of December of the previous year, 1670. May God will that such a happy day comes that it can be marked and cause those ones to be forgotten; but it will be difficult for the impression of misery that they have left to be obliterated so easily. I am astonished that I did not die of it.

---

[271] Mademoiselle's secretary and man of business, the successor to Guilloire. Rollinde was the choice of Lauzun.

[Lauzun was imprisoned in the fortress of Pinerolo. Mademoiselle devotes numerous pages, first, to her depression; second, to the minutiae of court life and her own life; and third, to military matters. Thereafter, the tone towards Lauzun shifts, as the last part of her memoirs was written after she had finally fallen out with him.]

Part III
(1680–1684)

Chapter 1
Lauzun's Release (1680–1681)

At the time when I went to the Carmelites every day, the abbot of La Trappe came to Paris: I saw him often, this man whose retirement and austerities were so much talked of at that time and who had assisted my father on his death bed.[272] It was said that he wanted to encourage me to become a Carmelite; but that never entered his head. He was too shrewd not to realize that people of my rank can do more good in the world than in seclusion, and that they save themselves by saving others, when they know how to use their rank to set good examples, and to assist the widow and the orphan with their purse and their protection. In this spirit, I built and endowed a hospital at Eu for the education of children, managed by the Sisters of Charity, called St Anne's Hospital. When I am there, I often go and see them at work, and I take pains to find out if it is well run. I also built a seminary for those same Sisters of Charity at Eu, where there are twelve of them, and they take soup to the sick, as in Paris, and teach poor children; all that is well endowed.

[Mme de Montespan persuaded Mademoiselle to donate Dombes and Eu to the duc du Maine, the eldest of her sons by Louis XIV. In return, Lauzun was to be released, but Mme de Montespan told her that the king forbade her to think of marrying him. Lauzun was allowed to go to Bourbon with Maupertuis and an escort of musketeers. Mademoiselle learnt that he had been on the best of terms there with Marshal d'Humières's wife.]

An amusing thing happened. M. de Belzunce, Mme de Nogent's brother-in-law, who had gone to see her [at Bourbon], called at Choisy on his way back.[273] I asked him if he had many letters for Paris; he named the people for whom he had any, amongst others

---

[272] Armand-Jean Le Boutheiller de Rancé (1626–1700), the brother of Mademoiselle's childhood friend Charlotte de Rancé. Shaken by the death of his mistress, Mme de Montbazon, and then by that of Gaston d'Orléans, whose first almoner he was, he withdrew in 1662 to the Cistercian abbey of La Trappe, of which he was titular abbot, reformed it, and made it famous for its austerity.

[273] Choisy was an estate that Mademoiselle had bought in 1678, during Lauzun's imprisonment. Lying on the west bank of the Seine, about 10 kilometres south of Paris, it is best remembered for its association with Louis XV and Mme de Pompadour.

Marshal d'Humières's wife. I said: 'Give it to me; I shall send it to her.' He did not think he should refuse, or that M. de Lauzun could mind. When he had gone, I opened it. I found a most affectionate letter: he spoke to her of a book she had given him, and said that he kissed it a thousand times a day, because, now that he could no longer see her, it was his only consolation, and that he expected everything from her and her efforts. I burnt the letter, and felt sorry for him for thinking that she could be of any use to him.

[Lauzun was moved to Chalon-sur-Saône.]

He behaved as badly at Chalon[274] as he had at Bourbon; for he sent to ask everyone to go and see him, and all who passed through, men and women, returned to Paris. The best of his friends, the comtesse de Chamilly, who is a decent woman, a gamester, whose mind and whose judgement are not of the first order, spoke of nothing but him, saying that she wrote to him and had had letters from him. I heard all that with much sorrow. [...]

The king allowed me to give some property to M. de Lauzun: at first, it was to be Châtellerault and other estates, but he refused. He preferred Saint-Fargeau, which was then leased for 22,000 livres; Thiers, which is a very fine estate in Auvergne; and 10,000 livres a year from the salt tax of Languedoc. As Saint-Fargeau is a duchy, I expected that it would merely have to be claimed. Instead of being well satisfied, I learnt that he was saying that I had given him so little that he had been reluctant to accept it.

[Lauzun was then moved to Amboise.]

I received letters from M. de Lauzun, who was at Amboise and was eager to come back. He said that the air of Amboise was killing him; that he did not know why it had been chosen, and he was bored there; he saw no one and, if God did not help him, he would be worse off than at Pinerolo. I often spoke about it to Mme de Montespan and M. Colbert, who said: 'You must be patient.' We knew everything he was doing; his conduct was thought ridiculous. The marquise d'Alluye[275] was relegated there, her husband being governor of the town; he was constantly in their house. A great many Parisians with houses in those parts, and who were taking holidays there, said that M. de Lauzun was always with them, and flirted with the ladies; in short,

---
[274] Mademoiselle writes 'Châlon'.
[275] The former Mlle de Fouilloux.

he was doing everything he could to make himself look ridiculous. At last, the king consented to his return, stipulating that he was to see him once only, and go to Paris or wherever he wished, except to court. That was something; but, as I feared that he would not behave well, I should have preferred him not to return. Mme de Montespan said: 'At court, one must always take; it is one thing after another.'

Chapter 2
Reunion and Final Break-Up (1681–1684)

On the day of M. de Lauzun's return, the king was due to dine at Versailles. Mme de Montespan told me that the king had said that if I did not want to go, I could stay behind [at Saint-Germain] and even see M. de Lauzun before he had seen the king, as I would perhaps like to talk to him. I answered that I would have to have taken leave of my senses to do any such thing and that people would laugh at me, and with good reason. We went and dined at Versailles; the king was in an excellent humour. We played at *trou-madame* for jewellery and clothes;[276] I won some. We stayed very late; we did not return until torchlight.

On arriving, I went to Mme de Montespan's apartments, where M. de Lauzun came after he had seen the king; he had on an old *justaucorps à brevet*,[277] dating back to long before his imprisonment (for they are changed every year), too short and almost all in rags, and a hideous wig. He threw himself at my feet, and did it with a good grace; then Mme de Montespan took us into her closet, and said: 'You will be very glad to talk to each other.' She went away, and I followed her. M. de Noailles said: 'You must go to see Monseigneur and the dauphine,[278] and Monsieur and Madame.' I stayed with Mme de Montespan. He came at a quarter to ten; he told me that no one could have been better received than he had by all those he had just mentioned to me, that he owed it to me, and that nothing good could ever happen to him except through me, to whom he owed everything. He made some very kind remarks to me; he was right to behave like that. I did not say a word; I was astounded. Barail was present. [...]

I was still at Saint-Germain, and, four days after M. de Lauzun's arrival, I went to Choisy, without letting him know. He came there next morning with Barail and La Hillière.[279] He said: 'I was amazed to see the queen with coloured ribbons all over her hair.'[280] 'Do you

---

[276] *Trou-madame* was a board game in which balls were rolled into winning and losing holes.
[277] An item of court dress worn only by those who had a patent (*brevet*) from the king.
[278] 'Monseigneur' was the dauphin's courtesy title. He had married in 1680.
[279] This is how Mademoiselle spells the name of the chevalier de La Ilhière, who served with Lauzun in the king's bodyguard.
[280] The fashion had begun when Mlle de Fontanges, the king's mistress, tied her hair with a ribbon on a windy day. The 'fontange' hairstyle persisted into the eighteenth century.

think it odd, then, that I, who am older, wear them?' He said nothing. I informed him that rank allowed one to wear them longer than other women; and that I wore them only in the country and in a dressing-gown. I realized that the habit of finding fault that he had before his imprisonment had not altered. The weather was very fine; we had a long walk; he was in an excellent humour. [...] When he left, he said: 'I am very sorry to be going: I am delighted with Choisy; but I shall have the honour of seeing you this evening,' for I was going back to Paris at eight. Barail came with his apologies for not coming back; but he had felt so tired, unaccustomed as he was to walking, that he was capable of nothing more, and was going to bed. I said to Barail: 'Is it true?' He said: 'I think so; I left him at Rollinde's house.'

Next morning, he came to the Luxembourg; there was a crowd. I scarcely spoke to him. [...] After he had gone, Mme de Langlée, his particular friend, and Mme de Valentinois came.[281] I said: 'You were very pleased to see M. de Lauzun again.' They said that I might well think so, and that, since his return, he had either dined or supped with them. Mme de Langlée said: 'Yesterday evening, he came to my house and threw himself into a chair, saying: "I am dying! If Mademoiselle lived here and made me walk as much every day as I have today, I should die." He could not move. I had had supper: a dish of pigeons was brought for him. He had to be fed with a fork, since he was unable to raise his arms.' This account and that visit, after his message, surprised me a little, I own.

[When Lauzun came back next day, after mass], I asked him: 'How are you? For yesterday evening you went to bed after leaving M. Colbert's, according to the message Barail brought me from you.' 'Yes, indeed, I was in bed at nine o'clock.' 'So you got up again to go to Mme de Langlée's?' 'What a story!' 'Tell her not to tell stories; for she and Mme de Valentinois came here, and it was they who told me of your tiredness and your joy that I was leaving today.' He was very embarrassed. [...] I went to Saint-Germain next day, to his great satisfaction.

[Their relations continued to be strained. He blamed her for meddling with his affairs and ruining his career; she disapproved of his attentions to other ladies, such as Mlle Fouquet.]

---

[281] Princes of Monaco were also ducs de Valentinois before their accession to the principality. Our research has discovered no living duchesse de Valentinois between 1678 and 1688. Has Mademoiselle made a mistake? Has her editor? We think she must have intended to write 'Valentinay'.

The marquise d'Alluye came and played cards with me, and, as she played, she spoke a great deal of Amboise and all they did: of the diversions they had, and of the outings, and she said: 'It is a great deal for a fastidious courtier like M. de Lauzun not to be bored in a small town.' I said: 'He informed me of all that, and we often spoke of you.' She began again: 'Do you remember Madame So-and-so (names I have forgotten); she was very pretty; we had ladies from Paris. As they liked fashion, M. de Lauzun dressed smartly; he did wonders, gave us collations, lost at forfeits, and sent for jewels from Blois; was that not genteel?' When I had finished playing (he had come there with the duc de la Force), they left. As he was leaving, I said to him, 'By the way, go and recount today's scene to Mlle Fouquet; you who never lie.'

[One day they quarrelled about a crackbrained scheme of his of becoming commander of the French army in Italy through the influence of the Duchess of Savoy, the former Marie-Jeanne de Nemours.]

He said to me: 'As you have not the necessary influence to obtain for me what I may hope for from the king, would you be sorry if she completed what you began and are abandoning? You should be obliged to her, if you think as highly of me as you say.' I answered abruptly: 'I have done or tried to do more for you than anyone else can ever do. If you have ruined everything by your misconduct, blame yourself, and I shall be delighted never to meddle with your affairs.'

We separated thus. Next day, he came back, meek, and with flattering looks and words; and every other day he was motivated by fits of respectfulness and gratitude; on the days in between, he was a raging ingrate. In all his behaviour, he appeared very grasping, which I did not believe, nor anyone who had known him before his imprisonment; for he appeared to be recklessly lavish, and on many occasions he did behave thus. But, in consequence of his extraordinary and underhand manners, he showed himself like this only on his good days, and people only knew his good moments: he knew his humour, and how to conceal it; but his imprisonment, instead of correcting him, had thrown him back on himself to such an extent that he could no longer control it.

One day, he upbraided Rollinde, at his own fireside, in front of Montaigu and La Hillière, for not having stopped me from buying Choisy and spending money on it, saying that he would have had all that money, which he would have made me give him. The gentlemen were quite taken aback. Rollinde said to him: 'You gave me to Mademoiselle as an honest man, and I should have been a rascal if I had had any other consideration than to serve her in her way, and had tried to presume to give her advice contrary to her satisfaction.' Next, he asked him: 'Where is the money for the string of pearls which Mme de Nogent told me that she had sold for 40,000 écus?' He said: 'You may ask her, Monsieur; she does what she pleases with her own money.' He asked me, on the day he saw my jewellery, whether he had not formerly seen me wearing a string of pearls. I said, yes, but I had sold it to build Choisy. He told me, one day when I was walking there: 'This is a very useless building; you only need a cottage here to come to and eat a chicken fricassee, not to sleep. All these terraces cost immense sums: what is the point of them?' Someone told him that it was not too fine for me. He swore that it was easy for those whom it cost nothing to talk. I told him that I had done nothing except on the advice of M. Colbert. He said: 'Will he pay for it for you? I have a legitimate grievance; you would have used this money better by giving it to me.' I replied mildly: 'I have given you, and caused you to be given,[282] enough for you to be satisfied still, and I have given enough, too, to redeem your bad conduct.' He went and gambled all over, playing for very high stakes. When he lost, he was in despair; he would come to me, grumbling.

One day, I was having some jewels set: two identical diamonds were needed. Rollinde said: 'It could be done with one or two of M. de Lauzun's; they will be replaced; there are some of the kind we need.' I would not; Barail urged me to: they were ordinary and useless. When he [Lauzun] came back, I said to Rollinde: 'I want to give him four diamonds as buttons for his wristbands. They will be very fine at 1000 pistoles the four.' Rollinde told him, and brought him some to choose; he took some, put them on his wristbands, and showed them to some ladies who were at cards with me. Next day, he said: 'Everybody thought them ugly and not worth the money.' Rollinde said: 'It will be better if you take the 1000 pistoles and buy some to your liking.' He told him: 'I have found some lovely ones; but I should need another two hundred pistoles.' I refused to give them to him. He took the money, and, a week later, as we were talking of

---

[282] When the marriage was broken off, Lauzun received 50,000 livres to pay his debts and was made Governor of Berry the following Easter. After his release from Pinerolo, he was given a further large sum.

jewellery at the card table, he said to Mme de Palaiseau, who was next to him: 'I have sold my diamonds that Mademoiselle gave me, to live on, for I was penniless.' Such things are unheard of; every day he played tricks, which everyone thought ludicrous. He went about in a hired coach, not wanting to own one till he was a duke and could put the ducal mantle on his arms. True, I had been promised that he would be made one; but these ways did not help, and he was laughed at.

[Mademoiselle went to Eu. Her relationship with Lauzun continued to be difficult. She travelled with the court to Chambord, and then went to Choisy, passing the winter of 1682–1683 between there, Paris, and Versailles.]

The court made a journey to Compiegne and then to Germany;[283] I did not go; I remained at Choisy. These journeys of the court had upset M. de Lauzun, and brought severe reproaches on me every day, instead of thanks; for he was never to speak to me without them. He told me one day that everyone was astonished at the way I treated him, and my poor opinion of him; that people said he ought to be all-powerful in my household, like the chevalier de Lorraine in Monsieur's; that he would have me better served than I was; that my furniture would be more elegant and more magnificent; that I ought not to employ anyone except at his choice; that, if I needed money, I ought to ask him for it; and that he would make my treasurer render better accounts than my people did. To that I replied: 'I think you are joking; I should be laughed at, and you have blamed Monsieur so much for allowing himself to be governed: would you have me fall into the same error? It would be pointless, when I needed money, to send to ask you for it.'

Another time, he told me that people thought it wrong that he should be lodging in Rollinde's house, not knowing which way to turn; that he would have thought that I should have arranged, as soon as he left prison, to furnish a house for him, and set him up in furniture and clothing, but that he found nothing; and that that is what compelled him to buy a house in the île Notre-Dame,[284] so as not to be like a beggar. If, however, I were to do the proper thing, I should turn out my pages and some of my people who are in Mme de Choisy's house; I should have a fine, well-furnished apartment made for him, and he would come and stay there sometimes; I should have

---

[283] The court went to Compiègne in 1683, and then to Alsace, Lorraine, and Burgundy. It did not, in fact, go to Germany.
[284] Now the île Saint-Louis.

meals sent in for him, and he would be able to bring some of his friends to eat there. That would look handsome, and I ought also to have a coach and six for his use alone, when he was staying in the apartment.

These remarks were not all made on the same day; he spaced them out, now reproaching and scolding, now wheedling; never for a quarter of an hour in the same way. At last, after I had said: 'But you are joking! These are crazy notions; it is not possible that you are really thinking of these things; but are you leaving the king out of account? Would he allow them? You really ought to be more careful about what you say, and realize that, if I wanted to do these things, you ought not to want me to, from the genuine affection you should have for me.' He said not another word.

[Mademoiselle went to Eu and to take the waters at Forges.]

M. de Lauzun came to Eu a day or two after I arrived; he made a habit of going hunting, which meant that he was not so bored as the year before. One day, as he was walking in the gallery with me, he said a great deal about his return to court and the disservices that were being done to him. People, he said, believed he was eager to get his hands on my property; that was not in his mind, and, if I took his advice, I should give all I had left to Mme de Montespan, to go to the comte de Toulouse afterwards. I should have her called Mme de Montpensier, so that she would no longer have to bear the name of that horrible man who was so hateful to her.[285] I should be given a pension larger than the income from my estates; I should have no more lawsuits, no more need of men of business; I should know at any moment how much I had; and I should be very happy. I said: 'The king and M. Colbert are not immortal; what guarantor would there be?' 'If that were to happen, would Mme de Montespan not be a good one?' 'I have given enough away; I shall give nothing more; and you are giving me bad advice.' He called to the comtesse de Fiesque, and said to her: 'Comtesse, listen to what I am telling Mademoiselle, and say whether she ought not to do it.' And he began what I have just said all over again, and added: 'I have put it in writing; the court will know that I am acting thus.'

[Matters went from bad to worse, not least because Mademoiselle felt that Lauzun had set out to bring about Mme de Montespan's coolness towards her; Lauzun felt that she was using her influence with the king to hold back

---

[285] Her husband, who had not accepted her relationship with Louis XIV tamely.

his military career. His gambling increased. The king left for the army on 22 April 1684. The final breach occurred on 4 May.]

I spent the day in Paris, without M. de Lauzun's coming to see me. I went to St Joseph's.[286] When I arrived, I met Mme de Montespan in the street, setting off; we said goodbye rather frigidly. Monsieur had remained in Paris for a few days. M. de Lauzun came to see me. I went up to him, smiling, and said: 'You must go to Lauzun or Saint-Fargeau; for, as you are not going with the king, it would be ridiculous for you to stay in Paris, and I should be very sorry that it should be thought that I was the cause of your staying.' He said: 'I am going, and I am saying goodbye to you, never to see you again in my life.' I replied: 'It would have been a very happy one, if I had never seen you; but better late than never.' 'You have ruined my fortune; you have blighted my life; you have stopped me from going with the king; you asked him for that.' 'Oh! As to that, it is false; he can tell you the facts himself.' He grew very angry, while I remained completely calm throughout. I said: 'Goodbye, then'; and went into my little room. I remained some time there; I went back; I found him still there. The ladies who were there said to me: 'Do you not want to play cards, then?' I went up to him, saying: 'This is too much; keep your resolution; go!' He withdrew, and went to Monsieur's to tell him that I had dismissed him like a rascal, and complained bitterly about me. When I told Monsieur what had passed, he thought him very much in the wrong. During the days he remained in Paris, he gambled. He left; his baggage was all ready, and I have never known or understood what all that was about.

[A short final section begins with brief remarks about people Mademoiselle has previously mentioned, and sketchily recounts some of the events of the next few years. Almost her closing thought is to complain that news of Lauzun's activities makes her angry.[287] After that, her text ends abruptly, in mid-sentence, at a point where, in December 1688, she has just returned from Eu.]

---

[286] This church still stands, in the rue de Vaugirard in the sixth arrondissement of Paris. It lies about half way between the Luxembourg, where Mademoiselle was living, and a house that had been owned for many years by Mme de Montespan, who spent more of her time there since falling from favour at court.

[287] For a succinct account of Lauzun's final years — he outlived Mademoiselle by three decades — see the seven-page 'Epilogue' to Vita Sackville-West's book, *Daughter of France*, details of which are in 'Further Reading'.

Further Reading

The best edition of the *Mémoires* is that of Adolphe Chéruel (*Mémoires de Mlle de Montpensier, petite-fille de Henri IV*, 4 vols (Paris: Charpentier, 1858–1859)). Chéruel worked with the original manuscript in what is now the Bibliothèque nationale de France. Previous editions, of which there were several, had been marred by a mixture of editorial interference and inaccurate transcribing that in some places was so reckless as to make the text unrecognizable when compared with Chéruel's. In his footnotes, he indicates the worst of these excesses, but he is not always reliable when it comes to identifying individuals or places. It is fortunate that Chéruel's edition is available in many good libraries; even so, a new and even more accurate edition is long overdue.

The only complete modern reprint, *Mémoires de Mlle de Montpensier, La Grande Mademoiselle*, 2 vols (Paris: Fontaine, 1985), has a brief introduction that includes insights into the publishing history of the text, but it suffers from numerous misprints and has no index. The extensive — but even so, abridged — version in one volume by Bernard Quilliet (*Mémoires de la Grande Mademoiselle*, Paris: Mercure de France, 2005), contains an introduction, good notes, and an index. Readers of French wanting an unabridged version of the early years can consult *La Grande Mademoiselle: Mémoires de 1627 à 1643*, edited by Chantal Thomas (Paris: Mercure de France, 2001), which reproduces Chéruel's text.

The *Mémoires* have been translated into English in their entirety only once (anonymously, a version published in three volumes by Colburn in London in 1848). It is an archaic rendering and, in any case, predates Chéruel's establishment of the text. A later version, by Grace Hart Seely (London: Eveleigh Nash & Grayson; New York: The Century Co., 1928), is, to quote the translator herself, 'a considerable abridgement'. It is preceded by a somewhat excited biographical sketch in the manner of much popular historical writing of the period, lending credence to half-truths and myths that more recent students of Mademoiselle would not entertain. Seely translates a little over one-eighth of the text, and while that, in itself, is understandable, she never indicates where omissions occur or gives any idea of what is omitted. She sometimes embroiders the original, albeit sympathetically, in such a way as to misdirect the innocent reader who does not wish to compare her version with the source text. It is all engagingly done, but, for these reasons, her work belongs in that middle ground where translation meets adaptation. The *Mémoires* have not been translated since.

A manuscript containing some of the correspondence of Mademoiselle and Mme de Motteville has been transcribed and published by Joan DeJean — the original text and an English translation on facing pages — under the title *Against Marriage: The Correspondence of La Grande Mademoiselle, Anne-Marie-Louise d'Orléans, duchesse de Montpensier* (Chicago: University of Chicago Press, 2002).

Two very readable lives of the Grande Mademoiselle in English, published over half a century ago, are still worth locating, viz. Francis Steegmuller, *La Grande Mademoiselle* (London: Hamish Hamilton, 1955) and Vita Sackville-West, *Daughter of France: The Life of Anne-Marie Louise d'Orléans, duchesse de Montpensier (1627–1693), la Grande Mademoiselle* (London: Michael Joseph, 1959). The charge that the latter is at least as much about Vita Sackville-West as about Mademoiselle, like many such witticisms, has some basis in truth. Finally, the most recent biography, by Vincent J. Pitts, *La Grande Mademoiselle at the Court of France 1627–1693* (Baltimore and London: Johns Hopkins University Press, 2000), is well researched and well written, even if at times it claims a little too much for its subject's direct influence on the course of French history and civilization. As a richly footnoted and serious academic study, it may not appeal to all tastes, but it deserves to be regarded as a *sine qua non* of Mademoiselle studies.

There are several lives in French, including Christian Bouyer, *La Grande Mademoiselle: Anne-Marie Louise d'Orléans, duchesse de Montpensier* (Paris: Albin Michel, 1986), aimed at a general readership while deriving from a rigorous consultation of available sources. It was reissued as *La Grande Mademoiselle: La tumultueuse cousine de Louis XIV* (Paris: Pygmalion, 2004) with a barely noticeable sprinkling of textual adjustments and, unfortunately, the omission of the half-dozen two-tone illustrations that graced the first edition. Bernardine Melchior-Bonnet's book *La Grande Mademoiselle* (Paris: Perrin, 1991) and Michel Le Moël's of the same title (Paris: de Fallois, 1994) are two of the numerous other biographies that have appeared over the last hundred years or so, most of which have their merits. The one by the duc de la Force, *La Grande Mademoiselle* (Paris: Hachette, 1952), is worth seeking out. Arvède Barine's study

La Jeunesse de la Grande Mademoiselle, 1627–1652 (Paris: BiblioBazaar, 2009), despite its date, is far from being the most recent: Cécile Vincens, a respected biographer who wrote as Arvède Barine, in fact died in 1908. Her book appeared in 1901 (Paris: Hachette) and was many times reprinted both in French and in English translation in the years before the Great War. Even though, to risk a truism, it does not benefit from more recent research, it can still be read pleasurably by anyone willing to exercise suitable critical detachment. Its sequel, published as *Louis XIV et la Grande Mademoiselle, 1652–1693* (Paris: Hachette, 1905) and also reprinted many times in both French and English, has not been reissued since the 1930s.

Readers of French should also consult the major critical account by the doyen of Mademoiselle studies, Jean Garapon, viz. *La Grande Mademoiselle mémorialiste: une autobiographie dans le temps* (Geneva: Droz, 1989). Garapon also adds considerably to our understanding of the princess in *La Culture d'une princesse: écriture et autoportrait chez Mlle de Montpensier* (Paris: Champion, 2003). Finally, a collection of essays by Denise Mayer (*Mademoiselle de Montpensier: Trois études d'après ses Mémoires* (Paris, Seattle, Tübingen: Papers on French Seventeenth-Century Literature/Biblio 17, 1989)), though more modest in scope, contains valuable observations.

Index

Aiguillon, Marie-Madeleine de Vignerot (1604–1675), marquise de Combalet, in 1638 duchesse d', niece of Cardinal Richelieu and aunt of the duc de Richelieu 5, 5 n. 12, 11 n. 21, 108, 168
AIX-EN-PROVENCE 137–39, 140, 140 n. 209
Albret, César, baron de Pons (1614–1676), Marshal d' 93, 117, 184
Alençon, Mlle d' *see* Orléans, Élisabeth d'
Alexander VII, Fabio Chigi (1589–1667), in 1655 Pope 134, 135
Alfonso VI (1643–1683), King of Portugal 1653–1667: xxi, 144–46, 162 n. 221
Alluye, Paul d'Escoubleau (d. 1690), marquis d', son of Charles, marquis de Sourdis 51, 201
Alluye, Bénigne de Meaux de Fouilloux d', wife of the foregoing, *see* Fouilloux
AMBOISE 201, 205
AMIENS 21, 33, 136
ANGERS 43
ANGOULÊME 132
Anjou, Gaston, duc d' *see* Orléans, Gaston-Jean-Baptiste, duc d'
Anjou, Philippe, duc d', Louis XIV's brother, *see* Orléans, Philippe, duc d'
Anjou, Philippe-Charles (1668–1671), duc d' 176, 176 n. 242, 182, 186
Anne of Austria (1601–1666), Queen of France, wife of Louis XIII: xx n. 13, xxix, xxx, 21, 22, 35, 81, 92, 98, 100–01, 103–06, 112, 113, 115–17, 121, 124, 128–33, 137, 140, 140 n. 207, 141, 142
    death xxx, 147
    and the Fronde 25 n. 41, 26–29, 31, 43
    and Gaston d'Orléans 14, 38, 122, 131
    and Louis XIII: 6, 6 n. 14
    and Mademoiselle xxi, 2, 4, 9, 11, 20, 25, 27, 29, 31, 33, 34, 99, 100, 106, 107
    pregnancy 9, 10
Anne Stuart (1665–1714), daughter of the Duke of York, in 1702 Queen of England 168, 168 n. 231
Anville *see* Damville
APT 141
ARLES 134, 137
Armentières, Henriette de Conflans (c. 1630–1712), called Mlle d' 133
Arnauld d'Andilly, Robert (1589–1674), Gaston's former secretary 96–98, 98 n. 144
Arnauld, Antoine, theologian (1612–1694), younger brother of Robert, called the Grand Arnauld 96, 97
ARPAJON *see* CHÂTRES
ARRAS 162
ARTENAY 49, 49 n. 79
ATH 197

AUGE xii
Augustin, Saint 95
Aumale, Suzanne d'Aumale de Haucourt, known as Mlle d' (d. 1688), later, wife of Frédéric, Marshal Schomberg 121, 121 n. 180
Austria, Anne of *see* Anne of Austria
Austria, Emperor of *see* Ferdinand III
Austria, Empress of *see* (1) Spain, Maria Anna of, first wife of Ferdinand III; (2) Austria, Maria Leopoldine of, second wife of Ferdinand III; (3) Mantua, Eleonora Gonzaga. princess of, third wife of Ferdinand III
Austria, Maria Leopoldine of (1632–1649), in 1648 Empress of Austria 32, 37, 37 n. 58
AUXERRE 78, 95
AVESNES (LES-AUBERT) 160, 161
AVIGNON 133, 134, 134 nn. 196–98, 135–37, 140, 140 n. 208, 141
Ayen, Anne d' *see* Noailles
Ayen, Louise Boyer d' *see* Noailles
Ayen, Anne-Jules de Noailles (1650–1708), comte d', son of the foregoing, in 1678 duc de Noailles 165 n. 227, 176, 197

Bachaumont, François le Coigneux de (1624–1702), councillor in the Paris parlement, son of President Le Coigneux 26
BAGNOLET 12, 70
Ballet d'Alcidiane, Le 114, 114 n. 165
BAPAUME 162
BAR-SUR-SEINE xii
Barail, Henri de (d. 1705) xxvii, 189, 189 n. 260, 197, 203, 204, 206
Barrillon, Antoine (1599–1672), sieur de Morangis, first cousin of Michel Le Tellier 26, 26 n. 46
Barrillon, Jean-Paul (1628–1691), nephew of the foregoing 26 n. 46
Bautru, Armand de *see* Nogent
Bautru, Charlotte de *see* Nogent
Bautru, Marie de *see* Rambures, marquise de
Bautru, Nicolas de *see* Nogent
Bavaria, Ferdinand-Marie (1636–1679), Elector of 81, 195
Bavaria, Henriette-Adelaide of Savoy (1636–1676), Electress of, wife of the foregoing 81, 195, 195 n. 268
Bavaria, Anne-Marie-Christine-Victoire of (1660–1690), daughter of Ferdinand-Marie and Henriette-Adelaide, in 1680 dauphine of France xxxi, 203
BAYONNE 141
BEAUCAIRE 133, 137
Beaufort, François de Vendôme (1616–1669), duc de, second son of César de Bourbon, duc de Vendôme 44, 47, 49, 56–58, 62, 70
BEAUJOLAIS xii, 124, 126

Beaumont, Mlle de (d. 1661) 10
BEAUNE 128
BEAUVAIS 88 n. 130
Beauvais, Catherine-Henriette Bellier (1615–1690), baronne de, first lady of the chamber to Anne of Austria 100
Bellefonds, Bernardin Gigault de (1630–1694), Marshal 187
Bellegarde, Roger de Saint-Lary (1563–1646), duc de, sometime superintendent of Gaston's household 76, 79
Belzunce, Armand (c. 1634–after 1699), marquis de Belzunce et de Castelmoron, who in 1668 married Anne de Caumont de Lauzun, sister of the comte de Lauzun 200
BERGUES 163
Beringhen, Henri (1603–1692), marquis de 42 n. 67
Beringhen, Anne du Blé (d. 1676), marquise de, in 1646 wife of the foregoing 42, 42 n. 67
Bermont, Martin de (d. 1686), councillor in the Paris parlement 45, 50, 59
Berville, M. de (d. 1656) 90, 90 n. 133
Béthune, Hippolyte (1603–1665), comte de, Sully's nephew xxiii n.17, 69, 84, 91, 93, 93 n. 142, 104, 107, 119
Béthune, Anne-Marie de Beauvillier (1610–1688), comtesse de, wife of the foregoing 84, 84 n. 123, 87, 91, 92, 104, 157, 158
Béthune, Henri, chevalier de (1632–1690), younger son of Hippolyte and Anne-Marie, in 1658 comte de Selles 119
Béziers, M. de *see* Bonzy, Pierre, abbé de
Blancmesnil, René Potier de (d. 1680) 24
BLAYE 12
BLÉNEAU 61
BLOIS xii n. 2, xiii, xviii, xxv, 6–8, 43, 44, 57, 58, 75 n. 109, 77, 79, 84, 95, 108–10, 130–32, 205
BOIS-LE-VICOMTE, château 23, 24, 38, 77, 109 n. 158
Bonneuil, Mlle de, maid of honour to Anne of Austria 116
Bontemps, Alexandre (1626–1701), Louis XIV's principal valet de chambre 180, 180 n. 244
Bonzy, Pierre (1631–1703), abbé de, in 1660 Bishop of Béziers 108, 144
BORDEAUX xxii, 12, 18, 43, 51, 74, 130 n. 193, 132, 133 n. 195
Bossuet, Jacques-Bénigne (1627–1704), Bishop of Condom, later Bishop of Meaux 166
Boucher (before 1640–after 1676), obstetric surgeon xxiii
Bouligneux, Jacques-Claude de la Palu (d. 1672), comte de, lieutenant of the guard to Anne of Austria 156
BOULOGNE (SUR MER) 164
BOURBON 84, 84 n. 122, 200, 201
Bourbon, Anne-Geneviève de *see* Longueville, duchesse de
Bourbon, Jeanne-Baptiste de *see* Fontevrault

Bourbon-Montpensier, Marie de (1605–1627), duchesse de Montpensier, who married Gaston d'Orléans in 1626: xxix, 1, 2, 81
BOURGOGNE (HÔTEL DE), Paris 121, 121 n. 177
Bouthillier, Marie de Bragelongne (1590–1673), comtesse de, wife of Claude Bouthillier de Chavigny (1581–1652), Surintendant des Finances under Richelieu 23, 45 n. 70, 75, 92
Brays, lieutenant-colonel, equerry to Mademoiselle xxiii n. 17, 90, 90 n. 133, 138 n. 203
Bréauté, Marie de Fiesque (1615–1680), marquise de 46, 46 n. 72, 52, 82
Brégis (or Brégy), Nicolas de Flesselles (1615–1689), comte de 116
BRESSE xii, 126
Brézé, Mlle de *see* Condé, Claire-Clémence de Maillé-Brézé, princesse de
Brienne, Louise Béon (d. 1655), comtesse de xxiii n. 17, 22
BRISSAC (HÔTEL DE), Paris 9, 9 n. 18
Brissac, François de Cossé (d. 1651), duc de 4 n. 7
Brissac, Élisabeth de Cossé (c. 1623–1679), Mlle de, daughter of François, later marquise de Biron 4, 4 n. 7
Brissac, Marguerite-Guyonne de Cossé de, daughter of François 4 n. 7
Brissac, Marie de Cossé de (1621–1710), daughter of François, in 1637 the wife of Marshal de la Meilleraye 4 n. 7
Brissac, Ursule-Anne de Cossé de, daughter of François 4 n. 7
Broussel, Pierre de (?1576–1654) 24, 69, 69 n.102, 190 n. 265
Brûlart, Nicolas (1627–1692), First President of the Dijon parlement xx
BRUSSELS 95
Bussillet *see* Messimieux

CAMBRAI 160 n. 218
Campion, Alexandre (1610–1670), gentleman of the comte de Soissons 6
Candale, Louis-Charles-Gaston de Nogaret de Foix (1627–1658), duc de Valette et de, son of Bernard, duc d'Épernon 74 n. 107, 113, 113 n. 162, 117, 118
Canillac, killed in a duel by Flamarens: possibly one of the sons of Gilbert de Beaufort-Canillac (d. 1622) 72
Carignan, Marie de Bourbon-Soissons (1606–1692), princesse de, daughter of Charles, comte de Soissons and mother of Eugène-Maurice, comte de Soissons 115
Carmelites 39 n. 62, 200
    of Aix 139
    of Avignon 136
    of Saint-Denis xxii, xxii n. 15, 44
    of the faubourg Saint-Jacques 38, 38 n. 61
    of the rue du Bouloi 182, 182 n. 247, 194
Castiglione, *The Courtier* vii
CATEAU-CAMBRÉSIS 161

Catharine (or Catherine) de' Medici *see* Medici

Catherine of Braganza (1638–1705), in 1662 wife of Charles II and Queen of England 163

Catherine the Great (1729–1796), in 1762 Empress of Russia vii

Cavalli, Pier Francesco (1602–1676), *Egisto* 19, 19 n. 38, 93 n. 140

Célestins:

  of Amiens 136, 137

  of Avignon 136

Chabannes, Antoine de (1411–1488), great-great-grandfather of Mademoiselle's maternal grandmother 83 n. 121

CHALON (SUR-SAÔNE) 201, 201 n. 274

CHAMBORD xxv, xxvii, 7, 77, 130, 131, 173, 173 n. 241, 207

Chamilly, Catherine Leconte de Nonant (d. 1693), in 1660 comtesse de 201

CHAMPIGNELLES 82, 82 n. 119

CHAMPIGNY-SUR-VEUDE xii, 8 n. 16, 23 n. 40, 105, 109, 109 n. 158, 110

Champlâtreux, Jean-Édouard Molé, marquis de, son of Mathieu Molé (?1608–1682) 55, 55 n. 84

CHANTILLY 6

CHARENTON 61, 188, 188 n. 259, 189, 189 n. 263

Charles I (1600–1649), in 1625 King of England vii, 13 n. 25, 18, 19 n. 37, 31, 81

Charles II (1630–1685), Prince of Wales, son of the foregoing, in 1649 King of England, restored in 1660: vii, xvii, 18, 19, 19 n. 37, 20, 21, 26, 31–34, 39, 40, 40 n. 65, 41, 42, 81, 86 n. 125, 88, 88 n. 130, 163, 163 n. 225, 164

Charles II (1661–1700), in 1665 King of Spain xxv

Charles VII (1403–1461), in 1422 King of France 83, 83 n. 121

Charles Leopold of Lorraine *see* Lorraine, Charles Leopold Nicolas Sixte de

Charles Lewis, Elector Palatine, *see* Karl Ludwig

CHARLEVILLE 105–07

Charny, Louis (1638–1692), chevalier (later, comte) de xxiii n. 17, 105, 105 n. 150, 132, 132 n. 194

Charost, Armand de Béthune (1641–1717), duc de 165, 176

CHARTRES 189

Chartres, Marie-Anne d'Orléans, Mlle de *see* Orléans

Châteauneuf, ?Louis-Joachim de Simiane, marquis de 136

Châteauneuf, marquise de, wife of the foregoing 136

Châtelet, M. du (perhaps Charles (c. 1623–1691), chevalier (in 1659, marquis) du Châtelet, from 1644 in the service of Gaston d'Orléans) 78

CHÂTELLERAULT xii, 201

CHÂTILLON 82, 82 n.119

Châtillon, Élisabeth-Angélique de Montmorency-Bouteville (?1627–1695), duchesse de 46, 65 n. 99, 69, 70, 88, 103, 121

CHÂTRES (nowadays ARPAJON) 47, 47 n. 73

Chavigny (Hôtel de), Paris 71, 71 n. 105
Chavigny, Léon Bouthillier (1608–1652), comte de 45, 45 n. 70, 46, 63, 71
Chemerault, Françoise de Barbezières (d. 1678), Mlle de, maid of honour to Anne of Austria, later Mme de la Bazinière 9, 12, 115, 115 n. 166
Chenonceaux 8
Chetrupe, Mme de *see* Stuppa
Chevreuse, Charlotte-Marie de Lorraine (1627–1652), known as Mlle de 76
Chilly 86, 87, 89, 91
Chiverni, Cécile-Élisabeth Hurault de (1618–1695), in 1645 wife of François-de-Paule de Clermont, marquis de Montglat xxiii n. 17, 14, 16, 84, 93, 133, 136
Choisy (le-Roi) 200, 200 n. 273, 203–07
Choisy, Jean de (d. 1660), in 1644 Gaston's chancellor 19
Choisy, Jeanne-Olympe Hurault de l'Hôpital (c. 1604–1669), Mme de, wife of the foregoing xxiii n. 17, 19, 74, 111
Choisy, Mme de, daughter-in-law of the foregoing, wife of Jean-Paul de Choisy (d. 1697) 207
Christina (1626–1689), Queen of Sweden 1632–1654: xv, 91–95, 108, 108 n. 156, 109–11, 114–16, 118
Christine de France (1606–1663), Duchess of Savoy, Mademoiselle's aunt and, in 1619, the wife of Victor Amadeus I: xxi, 2, 81, 124, 129, 138 n. 203
Cinq-Mars, Henri Coiffier d'Effiat (1620–1642), marquis de 12, 13, 13 n. 26, 14, 14 n. 29, 86 n. 127
Clement VII (1342–1394), in 1378 Anti-Pope 136 n. 202
Clement IX, Pope, *see* Rospigliosi
Cléry 47, 47 n. 75, 54
Clinchamp (or Clinchamps), baron de 47, 47 n. 76, 57, 58, 66
Clinchamp, Bernardin, baron de 47 n. 76
Clinchamps, Louis (1624–1680), sieur de 47 n. 76
Cœur, Jacques (1400–1456) 83, 83 n. 121
Colbert, Jean-Baptiste (1619–1683), Controller General of Finances xvi, 108, 163, 163 n. 224, 164 n. 226, 201, 204, 206, 208
Colbert-Croissy *see* Croissy, Charles Colbert, marquis de
Cologne xxiii
Colombes 173, 173 n. 239
Colombier, one of Mademoiselle's gentlemen 138
Combalet, Antoine de 5 n. 12
Combalet, Marie-Madeleine de Vignerot de *see* Aiguillon, Marie-Madeleine de Vignerot, duchesse d'
Combrailles xii
Comminges, Gaston (1613–1670), comte de, lieutenant of the queen's guards 28, 29, 34, 92, 93, 140, 141
Compiègne 21, 33, 34, 37, 155, 207, 207 n. 283

CONDÉ (HÔTEL DE), Paris 75
Condé, Charlotte-Marguerite de Montmorency, princesse de (1594–1650), mother of the Grand Condé 9, 10, 11 n. 20, 27, 29
Condé, Anne-Geneviève de Bourbon-Condé, daughter of the foregoing, *see* Longueville, duchesse de
Condé, Louis II de Bourbon (1621–1686), prince de, son of Charlotte-Marguerite, otherwise Monsieur le Prince, also called the Grand Condé xxiii n. 17, 29, 30, 81, 94, 101 n. 146, 102, 102 n. 147, 137, 188, 188 n. 257

    in the Fronde xvii, 35, 36, 39, 43, 44 n. 69, 45, 46, 47 n. 76, 48 n. 77, 51, 54, 56–59, 61–63, 67–70, 70 n. 103, 71, 72, 74, 74 n. 108, 105

    and Gaston d'Orléans 62, 63, 68, 72, 74, 74 n. 108

    relationship with Mademoiselle xvii, xx, xxi, 24, 35, 36, 36 n. 54, 37, 78, 83, 103, 191, 191 n. 267

    his marriage xxi, xxii, 13, 32, 38, 103

    and Mazarin 36, 37, 56, 63, 105

    military victories 24, 61, 107 n. 152

    and Spain xiii, 74 n. 107, 102 n. 147

Condé, Claire-Clémence de Maillé-Brézé (1628–1694), princesse de, wife of the foregoing xxi, xxii, 6, 29, 32, 38, 81, 103, 169
Condé, Henri-Jules de, son of Louis II and Claire-Clémence, *see* Duc, Monsieur le
CONFLANS 188, 189
Conti, Armand de Bourbon (1629–1666), prince de, son of Charlotte-Marguerite de Condé and brother of Louis II de Bourbon-Condé 35–37, 51, 54
Conti, Anne-Marie Martinozzi (1637–1672), princesse de, Mazarin's niece, wife the foregoing 123, 130, 132, 133
CORBEIL 86, 95
Corneille, Pierre (1606–1684) viii
    La Suite du Menteur 148, 149
COSNE 129
COURS-LA-REINE, Paris 18, 18 n. 34
Courtenay, Lucrèce-Chrétienne de Harlay (c. 1620–1675), princesse de 126
COURTRAI 163
Cramail, Adrien de Monluc (1568–1646), comte de 55
Cramail, Jeanne de Monluc de, daughter of the foregoing, *see* Sourdis
CRÉQUI (HÔTEL DE), Charenton 189, 189 n. 263
CRÉQUI (HÔTEL DE), Paris 189 n. 263
Créqui, Charles (1624–1687), comte (in 1662 duc) de 184, 189, 192
Créqui, Armande de Lusigny de Lansac (1637–1709), comtesse (in 1662 duchesse) de, wife of the foregoing 121, 159
Créqui, François de Blanchefort de (1629–1687), younger brother of Charles, Marshal 194

Créqui, Catherine de Rougé (1641–1713), wife of the Marshal 189, 194
Crèvecœur, Nicolas Gouffier (1620–1705), marquis de 8 n. 16
Crillon, Louis de Bertou (1608–1695), marquis de 135, 135 n. 200
Crillon, Marie d'Albertas (b. 1611), marquise de, wife of the foregoing 135, 136
Crofts, William (1611–1677), Baron, chamberlain to the Duke of York and later to Charles II: 88, 88 n. 130, 117
Croissy, Charles Colbert (1625–1696), marquis de 163, 163 n. 224, 164 n. 226
Croissy, Fouquet de, councillor in the parlement 45, 47, 50, 59
Cromwell, Oliver (1599–1658) 123

Damville, François-Christophe de Levis-Ventadour (1603–1661), comte de Brion, duc de, Monsieur's master of the horse 99, 116
DANNERY 76, 77
Dauphin *see* Louis de France
Dauphine *see* Bavaria, Anne-Marie-Christine-Victoire of
DAX 141
Denmark, Frederick of Holstein (1609–1670), Prince of xxi
Des Marais (or Des Marets), Nicolas Dauvet (1602–1678), comte 119
Des Marais (or Des Marets), Christine de Lantage d'Éguilly, comtesse, wife of the foregoing xxii, 119, 119 n. 175
Des Marais (or Des Marets), Marie-Anne, Mlle, daughter of Nicolas and Christine, wife of Henri de Béthune, comte de Selles xxii, 119
Des Noyers, restaurateur 91
DIEPPE 39
DIJON xx, 124
DOMBES xii, xiv, xviii, 59 n. 90, 124, 124 nn. 184 & 185, 125, 126, 126 n. 188, 127, 127 n. 191, 128, 133, 188, 200
DOMFRONT xii
DOUAI 162
DOVER 163, 166
Du Blé, Jacques *see* Huxelles, Jacques du Blé, baron d'
Du Breuil, Claude Damas (c. 1616–1691), marquis 126, 126 n. 188
Duc, Henri-Jules de Bourbon-Condé (1643–1709), called Monsieur le, son of the Grand Condé xxi, 13, 27, 188, 188 n. 257
Du Deffant, Mme (d. ?1675), mistress of the wardrobe to Madame, Mademoiselle's stepmother 188
DUNES, BATTLE OF THE xx, 119
DUNKIRK 119, 123, 163, 163 n. 223, 196

Edward (1625–1663), Prince Palatine of the Rhine xvi n. 9
Effiat, Antoine Coiffier de Ruzé (1581–1632), marquis de 86 n. 127, 87
Effiat, Marie Coiffier de Ruzé d' (1614–1633), daughter of the foregoing, in 1630 marquise de La Meilleraye 86 n. 127

Effiat, Jean Coiffier (1622–1698), abbé d', son of the foregoing 69
Elbène, Alphonse d' (d. 1665), in 1647 Bishop of Orleans, brother of Guy d'Elbène, Gaston d'Orléans's chamberlain 46, 55, 55 n. 85, 61
Elbeuf, Charles de Lorraine (1596–1657), duc d' 4
Elbeuf, Catherine-Henriette (1596–1663), duchesse d', illegitimate daughter of Henry IV and Gabrielle d'Estrées, known as Mlle de Vendôme, wife of the foregoing 142
Elisabeth Charlotte, duchesse d'Orléans, *see* Orléans, Elisabeth Charlotte, duchesse d'
Élisabeth de France (1602–1644), Queen of Spain, Mademoiselle's aunt and the mother of Maria Theresa, Queen of France 2, 80
Elizabeth Stuart (1596–1662), Electress Palatine, Queen of Bohemia 19 n. 37
ENGHIEN 147
Enghien, son of the Grand Condé, *see* Duc, Henri Jules de Bourbon-Condé, called Monsieur le
ENGLAND 21, 83, 88, 135, 135 n. 199, 163, 164
England, Queen of *see* (1) Henrietta Maria; (2) Catherine of Braganza; (3) Mary Beatrice of Modena; (4) Anne Stuart
Épernon, Bernard de Nogaret de la Valette (1592–1661), duc d', Governor of Guyenne xxvii, 18, 113 n. 162
Épernon, Marie de Cambout de Coislin (d. 1691), Richelieu's niece, in 1634 duchesse d', second wife of Bernard xxiii n. 17, 18, 41, 42, 87, 91
Épernon, Anne-Louise-Christine de Foix de la Valette (1624–1701), Mlle d', daughter of Bernard by his first wife Gabrielle-Angélique de Bourbon (1603–1627) xxii, xxiii, 4, 18, 113 n. 162, 193
ÉPÔNE, château of 189
Escars, Charles de la Renaudie (b. 1611), comte d'Escars et de Ségur 10 n. 19, 78, 84, 85, 92, 102
Escars, Charlotte de Hautefort (1620–1712), called Mlle d' 10, 10 n. 19
Escars, Françoise d' *see* Ségur
Escars, Marie d' *see* Hautefort
Esselin, Louis (1602–1662) 92, 92 n. 139
ESSONNE 92
Estrades, Godefroi d' 89 n. 132
Estrades, Marie de Lallier du Pin (d. 1662), in 1637 comtesse d' 89, 89 n. 132
ÉTAMPES 44, 47, 47 n. 73, 71
EU viii, xiv, xv, xxiii, 108, 130, 146, 178, 200, 207–09
ÉVRY 92 n. 138

Fauconberg, Thomas Belasyse (1627–1700), Viscount 123, 123 n. 183
Favier, Jacques, sieur de Boullay-Thierry, member of the conseil d'état and brother-in-law of President Viole 3
Ferdinand III (1608–1657), in 1637 Emperor of Austria (Holy Roman Emperor) xx, 20, 20 n. 39, 21, 22, 32

Ferdinand IV (1633–1654), son of the foregoing, in 1647 King of Hungary 32

Ferdinand of Austria (c. 1609–1641), Cardinal-Infante of Spain xx, xx n. 13, 11, 12, 14

Fienne (or Fiennes), Marc de Fruges (?1589–1654), vicomte de 42

Fiennes, Françoise de Fruges, comtesse des Chapelles, half-sister of the foregoing, known as Mme de 104

Fiesque, Anne Le Veneur (1585–1653), comtesse de xix, 15, 16, 16 n. 31, 17, 29, 29 n. 49, 41, 46, 82, 83

Fiesque, Charles Léon (1610–1658), comte de, son of the foregoing 13, 16 n. 31, 43–46, 62, 69

Fiesque, Gilonne-Marie-Julie d'Harcourt (1619–1699), comtesse de, wife of Charles Léon, mistress of Philibert, chevalier de Gramont xiv, 45, 46, 52, 55, 69, 78, 81, 84, 84 n. 124, 86, 91–93, 105, 117, 122, 122 n. 181, 133, 189, 198, 208

Fiesque, Jean-Louis (1641–1708), comte de, son of Charles Léon and Gilonne-Marie 17

Flamarens, Agésilas-Antoine de Grossolles (1610–1652), marquis de, chamberlain to Gaston d'Orléans 45, 49, 65 n. 99, 72

Flavacourt, François-Marie de Fouilleuse (d. 1679), in 1637 marquis de, Governor of Gisors 89

Fleix, Marie-Claire de Bauffremont (1618–1680), comtesse de, daughter of the marquise de Senecey and lady-in-waiting to Anne of Austria 101, 102, 130

FLORENCE viii, xxii

FONTAINEBLEAU 4, 22, 57, 81, 86, 91, 108, 110, 111, 120–23, 130, 130 n. 193, 143, 147, 197

Fontanges, Angélique de Scoraille de Roussille (1661–1681), Mlle de 203 n. 280

FONTEVRAULT 8, 8 n. 16, 80

Fontevrault, Jeanne-Baptiste de Bourbon (1608–1670), abbess of 80, 80 n. 116

FORGES-LES-EAUX xiii, 86, 89, 90, 104, 108, 119, 120, 144–47, 170, 171, 197, 208

Foucquet *see* Fouquet

Fouilloux, Bénigne de Meaux (c. 1638–1720), Mlle de, in 1667 marquise d'Alluye 121, 122, 201, 201 n. 275, 205

Fouilloux, Jacques de, ensign of the queen's guards, brother of the foregoing 112

Fouquerolles, Jeanne Lambert d'Herbigny (d. after 1667), marquise de xiii n. 3, 59

Fouquet, Nicolas (1615–1680), Surintendant of Finances 83 n. 121, 118 n. 172

Fouquet, Marie-Madeleine de Castile (1636–1716), Mme, second wife of the foregoing 118 n. 172

Fouquet, Marie-Madeleine (1656–1720), Mlle, daughter of the foregoing, later marquise de Crussol 204, 205
Fouquet, Basile (1622–1680), abbé, brother of Nicolas 103
Fourilles, René de Chaumejan (?1600–c. 1660), marquis de, lieutenant-colonel of the guards 137
Fourilles, Marie Testu de Frouville, in 1624 marquise de, wife of the foregoing 8
FRANCE:
 as a setting for novels xxiv, 40
 Charles II's liking for 40
France, Christine-Marie de *see* Christine de France
France, Élisabeth de *see* Élisabeth de France
France, Henriette-Marie de *see* Henrietta Maria
France, Louis de *see* Louis de France
France, Marie-Thérèse de *see* Marie-Thérèse de France
France, 'Nicolas' de (1607–1611), duc d'Orléans, second son of Henry IV xxix, 2, 2 n. 2
FRANCHART (hermitage) 121, 121 n. 176
Francis I (1494–1547), in 1515 King of France xxvi, 29 n. 50
Frontenac, Louis de Buade (1620 or 1622–1698), comte de, in 1672 Governor of New France (Canada) xiv, 78, 84, 116
Frontenac, Anne de la Grange-Trianon (1632–1707), comtesse de, wife of the foregoing xiv, 38, 45, 46, 52, 55, 75, 77, 78, 80, 84, 84 n. 124, 86, 91, 92, 105, 117, 122, 122 n. 181, 133
Froulai, Charles (1601–1671), comte de 108

Gaston de France *see* Orléans, Gaston-Jean-Baptiste, duc d'
GENEVA 124
George I (1660–1727), in 1714 King of England vii
Georges, Father, a Capuchin 44
Gesvres, Léon Potier (1620–1704), marquis (later, duc) de 145
Gesvres, Marie-Françoise du Val (1632–1702), marquise (later, duchesse) de, wife of the foregoing 186, 186 n. 252, 188
GIEN 61
GISORS 89, 178
Gondi, Jean-François de (1584–1654), Archbishop of Paris 6 n.14
Gondi, Jean-François Paul de *see* Retz
Gonzaga *see* (1) Gonzague ; (2) Mantua
Gonzague, Anne de (1616–1684), princesse palatine xvi, xvi n. 10, 130
Goulas, Nicolas (1603–1683), Gaston's secretary xix, xx, 41
Gourdon, Jean-Paul de (1621–1681), comte de Vaillac, captain of the guard to Philippe d'Orléans 112
Gourdon, Henrietta Douglas Gordon (1633–1673), called Mlle de, maid of honour to Anne of Austria and later to Henrietta Anne 116

Gourville, Jean Hérault de (1625–1703) 65
Gramont, Antoine II (c. 1570–1644), comte (in 1643 duc) de 4, 4 n. 8
Gramont, Antoine III (1604–1678), in 1641 Marshal, in 1644 duc de, ambassador to Madrid, son of Antoine II by his first marriage 4 n. 8, 132
Gramont, Philibert (1621–1707), chevalier de, later comte de, half-brother of Antoine III by their father's second wife 4 n. 8, 43, 46, 53, 93
Gramont, Anne-Louise de (d. 1666), later marquise de Feuquières, half-sister of Antoine III by their father's second wife 4, 4 n. 8
Gramont, Charlotte-Catherine (d. 1714), abbess of Notre-Dame du Ronceray in Angers, half-sister of Antoine III by their father's second wife 4, 4 n. 8
Gramont, Suzanne-Charlotte de (d. 1688), later marquise de Saint-Chamond, half-sister of Antoine III by their father's second wife 4, 4 n. 8
Gramont, Catherine-Charlotte (1639–1678), Mlle de, later Princess of Monaco, daughter of Antoine III: xxii, 4 n. 8, 157, 188
Grand Condé *see* Condé, Louis II de Bourbon, prince de
Grand Master of Artillery *see* La Meilleraye
Grasteau, councillor in the parlement 3
GRAVELINES 123
Grillon (family) *see* Crillon
Guéméné, Louis de Rohan (1598–1667), prince de, duc de Montbazon, Governor of the Île-de-France 69
Guéméné, Anne de Rohan (1604–1685), princesse de, wife of the foregoing xxvii, 123
Guiche, Marie-Charlotte de Castelnau (1647–1694), comtesse de, later duchesse de Gramont 150
Guilloire, Jacques, Mademoiselle's man of business after Préfontaine xxiii n. 17, 182, 182 n. 246, 186, 198 n. 271
GUISE (HÔTEL DE), Paris 15, 15 n. 30, 17
Guise, Charles de Lorraine (1571–1640), duc de xviii n. 11, 3 n. 4
Guise, Henriette-Catherine de Joyeuse (1585–1656), Mademoiselle's maternal grandmother, wife of (1) Henri, duc de Montpensier; (2) Charles de Lorraine, duc de xviii, xviii n. 11, 3, 3 n. 4, 17, 17 n. 33, 81, 86, 99
Guise, Henri de Lorraine (1614–1664), duc de, eldest son of the foregoing by her second husband 92, 94
Guise, Marie de Lorraine (1615–1688), called Mlle de, sister of Henri de Lorraine, duc de Guise 17, 17 n. 33, 81, 191
Guise, François de, brother of Henri de Lorraine, duc de Guise, *see* Joinville, François de Lorraine, prince de
Guise, Louis de, brother of Henri de Lorraine, duc de Guise, *see* Joyeuse, Louis de Lorraine, duc de
Guise, Roger de Lorraine (1624–1653), chevalier de, brother of Henri de Lorraine, duc de Guise 17, 17 n. 33, 81

Guise, Louis-Joseph de Lorraine (1650–1671), duc de, son of Louis, duc de Joyeuse, and husband of Mlle's half-sister Élisabeth d'Orléans 147, 172, 172 n . 238, 179, 183, 183 n. 249, 185

Guise, Élisabeth d'Orléans, duchesse de *see* Orléans

Guitaut, François de Comminges (1581–1663), comte de 36 n. 55

Guitaut, Guillaume de Pechpeyrou de Comminges (1626–1685), comte de 36, 36 n. 55, 37, 66

Guitry, Guy de Chaumont (c. 1630–1672), marquis de, Grand Master of the King's Wardrobe 150, 155, 181, 184, 188, 192, 195

Guitry, Jeanne de Caumont de La Force (c. 1637–1726), marquise de, wife of Guy II de Chaumont-Guitry, second cousin of the foregoing 188, 189

Habsburg *see* (1) Ferdinand III; (2) Ferdinand IV; (3) Leopold William

Hardouin de Péréfixe de Beaumont, Paul-Philippe (1606–1671), in 1662 Archbishop of Paris 187, 187 n. 254

Harlay de Champvallon, François (1625–1695), in 1671 Archbishop of Paris 182 n. 246

Haro, Don Luis de (1599–1661), Spanish Chief Minister 132

Hautefort, Marie d'Escars (1616–1691), called Mme de, in 1646 wife of Charles, Marshal Schomberg 9, 10, 10 n. 19, 11, 12

HAZEBROUCK 163 n. 223

Henrietta Anne *see* Orléans, Henrietta Anne, duchesse d'

Henrietta Maria (Henriette-Marie de France, 1609–1669), Queen of England, Mademoiselle's aunt, in 1625 wife of the future Charles I: vii, xiv, xxv, 2, 6 n. 14, 13 n. 25, 18–20, 26, 27, 32, 33, 39, 40, 42, 81, 86–89, 113, 116, 123, 168, 168 n. 232, 173, 173 n. 239

Henriette d'Angleterre *see* Orléans, Henrietta Anne, duchesse d'

Henry IV (1553–1610), in 1589 King of France vii, xxvi, xxix, 2, 2 n. 1, 13 n. 25, 27 n. 47, 29 n. 50, 80, 80 n. 116, 97, 106, 142

Henry VIII (1491–1547), in 1509 King of England 135 n. 199

HESDIN 164

Hesselin *see* Esselin

Hocquincourt, Charles de Monchy (1599–1658), in 1651 Marshal d' 43, 61

Hollac, Wolfgang Julius (1622–1698), Count Hohelohe-Neuenstein, called comte de 71, 77, 78, 102, 102 n. 147

Holy Roman Emperor *see* Ferdinand III

Hôpital, François (?1583–1660), Marshal de l' 63–65, 112, 118

Hôpital, Françoise Mignot de l' (1631–1711), second wife of the foregoing 112

Humières, Louis de Crevant (1628–1694), Marshal d' 200

Humières, Louise-Antoinette de la Châtre (1635–1723), wife of the foregoing 200, 201

Huxelles, Jacques du Blé (d. 1629), baron d' 42 n. 67

Huxelles, Louis Chalon du Blé (1619–1658), marquis d', son of the foregoing 123
Huxelles, Marie le Bailleul, marquise d' (1626–1712), wife of Louis 42 n. 67
Hyde, Anne *see* York, Duchess of

IF, CHÂTEAU D' 140, 140 n. 206
IRELAND xiv, 32
Irval, Jean-Antoine de Mesmes (1598–1673), seigneur d' 3

James I (1566–1625), in 1603 King of England xvi n. 9
James II (1633–1701), Duke of York, later King of England 1685–1688: xiv, 40, 40 n. 65, 42, 81, 86, 87, 168, 168 n. 231, 196
James Francis Edward (1688–1766), Prince, son of the foregoing xiv
Jansen (or Jansenius), Cornelius (1585–1638), in 1636 Bishop of Ypres 95, 97
JARGEAU 48, 48 n. 78, 49, 130
Jarnac, Guy Chabot (c. 1562–?1640), comte de 4 n. 11
Jarnac, Claire Chabot (1620–1691), Mlle de, daughter of the foregoing 4, 4 n. 11
Jarnac, Charlotte de (born c. 1630), sister of Claire 4, 4 n. 11
Jarnac, Marie (born c. 1630), sister of Claire 4, 4 n. 11
Jean-François, Jesuit Father (also called Jean-Antoine) 79, 79 n. 114
Jeannin de Castile, Nicolas (d. 1691) 117, 118, 118 n. 172
Jermyn, Henry (1605–1684), Lord 32, 33, 35, 40–42
Jodelet, Julien Bedeau (c. 1596–1660), actor, known as 94
JOINVILLE xii
Joinville, François de Lorraine (1611–1639), prince de 81
JOUARRE 95, 145
Joyeuse, Henriette-Catherine de *see* Guise
Joyeuse, Louis de Lorraine (1622–1654), duc de 17, 17 n. 33, 81

Karl Ludwig (1617–1680), Elector Palatine xvi n. 9

La Bazinière, Macé Bertrand de (d. 1688) 115 n. 166
La Bazinière, Françoise de Barbezières-Chemerault de, wife of the foregoing, *see* Chemerault
La Boulaye, Maximilien Échelard (1612–1688), son-in-law of the duc de Bouillon 65
LA BOURDAISIÈRE 7
La Bruyère, Jean de (1645–1696), writer and moralist viii
LA CASSINE 107, 107 n. 152
La Croix, M. de 66

Lafayette, Marie-Madeleine Pioche de la Vergne, comtesse de (1634–1693), *La Princesse de Clèves* xxiv
LA FÈRE 91, 91 n. 137
La Ferté, Henri de Senneterre (?1599–1681), Marshal de 38 n. 60, 71, 123
La Ferté, Madeleine d'Angennes de la Loupe (1629–1714), second wife of the Marshal 38, 38 n. 60
La Force, Jean Nompar de Caumont (1629–1699), duc de 205
La Guérinière, M. de, Mademoiselle's major-domo 76
La Hillière (or La Ilhière), Jean-François de Polastron (1625–1697), chevalier de, lieutenant in the king's guards, from 1656 attached to the household of Mademoiselle 203, 203 n. 279, 205
La Hillière, Mme de, wife of the foregoing 188
La Ilhière *see* La Hillière
La Lande, ?Jean de (b. after 1629), ensign 108
La Loupe, Catherine-Henriette, daughter of the baron de, *see* Olonne, comtesse d'
La Loupe, Madeleine, daughter of the baron de, *see* La Ferté, wife of the Marshal de
La Marck, Louise-Madeleine Échelard de (1659–1717), daughter of La Boulaye, later duchesse de Duras 158
LA MARFÉE 13, 13 n. 24
La Meilleraye, Charles de la Porte (1602–1664), marquis (and, in 1639, Marshal) de, Grand Master of the Artillery 4 n. 7, 67, 67 n. 101, 86 n. 127, 108, 108 n. 55
La Meilleraye, Marie de Cossé, second wife of the Marshal, *see* Brissac
La Mothe (or La Mothe-Argencourt), Madeleine de Conti d'Argencourt (c. 1638–1718), called Mlle de, maid of honour to Anne of Austria, later Mme de Barail 112, 122, 189 n. 260
La Mothe (or La Mothe-Houdancourt), Louise de Prie de (1624–1709), wife of Philippe, Marshal de La Mothe (1605–1657) and, later, governess to the children and grandchildren of Louis XIV: 176
LANDRECIES 156, 156 n. 215, 158, 160, 160 n. 218
Langlée, M. and Mme, near neighbours of Mademoiselle at Saint-Fargeau 82
Langlée, Catherine Roze de Cartabalan (c. 1620–1698), Mme de 204
Langres, Bishop of *see* La Rivière
Lannoi, Anne-Élisabeth de (1626–1654), later duchesse d'Elbeuf 4
LAON 141 n. 210
La Richardière, M. de, a Norman gentleman 145
La Rivière, Louis Barbier (1595–1670), abbé de, chaplain to Gaston d'Orléans, in 1655 Bishop of Langres 14, 21, 27, 32, 34, 35, 92
La Rochefoucauld, François VI (1613–1680), duc de, author of the *Maximes* xxii, 65, 66, 172 n. 237

La Rochefoucauld, François VII (1634–1714), prince de Marcillac, son of the foregoing, in 1680 duc de 65

La Roche-Giffard, Henri de la Chapelle (c. 1616–1652), marquis de 67

LA ROCHE-SUR-YON xii

La Salle, Louis de Caillebot (d. 1682), seigneur (in 1673 marquis) de, captain of the gendarmes in the king's guard, lieutenant-general 108

Lascaris-Castellar, Gaspard de (d. 1684) 134, 134 n. 198, 135–37

La Trappe, Armand-Jean de Boutheiller de Rancé (1626–1700), abbot of 4 n. 10, 200, 200 n. 272

La Trémouille, Marie-Charlotte (1632–1682), Mlle de, in 1662 Duchess of Saxe-Jena 109, 109 n. 159, 110

Launay-Gravé, Françoise Godet des Marais (died c. 1660), Mme de 91, 91 n. 136

LAUZUN 209

Lauzun, Antonin Nompar de Caumont (1633–1723), comte (in 1692 duc) de xiii n. 4, xviii, xxviii, 147, 158, 189 n. 260, 209 n. 287

    his arrest and imprisonment xiv, xxxi, 140 n. 206, 197–99, 201

    and Louis XIV xiii, xxx, 154, 179

    relationship with Mademoiselle xii, xiii, 148–56, 159–65, 167–71, 173, 174, 201–08

    possible marriage to Mademoiselle xi, xiv, xxx, 172, 172 n. 236, 175–97, 200, 206 n. 282

    final break with Mademoiselle xiv, 208, 209

    his military exploits and responsibilities xiii, xiv, 147, 154, 168, 168 n. 229, 179

    portrait of xiii, 148, 151, 156, 195

    relationships with other women xxii, 157, 162, 201

Laval, Guillaume de Sève de *see* Sève de Laval, Guillaume de

Laval, Marie Séguier (1618–1710), duchesse de 4 n. 9, 76, 76 n. 111

La Vallière, Gabrielle Glé de la Costardais (1648–1707), marquise de, lady-in-waiting to Maria Theresa 158, 158 n. 217, 159

La Vallière, Louise-Françoise le Blanc de la Baume (1644–1710), Mlle (in 1667 duchesse) de xxii, xxiii, 158, 158 n. 217, 166, 173

Lavardin, Marguerite de Rostaing de la Baume (d. 1694), in 1642 marquise de, widow in 1644 of Henri de Beaumanoir, marquis de Lavardin 84

La Vieuville, Charles Coskaër (1616–1689), marquis (later, duc) de 4

La Ville-aux-Clercs, Marie-Antoinette de Loménie de Brienne (1624–1704), called Mlle de, in 1642 marquise de Gamaches 4

LE CATELET 161

Le Coigneux *see* Bachaumont

Le Fèvre de la Barre, Antoine 63

LE HAVRE 36

Le Maître, Antoine (1608–1658), nephew of Robert Arnauld d'Andilly 96, 97

LENS 24
Leopold William (1614–1662), Archduke of Austria, younger brother of Ferdinand III, Governor of the Spanish Netherlands xx, 32, 32 n. 52
LE QUESNOY 161
Le Tellier, Michel (1603–1685), in 1643 Secretary of State for War, in 1677 Chancellor 125, 125 n. 186, 187, 187 n. 253
Le Tellier, François-Michel, son of the foregoing *see* Louvois
Le Tellier, Claude-Maurice (1642–1710), son of Michel Le Tellier, in 1675 Archbishop of Reims 187, 187 n. 253
LEUCATE 141 n. 211
Le Vau, Louis (1612–1670), Fouquet's architect 83 n. 121
Le Vau, Louis-François (1613–1676), brother of the foregoing, known as François, Mademoiselle's architect 83, 83 n. 121
L'Hôpital *see* Hôpital
LILLE 163
LIMOURS 5, 5 n. 13, 38, 75 n. 109, 95
Lixein, Henriette de Lorraine-Vaudémont (1605–1660), Mme de 86, 86 n. 126
Locke, John (1632–1704) xxvi
Lockhart, Sir William (?1621–1675) 123, 123 n. 183
Lomelino (or Lomellini), Stefano Maria (c. 1611–), commander of the Pope's military detachment in Avignon 135
Loménie de Brienne, Marie-Antoinette de *see* La Ville-aux-Clercs, Mlle de
LONDON 39
Longueville, Henri d'Orléans (1595–1663), duc de xxii, 12, 35–37, 91
Longueville, Anne-Geneviève de Bourbon-Condé (1619–1679), duchesse de, wife of the foregoing xxii, 9, 11, 11 n. 20, 74 n. 107, 91, 169
Longueville, Charles-Paris d'Orléans (1649–1672), comte de Saint-Pol, duc de, son of Anne-Geneviève xxi, 172, 172 n. 237, 180, 181
Longueville, Marie d'Orléans (1625–1707), known as Mlle de, in 1657 duchesse de Nemours xvii, 4, 9, 12, 42
LORRAINE, DUCHY OF xxvii, 109 n. 157, 150
Lorraine (family) 191; *see also* Guise
Lorraine, Charles IV (1604–1675), duc de 74, 86 n. 126, 109, 109 n. 157
Lorraine, François de (1609–1670), comte de Vaudémont, brother of the foregoing 109, 109 n. 157
Lorraine, Marguerite de (1615–1672), sister of the foregoing, in 1632 wife of Gaston d'Orléans xvi, xxiv, xxix, xxxi, 5, 5 n. 13, 25, 27, 28, 30, 33, 37, 40, 52, 74, 78–81, 86 n. 126, 93, 109 n. 157, 130–32, 141, 142, 147, 188, 188 n. 258
Lorraine, Charles Léopold Nicolas Sixte (1643–1690), son of François, in 1675 Charles V, duc de xxi, xxii, 109, 109 n. 157, 150, 151
Lorraine, Élisabeth Charlotte, duchesse de *see* Orléans, Élisabeth Charlotte d'

Lorraine, Philippe de Lorraine-Armagnac (1643–1702), chevalier de 140 n. 206, 147, 170, 185 n. 250, 207
Louis XIII (1601–1643), in 1610 King of France viii, xii, xv, xxvi, xxix, xxx, 2, 4, 5, 5 n. 13, 6, 9–11, 13, 13 n. 25, 14, 18, 27, 81, 92 n. 139
Louis XIV (1638–1715), in 1643 King of France viii, ix, xii, xvi, xxii, xxiii n. 17, xxv, xxvi, xxx, 13, 18, 18 n. 35, 20, 34, 41, 91, 92, 100–02, 104, 105, 108, 114, 117, 121, 123, 128, 137, 140, 142, 155–60, 163, 164, 166, 168, 169, 175, 178–81, 185, 186, 188, 195, 196, 203, 205, 208, 208 n. 285
    birth xxix, 11
    and the Fronde 25 n. 41, 26–29, 31, 35, 50, 51, 54–56, 59, 70, 70 n. 103, 73, 74, 74 n. 107, 106
    and Gaston d'Orléans 74 n. 108, 122, 131, 132, 138
    illness 119, 120
    and Lauzun xi, xiii, xiv, xxx, 147, 154, 177, 184, 201, 202
    and Mademoiselle xiii, xvi, xx, xxx, 74, 103, 106, 107, 112, 144, 145, 150, 151, 162, 167, 170–74, 182–84, 190–94, 198, 201
    and marriage to Mademoiselle xxi, 38, 103
    and Maria Theresa xviii, 130, 143, 159, 187
    his military exploits 100, 100 n. 145, 106, 139, 139 n. 204, 209
    and Mme de Montespan xiii, xiv, 200, 208, 208 n. 285
    and Philippe d'Orléans xiv, 115, 118, 119
    his search for a wife 124, 129
Louis de France (1661–1711), son of the foregoing, the Grand Dauphin xxx, xxxi, 154, 171–73, 186, 203, 203 n. 278
Louis XV (1710–1774), grandson of the Grand Dauphin, in 1715 King of France 200 n. 273
Louison *see* Roger de la Marbillière, Louison
Louvière, Jérôme de Broussel (d. 1658), sieur de 69, 69 n. 102
Louvois, François-Michel Le Tellier (1641–1691), marquis de, Secretary of State for War 156, 159, 182, 187 n. 253
LOUVRE, Paris viii, xxv, 2, 2 n. 3, 3, 12 n. 23, 18, 24, 25 nn. 42 & 43, 39, 75, 111–18, 123, 124, 181, 186, 190 n. 265
Lude, Charlotte-Marie de Daillon du *see* Roquelaure, duchesse de
Lude, Françoise de Daillon (c. 1623–1644), Mlle du, in 1642 marquise d'Avaugour 4, 87 n. 129
Lully, Jean-Baptiste (1632–1687), violinist and composer viii, 196 n. 269
LUXEMBOURG PALACE, Paris xxv, 24, 36, 37, 45, 62, 71, 74, 75, 81, 107 n. 154, 108, 111 n. 161, 113, 118, 119, 147, 180, 181, 184, 204, 209
LUXEMBURG xxv, 136, 136 n. 202
LUYNES (HÔTEL DE), Paris 26, 26 n. 44
LYON xx, xxvii, 13 n. 26, 79 n. 112, 92, 113, 124, 124 n. 185, 125, 126, 128, 129
Lyon, Archbishop of *see* Villeroy, Camille de Neufville de

Madame *see* (1) Bourbon-Montpensier, Marie de, Mademoiselle's mother; (2) Lorraine, Marguerite de, Mademoiselle's stepmother; (3) Orléans, Henrietta Anne, duchesse d', first wife of Philippe, duc d'Orléans; (4) Orléans, Elisabeth Charlotte, duchesse d', second wife of Philippe, duc d'Orléans

Mademoiselle xxiv, xxv; *see also* (1) Montpensier, Anne-Marie-Louise d'Orléans, duchesse de, La Grande Mademoiselle; (2) Orléans, Marie-Louise d', daughter of Philippe and Henrietta Anne

Maillé-Brézé, Mlle de *see* Condé, Claire-Clémence de Maillé-Brézé, princesse de

Maine, Louis Auguste de Bourbon (1670–1736), duc du xiv, 200

MALLEMORT 140, 140 n. 209

Mancini, Marie (1639–1715), in 1661 wife of Prince Lorenzo Colonna 102, 116, 116 n. 168, 121

Mancini, Marie-Anne (1649–1714), in 1662 duchesse de Bouillon 116 n. 168

Mancini, Olympe *see* Soissons, comtesse de

Mancini, Philippe-Jules *see* Nevers, Philippe-Jules Mancini, duc de

MANTES-LA-JOLIE 189 n. 261

Mantua, Charles III Gonzaga (1629–1665), Duke of 107

Mantua, Eleonor Gonzaga (1630–1686), princess of 37

MARAIS THEATRE, Paris 90, 91, 91 n. 135, 121 n. 177

Marais (family) *see* Des Marais

Marguerite de Lorraine *see* Lorraine, Marguerite de

Marguerite de Navarre (1492–1549), otherwise Marguerite d'Angoulême, sister of Francis I: vii

Marguerite de Valois (1553–1615), Queen of France 1589–1599, also called Queen Margot vii, xiv, 78

Maria Anna of Spain *see* Spain

Maria de' Medici *see* Medici

Maria Theresa (1638–1683), Infanta of Spain and, in 1660, wife of Louis XIV and Queen of France xv, 32, 142, 148, 151, 154–59, 161, 166–69, 171, 173, 176, 181, 196, 198, 203
    death xxxi
    wedding to Louis XIV xviii, xxx, 130, 132, 143
    and Mademoiselle 162–64, 172, 174, 182, 185, 186, 186 n. 251, 187, 189, 193, 194
    her piety and religious devotions 150, 153, 185, 187, 195

Marie-Thérèse de France (1667–1672) 170, 170 n. 235

Marion, Simon (1572–1628), grandfather of the Arnauld brothers 97

MARLOU (nowadays MELLO) 88, 88 n. 130

MARSEILLE xvii, 139, 140, 140 n. 208

Martinozzi, Anne-Marie *see* Conti, Anne-Marie, princesse de

Mary Beatrice of Modena (1658–1718), Queen of England 1685–1688: xiv

Mary Stuart (1631–1660), Princess Royal, daughter of Charles I of England and wife of William II of Orange 86, 86 n. 125, 87–89

Matha (or Mastas), Charles de Bourdeille (d. 1674), comte de, in 1640 captain of the regiment of guards 84, 108

Matomenis (or Matomesnil), M. de, gentleman of the county of Eu 146

Maulévrier, Édouard-François Colbert (1633–1693), comte de 164, 164 n. 226

Maupertuis, Louis de Melun (1635–1721), marquis de 200

Maure, Louis de Rochechouart (1602–1669), comte de 84 n. 122

Maure, Anne Doni d'Attichy (?1600–1663), comtesse de, wife of the foregoing 84, 84 n. 122, 133

Mazarin, Jules (Giulio Mazarini) (1602–1661), Cardinal xxx, 30, 31, 59, 60, 79 n. 113, 118, 120, 123, 125, 134 n. 198, 135, 137, 138, 142
    and Christina of Sweden 94, 108 n. 156, 114, 115
    and Condé 36, 37, 74 n. 108
    death xxx
    and the Fronde 26, 36, 43, 56, 64, 65 n. 99, 73
    and Gaston d'Orléans 35–37, 63, 74 n. 108, 79, 103, 122, 138 n. 203
    and Mademoiselle xxi, xxi n. 14, 21, 31, 73, 100–04, 107, 108, 113, 129
    negotiates wedding of Louis XIV: 130 n. 193, 132, 133
    unpopularity ix, 26, 27, 51, 54, 64

Medici, Catherine de' (1519–1589), wife of Henry II and, in 1547, Queen of France viii, 12 n. 23

Medici, Maria de' (1573–1642), in 1600 wife of Henry IV and Queen of France xii, xxv, xxix, 2, 2 n. 1, 3, 3 n. 4, 13, 18 n. 34, 80

MELLO see MARLOU

Menou, Louis de (c. 1595–after 1657), in 1648 Governor of Saint-Fargeau 83, 83 n. 120

Messimieux, Gabriel Bussillet (d. 1670) seigneur de, knight of honour of the parlement of Dombes 127, 127 n. 190, 128

MÉZIÈRES xii

MITRY-MORY 23 n. 40

Molé, Mathieu (1584–1656), First President of the Parlement and Keeper of the Seals 1651–1656: 51, 55, 55 n. 84, 56

Molé, Jean-Édouard, son of the foregoing, *see* Champlâtreux

Molière (Jean-Baptiste Poquelin) (1622–1673):
    Le Bourgeois gentilhomme 173 n. 241
    Psyché 196, 196 n. 269

Monaco, Honoré II Grimaldi (1597–1662), Prince of xxii, 4 n. 8

Monaco, Louis Grimaldi (1642–1701), Prince of, grandson of Honoré II: xxii, 4 n. 8

Monaco, Mme de *see* Gramont, Catherine-Charlotte de

Monaldeschi, Gian Rinaldo (c. 1626–1657), marquis, Queen Christina of Sweden's master of the horse 109–11
Mondevergue, gentleman in the service of Anne of Austria 20, 22
Monglat *see* Montglat
Monsieur *see* (1) Orléans, Gaston d'; (2) Orléans, Philippe d'
Monsieur le Duc *see* Duc, Monsieur le
Monsieur le Prince *see* Condé, Louis II de Bourbon, prince de
MONTAIGU xii
Montaigu, a friend of Lauzun 205
Montaigu, an ensign (cornet) in the king's light horse 106, 107
MONTARGIS 57, 57 n. 87, 82, 86
Montausier, Charles de Sainte-Maure (1610–1690), duc de, Governor of Angoulême and Saintonge 132, 184–88, 192
Montausier, Julie d'Angennes (1607–1671), duchesse de 121, 132, 133, 168
Montbazon, Marie de Bretagne-Avagour (1612–1657), in 1628 duchesse de 12, 89, 200 n. 272
Montbrun, Henri de 118
MONTEREAU 57, 57 n. 87
Montespan, Louis-Henri de Pardaillan de Gondrin (1640–1701), marquis de 208, 208 n. 285
Montespan, Françoise-Athénaïs de Rochechouart (1640–1707), marquise de, wife of the foregoing, mistress of Louis XIV xiii, xiv, 84 n. 122, 86 n. 128, 158, 164, 166, 173, 190, 200–03, 208, 209
Montglat, Françoise de Longuejoue (d. 1632), baronne de, governess to the children of Henry IV 2, 2 n. 2
Montglat, Jeanne de Harlay de *see* Saint-Georges, Jeanne de Harlay de
Montglat, François-de-Paule de Clermont (1620–1675), marquis de, son of Jeanne de Harlay, marquise de Saint-Georges 14, 16, 16 n. 32
Montglat, Cécile-Élisabeth Hurault de Chiverni de *see* Chiverni
MONTLOUIS-SUR-LOIRE 8 n. 16
MONTMÉDY 100, 100 n. 145, 101, 105
Montmort, Marie-Henriette de Frontenac (d. 1679), Mme de 75
MONTPELLIER 133
Montpensier, Henri de Bourbon (1563–1608), duc de, Mademoiselle's maternal grandfather xviii n. 11, 81
Montpensier, Henriette-Catherine de Joyeuse, duchesse de, wife of the foregoing, Mademoiselle's maternal grandmother *see* Guise
Montpensier, Marie de Bourbon, duchesse de, Mademoiselle's mother *see* Bourbon-Montpensier
Montpensier, Anne-Marie-Louise d'Orléans (1627–1693), duchesse de, the Grande Mademoiselle
    birth and childhood viii, xii, xxv, xxix, 1–18
    and Anne of Austria xxi, 2, 4, 9–11, 20, 22, 25, 27, 29, 31, 33, 34, 99–101, 106, 107, 142, 147

her character ix, xvii–xix, 3, 9, 31, 85, 138, 142, 153
and Charles, Prince of Wales, later Charles II: 18–21, 39, 42
    possible marriage to vii, xvii, xx, xxi, 31–35, 40, 41, 88, 163–65
and Christina of Sweden 91–95, 108–11, 114–16, 118
and Condé xvii, xx, xxi, 24, 35, 36, 36 n. 54, 37, 38, 46, 48, 59, 66, 71, 78, 83, 101 n. 146, 103, 191, 191 n. 267
death xiv, xxxi
and her estates and properties xii
    Bois-le-Vicomte 23, 23 n. 40, 24, 38, 109 n. 158
    Champigny 105, 109, 109 n. 158
    Choisy 200, 200 n. 273, 203–07
    Dombes xiv, 124–27, 127 n. 191, 128, 129, 133, 188, 200
    Eu viii, xiv, xv, xxiii, 108, 130, 145, 146, 200, 207–09
    Luxembourg palace, Paris xxv, 24, 75, 108, 111, 113, 119, 147, 181, 204
    Saint-Fargeau viii, xiii, xxiii, xxiv, 75–86, 95, 110, 129, 145, 201
and the Fronde ix, xi, xii, 24–31, 43, 61, 62
    the Faubourg Saint-Antoine xvii, xxi, 63–70, 70 n. 103, 71–73, 75, 99
    in Orleans xix, 44–46, 50, 51, 51 n. 81, 52–61, 74, 75, 99
and Gaston d'Orléans, her father viii, xii, xiii, xv, xvii, xx, 3, 5, 7, 8, 14–18, 21, 22, 24–33, 36–38, 40, 41, 44–46, 72, 74, 75, 77–80, 83, 84, 84 n. 124, 85, 86, 88, 94, 110, 122, 123, 131, 132, 137, 138, 138 n. 203
and members of the Guise family xviii, xviii n. 11, xxv, 3, 3 n. 4, 17, 147, 172, 183, 183 n. 249, 185
and her half-sisters xviii, 80, 131, 132, 141, 142, 147, 183, 187
and Henrietta Anne, Philippe d'Orléans's first wife xv, xxiii, 150, 166, 169
illnesses and medical treatments 35, 39, 41, 108, 147, 155
and Lauzun 147
    relationship with xii, xiii, xviii, 148–56, 159–65, 167–71, 173, 174, 201–08
    possible marriage to xi, xiv, xxx, 172, 172 n. 236, 175–97, 200, 206 n. 282
    final break with xiv, 208, 209
and Louis XIII: 10
and Louis XIV: xiii, xvi, xx, xxi, xxx, 11, 18, 38, 74, 100, 103, 106, 107, 112, 144, 145, 150, 151, 162, 167, 170–74, 182–84, 190–94, 198, 201
and Marguerite de Lorraine, her stepmother xv, 5, 25, 28, 33, 79, 80, 141, 142, 147, 188

and Maria Theresa 142, 157, 158, 162–64, 172, 174, 182, 185, 186, 186 n. 251, 187, 189, 193, 194
and Mazarin ix, xv, xxi, xxi n. 14, 21, 31, 36, 56, 73, 74 n. 108, 100–04, 107, 108, 113, 129
possible marriages (apart from Charles II, Philippe d'Orléans, and Lauzun) xiii, xvi, xx, xx n. 13, xxi, 6, 10–13, 20–22, 31, 37, 37 n. 58, 38, 79, 80, 103, 144–46, 149–51, 172, 196
her memoirs xi, xii, xiv, xv, xviii–xx, xxvii, xxvii n. 19, xxviii, 1, 3, 78, 130, 184
and Mme de Montespan xiii, xiv, 200, 202, 203, 208, 209
and Philippe d'Orléans 120, 121
    relationship with 18, 100, 101, 103–05, 111, 113–18, 124, 126, 193
    possible marriage to xxi, 112, 167–72, 172 n. 236, 173–75
physical characteristics xvii, xxv, 19, 20, 35, 99, 100
plays, actors and playwrights viii, ix, 9, 18, 19, 79, 79 n. 112, 90, 91, 91 n. 135, 93, 94, 112, 116, 116 n. 167, 121, 121 n. 177, 142, 146, 148, 149, 173, 173 n. 241, 196
and protocol xvi, 11, 32, 113, 114, 116, 142, 168, 195
and reading viii, xiv, xix, xxiv, 78, 84, 146
and religion ix, xi, 21, 22, 44, 89, 95–98, 128, 136, 136 n. 202, 137, 139, 141, 142, 146, 148, 154, 159, 173, 182, 194, 200
and Richelieu 5, 11, 14
superstition, horoscopes, and the supernatural xix, 52, 72, 77, 121, 121 n. 178, 162, 188, 189
travels:
    to Flanders 154–65, 196, 197
    to Forges xiii, 86, 89–91, 104, 108, 119, 120, 144, 145, 147, 170, 171, 197, 208
    to Lyon xx, 79 n. 112, 124, 125, 128, 129
    to Port-Royal-des-Champs 95–99
    to Sedan 99–108
    in the south of France xvii, 130–43
at wedding of Louis XIV and Maria Theresa xvi, xviii, 142, 143
writings:
    Divers Portraits xxiii, xxiii n. 17, 110
    Histoire de Jeanne-Lambert d'Herbigny, marquise de Fouquerolle xiii, xiii n. 4, xiv, xxiii, 78
    L'Histoire de la princesse de Paphlagonie xxiii, 133, 133 n. 195
    [*Letters to Mme de Motteville*] 142, 143, 211
    Nouvelles françoises, ou les Divertissements de la Princesse Aurélie xxiii

Réflexions morales et chrétiennes sur le Premier Livre de l'Imitation de Jesus-Christ xxiii

Réflexions sur les Huit Béatitudes du Sermon de Jesus-Christ sur la Montagne xxiii

Relation de l'isle imaginaire xxiii, 127 n. 190, 133 n. 195

MONTROND 48, 48 n. 77

Montsoreau, Bernard de Combes (1622–1669), comte de 190 n. 264

Montsoreau, Marie-Geneviève (c. 1639–1715), Mlle de, daughter of the foregoing, in 1677 marquise de Sourches 190 n. 264

Montsoreau, Louis-François du Bouchet (1645–1716), comte de, gentleman-in-ordinary to the king, son-in-law of Bernard de Combes and, in 1677, marquis de Sourches 190, 190 n. 264

Morangis *see* Barrillon

Mornay, René (d. 1691), abbé de Villarceaux 117

Morosini, Giovanni (1604–1676), Venetian ambassador to France from 1668 to 1671: 160, 161

MORTAIN xii

Mortemart, Gabrielle de Rochechouart, called Mlle de *see* Thiange

Motteville, Françoise Bertaut (1621–1689), Mme de xxiii, xxiv, 6 n. 14, 142, 143, 211

Navailles, Philippe de Montaut-Bénac (1619–1684), comte (later, duc) de 108, 144

Navailles, Suzanne de Baudéan, duchesse de, wife of the foregoing, *see* Neuillant, Suzanne de Baudéan, Mlle de

Nemours, Charles-Amédée de Savoie (1624–1652), duc de 44, 46, 48, 49, 56–58, 62, 65, 65 n. 99, 66

Nemours, Élisabeth de Vendôme (1614–1664), duchesse de, in 1643 wife of Charles-Amédée *see* Vendôme, Élisabeth de

Nemours, Marie-Jeanne-Baptiste de (1644–1724), daugher of Charles-Amédée and Élisabeth, in 1665 second wife of Charles Emmanuel II, Duke of Savoy 113, 113 n. 163, 114, 205

Nemours, Marie-Françoise de (1646–1683), daughter of Charles-Amédée and Élisabeth, in 1666 Queen of Portugal 113, 113 n. 163, 114, 162, 162 n. 221

Nemours, Marie d'Orléans de, wife of Henri, duc de Nemours, *see* Longueville

Neuburg, Philip William (1615–1690), Duke of, in 1685 Elector Palatine xxi, 79, 79 n. 114, 80

Neuillant, Suzanne de Baudéan (1626–1700), Mlle de, maid of honour to Anne of Austria and later to Maria Theresa, in 1651 the wife of Philippe de Montaut-Bénac, future duc de Navailles 18, 144

NEUVILLE-SUR-SAÔNE *see* VIMY

NEVERS 84 nn. 122 & 123

Nevers, Charles I Gonzaga, duc de (1580–1637), in 1627 Duke of Mantua xvi n. 9
Nevers, Philippe-Jules Mancini (1641–1707), duc de 184
Nevers, Diane-Gabrielle de Thiange (1656–1715), duchesse de, wife of the foregoing 184
NÎMES 133
Noailles, Anne de (1615–1678), comte d'Ayen, in 1663 duc de Noailles 89 n. 132, 165 n. 227, 194, 195, 203
Noailles, Louise Boyer (1631–1697), comtesse d'Ayen, in 1663 duchesse de Noailles 89, 89 n. 132, 130, 194
Nogent, Nicolas de Bautru (d. 1661), comte de 116 n. 169
Nogent, Armand de Bautru (d. 1672), comte de, son of the foregoing 181 n. 245
Nogent, Diane-Charlotte de Caumont de Lauzun (1632–1720), comtesse de, wife of Armand de Bautru 181, 181 n. 245, 184, 188–90, 198, 200, 206
Nogent, Charlotte Bautru (1641–1725), Mlle de, daughter of Nicolas, later marquise de Ranes 115, 116, 116 n. 169, 181 n. 245
Noirmoutier, Louis de la Trémouille (1612–1666), duc de, Governor of Charleville 105, 107
NOYON 155

Olonne, Catherine-Henriette d'Angennes de la Loupe (1634–1714), comtesse d' 38, 38 n. 60, 86, 117, 118
Olonne, Louis de la Trémouille (1626–1686), comte d' 117, 118
ORANGE 124
Orange, William II (1626–1650), Prince of 34, 86 n. 125
Orange, Mary, princess of, wife of the foregoing, *see* Mary Stuart
Orange, William of Nassau (1650–1702), Prince of, son of the foregoing, King of England in 1689: 86 n. 125
ORLEANS xii, xii n. 2, xviii, xix, xxvi, xxx, 43–47, 47 n. 75, 49, 49 n. 79, 50–53, 56, 56 n. 86, 58–61, 67, 68, 72, 74, 75, 78, 80, 83, 84, 95, 99, 108, 130
Orleans, Bishop of *see* Elbène
Orléans, Gaston-Jean-Baptiste (1608–1660), duc d', Mademoiselle's father xviii, xxiv, xxv, xxix, 2, 6, 7, 13, 13 n. 26, 18 n. 35, 19, 23 n. 40, 53 n. 82, 76, 79 n. 112, 80 n. 116, 81, 93, 97, 127, 134, 138 n. 203, 200 n. 272
    and Anne of Austria 6, 22, 38, 122, 131
    and Blois xxv, 6–8, 44, 45, 75 n. 109, 79, 131
    death xxx, 137–39
    and the Fronde xii, 25, 43, 44, 46, 48–50, 54–57, 59, 60, 62, 63, 63 n. 93, 64, 68–70, 72, 74
    and Henrietta Maria 33, 40, 88
    and Louis XIII: xii, 3–5, 14, 14 n. 27
    and Louis XIV: 74 n. 108, 120, 122, 130–32
    and Louison Roger 7, 7 n. 15, 8, 105 n. 150

and Mademoiselle viii, xiii, xv, xx, 5, 7, 8, 14–18, 21, 22, 24–33, 38, 40, 41, 44–46, 72, 74, 75, 77, 78, 80, 83, 84, 84 n. 124, 85, 86, 88, 94, 110, 122, 123, 131, 132, 138
 and Marguerite de Lorraine xxix, 5 n. 13, 27, 28, 30, 33, 78–80, 132
 and Mazarin 21, 35–37, 74 n. 108, 79, 102, 103, 122, 123
 and Richelieu xii, 5, 9, 14

Orléans, Anne-Marie-Louise d', eldest daughter of the foregoing, the Grande Mademoiselle *see* Montpensier, Anne-Marie-Louise d'Orléans, duchesse de

Orléans, Marguerite-Louise d' (1645–1721), called Mlle d'Orléans, daughter of Gaston and Marguerite de Lorraine, in 1661 Grand Duchess of Tuscany xviii, xxii, 27, 30, 131, 141, 142

Orléans, Élisabeth-Marguerite d' (1646–1696), called Mlle Alençon, daughter of Gaston and Marguerite de Lorraine, in 1667 duchesse de Guise xviii, xxv, 27, 131, 141, 142, 147, 172 n. 238, 179, 183, 183 n. 249, 185, 187, 188

Orléans, Françoise-Madeleine d' (1648–1664), called Mlle de Valois, daughter of Gaston and Marguerite de Lorraine, in 1663 first wife of Charles Emmanuel II, Duke of Savoy xviii, 80, 131, 138 n. 203, 141, 142

Orléans, Jean-Gaston (1650–1652), duc de Valois, son of Gaston and Marguerite de Lorraine 47, 47 n. 74

Orléans, Marie-Anne d'(1652–1656), called Mlle de Chartres, daughter of Gaston and Marguerite de Lorraine 93, 93 n. 141

Orléans, Philippe I (1640–1701), duc d', brother of Louis XIV: xxiii n. 17, xxiv, xxv, xxxi, 18 n. 35, 32, 100–03, 106, 107, 114, 121, 123, 138, 138 n. 203, 142, 155, 157, 158, 163, 164, 187, 197, 203
 birth xxix, 13
 and dress 100, 103, 104, 111, 116
 and Henrietta Anne, his first wife xxx, 152 n. 214, 166–68
 and Lauzun 157, 185, 209
 and the chevalier de Lorraine 147, 170, 185 n. 250, 207
 and Louis XIV: xv, 118–20, 186
 and Mademoiselle 18, 104, 105, 111, 113–18, 124, 126, 193
 possible marriage to Mademoiselle xxi, 112, 167–72, 172 n. 236, 173–75
 Mademoiselle's opinion of 100, 120

Orléans, Henrietta Anne (1644–1670), called Henriette d'Angleterre, in 1661 duchesse d', first wife of Philippe, duc d'Orléans xv, xxiii–xxv, xxx, 87, 113, 114, 114 n. 164, 116, 150, 154 n. 214, 157, 158, 162–64, 166–73, 188 n. 258

Orléans, Marie-Louise d' (1662–1689), daughter of Philippe and Henrietta Anne, in 1679 Queen of Spain xxiv, 168, 168 nn. 230, 233, & 234, 171

Orléans, Anne-Marie d' (1669–1728), called Mlle de Valois, daughter of Philippe and Henrietta Anne, Duchess of Savoy in 1684 xxv, 154, 154 n. 214, 168, 168 n. 234

Orléans, Elisabeth Charlotte (1652–1722), duchesse d', second wife of Philippe duc d'Orléans xiii, xiv, xvi, xxiv, xxv, xxxi, 197, 203

Orléans, Élisabeth Charlotte d' (1676–1744), daughter of Philippe and Elisabeth Charlotte, later duchesse de Lorraine xxv

Orléans, Nicolas, duc d' *see* France, 'Nicolas' de

Orval, François de Béthune (1598–1678), duc d', younger son of Maximilien, duc de Sully, master of the horse to Anne of Austria 133

Orval, Anne de Harville-Palaiseau (1626–1716), duchesse d', wife of the foregoing 133, 134, 136

Palaiseau, Anne de Comans (d. 1693), marquise de 207

PALAIS-ROYAL, Paris xxv, 18, 19, 21, 25–27, 36

Palatine (Elector) *see* Karl Ludwig

PARIS vii, xi–xiii, xxvi, 3, 8, 11, 14, 24, 29, 31, 43, 44, 49, 63–66, 72, 91, 108, 110, 111, 123, 129, 130, 137, 139, 143, 155, 167, 169, 171, 179, 184, 196, 198, 200–02, 205, 207, 209

Pascal, Blaise (1623–1662), *Provincial Letters* 97 n. 143

Paulet, Charles, secretary of the Chambre des Comptes under Sully 27 n. 47

Péguilin *see* Lauzun

Péréfixe de Beaumont *see* Hardouin de Péréfixe

PÉRONNE 34, 34 n. 53

PERPIGNAN xxiii, 141, 141 n. 211

Perrault, Charles (1628–1703), *Peau d'Âne* 161 n. 219

Peter of Alcantara, Saint (1499–1562) 150

Peter of Luxemburg, Saint (1369–1387), Bishop of Metz and Cardinal of Avignon 136, 136 n. 202

PETIT-BOURBON, SALLE DU (Paris) 121 n. 177

PETIT-BOURG 92, 92 n. 138, 95

Philip IV (1605–1665), King of Spain in 1621: xx, 12, 32, 72, 80

PINEROLO xiv, 140 n. 206, 199, 201, 206 n. 282

Plessis, César de Choiseul du Plessis-Praslin (1598–1675), Marshal du 103

POISSY 65, 65 n. 97, 89

POITIERS 79

Poland, John II Casimir (1609–1672), King of Poland in 1648: xxii, xxii n. 16

Poland, Ladislas IV (1595–1648), King of Poland in 1632: xxii, xxii n. 16

Pompadour, Antoinette Poisson (1721–1764), marquise de 200 n. 273

PONT (SUR-SEINE) 23, 75, 81, 95

PONT-DE-L'ARCHE 37, 37 n. 57

PONT DU GARD 134

Pontac, Arnaud de, First President of the parlement of Bordeaux 133 n. 195
Pontac, Louise de Thou (c. 1600–1681), Mme de, wife of the foregoing 133, 133 n. 195
PONTOISE 74 n. 107, 89
POPINCOURT 70
PORT-ROYAL (Paris) 96
PORT-ROYAL-DES-CHAMPS xxiii, 96, 97, 99
Portugal, King of *see* Alphonse VI
POUGUES 84, 84 n. 123
Pradelles, M. de, captain of the king's regiment of guards 105
Pradine, ?Paul de, lieutenant of Monsieur's guards 47, 50, 51, 54, 58
Préfontaine, Louis de, Mademoiselle's man of business xiv, 38, 38 n. 59, 44, 60, 61, 66, 77, 78, 84, 85, 94
Prince, Monsieur le *see* Condé, Louis II de Bourbon, prince de

Quinault, Philippe (1635–1688) 196 n. 269
    Le Feint Alcibiade 116, 116 n. 167
QUINTIN 141 n. 210

Rambures, Marie de Bautru (d. after 1689), marquise de 146, 154, 181 n. 245, 188, 189, 195
Rancé, Denis de Boutheiller de (c. 1582–after 1630) 4 n. 10
Rancé, Armand-Jean de Boutheiller de *see* La Trappe
Rancé, Charlotte (c. 1628–1697), Mlle de, in 1644 the wife of Gilbert-Antoine. comte d'Albon (c. 1620–1680), knight of honour to Henrietta Anne d'Orléans 4, 4 n. 10, 129 n. 192, 200 n. 272
Rancé, Marie de, later Mme de Rochemontais 4, 4 n. 10
Ranes, Nicolas d'Argouges (d. 1678), marquis de, Colonel-General of the King's Dragoons 116 n. 169
Raré (or Raray), Catherine d'Angennes de la Loupe (1607–1680), baronne de, governess to the daughters of Gaston d'Orléans and Marguerite de Lorraine 131
RATILLY 83, 83 n. 120
Recollects 150, 185
REIMS xxvii, 99
Remenecourt 158
Remenecourt, Mlle de, maid-of-honour to Marguerite de Lorraine xxiii, 38, 39
Retz, Jean-François Paul de Gondi (1613–1679), Cardinal de 44, 44 n. 69, 45, 48, 62, 69, 97, 105
REUILLY 70
RICHELIEU 8, 8 n. 16
Richelieu, Armand-Jean du Plessis (1585–1642), Cardinal xii, xx, xxv, xxix, 5, 5 n. 13, 6, 9–12, 14, 23 n. 40, 45, 95

Richelieu, Armand-Jean de Vignerot du Plessis (1629–1715), duc de, great-nephew of the Cardinal 23 n. 40, 109 n. 158, 188, 189

Richelieu, Anne Poussart de Fors du Vigean (1622–1684), in 1649 duchesse de, wife of the foregoing, lady-in-waiting to the queen in 1671 and to the dauphine in 1679: 189

Richelieu, Jean-Baptiste-Amador de Vignerot du Plessis (1632–1662), marquis de 122

Ricousse, Mme de, coiffeuse to Mme de Châtillon 89

Rochefort, Henri-Louis d'Aloigny (d. 1676), Marshal 156, 161, 190, 198

ROCROI 107, 107 n. 152

Roger de la Marbillière, Louison (1621–after 1657), Gaston's mistress 7, 7 n. 15, 8, 105 n. 150

Rohan-Chabot, Henri de Chabot (1616–1655), duc de, called the duc de Rohan 45, 47, 48, 50, 63, 66, 69, 74

Rohan-Guéméné, Marie-Eléonore de (1629–1682) 89, 89 n. 132

Rollinde, Mademoiselle's man of business in succession to Guilloire 198, 198 n. 271, 204–07

Roncherolles, Pierre (born c. 1610), marquis de, Governor of Landrecies 156

Roncherolles, Charles (c. 1635–after 1699), marquis de, son of the foregoing 156

Roquelaure, Charlotte-Marie de Daillon du Lude (1635–1657), in 1653 duchesse de 87, 87 n. 129, 111

Rospigliosi, Giulio (1660–1669), chevalier, in 1657 Cardinal and, in 1667, Pope Clement IX: 135

ROUEN 30, 37 n. 57, 90, 91 n. 135

Rousseau, Jean-Jacques (1712–1778) xi

Roye, Frédéric-Charles de la Rochefoucauld (1633–1690), comte de 132

RUEIL *see* RUEL

RUEL (nowadays RUEIL-MALMAISON) 11, 11 n. 21, 26, 27, 31, 168

Rupert (1619–1682), Prince Palatine of the Rhine xvi n. 9, 19, 19 n. 37

Saint-Aignan, François de Beauvillier (1610–1687), comte (in 1663 duc) de 84 n. 123, 108, 144, 144 n. 212

Saint-Aignan, Antoinette Servien (1617–1680), comtesse (in 1663 duchesse) de, wife of the foregoing 108

Saint-Aunais, Henri de Bourcier de Barry (1590–after 1665), marquis de 141, 141 n. 211

Saint-Aunais, Charles de Bourcier de Barry (1638–after 1667), marquis de, son of the foregoing 141, 141 n. 211

SAINT-CLOUD 99, 166, 169

Saint-Cyran, Jean Duvergier de Hauranne (1581–1643), abbot of 95, 96

SAINT-DENIS (north of Paris) xxii, xxii n. 15, 16, 36, 61, 169

SAINT-DENIS (east of Orleans) 48, 48 n. 78

SAINTES 132
SAINT-FARGEAU viii, ix, xiii, xxiii, xxiv, 61, 75–80, 82, 82 n. 119, 83, 84, 84 nn. 122 & 124, 86, 95, 110, 129, 133, 145, 201, 209
Saint-Fargeau, bailli de 76 n. 110, 77
Saint-Georges, Hardouin de Clermont (c. 1582–1633), seigneur de 2
Saint-Georges, Jeanne de Harlay de Montglat de (d. 1643), in 1598 wife of the foregoing 2, 6, 8, 14, 15, 119 n. 175
Saint-Georges, Victor de Clermont de (c. 1622–after 1643), baron de Rupt 16, 16 n. 32
SAINT-GERMAIN (EN-LAYE) xxv, 9, 10, 11 n. 21, 14, 26–28, 29, 29 n. 50, 31, 32, 65 n. 97, 148, 166, 168, 171, 174, 197, 198, 203, 204
SAINT-GERMAIN-dES-PRÉS 113
SAINT-JEAN-DE-LUZ 130 n. 193, 141
Saint-Jean-de-Lyon, François d'Albon (1623–1705) comte de 129, 129 n. 192
Saint-Louis, Anne de Taillefer (c. 1621–c. 1669), Mlle de, maid of honour to Anne of Austria 9, 10
SAINT-MESMIN 58, 58 n. 89
Saintôt, Nicolas (c. 1632–1713) 167
Saint-Pol *see* Longueville, Charles-Paris, duc de
SAINT-QUENTIN 91 n. 137, 155, 156, 156 n. 215
Saint-Quentin, M. de, gentleman-in-waiting to Gaston d'Orléans 120
Saint-Simon, Claude de Rouvroy (1607–1693), duc de 12
Saint-Simon, Louis de Rouvroy (1675–1755), duc de, son of the foregoing, the memorialist xi, xvi
    Mémoires xiv n. 6, xxv n. 18
SAINT-VENANT 163, 163 n. 223
Sales, Saint François de ix
SALON (DE-PROVENCE) 137
Sanguin, Marie de Bordeaux, in 1647 Mme 117
Santinelli *see* Sentinelli
Saugeon *see* Saujon
Saujon, César-Louis de Campet (1600–after 1660), baron, captain of the guard to Gaston d'Orléans xxvii, 37, 37 n. 58, 39 n. 62, 59, 59 n. 90, 84, 126
Saujon, Anne-Marie de Campet de (1618 *or* 1628–1694), half-sister of the foregoing xxiii, xxvii, 39, 39 n. 62
SAUMUR 8, 8 n. 16, 79
Savoy, Victor Amadeus I (1587–1637), in 1630 Duke of Savoy 81
Savoy, Christine-Marie, Duchess of, wife of the foregoing, *see* Christine de France
Savoy, Maurice (1593–1657), Prince of, brother of Victor Amadeus I, later Prince of Oneglia 81
Savoy, Charles Emmanuel II (1634–1675), son of Victor Amadeus I and Christine-Marie, in 1638 Duke of Savoy xxi, 81, 124, 138 n. 203, 144

Savoy, Marie-Jeanne de Nemours, Duchess of, second wife of the foregoing, see Nemours, Marie-Jeanne-Baptiste de

Savoy, Henriette-Adelaide of, daughter of Victor Amadeus I and Christine-Marie, see Bavaria, Henriette-Adelaide of Savoy, Electress of

Savoy, Louise-Christine of (1629–1692), daughter of Victor Amadeus I and Christine-Marie and wife of Prince Maurice of Savoy 81

Savoy, Marguerite-Yolande of (1635–1663), daughter of Victor Amadeus I and Christine-Marie 81, 124, 129

Savoy, Victor Amadeus II (1666–1732), son of Charles Emmanuel II, in 1675 Duke of Savoy xxv

SCOTLAND 39

Scudéry, Madeleine (1607–1701), Mlle de 133

SEDAN 6, 13, 13 n. 24, 99, 100 n. 145, 101 n. 146, 104, 104 n. 148, 107, 107 n. 152, 108

Segrais, Jean Regnault de (1624–1701) xxiii, 182 n. 246

Séguier, Pierre (1588–1672), in 1635 Chancellor of France 4, 4 n. 9, 6 n. 14, 25, 26, 113

Séguier, Charlotte, Mlle de, daughter of Pierre, see Sully, duchesse de

Séguier, Marie, Mlle de, daughter of Pierre, see Laval, duchesse de

Ségur, Françoise d'Escars, Mlle de, in 1652 vicomtesse de Château-Rocher 10 n. 19, 92

Senecey, Marie-Catherine de la Rochefoucauld (1588–1677), marquise de 29

SENLIS 155

Sentinelli (or Santinelli), Francisco Maria (1627–1697), Count 110

Sentinelli (or Santinelli), Ludovico, captain of Queen Christina's guards, brother of the foregoing 109–11

Servien (or Servient), Abel de (1593–1659), marquis de Sablé 83 n. 121, 93

Sève de Laval, Guillaume de 127, 127 n. 191

Sévigné, Marie de Rabutin-Chantal (1626–1696), marquise de 42 n. 67, 84

SOISSONS (HÔTEL DE), Paris 9 n. 18, 12 n. 23

Soissons, Charles de Bourbon-Condé (1566–1612), comte de 12 n. 23

Soissons, Anne de Montafié (1577–1644), comtesse de, wife of the foregoing 9, 12

Soissons, Louis de Bourbon (1604–1641), comte de, son of Charles and Anne xx, 6, 12, 13, 13 nn. 24 & 25

Soissons, Olympe Mancini (1640–1708), wife of Eugène-Maurice de Savoie (1635–1673), comte de Soissons 112, 121, 166

Sophia, Duchess of Hanover (1630–1714) vii

Soubise, François de Rohan (1631–1712), prince de 156

Sourches, Jean du Bouchet (c. 1620–1677), marquis de, in 1643 Grand Provost of France 108, 108 n. 155, 190 n. 264

Sourches, Louis-François du Bouchet de, son of the foregoing, see Montsoreau

Sourdis et d'Alluye, Charles d'Escoubleau (1588–1666), marquis de 49, 51, 54, 55, 59–61

Sourdis et d'Alluye, Jeanne de Monluc de Cramail, marquise de, wife of Charles d'Escoubleau de Sourdis 55

Spain, Infanta of *see* (1) Spain, Maria Anna of ; (2) Maria Theresa, Queen of France

Spain, Maria Anna of (1606–1646), sister of Philip IV and first wife of Ferdinand III, Emperor of Austria 20, 20 n. 39

Spain, Queen of *see* Élisabeth de France

Stuppa, Pierre (d. 1701), captain of the Swiss guards 159

Stuppa, Anne-Charlotte de Gondi (1630–1694), wife of the foregoing, whom Mademoiselle calls Mme Chetrupe 159

SULLY (SUR-LOIRE) 77, 79

Sully, Maximilien de Béthune (1559–1641), duc de 27 n. 47

Sully, Maximilien-François de Béthune (1615–1661), duc de, grandson of the foregoing 117

Sully, Charlotte Séguier (1622 or 1623–1704), duchesse de, wife of Maximilen-François 4, 4 n. 9, 76, 76 n. 111, 79, 84

TARASCON 133, 137

Tarente, Amélie de Hesse-Cassel (1625–1693), princesse de 109

Tavannes, Jacques de Saulx (1620–1683), comte de 45

Theresa, Saint 98, 98 n. 144

Thiange, Claude-Léonor de Damas (c. 1620–1702), marquis de 86, 126 n. 188

Thiange, Gabrielle de Rochechouart (1631–1693), Mlle de Mortemart, in 1655 marquise de, wife of the foregoing xxiii n. 17, 86, 86 n. 128, 87, 157–59, 188

Thiange, Diane-Gabrielle de, daughter of Claude-Léonor and Gabrielle, *see* Nevers, duchesse de

THIERS 201

Thou, François-Auguste de (1607–1642) 13, 13 n. 26, 14, 133 n. 195

THOUARS 109 n. 158, 110

Thury, Louis d'Harcourt (c. 1630–1699), marquis de, lieutenant in the queen mother's light horse 117

Tillières, Henri Le Veneur (d. 1687), comte de 16 n. 31

Tillières, Claude Rouault (b. after 1613), in 1638 comtesse de, wife of the foregoing 15, 16 n. 31

TOULON 137, 138

TOULOUSE 133, 141

Toulouse, Louis-Alexandre de Bourbon (1678–1737), comte de, youngest son of Mme de Montespan by Louis XIV: 208

TOURNAI 162, 197

TOURS 7, 8

Toury 108
Trévoux 124 n. 184, 126, 127, 127 n. 191, 128
Trivelin, Domenico Locatelli (d. 1671), actor, known as 94
Tuileries (palace and gardens) 2, 2 n. 3, 12 n. 23, 18 n. 34, 24, 25, 39, 61, 74, 181, 184, 185, 192, 193, 195, 196
Turenne, Henri de la Tour-Auvergne (1611–1675), vicomte de 61, 68, 70 n. 103, 71, 104 n. 148, 117, 144–46
Turin 138 n. 203, 144
Tuscany, Cosimo III de' Medici (1642–1723), Grand Duke of xxii

Urban VI, Bartolomeo Prignano (1318–1389), in 1378 Pope 136 n. 202
Uzès, François de Crussol (1602–1680), duc d' 130
Uzès, Marguerite d'Apchier (c. 1618–1708), in 1636 duchesse d', wife of the foregoing 130

Valavoir, François-Auguste (?1619–after 1676), marquis de 135
Val-de-Grâce 6, 6 n. 14, 96, 123, 123 n. 183
Valentinay, Catherine Coudreau (1638–after 1691), wife of Louis I Bernin, sieur de, controller general of the king's household 204 n. 281
Valentinois, Mme de 204, 204 n. 281
Vallot, Antoine (1594–1671), first physician to the king 166
Valois, Marguerite de *see* Marguerite de Valois
Valois, duc de *see* Orléans, Jean-Gaston d'
Valois, Mlle de *see* (1) Orléans, Françoise-Madeleine d' (2) Orléans, Anne-Marie d'
Valon, François de la Baume, seigneur de, brigadier (later, lieutenant-general) in Monsieur's regiment 47, 66
Vandy, Catherine d'Apremont (b. ?1619), called Mlle de xxiii n. 17, 84, 92, 127, 132, 133
Vantelet, one of Mademoiselle's equerries 53
Vendôme, Françoise de Lorraine (1592–1669), duchesse de 10, 11
Vendôme, Élisabeth de (1614–1664), daughter of the foregoing, sister of the duc de Beaufort, in 1643 duchesse de Nemours 11, 11 n. 20, 62, 64, 65
Vendôme, Mlle de *see* Elbeuf, Catherine-Henriette, duchesse de
Venice 144
Versailles vii, ix, xiv, xxv, 147, 166, 167, 175, 176, 184, 194, 197, 203, 207
Vieuville *see* La Vieuville
Vilaine *see* Villènes
Villarceaux *see* Mornay
Villefranche (sur-Saône) 124, 124 n. 184
Villènes (or Vilaine), Charles-Nicolas Bourdin (d. 1676), marquis de 52
Villeneuve (lès-Avignon) 134
Villeroy, Nicolas de Neufville (1597–1685), Marshal de 73, 121 n. 179, 125 n. 187, 157 n. 216, 189 n. 262

Villeroy, Catherine de Neufville (1639–1707), Mlle de, daughter of Nicolas, maid of honour to Anne of Austria, in 1660 comtesse d'Armagnac 121, 121 n. 179

Villeroy, François de Neufville (1644–1730), marquis (later, duc and Marshal) de, son of Nicolas 157, 157 n. 216

Villeroy, Camille de Neufville de (1606–1693), Archbishop of Lyon, brother of Nicolas 125, 125 n. 187, 189, 189 n. 262

Villeroy, Ferdinand de Neufville de (1611–1690), Bishop of Chartres, brother of Nicolas 125 n. 187, 189, 189 n. 262

VIMY (nowadays NEUVILLE-SUR-SAÔNE) 125, 125 n. 187

VINCENNES xxii, 68, 118, 118 n. 173

Viole, Pierre, président 69

Visé, Antoine de (1599–1676) 53, 53 n. 82

Visé, Jean Donneau de (1638–1710), author and journalist, son of the foregoing 53 n. 82

Vivonne, Antoinette de Mesmes (1641–1709), duchesse de 121

Voltaire (pseudonym of François-Marie Arouet, 1694–1778), *Le Siècle de Louis XIV* xxi, xxi n. 14

Wales, Prince of *see* Charles II
William III, King of England *see* Orange, William of Nassau, prince of
Wilmot, Henry (1612–1658), in 1652 Earl of Rochester 39
WORCESTER, BATTLE OF 39, 39 n. 63

York, Anne Hyde (1638–1671), Duchess of 168 n. 231, 196
York, Duke of *see* James II

MHRA New Translations

The guiding principle of this series is to publish new translations into English of important works that have been hitherto imperfectly translated or that are entirely untranslated. The work to be translated or re-translated should be aesthetically or intellectually important. The proposal should cover such issues as copyright and, where relevant, an account of the faults of the previous translation/s; it should be accompanied by independent statements from two experts in the field attesting to the significance of the original work (in cases where this is not obvious) and to the desirability of a new or renewed translation.

Translations should be accompanied by a fairly substantial introduction and other, briefer, apparatus: a note on the translation; a select bibliography; a chronology of the author's life and works; and notes to the text.

Titles will be selected by members of the Editorial Board and edited by leading academics.

Alison Finch
General Editor

Editorial Board

Professor Malcolm Cook (French)
Professor Alison Finch (French)
Professor Ritchie Robertson (Germanic)
Dr Mark Davie (Italian)
Dr Stephen Parkinson (Portuguese)
Professor David Gillespie (Slavonic)
Professor Derek Flitter (Spanish)
Dr Jonathan Thacker (Spanish)

Published titles

1. *Memoirs of Mademoiselle de Montpensier (La Grande Mademoiselle)* (P. J. Yarrow. Edited by William Brooks. 2010)

For details of how to order please visit our website at:
www.translations.mhra.org.uk

www.ingramcontent.com/pod-product-compliance
Lightning Source LLC
Chambersburg PA
CBHW071425150426
43191CB00008B/1044